```
' Force variable declaration.
Option Explicit

' Dimension event class.
Dim X As New clsEvents

' Macro to set the selected line's color property to red.
Sub Ch02_SetObjectProperty()

    Dim objLine As AcadLine      ' Line object.
    Dim varPickPoint As Variant  ' User pick point.

    ' Ask the user to select a line.
    ThisDrawing.Utility.GetEntity objLine, varPickPoint, "Se...

    ' Set the line's color to red.
    objLine.Color = acRed

    ' Tell the user.
    MsgBox "Line color property set to red."

End Sub


' Macro to get a selected line's color.
Sub Ch02_GetObjectProperty()

    Dim intColor As Integer       ' Line color.
    Dim objLine As AcadLine       ' Line object.
    Dim varPickPoint As Variant   ' User pick poin...

    ' Ask the user to select a line.
    ThisDrawing.Utility.GetEntity objLine, varPic...

    ' Get the line's color.
    intColor = objLine.Color

    ' Show the user.
    MsgBox "Line color property is currently " &...

End Sub


' Macro to move a line from 0,0,0 to 2,2,0.
Sub Ch02_UseObjectMethod()

    Dim objLine As AcadLine       ' Line object.
    Dim dblPoint1(2) As Double    ' Base point.
    Dim dblPoint2(2) As Double    ' Point to move...
    Dim varPickPoint As Variant   ' Use a Variant

    dblPoint1(0) = 0#             'X value of the
    dblPoint1(1) = 0#             'Y value of the
    dblPoint1(2) = 0#             'Z value of the

    dblPoint2(0) = 2#             'X value of the
    dblPoint2(1) = 2#             'Y value of the
    dblPoint2(2) = 0#             'Z value of the

    ' Ask the user to select a line.
    ThisDrawing.Utility.GetEntity objLine, varPickPoint, "Selec

    ' Move the line from the base point to the new point
    objLine.Move dblPoint1, dblPoint2

End Sub


' Macro that iterates the entire Layers collection and displays the layers to the user.
```

VBA for AutoCAD

Paul Richard

P9-DHF-452

Publisher

The Goodheart-Willcox Company, Inc.

Tinley Park, Illinois

www.g-w.com

Expanded Table of Contents

Chapter 5
Creating AutoCAD Entities 163

Chapter 6
Editing AutoCAD Entities 193

Chapter 7

Selection Sets 217

Chapter 10
Views and Viewports 281

Chapter 11
Blocks, Block Attributes, and Xrefs 303

Chapter 13

Controlling Pull-Down Menus and Toolbars . . . 367

Chapter 14

Programming Using VBA Forms 395

Chapter 15
Utilizing ActiveX and Programming with AutoCAD Events 409

Student CD
    Appendix A Objects
    Appendix B Properties
    Appendix C Methods
    Appendix D Events
    Text Code Examples
    Required Files

CHAPTER 1

Introduction to Visual Basic for Applications

Learning Objectives

After completing this chapter, you will be able to:

- Describe the different data types used in VBA.
- Explain the different program structures in VBA.
- Describe a procedure and how it is used.
- Determine the scope of variables and procedures.
- Describe the different coding conventions commonly used in VBA.
- Handle and manage errors in VBA.

This chapter introduces the basics of the Visual Basic programming language. The intent of this chapter is to provide a quick overview of the key concepts and features of Visual Basic. The chapter is not intended as a definitive guide to Visual Basic, but rather as a reference so that you can quickly get started creating VBA macros for use in AutoCAD.

Introduction to Visual Basic for Applications

Visual Basic is a graphic implementation of the BASIC programming language that has been around for years. It is called "visual" because of the graphical interface and "basic" because of its ease of use. Visual Basic has been built into AutoCAD since release 14 as *Visual Basic for Applications (VBA).* In fact, VBA exists in most of the major Microsoft Office programs, including Word, Excel, and Access. Because of this, VBA can be used to share data between all of these applications. This concept is often referred to as ActiveX Automation, or simply *ActiveX.* ActiveX is a very powerful tool that is discussed further in later chapters.

Visual Basic for Applications is based on the full version of Microsoft's Visual Basic (VB). Because of this, most of the data types, operators, decision structures, loop structures, and procedure types that are found in Visual Basic are included in VBA. This chapter briefly covers most of these concepts and features, but for more in depth coverage, you should consult a more comprehensive book dedicated to the VB programming language. The main objective of this text is to explore how VBA can be used with the AutoCAD ActiveX Object Model to program AutoCAD, not to teach all of the aspects of the VB programming language.

Variables and Data Types

In VBA, it is normal to explicitly declare variables to be a specific data type before they are used in your program. The syntax for declaring a variable is:

Dim *variable* As *data type*

Dim is short for "dimension" because you are "dimensioning" the variable to a specific data type. For example:

Dim IntValue As Integer

The variable *intValue* can now only store an integer value, as indicated by **Integer**.

A variable may be declared anywhere in your program, as long as it is declared before a value is assigned to the variable. A variable may also be assigned different values as long as the values are of the same data type. The basic VBA data types are shown in **Figure 1-1.**

After a variable is declared, or "dimmed," it can then be set to a value using the **=** (equals) assignment operator:

```
' Set integer value to 1.
intValue = 1
```

Figure 1-1.
Basic VBA data types.

Data Type	Range	Used For
String	0 to 2 billion text characters	Text characters.
Integer	–32,768 to +32,767	Small integer values.
Long	–2,147,483,648 to +2,147,483,647	Large integer values.
Single	1.4E–45 to 3.4E+48	Single precision floating point numbers.
Double	4.94E–324 to 1.8E+308	Double precision floating point numbers.
Currency	–922,337,203,685,477.5808 to +922,337,203,685,477.5807	Monetary values.
Date	1/1/100 to 12/31/9999 or 0:00:00 to 23:59:59	Date and time values.
Byte	0 to 255	Positive integers.
Boolean	1 or 0	True or false values.
Variant	All of the above.	The default data type; can be set to anything.

The first line of this example is known as a programming comment, as indicated by the preceding apostrophe. *Programming comments* describe what is intended by the programmer. In other words, a comment is a brief explanation of what is going on in the code. Comments help make your code easier to understand and maintain. Comments and other coding conventions are described in detail in the Coding Conventions section later in this chapter.

If you try to assign a different data type than the data type for which the variable was dimensioned, a *type mismatch* error message is generated, as shown in **Figure 1-2.** This built-in data validity checking provides better control over your program's behavior and reduces the chance of run-time errors.

Unfortunately, declaring variables explicitly in VBA is not a requirement. In fact, a variable that is not declared explicitly is considered a **Variant** data type. A *variant variable* can be set to many different data types at program run time. This might seem convenient at first, but ultimately it leads to sloppy and error-prone programs. Luckily, there is an option in the **Visual Basic Editor** to make variable declaration a requirement. Or, you can add the **Option Explicit** statement at the top of each form, module, and class in your program.

```
Option Explicit
```

There are other productivity tools in the **Visual Basic Editor** that make declaring variables explicitly even more appealing. These tools and others are discussed in Chapter 3.

In the AutoLISP programming language, variables are not declared as a data type before being used in a program.

AutoLISP vs. VBA

Caution

Although you can declare multiple variables on the same line, a common mistake is to try the code:

```
Dim intValue1, intValue2, intValue3 As Integer
```

This method will only set the last variable, *intValue3*, to be an **Integer** data type. The other two variables, *intValue1* and *intValue2*, will default to a **Variant** data type. You must use the **As** *type* identifier for each variable in your program. The correct syntax for declaring multiple variables on the same line is:

```
Dim intValue1 As Integer, intValue2 As Integer, intValue2 _
    As Integer
```

Figure 1-2.
A type mismatch error.

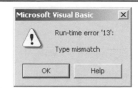

It is possible to use shorthand when declaring a variable by appending what is known as a *type declaration character* to the end of the variable name and omitting the **As** *type* identifier. For example, the variable name *intValue%* has a percentage sign appended to the name so it is automatically dimensioned as an **Integer** data type. The type declaration characters are:

%	**Integer**
&	**Long**
!	**Single**
#	**Double**
$	**String**
@	**Currency**

Early Binding vs. Late Binding

Declaring a variable to be a particular data type is called *binding*. When you declare a variable explicitly, as in the example shown in the previous section, it is called *early binding*. This is because the variable's data type is resolved before the program is run.

There are two generic data types—**Object** and **Variant**—that allow the variable's data type to remain unresolved until the program is run. The **Object** *data type* can be used to represent any object type in the ActiveX object model. ActiveX and the ActiveX object model are explained in Chapter 2. A **Variant** *data type* typically represents the basic data types listed in **Figure 1-1**.

When **Object** or **Variant** data types are used, it is referred to as *late binding*. Late binding of variables causes programs to run slower because validity checking is done while the program is running. Late binding also increases the possibility of run-time errors. Early binding is preferred to late binding because it provides validity checking during design time and reduces the possibility of run-time errors. *Design time* is before the program is run. *Run time* is when the program is running.

Data Conversion

Sometimes, it is necessary to convert one particular data type into another. VBA provides all of the data conversion functions shown in **Figure 1-3.** For example, to convert an **Integer** data type into a **String** data type, you can use the **CStr** function:

```
Dim intValue As Integer
Dim strValue As String

intValue = 123
strName = CStr(intValue)
```

Figure 1-3.
VBA data conversion functions.

Function	Converted Data Type
CStr	String
CInt	Integer
CLng	Long
CSng	Single
CDbl	Double
CCur	Currency
CDate	Date
CByte	Byte
CBool	Boolean
CVar	Variant

The *strName* variable now contains the string value 123, which was converted from the integer 123.

An **Integer** data type may be exchanged with a **String** data type, and vice versa, without an explicit conversion. The data conversion for **Integer** and **String** data types takes place automatically. For example:

```
Dim intValue as Integer
Dim strValue as String

Set string value to "123"
strValue = "123"
intValue = strValue
```

The value of *intValue* is now the integer 123.

Caution

When converting variables, make sure the converted value is within the range of valid values for the new data type or a run-time error will occur. For instance, this code will generate a type mismatch error:

```
Dim intValue as Integer

' Try to convert the string "abc" to an integer value.
intValue = CInt("abc")
```

Obviously, there is no valid integer value that represents the string abc.

The VBA conversion functions outlined above are similar to the AutoLISP conversion functions shown in **Figure 1-4**.

AutoLISP vs. VBA

Figure 1-4.
AutoLISP data conversion functions.

AutoLISP Function	Description
(angtof *string* [*mode*])	Converts a string representing an angle into a real (floating-point) value in radians.
(angtos *angle* [*mode* [*precision*]])	Converts an angular value in radians into a string.
(ascii *string*)	Returns the conversion of the first character of a string into its ASCII character code (an integer).
(atof *string*)	Returns the conversion of a string into a real number.
(atoi *string*)	Returns the conversion of a string into an integer.
(chr *integer*)	Returns the conversion of an integer representing an ASCII character code into a single-character string.
(cvunit *value from to*)	Converts a value from one unit of measurement to another.
(distof *string* [*mode*])	Converts a string that represents a real (floating-point) value into a real value.
(itoa *int*)	Returns the conversion of an integer into a string.
(rtos *number* [*mode* [*precision*]])	Converts a number into a string.
(trans *pt from to* [*disp*])	Translates a point (or a displacement) from one coordinate system to another.

Variable Naming Conventions

You may have noticed in the examples thus far that all of the variable names have a three-character, descriptive prefix indicating their data type. This is known as *Hungarian notation* after Microsoft programmer Charles Simonyi, who is from Hungary. Hungarian notation is a voluntary variable naming convention that makes VB/VBA code easier to understand and maintain. This naming convention is used by a large percentage of the VB community and its use is promoted in this book. The unofficial list of prefixes and their data types is shown in **Figure 1-5.**

Figure 1-5.
Hungarian notation prefixes.

Prefix	Data Type
str	String
int	Integer
lng	Long
sng	Single
dbl	Double
cur	Currency
dtm	Date
byt	Byte
bln	Boolean
var	Variant
obj	Object

Constants

Constants are values assigned to a descriptive name that, once assigned, can never be changed within the program. Constants are used to make your program easier to understand and maintain. They also help reduce programming errors. A constant is declared and assigned a value at the same time. For instance, to set a constant to be the value of pi (π), enter:

```
Const Pi = 3.1415926536
```

Now, whenever the value of pi is needed in your program, simply reference the constant *Pi*:

```
dblCircumference = Pi * dblDiameter
```

Using a constant for pi in this manner gives you two advantages. First, you do not have to enter 10 digits each time the value of pi is needed, thus eliminating the risk of a typo. Second, if you decide to change the value of pi, you only have to change it in the one spot where it was originally declared. In fact, if you try to change the value of a constant anywhere else in a program, an error message is generated like the one shown in **Figure 1-6.**

There are a number of constants provided by VBA and AutoCAD to help make your program easier to understand and maintain. For instance, AutoCAD provides constants that represent the first seven colors in AutoCAD:

acRed = 1
acYellow = 2
acGreen = 3
acBlue = 4
acCyan = 5
acMagenta = 6
acWhite = 7

All of the AutoCAD constants have the ac prefix, while the VBA constants are prefixed with vb.

Figure 1-6.
A constant assignment error message.

There is another special type of constant referred to as an enumerated constant, or enum for short. An *enum* is a Visual Basic data type that is basically a collection of related constants. They look and behave similar to the constants described in this section. In fact, the enums provided by AutoCAD all have the same ac prefix used for AutoCAD constants. For example, AutoCAD provides an enum named **AcAngleUnits** that includes four constants that represent different angular unit settings:

acDegrees	Degrees
acDegreeMinuteSeconds	Degrees/minutes/seconds
acGrads	Gradians
acRadians	Radians

You must specify one of these four enums when converting angles using the **AngleToReal** method introduced in Chapter 4.

Arrays

An *array* is a collection, or list, of values of the same data type that is treated as a single unit. Each value, or *element*, in an array is referenced by its location in the list. An element's location is referred to as its *index*. In theory, an array can contain an infinite number of elements. However, the number of elements is usually limited due to memory considerations.

There are two types of arrays in VBA—fixed length and dynamic. A *fixed length array* is used when you know how many elements are needed in an array, and that this number will not change. A *dynamic array* is used when you do not know how may elements are needed or if the number of elements will change.

Fixed-Length Array

For an example of using a fixed-length array, consider a point drawn in 3D space in AutoCAD. A 3D point is represented by a fixed-length array that is three elements in length. One element is for the X-axis value, one element is for the Y-axis value, and one element is for the Z-axis value. The array will never need to be longer than three elements because no more than three coordinates are needed to define a point in AutoCAD. A point in AutoCAD is considered a **Double** *data type* because it is a large floating-point value. A small floating-point value is considered a **Single** *data type.* To dimension an array of double data type elements that is three elements long, enter:

```
Dim dblPoint(0 to 2) as Double
```

The 0 and 2 specify the lower and upper bounds of the array. Arrays are zero based in VBA, so the first element is always referenced via the 0 index. The lower bound is implied as 0 and does not necessarily have to be specified:

```
Dim dblPoint(2) as Double
```

This has the same effect as the previous example. Now, suppose you need to create a variable to hold the point (2.0, 4.0, 0.0). This is entered as:

```
' Set each element of an array to the proper coordinate value (X,Y,Z).
Dim dblPoint(2) as Double
dblPoint(0) = 2.0        'X
dblPoint(1) = 4.0        'Y
dblPoint(2) = 0.0        'Z
```

Notice how each index is set to the appropriate coordinate value of the point.

Dynamic Array

Sometimes, you might not know how large an array needs to be until the program is running. An array dimensioned at run time, not when the program is designed, is considered dynamic. To declare a dynamic array, do not specify the number of elements. Simply leave the parentheses empty:

```
Dim strDaysToXmas() As String
```

You can then dimension the array "on the fly," or dynamically, with the **ReDim** statement:

```
ReDim strDaysToXmas (1)

' The first day of Christmas my true love gave to me...
strDaysToXmas(0) = "A partridge in a pear tree"
```

Remember, arrays are *always* zero based in VBA! A dynamic array can be dimensioned as many times as needed. However, each time you use the **ReDim** statement to dimension an array, the previous contents are *erased* and all information is lost. For example, if another string of text is added to the string array *strDaysToXmas* using the **ReDim** statement, the first string is erased from memory:

```
ReDim strDaysToXmas (2)

' The second day of Christmas my true love gave to me...
strDaysToXmas(1) ="Two turtle doves"
```

The first element in the array *strDaysToXmas* (0) is now an empty string. Thankfully, there is a way to prevent this from happening.

The **Preserve** keyword allows you to preserve the contents of a dynamic array when using the **ReDim** statement:

```
ReDim Preserve strDaysToXmas (3)

' The third day of Christmas my true love gave to me...
strDaysToXmas(2) = "Three French hens"
```

The contents of the first two elements in the string array are still set to A partridge in a pear tree and Two turtle doves.

Multidimensional Array

An array can also be multidimensional, forming a matrix. For instance, to create an array of integers that is $3 \times 3 \times 3$, enter:

```
Dim intMatrix(2, 2, 2) As Integer
```

Remember, an array is 0 based, so the previous example can also be dimensioned in longhand:

```
Dim intMatrix(0 to 2, 0 to 2, 0 to 2) As Integer
```

AutoLISP vs. VBA

Arrays in VBA are a lot like lists in AutoLISP...but *much* easier to use. At last, you can forget about such AutoLISP functions as **CAR**, **CDR**, **CADR**, **CADDR**, and so on. To access the contents of an element in a VBA array, all you need to know is its index:

```
MsgBox strDaysToXmas(0)
```

This line of code displays the VBA message dialog box with the value of the first element (remember VBA arrays are zero based) in the *strDaysToXmas* string array, as seen in **Figure 1-7.**

The VBA **MsgBox** function is used extensively in this text because of its flexibility and ease of use. It is discussed in more detail later.

VBA also provides tools that allow you to process all of the elements in an array quickly and easily. There is even a VBA **For Each...** loop structure that works almost exactly like its AutoLISP counterpart, the **(foreach)** function. This and other array manipulation tools are discussed later in this chapter.

Figure 1-7.
A VBA message box example.

Let's Review...

VBA Basics

- Visual Basic for Applications (VBA) is the graphic version of the BASIC programming language.
- VBA is a subset of the full version of Microsoft's Visual Basic (VB) programming language that exists in many Microsoft Office applications.
- If the **Option Explicit** statement is used in VBA, variables must be explicitly declared as a specific data type.
- A variable's data type can be determined before a program is run (early binding) or when a program is running (late binding).
- It is possible to convert between data types using predefined VBA functions.
- Hungarian notation is the descriptive variable naming convention that allows you to determine the declared data type for the variable.
- A constant data type can only be assigned a value once in a program.
- An array is a collection of values of the same data type that is treated as a single unit.
- Arrays can be dynamic, which allows the number of elements contained within an array to be specified at program run time.

Using Hungarian notation, dimension variables for each of the following values using the correct data type. Create variable names that describe the type of data it contains. For example, a variable that will hold the string value Exercise 1-1 can be dimensioned:

    Dim strExercise As String

1. Visual Basic
2. 1
3. 250000000000
4. 2.5
5. $10.50
6. 12/12/05
7. 2.5E+50
8. True *or* False
9. two hundred fifty six *or* 256 *or* $256.00

Operators

Operators allow you to perform different data operations in your program. You have already seen the **=** (equals) assignment operator, which assigns a value to a variable. VBA has many more operators that can be broken down into several categories— arithmetic operators, comparison operators, concatenation operations, and logical operators. These are explained in the following sections.

Arithmetic Operators

Arithmetic operators are used to perform mathematical calculations. VBA contains the arithmetic operators shown in **Figure 1-8**.

Comparison Operators

Comparison operators are used to perform comparisons and return a Boolean value of true or false. The table shown in **Figure 1-9** contains a list of the comparison operators and the conditions that determine whether the result is **True** or **False**.

Figure 1-8.
VBA arithmetic operators.

Operator	Description	Syntax
+	Used to find the sum of two numbers.	A = B + C
−	Used to find the difference between two numbers.	A = B − C
*	Used to multiply two numbers.	A = B * C
/	Used to divide two numbers and return a floating-point result.	A = B / C
\	Used to divide two numbers and return an integer result.	A = B \ C
^	Used to raise a number to the power of an exponent.	A = B ^ C
Mod	Used to divide two numbers and return only the remainder.	A = B **Mod** C

Figure 1-9.
VBA comparison operators.

Operator	True	False
< (less than)	4 < 5	5 < 4
<= (less than or equal to)	4 <= 4	5 <= 4
> (greater than)	5 > 4	4 > 5
>= (greater than or equal to)	5 >= 4	4 >= 5
= (equal to)	4 = 4	4 = 5
<> (not equal to)	4 <> 5	5 <> 5

Figure 1-10.
VBA concatenation operators.

Operator	Description	Syntax
&	Used to force string concatenation of two expressions.	"abc123" = "abc" **&** "123"
+	Formerly used to force string concatenation of two expressions. Use of this operator is now discouraged.	"abc123" = "abc" **+** "123"

Concatenation Operators

Concatenation operators are used to combine strings. VBA contains the two concatenation operators shown in the table in **Figure 1-10.** It is recommended that you use the **&** operator instead of the **+** operator whenever possible to eliminate any confusion with the **+** operator being used in an arithmetic expression.

Logical Operators

Logical operators are used to perform logical operations. They are used to combine two or more comparison tests into a single compound comparison expression that returns a Boolean value of **True** or **False**. Comparisons are evaluated from left to right unless explicitly indicated by parentheses. VBA contains the logical operators shown in the table in **Figure 1-11.**

Figure 1-11.
VBA logical operators.

Operator	Description	Syntax
And	Used to perform a logical conjunction on two expressions.	A = B **And** C
Eqv	Used to perform a logical equivalence on two expressions.	A = B **Eqv** C
Imp	Used to perform a logical implication on two expressions.	A = B **Imp** C
Not	Used to perform a logical negation on an expression.	A = **Not** B
Or	Used to perform a logical disjunction on two expressions.	A = B **Or** C
Xor	Used to perform a logical exclusion on two expressions.	A = B **Xor** B

A detailed explanation of the different logical operators is beyond the scope of this textbook. Refer to a comprehensive Visual Basic textbook for additional information regarding logical operators.

Exercise 1-2

Evaluate the following expressions for the value of the variable to the left of the **=** assignment operator. Assume the variable names and their values are initialized as:

```
intCounter = 10
lngDistance1 = 250.5
strFirstName = "John"
strLastName = "Smith"
```

1. lngDistance2 = intCounter * 25 + 50.0
2. blnResult1 = lngDistance2 > lngDistance1
3. intNewCounter = intCounter ^ 3
4. blnResult2 = intNewCounter <> lngDistance2
5. strNewName = strFirstName & " " & strLastName *(Note the use of the two quotes with the space between them. This allows the first and last name to be separated by a space.)*
6. lngResult = lngDistance1 Mod 2   250 / 2
7. blnResult3 = blnResult1 And blnResult2

Decision Structures

Decision structures provide a means of testing a condition, or multiple conditions, in your program and then performing different operations based on the result. This allows you to create branches in your program that control the flow of program execution.

If...Then Decision Structure

The basic **If...Then** decision structure tests a condition and evaluates whether the condition is **True** or **False**. If the condition is **True**, the next statement after **Then** is executed. If the condition is **False**, the next statement is skipped. The syntax is:

If *condition* Then *statement*

The condition can be any expression that results in a numeric value when evaluated. In VBA, **True** is *always* any nonzero value, whereas **False** is *always* zero. The statement following **Then** can be any valid VBA code. An example of the basic **If...Then** structure is:

```
' If the counter is greater than 10, tell the user in a message box.
If intCounter > 10 Then MsgBox "Counter is greater than ten!"
```

Figure 1-12.
An example of a
message box used
with an **If…Then**
decision structure.

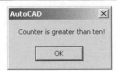

In this example, the integer variable *intCounter* is tested to see if its value is greater than 10. If it is greater, the condition is **True** and the code after **Then** is executed. In this case, a message box is displayed informing the user of the situation, **Figure 1-12**. If *intCounter* is less than or equal to 10, the code after **Then** is disregarded and control goes to the next line of the program.

It is also possible to test a condition and execute multiple lines, or a *block*, of code using the **If…Then** structure:

```
If condition Then
    statement1
    statement2
    statement3
End If
```

The **End If** statement indicates the end of the block of code. An example of **If…Then** and **End If** to execute a block of code is:

```
' If the counter is greater than 10, tell the user and reset the counter to 0.
If intCounter > 10 Then
    MsgBox "Counter is greater than ten!"
    intCounter = 0
End If
```

In this example, all of the statements after **Then** and before **End If** are executed when the condition of *intCounter* greater than 10 is **True**.

If…Then…Else Decision Structure

The **If…Then…Else** decision structure provides a way to execute one of two blocks of code depending on whether the evaluated condition is **True** or **False**. The syntax is:

```
If condition Then
    statement
Else
    statement
End If
```

If the condition is evaluated and found to be **True**, the block of code between **Then** and **Else** is executed. If the condition is **False**, the block of code between **Else** and **End If** is executed.

An example of the **If…Then…Else** structure is:

```
' If the counter is greater than 10, tell the user it is greater. If not, tell the
' user the counter is less than 10.
If intCounter > 10 Then
    MsgBox "Counter is greater than ten!"
Else
    MsgBox "Counter is less than ten!"
End If
```

Figure 1-13.
An example of a
message box used
with an **If...Then...Else**
decision structure.

In this example, if the *intCounter* variable is greater than ten, a message box is displayed indicating this to the user. Otherwise, a message box is displayed informing the user that the *intCounter* variable is less than ten, as shown in **Figure 1-13.**

The **If...Then** and **If...Then...Else** decision structures work similar to the AutoLISP **(if)** function, but again, in VBA the concept is somewhat simplified. In AutoLISP, you need to use the **(progn)** function to indicate blocks of code. In VBA, however, the **Else** and **End If** statements indicate the block of code by default. VBA also offers you more conditional testing options than AutoLISP. The **If...Then...ElseIf** decision structure discussed in the next section allows you to test as many conditions as you want. In AutoLISP, you can only test one condition.

AutoLISP vs. VBA

If...Then...ElseIf Decision Structure

The **If...Then...ElseIf** decision structure allows you to test multiple conditions within the same structure. This allows you to execute one of several blocks of code based on the evaluated condition. The syntax is:

```
If condition1 Then
    statement
ElseIf condition2 Then
    statement
ElseIf condition3 Then
    statement
Else
    statement
End If
```

Each condition is tested in order from the first to the last until an evaluated condition is **True**. Then, all of the statements between **Then** and the next **ElseIf** or **Else** are executed. Control is then passed to the line following the **End If** at the end of the structure skipping any remaining conditions. If all the conditions are **False**, the statements between **Else** and **End If** are executed. This allows you to create a "default" condition.

An example of the **If...Then...ElseIf** structure is:

```
' Test the value of the counter using increments of five and
' tell the user in which range the value falls.
If intCounter < 5 Then
    MsgBox "Counter is less than five!"
ElseIf intCounter < 10 Then
    MsgBox "Counter is between five and ten!"
ElseIf intCounter < 15 Then
    MsgBox "Counter is between ten and fifteen!"
Else
    MsgBox "Counter is over fifteen!"
End If
```

Figure 1-14.
An example of a message box used with an **If...Then...ElseIf** decision structure.

The *intCounter* variable is first checked to see if it is less than five, then if it is less than ten, and so on. Depending on which condition is **True**, a message box is displayed indicating the range in which the value falls, **Figure 1-14.**

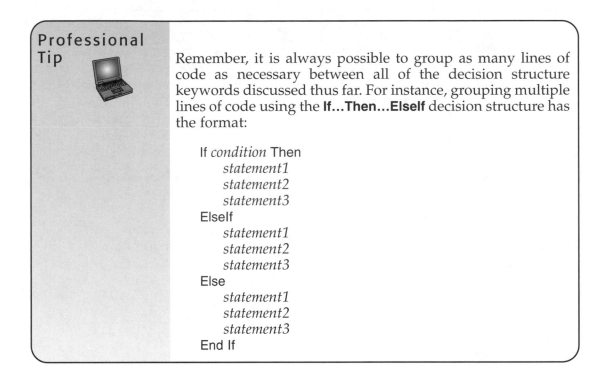

Professional Tip

Remember, it is always possible to group as many lines of code as necessary between all of the decision structure keywords discussed thus far. For instance, grouping multiple lines of code using the **If...Then...ElseIf** decision structure has the format:

```
If condition Then
        statement1
        statement2
        statement3
ElseIf
        statement1
        statement2
        statement3
Else
        statement1
        statement2
        statement3
End If
```

Top-Down Conditional Testing

The previous example is called ***top-down conditional testing.*** The top-down approach to conditional checking is sometimes referred to as *waterfall* or *cascade* programming because, like water falling over a waterfall, code is executed as control falls through the program. This concept is even more evident with the **Select Case...** decision structure described in the next section.

Looking at the previous example, you can see that the top-down order of the conditional testing is very important to the outcome. If the same structure first checked to see if the *intCounter* variable was less than 15, the functionality of the structure changes completely. For example, a value of 4 would result in the message box that indicates the value is between 10 and 15, which is incorrect. This top-down structure also allows the **Else** keyword to be used as a default for any condition where the value of the variable is over 15.

Select Case... Decision Structure

The **Select Case...** decision structure provides the same functionality as the **If...Then...ElseIf** decision structure. It should be used when many different conditions need to be tested. The syntax is:

```
Select Case condition
    Case condition1
        statement
    Case condition2
        statement
    Case condition3
        statement
    Case condition4
        statement
    Case Else
        statement
End Select
```

The test condition is evaluated once at the beginning of the **Select Case...** decision structure. The result of the evaluation is then passed down to the included **Case** statements where each condition is tested until a match is found. Once a match is found, the statements for that case are executed, the **Select Case...** structure is exited, and control is passed to the line after **End Select**. All other **Case** statements after the conditional match are disregarded.

The **Case Else** statement is optional and can be used when a default condition is desired. The code for the **Case Else** condition executes if no other matches are found.

An example of the **Select Case...** structure is:

```
' Determine which color is represented by the integer variable intColor by
' comparing its value with the AutoCAD color constants and display a
' message box informing the user.
Select Case intColor
    Case acRed
        MsgBox "Color selected is red!"

    Case acYellow
        MsgBox "Color selected is yellow!"

    Case acGreen
        MsgBox "Color selected is green!"

    Case acCyan
        MsgBox "Color selected is cyan!"

    Case acBlue
        MsgBox "Color selected is blue!"

    Case acMagenta
        MsgBox "Color selected is magenta!"

    Case acWhite
        MsgBox "Color selected is white!"

    Case Else
        MsgBox "Invalid color selected!"
End Select
```

The variable *intColor* is first evaluated and its value compared with the first seven AutoCAD color constants until a match is found. If no match is found, a message box with the message Invalid color selected! is displayed, as shown in **Figure 1-15.**

Figure 1-15.
An example of a
message box used
with a **Select Case...**
decision structure.

As you can see, the **Select Case...** decision structure is very similar to the **If...Then...ElseIf** decision structure. However, there is one major difference. The **Select Case...** structure can only evaluate *one* condition at the top of the decision structure, whereas the **If...Then...ElseIf** structure can evaluate multiple conditions. This is an important consideration when deciding which structure to use in your program.

AutoLISP vs. VBA

The **Select Case...** decision structure is very similar to the AutoLISP **(cond)** function. In AutoLISP, the example on the previous page looks like:

```
; Determine which color is represented by the integer variable intColor by
; comparing its value with the AutoCAD color constants and then display a
; message box informing the user.
(cond
     ((intColor = 1)
          (alert "Color selected is red!")
     )
     ((intColor = 2)
          (alert "Color selected is yellow!")
     )
     ((intColor = 3)
          (alert "Color selected is green!")
     )
     ((intColor = 4)
          (alert "Color selected is cyan!")
     )
     ((intColor = 5)
          (alert "Color selected is blue!")
     )
     ((intColor = 6)
          (alert "Color selected is magenta!")
     )
     ((intColor = 7)
          (alert "Color selected is white!")
     )
     (T
          (alert "Invalid color selected!")
     )
); end cond
```

Notice that both programming languages allow you to specify a default value that *always* evaluates to true and is *always* the last condition in each structure. These decision structures rely heavily on the waterfall or cascade approach to program execution explained earlier.

Loop Structures

Loop structures provide a means of repeating one or more statements. The number of times the statements are repeated is determined by one of the following:

- Number specified explicitly.
- Number of items in an array or collection.
- Conditional statement.

For…Next Loop Structure

If you know exactly how many times you want to repeat a block of statements, you can use the **For…Next** loop structure. This structure relies on an automated counter variable that can be changed either in positive or negative increments, depending on your needs. The syntax is:

```
For counter = start number To end number Step increment
    statement1
    statement2
    statement3
Next counter
```

The **Step** keyword is optional. If it is omitted, by default the value of the counter is increased by one each time.

An example of the **For…Next** loop structure is:

```
' Display a message box ten times (1 to 10).
For intCounter = 1 To 10
    MsgBox "Counter = " & intCounter
Next intCounter
```

This example will display a message box ten times, each time displaying the incremented counter concatenated to the phrase Counter = using the **&** operator introduced earlier. Notice that the **Step** keyword is not included in the code. Therefore, the increment is 1. The last number displayed is 10, as seen in **Figure 1-16.** Once the value of *intCounter* is greater than 10, the program exits the loop. The next line of code after the loop is then executed.

To process the same loop structure in reverse, you could use the **Step** keyword with a negative increment value:

```
' Display a message box ten times (10 to 1).
For intCounter = 10 To 1 Step –1
    MsgBox "Counter = " & intCounter
Next intCounter
```

This example also displays a message box ten times. However, this time the counter *decreases* from 10 in increments of 1. The last number to be displayed is 1, as seen in **Figure 1-17.**

Figure 1-16.
An example of a message box used with a **For…Next** decision structure.

Figure 1-17.
An example of a
message box used
with **For...Next**
decision structure
shown in **Figure 1-16,**
but with a negative
increment.

AutoLISP vs. VBA

The **For...Next** loop structure is similar to the AutoLISP **(repeat)** function. The only major difference is that there is no "step" option in AutoLISP. In AutoLISP, the example on the previous page looks like:

```
; Display an alert box ten times.
(setq intCounter 1)
(repeat 10
    (alert (strcat "Counter = " intCounter))
    (setq intCounter (1+ intCounter))
)
```

Notice that in AutoLISP you must increase the counter in code. An automatic increase function is not provided in AutoLISP as it is in VBA.

For Each...Next Loop Structure

The **For Each...Next** loop structure allows you to process each item in an array without regard to the number of elements contained within. The syntax is:

```
For Each element In array
    statement1
    statement2
    statement3
Next element
```

When processing an array, the element variable must be declared as a variant data type.

An example of the **For Each...Next** loop structure is:

```
' Display all items in an array.
For Each varItem In strDaysToXmas
    MsgBox varItem
Next
```

A message box is displayed with each string item in the array ending with the last item. There is no need to know the length of the array; it is calculated for you. In this example, the array *strDaysToXmas* contains the verses to the "12 days of Christmas" and the last item is "12 drummers drumming," as seen in **Figure 1-18.**

Figure 1-18.
An example of a
message box used
with a **For Each...Next**
decision structure.

AutoLISP vs. VBA

The **For Each...Next** loop structure is very similar to the AutoLISP **(foreach)** function. In AutoLISP, the example on the previous page looks like:

```
; Display all items in a list.
(foreach strXmasDay lstDaysToXmas
    (alert strXmasDay)
)
```

Do While... Loop Structure

The **Do While...** loop structure repeats a block of code while a condition statement is true, or nonzero. Once the condition is false, the block of code is skipped and the next line after **Loop** is executed. The syntax is:

```
Do While condition
    statement1
    statement2
    statement3
Loop
```

An example of the **Do While...** loop structure is:

```
' Display a message box while the counter is less than 10.
' Initialize the counter to 1.
intCounter = 1
Do While intCounter < 10
    MsgBox "Counter = " & intCounter
    IntCounter = intCounter + 1
Loop
```

The message box is displayed nine times while *intCounter* is less than 10. The last number displayed is 9, as seen in **Figure 1-19.** Once *intCounter* is equal to 10, the block of code that displays the message box is skipped because the conditional statement is false.

Figure 1-19.
An example of a message box used with a **Do While...** decision structure.

The **Do While...** loop structure is very similar to the AutoLISP **(while)** function. In AutoLISP, the example on the previous page looks like:

```
; Display a message box while the counter is less than 10.
; Initialize the counter to 1.
(setq intCounter 1)
(While (intCounter < 10)
    (alert (strcat "Counter = " intCounter))
    (setq IntCounter (1+ intCounter))
)
```

Do...Loop While Loop Structure

The **Do...Loop While** loop structure works the same as the **Do While...** structure except for one difference—the conditional test is at the bottom of the structure. Therefore, the block of code within the structure is always executed at least once. The syntax is:

```
Do
    statement1
    statement2
    statement3
Loop While condition
```

As you can see, this structure is basically the **Do While...** loop structure except flipped upside down.

An example of the **Do...Loop While** loop structure is:

```
Do
    MsgBox "Counter = " & intCounter
    IntCounter = intCounter + 1
Loop While intCounter < 10
```

This example is very similar to the example used to explain the **Do While...** loop structure, but do not be deceived. After initializing *intCounter* to 1, the block of code repeats ten times, as opposed to repeating nine times as seen in the earlier example. This is because even though the value of *intCounter* reaches 10 in both examples, the conditional test is not executed until the end of the structure in this example.

Do Until... Loop Structure

The **Do Until...** loop structure is very similar to the **Do While...** loop structure except the block of code within the structure is executed *until* the conditional statement is true. In the **Do While...** loop structure the block of code is executed *while* the conditional statement is true. The syntax is:

```
Do Until condition
    statement1
    statement2
    statement3
Loop
```

An example of the **Do Until...** loop structure is:

```
Do Until intCounter = 10
    MsgBox "Counter = " & intCounter
    IntCounter = intCounter + 1
Loop
```

If the *intCounter* variable is initialized to 1, this example produces the same result as the example used to explain the **Do While...** loop structure. The message box is displayed nine times until *intCounter* is equal to 10.

Do...Loop Until Loop Structure

The **Do...Loop Until** loop structure works the same as the **Do Until...** structure except for one difference. The conditional test is at the bottom of the structure, similar to the **Do...Loop While** structure. Therefore, the block of code within the structure is executed at least once, just as with the **Do...Loop While** structure. The syntax is:

```
Do
    statement1
    statement2
    statement3
Loop Until condition
```

The **Do...Loop Until** loop structure is basically the same as the **Do Until...** loop structure except flipped upside down. An example of the **Do...Loop Until** loop structure is:

```
Do
    MsgBox "Counter = " & intCounter
    IntCounter = intCounter + 1
Loop Until intCounter = 10
```

In this example, if the *intCounter* variable is initialized to 1, the block of code is repeated ten times until *intCounter* is equal to 10.

Professional Tip

A loop structure can be exited at any time by using either the **Exit Do** or the **Exit For** statements. The exiting of a loop structure is typically determined by a conditional test. The syntax to exit a **Do While...** loop structure is:

```
Do While condition
    statement1
    If condition Then Exit Do
    statement2
Loop
```

If the condition is true, the loop is exited immediately and control is passed to the next line in your program after **Loop**. None of the other statements in the loop will be executed. The syntax used to exit a **For...Next** loop structure is similar:

```
For counter = start number To end number
    statement1
    If condition Then Exit For
    statement2
Next counter
```

Nested Control Structures

It is possible to include control structures within other control structures. This is considered *nesting.* One common example of nesting is including a decision structure within a loop structure:

```
For intCounter = 1 to 10
    If intCounter < 5 Then
        MsgBox "Counter is less than five!"
    Else
        MsgBox "Counter is greater than five!"
    End If
Next intCounter
```

Notice the indentation in the above code. When nesting control structures, it is common to indent each nested structure to visually define where one structure starts and another structure ends. This makes your code much easier to understand. In the above code, you can clearly see that the **If...Then...Else** structure is nested within the **For...Next** structure.

Let's Review...

Operators, Decision Structures, Loop Structures, and Nested Control Structures

- Operators allow you to perform different data operations in a program.
- Decision structures allow you to perform different operations based on one or more conditional tests.
- Loop structures allow you to repeat a block of code multiple times. The number of times the code repeats is determined by either a specific number or a conditional test.
- Control structures can be nested.

Exercise 1-3

Using the control structures described in this chapter, create the code necessary for each of the following scenarios.
1. Check to see if the integer variable *intValue* is greater than 25. If so, display a message box that says Value is greater than 25! Otherwise, display a message box that says Value is less than 25!
2. Display a message box ten times that contains the values 100 through 1000 in increments of 100.
3. Given the string array *strStudents* of unknown length that contains the names of all the students in a class, display a message box with each name.
4. Given the integer array *intArray* that contains 20 integer values, check each value to see if it is equal to 99. If a value of 99 is found, display a message box that says Value of 99 found! and immediately stop checking any more array items.

Procedures

Whenever you construct a complex computer program, it is best to break up the program into small chunks that perform certain tasks. This is often referred to as *modular programming.* The modular approach to programming makes your code much easier to understand and maintain.

Procedures help facilitate modular programming. A *procedure* is programming code that is grouped together and assigned a unique name that can then be referenced anywhere in the program. When you reference, or invoke, a procedure, all of the code contained in the procedure is executed. This process is typically known as *calling* a procedure. There are two types of procedures in VBA—**Subs** and **Functions**.

Sub Procedures

A **Sub** *procedure* is the most basic procedure type. It is simply a named collection of programming code that, when called, is executed. Control is returned to the program when the **Sub** is complete. The syntax for a **Sub** procedure is:

```
Sub SubName()

    statement1
    statement2
    statement3

End Sub
```

In this example, the **Sub** name is *SubName*. All of the code between the **Sub** declaration and the **End Sub** statement is run when the **Sub** is called in the program.

To call a **Sub**, simply enter the name of the **Sub** in your program:

```
SubName
```

When the program comes to this line, the *SubName* code is executed and control is then passed back to the next line in the program.

A classic example of a **Sub** is:

```
' Subroutine that displays a message box with "Hello World."
Sub HelloWorld()

    ' Display message box with "Hello World."
    MsgBox "Hello World!"

End Sub
```

The *HelloWorld* **Sub** can now be called from a main **Sub**, or any other procedure for that matter:

```
' Main program.
Sub Main()

    ' Call the HelloWorld Sub.
    HelloWorld

End Sub
```

Figure 1-20.
An example of a message box used with a **Sub** procedure.

When the *Main* **Sub** is run and execution gets to the line of code that calls the *HelloWorld* **Sub**, the program enters the *HelloWorld* **Sub** and executes each line of code until **End Sub** is encountered. In this example, the message box shown in **Figure 1-20** is displayed. When the **Sub** is exited, control transfers back to the next line of code in the original *Main* **Sub**.

AutoLISP vs. VBA

A **Sub** procedure in VBA is basically the same thing as a function defined in AutoLISP using **(defun)**. In AutoLISP, the example on the previous page looks like:

```
; Display message box with "Hello World."
(defun HelloWorld()

    ; Display message box with "Hello World."
    (alert "Hello World!")

)
```

First, you must define the function *HelloWorld*. You can then call the *HelloWorld* function anywhere in the program:

```
; Main program.
(defun Main()

    ; Call the HelloWorld function.
    (HelloWorld)

)
```

Of course, you have to wrap the function call in parentheses. This *is* AutoLISP, after all!

Function Procedures

A **Function** *procedure* is the same as a **Sub** procedure except that it returns a value. Because of this, the syntax for a **Function** procedure is a bit different:

```
Function FunctionName(Argument as Integer) As Integer

    Dim ReturnValue As Integer

    statement1
    statement2
    statement3

    FunctionName = ReturnValue

End Function
```

A **Function** returns a value by assigning the return value to the **Function** name, typically at the end of the procedure. This means that the **Function** has to be declared as the same data type as the value being returned. In the example above, the **Function** has been declared as an **Integer** because that is the type of return value desired. The variable between the parentheses in the **Function** definition is referred to as an argument and is discussed later in this chapter. An example of calling a **Function** is:

```
Sub Main ()

    Dim intFunctionValue As Integer
    intFunctionValue = FunctionName(1)

End Sub
```

When the program comes to the assignment operator, the *FunctionName* **Function** is called and its return value is assigned to the *intFunctionValue* variable. As a rule, the variable being assigned to a **Function** return value must always be the same data type as the **Function**.

An example of a typical **Function** is:

```
' Function to calculate area based on width × height.
Function AreaCalc(dblWidth as Double, dblHeight as Double) as Double

    Dim dblArea as Double

    ' Get area by multiplying width x height.
    dblArea = dblWidth * dblHeight

    ' Return total to calling function.
    AreaCalc = dblArea

End Function
```

You can now call the *AreaCalc* **Function** from any procedure and calculate an area:

```
' Main program.
Sub Main()

    Dim dblWidth As Double
    Dim dblHeight As Double
    Dim dblArea as Double

    ' Assign the width and height.
    dblWidth = 10.0
    dblHeight = 5.0

    ' Calculate area using AreaCalc function.
    dblArea = AreaCalc(dblWidth, dblHeight)

    ' Display area for user.
    MsgBox "Total area = " & dblArea

End Sub
```

The values contained in the *dblWidth* and *dblHeight* variables are used by the *AreaCalc* **Function** to calculate the area and return it to the calling **Sub** *Main* where the area value is stored in the *dblArea* variable. This value is then displayed to the user in a message box, as seen in **Figure 1-21.**

In this example, the width and height are passed to the *AreaCalc* function as parameters, or arguments. Arguments are discussed in the next section. Because of their dynamic nature, most functions rely on arguments. **Functions** are very versatile, especially when you utilize arguments. One **Function** definition can be used with many different argument values to calculate and return different results.

Figure 1-21.
An example of a
message box used
with a **Function**
procedure.

AutoLISP vs. VBA

Functions in VBA are a bit different from functions in AutoLISP. An AutoLISP function simply returns the result of the last expression evaluated. In AutoLISP, the example on the previous page looks like:

```
; Function to calculate area based on width x height.
(defun AreaCalc (dblWidth dblHeight / dblArea)

    ; Get area by multiplying width x height.
    (setq dblArea (* dblWidth dblHeight))

    ; Return total to calling function.
    dblArea

)
```

You can then call the *AreaCalc* function anywhere in your program:

```
; Main program.
(defun Main(/ dblWidth dblHeight dblArea)

    (setq dblWidth 10.0)
    (setq dblHeight 5.0)

    ; Calculate area using AreaCalc function.
    (setq dblArea (AreaCalc dblWidth dblHeight))

    ; Display area for user.
    (alert (strcat "Total area = " dblArea))

)
```

Professional Tip

Modular programming using procedures is one of the best ways to create robust programs. Not only does it reduce repetitious code, but it also reduces bugs (i.e. less code = less bugs).

Procedure Arguments

In the **Function** examples above, the variables between the **Function** parentheses are considered arguments, or parameters, of the function. *Arguments* are values that are "passed" to a procedure that can then be used within the procedure itself. They are typically variables, but arguments can also be constants or even expressions. A procedure can have multiple arguments, if necessary. Multiple arguments are always separated by commas.

By default, arguments are passed to a procedure using a method called *by reference,* usually abbreviated in code as **ByRef**. Passing a variable by reference allows you to change the original value of the variable in memory. When a variable that is passed by reference is changed in your procedure, it affects all references to that variable in the calling procedure, and maybe beyond, depending on the scope of the variable. Variable scope is discussed a little later in this chapter.

The syntax for declaring a **Function** whose arguments will be passed by reference is:

```
Function FunctionName(ByRef Argument As DataType) As Integer

    statement1
    statement2
    statement3

End Function
```

Since passing arguments by reference is the default, you may omit the **ByRef** keyword with the same result:

```
Function FunctionName (Argument As DataType) As Integer

    statement1
    statement2
    statement3

End Function
```

An example of a typical **Function** that relies on arguments is the *AreaCalc* **Function** presented earlier. This **Function** utilizes two arguments that are both declared to be the double data type:

```
' Function to calculate area based on width × height.
Function AreaCalc (dblWidth as Double, dblHeight as Double) as Double

    Dim dblArea as Double

    ' Get area by multiplying width × height.
    dblArea = dblWidth * dblHeight

    ' Return total to calling function.
    AreaCalc = dblArea

End Function
```

In this example, if either the *dblWidth* variable or the *dblHeight* variable is changed within the *AreaCalc* function, its value is also changed in the calling procedure. Remember, by default, argument variables are *always* passed by reference.

AutoLISP vs. VBA

AutoLISP argument variables are declared by listing them before the forward slash (/) when the function is defined. Multiple argument variables are separated by spaces. The AreaCalc function seen earlier is a good example:

```
; Function to calculate area based on width x height.
(defun AreaCalc (dblWidth dblHeight / dblArea)
```

It is also possible to pass a variable *by value,* usually abbreviated in code as **ByVal**. The by value method makes a copy of the argument variable so that any changes made in the procedure only affect the copy and not the original variable. The syntax for declaring a **Function** whose arguments will be passed by value is:

```
Function FunctionName (ByVal Argument As DataType) As Integer

    statement1
    statement2
    statement3

End Function
```

An example of passing an argument by value is:

```
' Function to get the square root of a number.
Function GetSquareRoot (ByVal dblNumber as Double) as Double

    ' If invalid number entered exit the function.
    If dblNumber < 0 Then
        Exit Function
    ' Get the square root and return it.
    Else
        GetSquareRoot = Sqr(dblNumber)
    End If

End Function
```

Because the argument variable *dblNumber* is declared as **ByVal**, a copy is used within the *GetSquareRoot* **Function** and the original value of the variable in the calling procedure is maintained.

AutoLISP vs. VBA

AutoLISP argument variables are *always* passed by value. You always get a copy of whatever is stored in an AutoLISP argument variable while the value of the original variable in the calling procedure is maintained.

Professional Tip

The *GetSquareRoot* **Function** is elegant in its simplicity. A simple **If...Then...Else** decision structure is used to first determine if an invalid negative number was passed to the **Function**. If so, it is immediately dealt with by exiting the **Function** using the **Exit Function** statement. Otherwise, the square root is calculated and returned. The best part is that all of this is done within the decision structure itself.

Figure 1-22.
A type mismatch
error.

Argument Data Types

As seen, it is always necessary in VBA to declare the data type of an argument. In the following example, the data type of the **Sub** argument is declared as an integer.

Sub *SubName(Argument* as Integer)

This means that when the **Sub** is called in your program, an integer value must be passed in the argument:

```
Sub Main ()

    Dim intValue as Integer

    ' Set intValue to 1.
    intValue = 1

    ' Call the Sub with intValue as the argument.
    SubName(intValue)

End Sub
```

If the correct data type is not passed in the argument, the run-time error shown in **Figure 1-22** is displayed.

Declaring an argument data type also allows you to take advantage of the **Auto Quick Info** feature in the AutoCAD **Visual Basic Editor**, which is discussed in Chapter 3. The **Auto Quick Info** feature is a real time-saver that prompts you for the correct variable data type as you are writing code.

Calling a Procedure with Arguments

Subs and **Functions** can be called using different methods. To call a **Function** that has one or more arguments, it is necessary to enclose the arguments in parentheses and separate multiple arguments with commas:

intFunctionValue = FunctionName (intValue1, intValue2)

A **Sub** that has one or more arguments can be called using one of two different methods. The first method does not require that the arguments be enclosed in parentheses:

SubName intValue1, intValue2

Using this method, a space separates the **Sub** name and the first argument with additional arguments separated by commas. The second method of calling a **Sub** that has one or more arguments is:

Call SubName(intValue1, intValue2)

This method requires that you use the **Call** keyword and enclose all of the arguments in parentheses. Because it requires less code, the first method of calling a procedure is used more often, but either method is valid. You can use whichever method you prefer.

Calling functions with arguments in AutoLISP is similar to how it is done in VBA, except commas are not needed to separate function arguments. For example, the call to the AutoLISP *AreaCalc* function seen earlier had two arguments, *dblWidth* and *dblHeight*. When the function is called, the arguments are simply separated by spaces:

```
; Calculate area using AreaCalc function.
(setq dblArea (AreaCalc dblWidth dblHeight))
```

Also, remember that the *dblWidth* and *dblHeight* argument variable values cannot be changed in the function because they are always passed by value.

Variable Scope

All of the variables and constants you declare in your program have a particular lifetime, or scope. The *scope* of a variable determines where and when you can retrieve or set the value of the variable.

Local Variables

A variable that is declared within a procedure is considered a *local variable* because its value can only be set or retrieved from within the procedure in which the variable is declared. Once you exit the procedure, the value of the variable is erased.

Every local variable has its own unique memory space. This enables you to use variables with the same name in multiple procedures without worrying about what effect they have on each other. For example:

```
Sub SubName1()

    Dim intCounter As Integer
    IntCounter = 1

    statement1
    statement2
    statement3

End Sub

Sub SubName2()

    Dim intCounter As Integer
    IntCounter = 2

    statement1
    statement2
    statement3

End Sub
```

The variable *IntCounter* is used in each **Sub**, yet the value of each is set independent of each other. Setting *IntCounter* in one **Sub** has no affect on the value of *IntCounter* in the other **Sub**.

Module and Form Variables

A variable that is declared outside of all procedures in your program is said to be a *module variable* or *form variable*. Modules and forms are discussed in detail in Chapter 14. When a variable is declared outside of a procedure, it can be used by all procedures that are part of that module or form. The scope of a variable of this type is considered larger than a local variable because any procedure in the same module or form can set or retrieve its value.

In the following example, each **Sub** is referencing the same variable.

```
Dim intCounter As Integer

Sub Form1()

    intCounter = 1

    statement1
    statement2
    statement3

End Sub

Sub Form2()

    intCounter = intCounter + 1

    statement1
    statement2
    statement3

End Sub
```

Calling the *Form1* **Sub** first sets the value of *intCounter* to 1. A call to *Form2* directly thereafter will increase the value of *intCounter* by 1 so that it is now equal to 2. Subsequent calls to *Form2* will continue to increase *intCounter* by 1 each time.

Global Variables

The **Public** keyword allows you to increase the scope of a variable so that the variable can be referenced anywhere in your application. The syntax is:

```
Public intCounter As Integer
```

Simply replace the **Dim** keyword with the **Public** keyword. A variable used in this type of all-encompassing scope is considered a *global variable*.

Private Variables

The **Private** keyword ensures that the scope of a variable is limited to the module or form in which the variable is declared. This is called a *private variable*. The keyword is implied by default, but its use is encouraged to make the scope of a variable distinguishable and your code easier to understand. The syntax is similar to that of the **Public** keyword:

```
Private intCounter As Integer
```

Static Variables

The **Static** keyword affects the scope of a variable in a unique fashion. It allows you to declare a local variable whose value is not erased when you exit a procedure. A variable used in this manner is called a *static variable*. The variable retains the value it was last set to when the procedure is called the next time. Usage of the **Static** keyword is:

```
Sub SubName()

    Static intCounter As Integer

    intCounter = intCounter + 1

    statement1
    statement2
    statement3

End Sub
```

Each time *SubName* is called the *intCounter* variable will be increased by 1, even though it is local. If a variable is declared in another **Sub** with the same name, the value of the second variable would have no effect on the value of the first variable.

AutoLISP vs. VBA

Variable scope in AutoLISP is a bit more simplified; scope is either global or it is not global. The only way to limit the scope of an AutoLISP variable to a particular function is to include it between the parentheses after the forward slash (/) when the function is defined. Using the *AreaCalc* function as an example:

```
; Function to calculate area based on width x height.
(defun AreaCalc (dblWidth dblHeight / dblArea)
```

The *dblArea* variable is considered local to the *AreaCalc* function. To make an AutoLISP variable global, simply do not include its name in the function definition.

As in VBA, once a variable is global, it can be changed anywhere in a program. Although with AutoLISP the risk increases. *Any* AutoLISP program that is loaded can access and change *any other* AutoLISP global variable!

Procedure Scope

Procedures also have a scope. Both the **Public** and **Private** keywords can be used when defining a **Sub** or **Function**. By default, a procedure is considered to be **Public**, or global, so it can be used anywhere in your program. To provide clarity, you should try to always explicitly declare a procedure's scope.

The syntax for declaring a **Public Sub** is:

```
Public Sub SubName()

    statement1
    statement2
    statement3

End Sub
```

A **Public Function** is declared similarly:

```
Public Function FunctionName() As Integer

    statement1
    statement2
    statement3

End Sub
```

Just like a **Private** variable, a **Private** procedure can only be used in the module or form in which the procedure is declared. **Private** procedures are use exclusively on forms in VBA.

To declare a **Private Sub**:

```
Private Sub SubName()

    statement1
    statement2
    statement3

End Sub
```

A **Private Function** is declared similarly:

```
Private Function FunctionName() As Integer

    statement1
    statement2
    statement3

End Sub
```

Coding Conventions

There are a number of different coding conventions to keep in mind when writing VBA programs. Some conventions do not affect functionality and are only meant to enhance the readability of your code. However, other conventions may generate errors if they are violated. The following sections explain both types.

Case Sensitivity

VBA is case sensitive. All variables, constants, arrays, and procedures you declare must match their declaration exactly when they are used in your program. Fortunately, there are tools in AutoCAD's **Visual Basic Editor** that help facilitate this requirement. There is an autocorrect feature that automatically fixes misspelled and wrong-case variables while you are typing. There is a catch; in order to use autocorrect you must use the **Option Explicit** statement mentioned earlier in this chapter. This statement forces you to explicitly declare all the variables in your program. You can see how declaring variables explicitly is advantageous. Autocorrect and other tools are discussed in detail in Chapter 3.

Adding Comments to Your Code

Besides good error trapping (discussed later), commenting your code is possibly the most important concept discussed in this chapter. It is crucial that you add explanatory comments to your code so when you, or most likely someone else, must update the code or fix any bugs, your intentions for the code can be easily understood. Adding comments is an easy suggestion to ignore, especially when you are programming in the heat of the moment. It is easy to tell yourself to add comments later when the program is finished, but it never happens. Take the time when you are writing your code to add explanatory comments. The time saved when the code must be updated will be multifold.

There are two different conventions generally used to add comments to VBA programs. You can add general comments on individual lines in your code or you can add specific comments at the end of a single line of code. Both methods rely on the apostrophe (') character to indicate a comment. When an apostrophe is encountered in the program, everything that follows on the same line is ignored. Examples of both styles are:

```
' This is a comment that resides on its own line.
' You can write as many lines as you need to explain the related block of code.
Dim intCounter As Integer      ' Or, you can comment on the same line like this.
intCounter = 0        ' Initialize counter to 0—this comment explains the line of code.
```

Remember, you can never have too many comments!

AutoLISP vs. VBA

Program comments in VBA are very similar to program comments in AutoLISP. All that is different is that an apostrophe (') is used to indicate a comment in VBA whereas the semicolon (;)is used in AutoLISP.

Writing Statements on Multiple Lines

Sometimes it is necessary to continue a long statement on the next line in your program. This helps make your code easier to read because it can all be seen on your screen or on a printout at one time. Line continuation is achieved by using the underscore (_) character preceded by a space at the end of the statement you want to continue. For example:

```
MsgBox "The integer values of the first seven AutoCAD colors are: " & _
    vbCrLf & vbCrLf & "Red: " & acRed & vbCrLf & "Yellow: " & acYellow & _
    vbCrLf & "Green: " & acGreen & vbCrLf & "Cyan: " & acCyan & _
    vbCrLf & "Blue: " & acBlue & vbCrLf & "Magenta: " & acMagenta & _
    vbCrLf & "White: " & acWhite
```

All five lines of code are considered as one argument to the **MsgBox** function. It is common to indent lines that are continued so that it is apparent they are associated with the preceding line.

Professional Tip

The **vbCrLf** constant shown in the above example is a line feed character that acts somewhat like the [Enter] key on the keyboard. Text that follows the **vbCrLf** constant is displayed on the next line, as shown in the message box in **Figure 1-23.**

Figure 1-23.
Line feeds are used
to display multiple
lines of text in a
VBA message box.

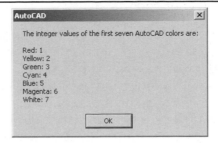

Caution

Comments may not follow a line continuation character on the same line of code.

Exercise 1-4

Create VBA procedures with the names given that perform the described tasks.
1. Create a sub named *WeekDays* that displays the name of each day of the week using a VBA message box. Use an array to store the name of each day.
2. Create a function named *GetCircumference* that accepts a circle diameter as an argument and returns the circle's circumference. *Hint:* circumference = pi × diameter.

Error Handling

Proper error handling is one of the most important aspects in determining how your program is perceived by users. No one likes a program that crashes, especially when they become stuck in AutoCAD's **Visual Basic Editor** in debug mode with an error message like the one shown in **Figure 1-24.**

This means nothing to the user. In fact, they probably find it quite annoying. Fortunately, there are a number of ways to exit a VBA program gracefully when errors occur. You can even choose to ignore errors if you wish and simply continue executing your program.

Figure 1-24.
Without proper
error handling, the
user may be faced
with a confusing
error message such
as this one.

On Error Goto... Statement

The **On Error Goto...** statement allows you to jump to another section of your program if an error occurs, avoiding the dreaded program crash. This is achieved using a label that identifies a line of code in the program. Labels can be any combination of characters that starts with a letter and ends with a colon (:). Labels must also start in the first (left-hand) column in the program. Using VBA labels, you can create blocks of code at the end of your procedures that can be used to respond to different error conditions. You can then inform the user what has happened, do some cleanup if necessary, and exit your program gracefully.

An example of a typical error handling label is:

```
ErrorHandler:
```

To jump to this line in the code, put the following statement somewhere in the program before where the *ErrorHandler* label is defined:

```
On Error Goto ErrorHandler
```

Now, if an error occurs anywhere in your program, execution will jump to the *ErrorHandler* label and skip the rest of the program code. A typical error handling structure is shown below. Notice the use of comments to explain the code.

```
Sub SubName()

    ' Implement error handling.
    On Error Goto ErrorHandler

    ' Execute some code.
    ' Go to the ErrorHandler label if something goes terribly wrong.
    statement1
    statement2
    statement3

' Exit program here when everything works as expected.
Exit Sub

' Here is our error handler block. Code execution only gets to this
' point when something bad happens.
ErrorHandler:

    ' Tell the user an error has occurred.
    MsgBox "An error has occurred. Program exiting."

    ' Do some cleanup if necessary and end the program.
    statement1
    statement2
    statement3

End Sub
```

An **Exit Sub** statement typically precedes an error handler label name, as shown above. This is the mechanism used to make the program execution stop, or exit, the **Sub** unless the error handler is explicitly called. If the **Exit Sub** statement does not precede the label, all of the code in the error handler is executed each time the program is run.

A real world example of error handling in VBA is:

```
' Try to open a file.
Sub OpenFile (strFileName As String)

    ' Implement error handling.
    On Error Goto ErrorHandler

    ' Try to open file.
    Open strFileName For Input As #1

' Exit program here when everything works as expected.
Exit Sub

' Here is our error handler block. Code execution only gets to this point
' when something bad happens.
ErrorHandler:

    ' Tell the user something went wrong.
    MsgBox "File " & strFileName & " could not be opened for input."

End Sub
```

When an error occurs trying to open the file name passed in the *strFileName* argument, the user will see the message shown in **Figure 1-25** and program execution will stop.

Sometimes, it is necessary to have more than one error handler defined for different situations. For example:

```
Sub SubName()

    statement1
    statement2
    statement3

' Exit program here when everything works as expected.
Exit Sub

' Here is our first error handler block.
ErrorHandler1:

    ' Tell user an error has occurred.
    MsgBox "An error has occurred. Program exiting."

    ' Do some cleanup if necessary and exit the program.
    statement1
    statement2
    statement3

' Exit program here so the second error handler does not run.
Exit Sub

' Here is our second error handler block.
ErrorHandler2:
```

Figure 1-25.
This error message was generated by error handling because the file could not be opened; the program exited gracefully.

```
        ' Tell the user some other error has occurred.
        MsgBox "Another error has occurred. Program exiting."

        ' Do some cleanup if necessary and exit the program.
        statement1
        statement2
        statement3

    End Sub
```

Adding an **Exit Sub** statement for the first error handler allows the use of a second error handler. In this way, if the first error handler is called, program execution will not cascade through the second error handler and run the wrong code.

Only one error handler can be active at any given time. The order in which the error handlers are referenced using the **Goto** statement determines which one is active. For example, the following code sets the first error handler active, executes a block of code, then sets the second error handler active for the rest of the program.

```
    Sub SubName()

        statement1
        statement2
        statement3

        ' Activate first error handler.
        On Error Goto ErrorHandler1

        statement4
        statement5
        statement6

        ' Activate second error handler. First error handler disabled!
        On Error Goto ErrorHandler2

        statement7
        statement8
        statement9

    ' Exit program here when everything works as expected.
    Exit Sub

    ' Here is our first error handler block.
    ErrorHandler1:

        ' Tell the user an error has occurred.
        MsgBox "An error has occurred. Program exiting."

        ' Do some cleanup if necessary and exit the program.
        statement1
        statement2
        statement3

    ' Exit program here so the second error handler does not run.
    Exit Sub

    ' Here is our second error handler block.
    ErrorHandler2:

        ' Tell the user some other error has occurred.
        MsgBox "Another error has occurred. Program exiting."
```

```
' Do some cleanup if necessary and exit the program.
statement1
statement2
statement3

End Sub
```

> **Caution**
>
> The **Goto** statement should be used sparingly. It is a throwback to the original Quick Basic programming language. Use of this statement has been discouraged for years because it makes a program more difficult to understand and/or debug when something goes wrong. Most VBA programmers used the **Goto** statement primarily for error handling only.

Resume Next Statement

Sometimes it is not necessary to handle errors explicitly, rather they can be simply ignored. This can be achieved by using the **Resume Next** statement. Using **Resume Next** allows the line of code that created the error to be bypassed and the next line code executed. Most typically, it is used in conjunction with the **On Error** statement:

```
On Error Resume Next
```

When execution of the code gets to this statement, any active error handlers are disabled. If an error is encountered, it is ignored and execution simply continues to the next line of code in the program.

Introduction to the VBA Err Object

VBA provides a powerful tool called the **Err** object for handling run time errors when they occur in your program. When an error occurs, the **Err** object returns a unique error number that you can identify and respond to accordingly. Even better, the **Err** object returns a text description of the error. The **Err** object and all of the other VBA objects are explained in detail in Chapter 2.

AutoLISP vs. VBA

AutoLISP provides a similar, although a little less powerful, method of error handling via the **(*error* msg)** function. Like the **Err** object in VBA, the **(*error*)** function automatically returns a description of an error when it occurs. All that is necessary is that the **(*error*)** function is not set to nil. The easiest way to do this is define an **(*error*)** function with one argument:

```
; Define our own error handling function.
(defun *error* (msg)

    ; Tell user what happened.
    (alert (strcat "Error: " msg))

    (princ)

)
```

Now, if an error occurs in the AutoLISP program, the **(*error*)** function is called so the user is informed and the program exits gracefully.

Whether working in AutoLISP or VBA, errors will occur. How you handle them can make the difference between a good program and a bad one.

Let's Review... Procedures, Procedure Arguments, Variable Scope, Coding Conventions, and Error Handling

- It is good programming practice to break up a program into small manageable chunks of related code that perform certain tasks called procedures.
- There are two types of procedures in VBA—**Subs** and **Functions**. A **Function** returns a value while a **Sub** does not.
- A procedure can have values passed to it as parameters or arguments.
- Arguments can be passed either by value or by reference. The **ByValue** statement passes a copy of the argument variable, whereas the **ByRef** statement passes the original argument variable.
- By default, argument variables are *always* passed by reference in VBA.
- All variables and procedures have a particular scope, or lifetime.
- Always comment your code!
- Error handling in VBA allows a program to exit gracefully when an error is encountered.

Chapter Test

Answer the following questions on a separate sheet of paper.

1. For what does the acronym VBA stand?
2. What does it mean to *dimension* a variable?
3. What is a variant data type and why should its use be avoided if possible?
4. Define the terms *early binding* and *late binding*.
5. Why is early binding of variables preferred over late binding of variables?
6. Write the code necessary to convert the string variable named *strName* to an integer variable named *intValue*.
7. Provide variable names for the following data values using Hungarian notation:
   A. Harley Davidson
   B. 15
   C. 999999999999999
   D. 3.75
   E. $100.00
   F. 12/25/00
   G. 10101010
   H. True *or* False
8. Describe what a *constant data type* is and why it might be used.
9. What is an *array data type?*
10. Which VBA statement allows you to change the size of an array at run time?
11. Evaluate the following expressions:
    A. 5.0 * 0.5 =
    B. 3.0 / 2.0 =
    C. 3.0 \ 2.0 =
    D. 3.0 Mod 2 =

12. What is a *comparison operator* and how is it used?
13. Explain what a *decision structure* is and give an example.
14. Which type of program structure allows you to repeat a block of code multiple times?
15. Which loop structure will process every item in an array or collection?
16. What is a VBA *procedure* and why is it used?
17. Describe the differences between a **Sub** procedure and a **Function** procedure.
18. What is the difference between passing procedure arguments *by reference* and passing arguments *by value?*
19. List the three different levels of variable scope and explain each.
20. Explain the advantages of adding explanatory comments to a program.
21. Which character allows you to continue a line of VBA code on the next line?

Programming Problems

Create VBA procedures with the names given that perform the described tasks. Write your code on a separate sheet of paper.

1. Write a **Sub** named *AcadColors* that displays the names of the first seven colors in AutoCAD (red, yellow, green, cyan, blue, magenta, and white) using a VBA message box. Use an array to store the name of each color and a loop structure to display the message box.
2. Write a **Function** named *ColorName* that accepts an integer argument representing one of the first seven AutoCAD color numbers. When the function is run, it should display a VBA message box with the integer value and its corresponding color name (1=red, 2=yellow, 3=green, 4=cyan, 5=blue, 6=magenta, 7=white).
3. Write a **Function** named *DegToRad* that converts degrees to radians. The degree value to convert should be passed as an argument to function. Display the result in a VBA message box. Hint: radians = $\pi \times$ (degrees $\div$ 180).
4. Create an error handler named *ErrorHandler* for the function *ColorName* created in Problem 2 that checks for an invalid color number argument when the function is called (i.e. negative numbers, etc.). If an invalid color number is passed in the argument, the error handler should display a VBA message box informing the user and exit the function gracefully.

The code examples in this chapter are supplied on the Student CD. A—First, open the **Open VBA Project** dialog box by selecting **Load Project...** from the **Macro** cascading menu in AutoCAD's **Tools** pull-down menu. B—Next, select the project Example Code.dvb and pick the **Open** button. C—Finally, display the **Macros** dialog box by picking **Macros...** from the **Macro** cascading menu in AutoCAD's **Tools** pull-down menu. Then, select the macro you wish to run and pick the **Run** button.

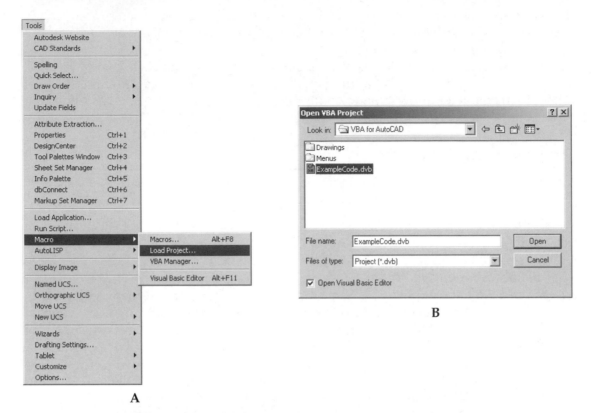

A

B

C

CHAPTER 2

Understanding Object-Oriented Programming

Learning Objectives

After completing this chapter, you will be able to:

- Explain Object-Oriented Programming.
- Interpret and use the VBA **Err** object.
- Define ActiveX Automation.
- Describe program events and how they are used.

Understanding Object-Oriented Programming

You have probably heard the term *object-oriented programming* in the past and wondered what it means. There is no need to be intimidated, because object-oriented programming is not difficult. In fact, object-oriented programming makes it easy to create powerful programs because most of the work has been done for you in the form of predefined programming objects. You simply need to reference these predefined objects in your VBA programs to create object-oriented programs.

The term *object* has been used to describe many different things in the programming world. For the purpose of this text, an *object* is a predefined programming component consisting of *properties* and *methods* that exists with other predefined *objects* in a hierarchy known as an object model. *Object properties* are the data that describe and define the object, similar to the properties of an entity in an AutoCAD drawing that can be accessed via the **Properties** window. *Object methods* are the functions, or procedures, that can be used to manipulate the object. The concept of the object model is described in the next section; object properties and object methods are explained in detail later in this chapter.

Professional Tip

Do not confuse an object with an AutoCAD drawing entity, which is often called an "object." In this text, lines, circles, splines, text, etc., created in AutoCAD are called *entities*.

Object Model

So, what exactly is an object model? An *object model* is the hierarchy of objects that represents an application. All data and functions of an application are represented by objects. The application is the top-level object in the hierarchy. All of the subobjects that make up the application reside directly below it in various branches of related groups.

The objects that make up a particular object model are always accessed through the application, or root, level object. An object that is nested deep in the object model hierarchy must be referenced through all of the objects in its particular branch, starting at the root object. In fact, this is the key to ActiveX Automation. All ActiveX-compliant programs can access the objects for other ActiveX-compliant programs via their root object because the root object has been "exposed," or made public. Because of this, the object model for each ActiveX-compliant program is very similar.

The ActiveX object model for AutoCAD is shown in **Figure 2-1.** Study the hierarchy closely. Notice that in addition to the objects that represent drawing entities, there are also objects that represent the AutoCAD menus and preferences used by AutoCAD. The **Preferences** object is used to control all of the settings found in AutoCAD's **Options** dialog box.

The top four objects directly below the AutoCAD root object are shown in **Figure 2-2.** All of the other AutoCAD objects are referenced through one of these four objects. For instance, to change the size of the AutoCAD mouse cursor to be full screen, or 100%, the **CursorSize** property of the **Display** object is set to 100. The **Display** object is a member of the **Preference** object, which in turn belongs to the **Application** object. Therefore, the code is:

```
Application.Preferences.Display.CursorSize = 100
```

The **.** (period) is used to designate each level in the object hierarchy. In other words, a period represents a branch in the object tree. In this example, **CursorSize** is considered a property of the **Display** object.

Object Variables

A variable can be declared to be a specific object type. The declaration process is very similar to declaring a variable to be a specific data type, as described in Chapter 1. Simply dimension the variable as the object type you want to use in the program with the **Dim** statement and the object class name:

```
Dim objLine As AcadLine
```

This statement declares the variable named *objLine* to be a **Line** object, as indicated by the **AcadLine** class name. The *object class name* is how the object is represented internally in the AutoCAD object model. A list of all of the AutoCAD object class names is automatically provided when you declare a variable. A complete list of class names is provided in Appendix A.

Once the variable *objLine* is declared as a **Line** object, it can only be assigned to a **Line** object in the program. A run-time error will be generated if any other data type is assigned to the variable. All of the rules for declaring and using object variables are the same as the rules for declaring and using data variables.

Figure 2-1.
The ActiveX object model for AutoCAD.

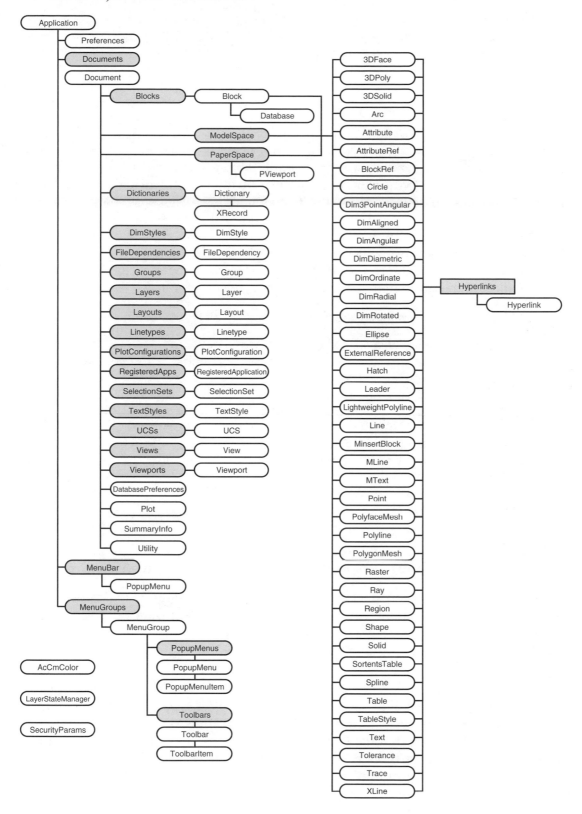

Figure 2-2.
Top four AutoCAD
objects.

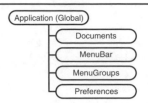

Professional Tip

The typical naming convention for object variables is to prefix the variable name with *obj* to indicate an object data type. This makes it easy to identify object data types in your program. See the section Variable Naming Conventions in Chapter 1 for the complete list of suggested variable prefixes.

Unlike data type variables, which are assigned a value using the **=** assignment operator, object type variables are assigned a reference to a particular object type using a combination of the **Set** statement and the **=** assignment operator:

    Set objLine = ThisDrawing.ModelSpace.AddLine (dblPoint1, dblPoint2)

In this example, the variable *objLine* now references a new **Line** object that starts at the coordinate value stored in the variable *dblPoint1* and ends at the coordinate value stored in the variable *dblPoint2*.

Using the **Set** statement to assign an object variable creates a *reference* to an object, not a copy. Therefore, more than one object variable can, in fact, reference the same object. This can lead to unexpected results, so VBA provides a way to de-reference a variable by setting it to nothing, literally. The **Nothing** keyword breaks the link between the object variable and the actual object.

    Set objLine = Nothing

In this example, the object variable *objLine*, which referenced a **Line** object, is set to nothing. De-referencing object variables is a good practice because it reduces program resources by freeing up any memory that was allocated to the referenced object.

VBA also provides a generic **Object** data type that can be assigned to any object type at program run time. This is similar to the catchall **Variant** data type described in Chapter 1, which can be assigned to any data type at program run time. The *objLine* object variable above could have also been declared as:

    Dim objLine As Object

The *objLine* object variable can now reference any object type at run time, not just a **Line** object. This forces VBA to wait until your program is running to determine the object type that the object variable is referencing. This is an example of late binding, which is discussed in Chapter 1. Late binding of object variables is discouraged because it makes your program slower and more difficult to maintain.

Always use the most-specific object type possible when declaring an object variable so you can take advantage of early binding. Early binding of variables makes your programs run faster and also allows you to take advantage of some time-saving features in the **Visual Basic Editor**. The **Visual Basic Editor** is discussed in detail in Chapter 3.

Object Properties

Every object has specific properties associated with it, just like AutoCAD drawing entities have properties. In fact, an AutoCAD drawing entity is just another object in VBA. Using VBA, you can access all of the same entity properties that are displayed in AutoCAD's **Properties** window and then some. For example, to change the color of a line to red using VBA, simply set the **Color** property of the **Line** object.

```
' Macro to set the color property of selected lines to red.
Sub Ch02_SetObjectProperty ()

    ' Declare a line object.
    Dim objLine As AcadLine
    ' Use variant to get a user pick point.
    Dim varPickPoint As Variant

    ' Ask the user to select a line in the drawing area.
    ThisDrawing.Utility.GetEntity objLine, varPickPoint, "Select line: "

    ' Set the line's color to red.
    objLine.Color = acRed

    ' Tell user.
    MsgBox "Line color property set to red."

End Sub
```

Once the line is selected, the AutoCAD color constant introduced in Chapter 1 is used to set its color to red.

The utility object provides a number of entity selection methods, including the **GetEntity** method shown in the above code. Many of the methods are similar to the selection functions used in AutoLISP. Object methods are discussed in detail in the next section.

The above example is a little simpler than using AutoLISP to do the same job. Finally, you can forget all of those DXF codes that took you so long to learn!

AutoLISP vs. VBA

ThisDrawing in the example above is a special object that represents the current document object, or the current AutoCAD drawing. It is simply an alias for the **Application.Document** object in the AutoCAD object model. You will see it used extensively in most of the examples in this book and the sample code included with AutoCAD.

An object's properties can also be queried. This allows you to examine what a particular property is set to without changing it. The process is simply the reverse of the previous example:

```
' Macro to get a selected line's color.
Sub Ch02_GetObjectProperty()

    ' Line color.
    Dim intColor As Integer
    ' Declare a line object.
    Dim objLine As AcadLine
    ' Use variant to get a user pick point.
    Dim varPickPoint As Variant

    ' Ask the user to select a line in the drawing area.
    ThisDrawing.Utility.GetEntity objLine, varPickPoint, "Select line: "

    ' Get the line's color.
    intColor = objLine.Color

    ' Show user.
    MsgBox "Line color property is currently " & intColor

End Sub
```

In this example, the *intColor* variable will be set to the color of the selected line.

The properties of a **Line** object are shown in **Figure 2-3.** Most of the objects representing AutoCAD drawing entities share similar properties. For example, a line, circle,

Figure 2-3.
The properties of a line object.

Property	Description
Angle	Counterclockwise rotation from the X axis.
Application	Application object to which the line belongs.
Color	Color of the line.
Document	Document object to which the line belongs.
Delta	Change from start to end.
EndPoint	Ending point.
Handle	Numeric AutoCAD handle.
HasExtensionDictionary	Extension dictionary attached.
Hyperlinks	Hyperlink attached.
Layer	Layer on which the line resides.
Length	Length of the line.
Linetype	Linetype assigned to the line.
LinetypeScale	Linetype scale of the line.
Lineweight	Lineweight of the line.
Normal	Normal view plane.
ObjectID	Object ID of the line.
OwnerID	Object ID of the owner.
PlotStyleName	Plot style name.
StartPoint	Starting point.
Thickness	Thickness of the line.
Visible	Visibility of the line.

and arc all have a **Layer** property in VBA. Therefore, the objects that represent these entities all have a layer property.

Objects that represent nongraphic AutoCAD elements, like the **Plot** or **Preferences** object, have very different properties. Obviously, neither of these objects has a **Layer** property. Instead, they have other properties that are unique to what they represent in AutoCAD.

There are a few properties that are shared by all AutoCAD objects. These include **Application**, **Document**, and **ObjectID**. Their usage is described later.

Professional Tip

For a complete list of all AutoCAD objects and their properties, refer to *ActiveX and VBA Reference* in the AutoCAD online documentation.

Object Methods

As defined earlier, an object consists of two parts—properties and methods. Methods are actions that you can perform on objects. If a property is considered *static*, a method is *dynamic*. For instance, suppose you want to move the **Line** object (line entity) in the previous example. A **Line** object has a **Move** method that can be used to move the **Line** object:

```
' Macro to move a line from base point 0,0,0 to new point 2,2,0.
Sub Ch02_UseObjectMethod ()

    ' Line color.
    Dim objLine As AcadLine
    ' Base point.
    Dim dblPoint1(2) As Double
    ' Point to move to.
    Dim dblPoint2(2) As Double
    ' Use variant to get a user pick point.
    Dim varPickPoint As Variant

    ' X value of base point.
    dblPoint1(0) = 0.0
    ' Y value of base point.
    dblPoint1(1) = 0.0
    ' Z value of base point.
    dblPoint1(2) = 0.0

    ' X value of new point.
    dblPoint2(0) = 2.0
    ' Y value of new point.
    dblPoint2(1) = 2.0
    ' Z value of new point.
    dblPoint2(2) = 0.0

    ' Ask the user to select a line in the drawing area.
    ThisDrawing.Utility.GetEntity objLine, varPickPoint, "Select line"

    ' Move the line from the base point to the new point.
    objLine.Move dblPoint1, dblPoint2

End Sub
```

Figure 2-4.
The methods of a line object.

Method	Action
ArrayPolar	Creates a polar array of the object.
ArrayRectangular	Creates a rectangular array of the object.
Copy	Copies the object.
Delete	Erases the object.
GetBoundingBox	Gets the bounding box of the object.
GetExtensionDictionary	Gets the object's extension dictionary.
GetXdata	Gets the object's xdata.
Highlight	Highlights the object.
IntersectWith	Gets the intersection points with another object.
Mirror	Mirrors the object.
Mirror3D	Mirrors the object in 3D space.
Move	Moves the object.
Offset	Offsets the object.
Rotate	Rotates the object.
Rotate3D	Rotates the object in 3D space.
ScaleEntity	Scales the object.
SetXData	Sets the object's xdata
TransformBy	Transforms the object.
Update	Updates the object.

In this example, the starting point of the move operation is defined as the coordinate point (0,0,0). The second point is defined as (2, 2, 0). The same entity selection method that was used in the properties example earlier is used to select the line. The **Move** method of the selected **Line** object is then invoked with the starting point variable *dblPoint1* and second point variable *dblPoint2* as arguments. All of the methods for the **Line** object are shown in **Figure 2-4.**

The syntax for invoking an object method with arguments is the same syntax used for a **Sub** with arguments. The arguments are simply separated with commas. You will find that most object methods have arguments because of their dynamic nature.

Most of the objects that represent AutoCAD drawing entities share similar methods, just as they share similar properties. Obviously, **Line**, **Circle**, and **Arc** objects all have **Move** methods. These objects also have **Copy**, **Mirror**, and **Rotate** methods. As you can see, all of the commands that you would use in the AutoCAD drawing editor to manipulate drawing entities exist as object methods in VBA.

Professional Tip

An object method is simply a **Sub** that is part of a particular object. Just like a **Sub**, a method can have multiple arguments. In fact, because of their dynamic nature, most methods have at least one argument, if not many. The method's name and its arguments are considered its *signature.*

Object Collections

An *object collection* is a predefined group of the same type of objects, similar to a VBA array. The AutoCAD object model has many object collections. For example, there is a **Blocks** collection that contains all of the blocks defined in a drawing, a **Layers** collection that contains all of the layers, and a **Linetypes** collection for linetype definitions. In fact, all of the named AutoCAD objects are stored as collections.

In the AutoCAD object model diagram shown in **Figure 2-1**, all of the object collections are shaded. Notice that there is a **ModelSpace** collection and a **PaperSpace** collection. This is how all of the AutoCAD drawing objects are organized. An object in model space is stored in the **ModelSpace** collection while a paper space object is stored in the **PaperSpace** collection. There are other collections as well. The **Drawings** collection is used to manage all of the open drawings. A **Layouts** collection is used to manage drawing layouts. The **FileDependencies** collection keeps track of all of a drawing's dependent files.

As you can see, VBA collections are used extensively throughout the AutoCAD object model. It is a good thing that VBA provides some easy, yet powerful, means of working with collections. The next few sections introduce accessing and managing VBA collections.

All of the AutoLISP symbol tables are implemented as object collections in VBA, as seen in **Figure 2-5**.

AutoLISP vs. VBA

Figure 2-5.
AutoLISP symbol tables vs. VBA object collections.

AutoLISP Symbol Table	VBA Object Collection
APPID	**RegisteredApps** (registered applications collection)
BLOCK	**Blocks** (blocks collection)
DIMSTYLE	**DimStyles** (dimension styles collection)
LAYER	**Layers** (layers collection)
LTYPE	**LineTypes** (linetypes collection)
UCS	**UCSs** (user coordinate systems collection)
VIEW	**Views** (views collection)
VPORT	**Viewports** (viewports collection)

Iterating Object Collections

VBA provides a simple means of stepping through each object in a collection so that you can access the object's properties and methods. This process is typically referred to as iteration. *Iteration* allows you to process a group of similar objects at one time. For instance, you can iterate the **Layers** collection to list all of the layer names in the current drawing:

```
' Macro that iterates the entire layer collection
' and displays the layer names to the user.
Sub Ch02_IterateCollection()

    ' List of layer names.
    Dim strLayers As String
    ' Layer object.
    Dim objLayer As AcadLayer

    ' Initialize string.
    strLayers = ""

    ' Iterate all layers in the drawing's layer collection.
    For Each objLayer In ThisDrawing.Layers
        strLayers = strLayers & objLayer.Name & vbCrLf
    Next

    ' Display to user.
    MsgBox "Layers in drawing: " & vbCrLf & vbCrLf & strLayers

End Sub
```

In this example, the *objLayer* variable is declared as an AutoCAD **Layer** object. Each **Layer** object in the **Layers** collection is stored in the variable *objLayer* as the collection is iterated using the **For Each...** loop. Each **Layer** object's **Name** property is then concatenated to the *strLayers* string along with a new line, or carriage control character, using the **vbCrLf** constant. A message box then displays the list of layers, as shown in **Figure 2-6.**

AutoLISP vs. VBA

Using AutoLISP to perform the iteration operation shown above involves dragging out the dreaded DXF codes, not to mention association lists.

Professional Tip

For a complete list of all AutoCAD object collections, refer to *ActiveX and VBA Reference* in the AutoCAD online documentation.

Figure 2-6.
A VBA message box showing the list of layers in the drawing. This was created by iterating an object collection.

Adding Objects to and Removing Objects from Object Collections

Adding an object to an object collection is easy. You just add the object to the desired collection using the collection's **Add** method. For instance, the following code adds a new layer named WALL to the current drawing's **Layers** collection.

```
' Macro that adds the layer named WALL to the layer collection.
Sub Ch02_AddToCollection1()

    ' Add WALL layer to the Layer collection.
    ThisDrawing.Layers.Add ("WALL")

    ' Tell user.
    MsgBox "WALL layer added to Layer collection."

End Sub
```

After the layer is added to the **Layers** collection, you can then set any of its properties to match your standards. In order to do this, though, you have to revise the code example above to get a reference to the newly created **Layer** object as it is added. Then, you can set its **Color** property.

```
' Macro that adds a layer named WALL to the layer collection
' and sets its color property to red.
Sub Ch02_AddToCollection2()

    ' Layer object.
    Dim objLayer As AcadLayer

    ' Add WALL layer to the Layer collection.
    Set objLayer = ThisDrawing.Layers.Add("WALL")

    ' Tell user.
    MsgBox "WALL layer added to the layer collection."

    ' Set layer color to red.
    objLayer.Color = acRed

    ' Tell user.
    MsgBox "WALL layer color set to red."

End Sub
```

In the example above, the VBA **Set** statement is used to get a reference to the newly created **Layer** object. Once you get a reference to an object, you can set any of its properties or use any of its methods. See the section Object Variables earlier in this chapter for information about referencing objects using the **Set** statement.

Removing an object from a collection is achieved using an object collection's **Delete** method. For instance, to remove all **Layer** objects from the **Layers** collection:

```
' Macro to delete all unreferenced layers.
Sub Ch02_RemoveFromCollection()

    ' Layer object.
    Dim objLayer As AcadLayer

    On Error Resume Next

    ' Delete all unreferenced layers.
    For Each objLayer In ThisDrawing.Layers
        objLayer.Delete
    Next objLayer

End Sub
```

Referencing a Specific Object in an Object Collection

There are two ways to reference an object directly in an object collection—by index and by name. Referencing an object by its index is similar to referencing an item in an array. Simply specify the desired index:

```
' Macro that references the 1st layer in the layer collection.
Sub Ch02_ReferenceCollectionItem1()

    ' Layer object.
    Dim objLayer As AcadLayer

    ' Reference the first layer in the Layers collection.
    Set objLayer = ThisDrawing.Layers.Item(0)

    ' Tell the user.
    MsgBox "Layer name: " & objLayer.Name

End Sub
```

The message box shown in **Figure 2-7** is displayed when you run the Ch02ReferenceCollectionItem1 macro.

If you know the name of the object you wish to reference, you can supply it as a string argument instead of specifying the index number. The following code gets the **Layer** object for the WALL layer:

```
' Macro to get the layer object for a layer named WALL.
Sub Ch02_ReferenceCollectionItem2()

    ' Layer object.
    Dim objLayer As AcadLayer

    ' Get WALL layer.
    Set objLayer = ThisDrawing.Layers.Item("WALL")

    ' Tell the user.
    MsgBox "Layer name: " & objLayer.Name

End Sub
```

Figure 2-7.
A VBA message box showing the layer name of the first layer in the layer collection.

AutoCAD	✕
Layer name: 0	
OK	

Figure 2-8.
A VBA error message indicating the run-time error. This error means that the layer name does not exist.

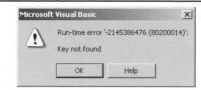

If the WALL layer name does not exist in the current drawing, you will get an error when you run the Ch02_ReferenceCollectionItem2 macro, **Figure 2-8.** Errors like this can be avoided using the VBA **Err** object, which is discussed in the next section.

Let's Review...

- An object in VBA is a predefined programming component that has properties and methods.
- An object model is the hierarchy of objects that represents an ActiveX application.
- An object property is an attribute assigned to an object that can be set or retrieved.
- An object method is a procedure associated with an object.
- An object collection is a predefined group of the same type of objects.
- A method's name and its arguments are considered its signature.

Exercise 2-1

Open the AutoCAD online documentation by selecting **Help** from the **Help** pull-down menu. Then, pick the **Contents** tab and double-click on the entry **ActiveX Automation and VBA**. Pick **ActiveX and VBA Reference** on the right-side of the help screen to display the **Developer Documentation** screen. Finally, pick **Object Model** on the right-side of the screen to display the AutoCAD object model diagram.

List all of the properties and methods for the following AutoCAD object types. *Hint:* Pick on any object in the object model diagram to retrieve all of its properties and methods, along with its complete description.
1. Arc
2. Circle
3. Text
4. Mtext
5. Mline
6. Layer
7. TextStyle
8. Document
9. Application

Figure 2-9.
A Windows-generated VBA error message may not be informative for the average user.

Figure 2-10.
A custom VBA error message can be more informative to the average user. This one indicates that the disk drive door is open, with a humorous nod to 2001: A Space Odyssey.

VBA Err Object

The VBA **Err** object provides you with the ability to determine which error has occurred when your program is running. This information can then be used with the error handling techniques described in Chapter 1 so that your program can react in a way that does not confuse or annoy the user. This approach to error management and control is often referred to as exiting a program "gracefully."

As emphasized earlier, users do not like it when a program crashes. They *really* do not like it when a program crashes and a confusing, Windows-generated error message is displayed like the one shown in **Figure 2-9.** Fortunately, the **Err** object allows you to "trap" these messages before they are displayed, determine exactly what is going on, and then display your own, user-friendly error message, like the one shown in **Figure 2-10.**

The **Err** object has a number of properties that you can analyze in the error handling section of your code so that the program can react accordingly. The properties most often examined are **Err.Number** and **Err.Description**. These two properties are all you need to create effective error handlers. They are discussed in the next sections with examples of how they can be utilized in your code.

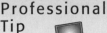

Professional Tip

For information about the **Err** object properties and methods, consult a comprehensive Visual Basic book.

Err.Number Property

The **Err.Number** property is set to a unique number, known as an *error code,* when a run-time error occurs. There are over 80 error codes defined in VBA. Descriptions of these error codes can be found in the VBA online documentation. A few typical error codes and their descriptions are shown in **Figure 2-11.** Utilizing this error number information in your code is easy.

Figure 2-11.
Typical VBA error codes and their description.

Error Code	Description
7	Out of memory.
11	Division by zero.
51	Internal error.
53	File not found.
57	Disk drive unavailable.
58	File already exists.
321	Invalid file format.
482	Printer error.
744	Search text not found.
31004	No object.
31036	Error saving to file.

A typical programming approach is to simply trap for particular error codes in your error handler code using the VBA **Case** statement. For example, the following error handler checks for a few common error codes that might occur when trying to copy a file and then displays a message that the user can actually understand:

```vba
Sub SubName()

    ' Implement error handling.
    On Error Goto ErrorHandler

    ' Execute some code.
    ' Go to the ErrorHandler label if something goes terribly wrong.
    statement1
    statement2
    statement3

' Exit program here when everything works as expected.
Exit Sub

' Here is our error handler block. Code execution only comes
' here when something bad happens.
ErrorHandler:

    ' Get error number from Err object.
    ErrorNumber = Err.Number

    ' Check error number and display message accordingly.
    Select Case
        ' Check for expected error codes.
        Case 53
            MsgBox "File not found. File not copied."
        Case 57
            MsgBox "Disk drive unavailable. File not copied."
        Case 58
            MsgBox "File already exists. File not copied."

        ' Must be something else. Display a generic, default message.
        Case Else
            MsgBox "Problem encountered while copying file. File not copied."
    End Select

End Sub
```

Figure 2-12.
A generic error
message can be
displayed by the
error handler.

It is always good practice to leave yourself an "out" by including a **Case Else** statement. In this example, the default message box shown in **Figure 2-12** is displayed whenever the error number is not 53, 57, or 58. Using this approach, you can check a handful of error codes and display a default message for the rest.

Professional Tip

The **Err** object's properties are all set to zero or empty strings when a procedure is either exited or a new **Resume** or **On Error...** statement is used in your code. It is also possible to reset the **Err** object manually using the **Err.Clear** method:

```
' Clear the Err object.
Err.Clear
```

This approach is explored later in the book in some code examples that utilize what is referred to as *inline error handling*. This involves checking and responding to an error on the line on which it occurs in the program. Using this method of error handling requires that you reset the **Err** object manually.

Err.Description

The **Err.Description** property is a little less used than the **Err.Number** property because it provides information that is not easily understood. However, the **Err.Description** property does provide a "quick and dirty" way of supplying the user with information about the error that just occurred. One common approach to using **Err.Description** is to simply display its value in a message box:

```
Sub SubName()

    ' Implement error handling.
    On Error Goto ErrorHandler

    ' Execute some code.
    ' Go to the ErrorHandler label if something goes terribly wrong.
    statement1
    statement2
    statement3

' Exit program here when everything works as expected.
Exit Sub

' Here is our error handler block. Code execution only comes
' here when something bad happens.
ErrorHandler:

    ' Check if description is provided and then display.
    If Err.Description <> "" Then
        MsgBox Err.Description
    End If

End Sub
```

Notice that the error handler first determines if an error description is provided by checking to see if it is an empty string. An error can occur that does not set the **Err** object **Description** property.

ActiveX Automation

ActiveX Automation is simply a means of programming using a predefined ActiveX object model that allows you to share data between various Windows-based applications. ActiveX Automation can be used to share data between AutoCAD and other Microsoft Windows programs, like Word, Excel, and Access, because each application's object model is exposed, or made public, to all of the other ActiveX applications. This is done through each application's "root" object, which is typically the application itself. Once this root object is made public, all of the other data objects in its object model can be accessed through the object hierarchy.

The easiest way to exploit ActiveX Automation is to use Visual Basic for Applications (VBA) because it is built into most ActiveX-compliant programs, but it is possible to use other programming languages. These languages include Visual Basic, C/C++, Java, and others. There are a few things to consider when deciding which programming language to use to create an ActiveX application, as described next.

A program written using VBA runs in the same memory space as the application that was used to create it. This is considered *in-process* and grants the best application performance. This also means that the host application must be running in order to use your program. For instance, a program written using AutoCAD VBA needs to be run from within AutoCAD. This is fine for most cases, but sometimes you may want to create a program that does not require a host application to be running in order to use the program.

Programs that do not rely on a host application are considered to be *out-of-process* and perform a little slower. To write an out-of-process ActiveX application, you cannot use VBA. You must use either stand-alone Visual Basic or one of the other languages mentioned above.

Consider the diagram shown in **Figure 2-13** that displays the concepts of in-process and out-of-process. Notice that VBA for AutoCAD is shown as being part of AutoCAD, or in-process. The other applications all communicate with AutoCAD via the ActiveX Automation Interface across what is called the "process boundary." In other words, they are out-of-process.

The objects, properties, and methods exposed by ActiveX Automation are contained in a type library. A *type library* is a file or part of a file that describes the object model for an ActiveX application.

Figure 2-13.
The relationship of in-process and out-of-process applications.

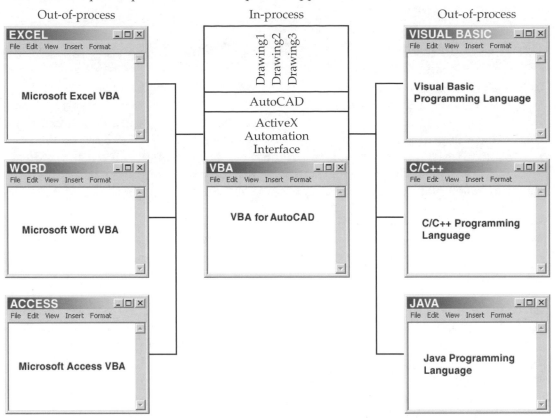

Before you can use the object model exposed by an application, you must first reference its type library. The reference is automatically set in AutoCAD VBA. For the other programming languages and development environments mentioned you must reference this type library explicitly.

Understanding Program Events

Besides properties and methods, objects also have another unique quality...they can talk to each other! An object can react to actions, or *events,* that occur when a program is running and then send a public broadcast message to the rest of the program indicating that an event has occurred. It is as though the object is saying "Hey program! Something is happening over here! You better do something!" As the programmer, you have the option of making the program listen to the object's request or ignore it.

It is even possible to create a uniquely named **Sub** procedure that is automatically executed if a particular event occurs when a program is run. Most of this process is automated; you just have to write the code that reacts to the event. This type of **Sub** is often referred to as an *event handler.* A prime example of a program that uses events is one that relies on dialog boxes, which are known as forms in VBA.

You may have used the Dialog Control Language (DCL) to create AutoLISP programs that employ dialog boxes. In DCL, you define a dialog box with different "tiles" (buttons, list boxes, etc.) that produce an "action request" if they are changed when the program is run. You can then associate a "callback function" with that action request. For example, you might associate an **OK** button tile with a function that exits your program cleanly. When the user picks the **OK** button in the dialog box, the "exit" function is executed. This is a form of event-driven programming.

Using VBA, programming with events is much easier. In VBA, a button is just another object, one referred to as a *control.* VBA has many controls, such as list boxes, text boxes, radio buttons, and so on. Every control has unique events built into it as **Subs**. When you add a control to a form in VBA, all of these **Subs** are added automatically. You just have to fill them in with your code. It is as simple as that. For instance, a button control has a "right click" event associated with it whose **Sub** is called **Right_Click**. Whatever code you add to the **Sub** named **Right_Click** is executed when someone right clicks the mouse when your program is run. Each VBA control has multiple, preprogrammed events associated with it. You just pick which events you want to react to and which events you want to ignore. Forms, controls, and their events are discussed in more detail in Chapter 14.

AutoCAD Events

There are other events in VBA besides the events associated with forms and controls. These events are created, or "raised," by AutoCAD itself. There are three different levels of events in AutoCAD:

- Application level
- Document level
- Object level

Application level events are events related to the AutoCAD application and its environment. These include opening and saving drawings, changes to AutoCAD's preferences, and changes to the AutoCAD window itself. It is even possible to write code that can react to any AutoCAD command via the application level events.

Document level events are events related to the current drawing in AutoCAD. These include running a LISP routine, creating or erasing a drawing entity, or plotting.

Object level events are events related to individual drawing entities in AutoCAD. These events allow you create drawing entities, like lines, circles, etc., that can let your program know when they have been modified in any manner (moved, scaled, erased, etc.).

As you can see, this is pretty powerful stuff. The possibilities are endless. See Chapter 15 for more information about how to program using AutoCAD events.

Let's Review...

- The VBA **Err** object contains information about the last error that occurred in a program.
- ActiveX Automation allows you to share data between different Windows-based ActiveX applications, like AutoCAD, Word, Excel, and Access.
- Programs written with VBA for AutoCAD offer the best performance because they run in the same memory space as AutoCAD, or in-process.
- Programming with events allows you to create code that can react to certain actions that occur when your program is running.
- It is possible to write code in VBA for AutoCAD that reacts to different AutoCAD events.

Chapter Test

Answer the following questions on a separate sheet of paper.

1. What is an *object* as it relates to VBA?
2. Define *Object-Oriented Programming*.
3. What is an *object model*?
4. List the top four objects in the AutoCAD object model.
5. Which punctuation symbol is used to designate a branch in the object model tree?
6. Describe what an *object property* is and give an example.
7. What is the **ThisDrawing** object?
8. Describe what an *object method* is and give an example.
9. What is an *object collection*?
10. Describe what *ActiveX Automation* is and give an example of how it might be used.
11. What is the difference between a program that runs *in-process* and a program that runs *out-of-process*?
12. What is a *type library*?
13. What does it mean to *program with events*?
14. What is an *event handler*?
15. List the three different levels of events in AutoCAD and give an example of each.

Programming Problems

Create VBA procedures with the names given that perform the described tasks. Write your code on a separate sheet of paper. *pro*

1. Write a **Sub** named ChangeLayer that prompts the user to select any type of entity in a drawing and put it on a layer named DOOR.
2. Write a **Sub** named MoveObject that prompts the user to select any type of entity and move it four units to the right on the X axis. *— move 4 units*
3. Write a **Sub** named ChangeRadius that prompts the user to select a circle and change its radius to 2.0 inches.
4. Write a **Sub** named MirrorText that prompts the user to select a string of single line text and mirror it vertically about the drawing origin (0,0,0).

EXAMPLE CODE

CHAPTER 3

VBA Projects and Macros

Learning Objectives

After completing this chapter, you will be able to:

- Create and load a VBA project using AutoCAD's **VBA Manager**.
- Use all the features in the VBA Integrated Development Environment (IDE).
- Create and run VBA macros.
- Debug VBA macros using the debugging tools in the VBA IDE.
- Run VBA code statements on the AutoCAD command line.

VBA Projects and Macros

In VBA, a program is called a project. A VBA *project* is a collection of one or more different modules (collections of procedures), and often forms (dialog boxes), that performs a given function or functions. These functions are referred to as macros in AutoCAD and other ActiveX applications. A *macro* is simply a **Sub** that is declared **Public** in a VBA project.

VBA projects reside either within a drawing or as a named file on your computer system with a .dvb file extension. When a project resides within a drawing, it is considered *embedded.* Each time a drawing that contains an embedded project is opened, the project is loaded automatically and all of its macros are available.

A project can also be saved to a DVB file so that it can be used in multiple drawings and on multiple computer systems. A project of this type is referred to as *global.* A global project must be loaded into AutoCAD before any of the project's macros are available. Once a project is loaded, all of its macros can be run from any open or new drawing.

VBA Manager

The AutoCAD **VBA Manager** is the main source of control over your VBA projects and macros. It is used for creating new projects, loading and unloading existing projects, and other project management tasks. It is also a portal to the **Visual Basic Editor** and the **Macros** dialog box used for editing and managing your project macros. Access the **VBA Manager** and all of the other VBA tools by selecting **Macros** in the AutoCAD **Tools** pull-down menu. Then, select **VBA Manager...** in the cascading menu to open the **VBA Manager**.

Unless a drawing has an embedded project or you are using the special acad.dvb project that loads automatically, the first time you open the **VBA Manager** it looks like **Figure 3-1.** No projects appear in the **Projects** list box. You must either create a new project or load an existing project. Both processes are explained in the following sections.

Creating a New Project

To create a new project, pick the **New** button in the **VBA Manager**. The new project has the name ACADProject and its location listed as Global1, as shown in **Figure 3-2.** This is the default name and location provided by AutoCAD until the project is saved using either the **VBA Manager** or the **Visual Basic Editor**. Note that a project is stored *only* in the drawing until it is either saved to a file or embedded in the drawing, which are described later in this chapter. All project information will be lost if you exit AutoCAD without first saving the project.

Figure 3-1.
The AutoCAD **VBA Manager**.

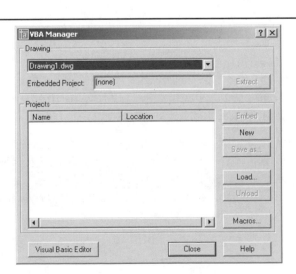

Figure 3-2.
A new project is created in the **VBA Manager**.

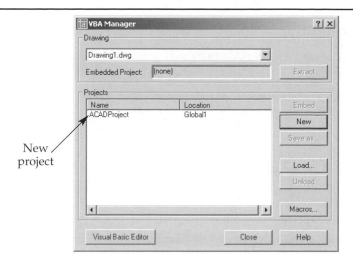

New project

Saving a Project

To save a project as a DVB file, highlight the project in the **Projects** list in the **VBA Manager**. Then, pick the **Save as...** button. The **Save As** dialog box is displayed. The default file name is Project.dvb.

As you may have guessed, it is always a good idea to give the project a descriptive file name. Enter a file name and navigate to the folder where you want the file stored. Then, pick the **Save** button to return to the **VBA Manager**. In **Figure 3-3,** the project has been saved as MyMacros.dvb.

The project name—ACADProject—can only be renamed in the **Properties** window of the **Visual Basic Editor**. The **Visual Basic Editor** is described in detail later in this chapter.

Figure 3-3.
The new project has been saved as MyMacros.dvb.

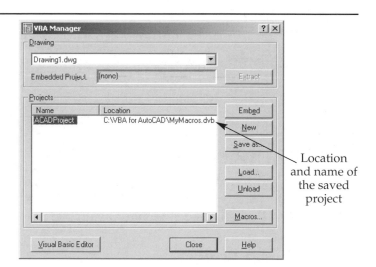

Location and name of the saved project

Figure 3-4.
This warning appears when you load a project that contains macros.

Project name and path

Uncheck to prevent the display of this warning in the future

Pick to load the project with macros disabled

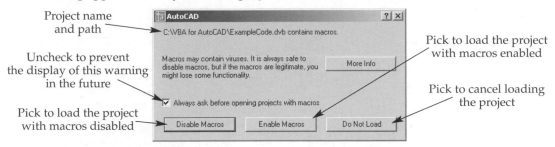

Pick to load the project with macros enabled

Pick to cancel loading the project

Loading a Project

To load an existing project, pick the **Load...** button in the **VBA Manager** to display the **Open VBA Project** dialog box. Then, locate the project you want to load, highlight it, and pick the **Open** button.

The first time you load a project, the dialog box shown in **Figure 3-4** is displayed. Do not be alarmed! You may have seen a similar dialog box when opening files in other Windows applications, such as Word or Excel. Computer viruses can be transmitted via VBA macros. This warning is meant to remind you of the virus potential. You can choose to load the project with macros disabled, to load the project with macros enabled, or not to load the project. Always practice "safe computing." If you do not know the history or origin of a project, it is always best not to load the project.

This warning dialog box can be disabled by unchecking the **Always ask before opening projects with macros** check box. It can also be disabled via the **Options** dialog box opened from the **Macros** dialog box discussed later in this chapter.

Professional Tip

The ExampleCode.dvb VBA project supplied with the book is for you to use and modify. This project contains all of the code examples in the book. The best part is that code from these examples can be cut and pasted directly into your own projects.

Unloading a Project

To unload a project, highlight the project you wish to unload in the **Projects** list in the **VBA Manager**. Then, pick the **Unload** button. When a project is unloaded, it is removed from the **VBA Manager** and no longer available.

Embedding a Project

Embedding a project makes it part of the current drawing. An embedded project is loaded automatically each time the drawing is opened. To embed a project into the current drawing, highlight the name in the **Projects** list in the **VBA Manager**. Then, pick the **Embed** button.

Look at **Figure 3-5.** There are two projects with the same name loaded in the current AutoCAD session, but with different locations. The location of an embedded project is the associated drawing, Drawing1 in this case. The location of the second project shown in the figure is the MyMacros.dvb file that was saved earlier.

Figure 3-5.
There are currently two projects loaded—one embedded project and one external DVB file. Both projects have the same name, but notice that the locations are different.

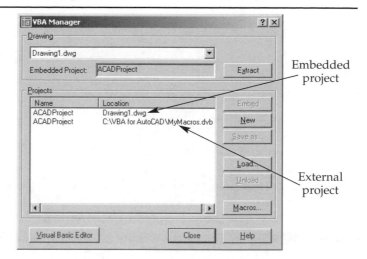

A drawing can contain only one embedded project at a time. If a drawing already contains an embedded project, you must extract it before a different project can be embedded into the drawing. Extracting a project is discussed in the next section.

Professional Tip

After embedding a project in a drawing, unload the original project that was loaded from a file to eliminate any confusion.

Extracting a Project

To remove an embedded project from a drawing, it must be extracted. An embedded project can be exported to a DVB file during the extraction process so that the project information is saved.

To extract a project, select the **Extract** button in the **VBA Manager**. The dialog box shown in **Figure 3-6** is displayed. This dialog box allows you to save the embedded project as a DVB file before it is removed from the drawing. If you pick the **No** button, the project is removed from the drawing but not saved. If you pick the **Yes** button, the **Save As** dialog box appears. Enter a project name and pick the **Save** button.

Figure 3-6.
When extracting a project, you are given the option of saving (exporting) the project before it is removed.

VBA Projects and Macros, and the VBA Manager

- A program in VBA is a collection of one or more modules and forms that are managed as a project.
- A VBA project can exist in a drawing (embedded) or as a stand-alone project in a DVB file.
- Stand-alone VBA projects must be loaded in AutoCAD before any macros are available.
- The special project file named acad.dvb is loaded automatically, if the file is in the AutoCAD search path.
- A macro is a **Public Sub** in a VBA project that can be run from within AutoCAD.
- The AutoCAD **VBA Manager** is the main source of control over VBA projects and macros.

Exercise 3-1

Using Windows Explorer, create a folder named VBA for AutoCAD. Also, create a subfolder named Drawings. Then, complete the following steps.
1. Start a new drawing in AutoCAD and open the **VBA Manager**.
2. Create a new project, which will be named ACADProject.
3. Save the project as MyMacros.dvb in the VBA for AutoCAD folder.
4. Embed the MyMacros.dvb project in the current drawing.
5. Unload the original ACADProject, leaving only the embedded ACADProject.
6. Close the **VBA Manager**.
7. Save the current drawing as ex03-01.dwg in the Drawings subfolder and quit AutoCAD.
8. Start AutoCAD and open ex03-01.dwg. When prompted, enable the macros.
9. Open the **VBA Manager**. Notice that the location of the project now includes the entire path to the drawing file.
10. Extract the ACADProject project and save it as ex03-01.dvb in the VBA for AutoCAD folder. Notice that after extracting the project, no projects are listed in the **VBA Manager**.
11. Close the **VBA Manager**, save the changes to the drawing, and quit AutoCAD.

Visual Basic Editor

The **Visual Basic Editor** is sometimes referred to as an Integrated Development Environment. This is because the *Integrated Development Environment (IDE)* is where all of your program development is done. In fact, *IDE* is a generic term used to describe the development environments for many programming languages.

Once a project is loaded, you can open the **Visual Basic Editor** by picking the **Visual Basic Editor** button in the **VBA Manager**, selecting **Visual Basic Editor** from the **Macros** cascading menu in the **Tools** pull-down menu, or using the [Alt][F11] key combination. The IDE for VBA—the **Visual Basic Editor**—appears as shown in **Figure 3-7.** The components that make up the **Visual Basic Editor** are discussed in detail in the following sections.

Figure 3-7.
The VBA Integrated Development Environment—the **Visual Basic Editor**.

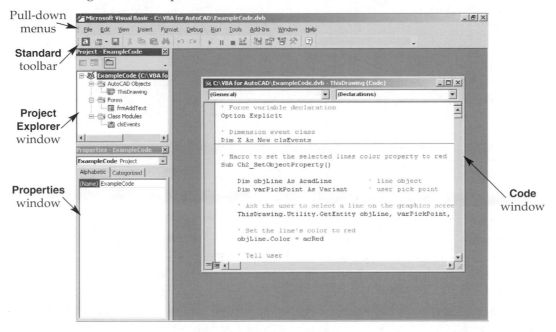

Figure 3-8.
The **Project Explorer** window is used to navigate through a project.

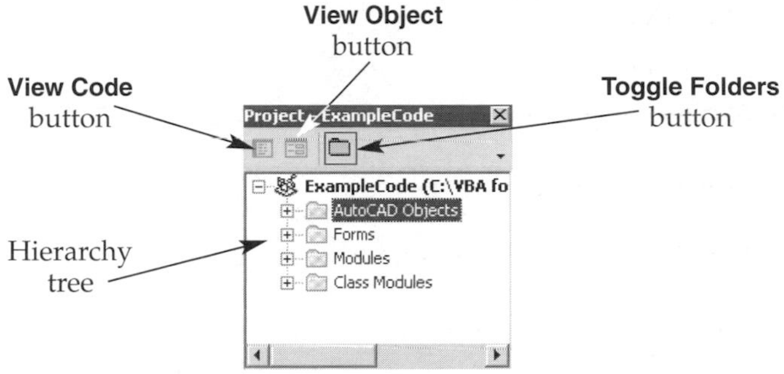

Project Explorer Window

The **Project Explorer** window is, by default, located at the top-left corner of the **Visual Basic Editor**. It is used to navigate through the components of a project, **Figure 3-8.** This is your portal to all of the code and forms (dialog boxes) that make up a project.

The three buttons at the top of the **Project Explorer** allow you to switch display modes. When the **View Code** button is selected, the **Code** window is displayed in the **Visual Basic Editor** where code can be edited. When the **View Object** button is selected, the **Object** window is displayed for the item selected in the tree. This button is used to display a form graphically so it can be edited. The **Toggle Folders** button is used to turn on and off the display of the folders in the tree. The items contained within the folders are always displayed.

Figure 3-9.
The **Properties** window is used to change various properties of project objects.

Properties - frmExampleCode [X]

frmExampleC(UserForm ◄──── Selected object

Alphabetic	Categorized
(Name)	frmExampleCc
BackColor	&H8000000
BorderColor	&H8000001
BorderStyle	0 - fmBorderSt
Caption	UserForm1
Cycle	0 - fmCycleAllF
DrawBuffer	32000
Enabled	True
Font	Tahoma
ForeColor	&H8000001
Height	180
HelpContextID	0
KeepScrollBarsVi	3 - fmScrollBar
Left	0
MouseIcon	(None)
MousePointer	0 - fmMousePo

Property ────► (Name)

Current value or setting ────► frmExampleCc

Properties Window

The **Properties** window is, by default, located below the **Project Explorer** window. This window is somewhat parallel to the AutoCAD **Properties** window. In AutoCAD, the **Properties** window controls the properties of a selected entity, such as its layer, color, and linetype. In VBA, the **Properties** window is used to control the properties of different program objects like forms (dialog boxes) and controls. For example, the form's name, background color, and size can be set using the **Properties** window in the **Visual Basic Editor**, **Figure 3-9**. Forms and controls are discussed in detail in Chapter 14.

Debug Windows

The **Immediate**, **Locals**, and **Watch** windows are provided to help debug a program. These windows allow you to inspect the values of variables and expressions at program run time. However, they are not displayed by default. To display any of these windows, select the appropriate entry—**Immediate Window**, **Locals Window**, **Watch Window**—from the **View** pull-down menu in the **Visual Basic Editor**. Program debugging is discussed in detail later in this chapter.

Professional Tip

All of the windows discussed thus far can be moved, sized, and turned on or off using the standard Windows methods. You can also control their visibility using the **View** pull-down menu in the **Visual Basic Editor**. For instance, you may want to turn off any debug windows at design time to allow the **Code** window to be larger.

Code Window

Because you spend most of your time writing code, the **Code** window is probably the most important part of the **Visual Basic Editor**. See **Figure 3-10**. There can be as many **Code** windows open as there are modules in your project. The **Window** pull-down menu in the **Visual Basic Editor** provides the normal Windows display modes and navigation features. Use features such as **Tile Vertically** and **Cascade** to your advantage.

As mentioned previously, there are many handy features included with the VBA IDE that make writing code easier and faster. These features are explained in the following sections.

Figure 3-10.
The **Code** window is where code can be added to the project.

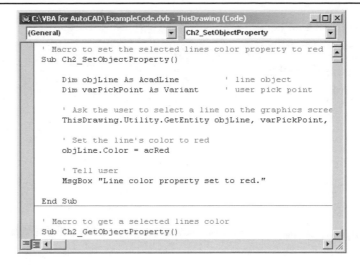

Object and Procedure Boxes

The **Object** and **Procedure** boxes are located at the top of the **Code** window. See **Figure 3-11.** The **Object** box lists the objects and controls contained in a project. The **Procedure** box lists the procedures available for a project's objects and controls. These boxes provide a means of navigating through your code and, in the case of forms, provide automated procedure naming and creation. Automated procedure naming and creation are discussed in Chapter 14.

Figure 3-11 shows the objects and procedures for a standard module that simply consists of procedures or macros. A standard module always contains a (General) object and a (Declarations) procedure. As you add procedures to a module, they are listed in the **Procedure** box. All of the procedures listed in the figure are also macros in AutoCAD.

Figure 3-11.
The **Object** and **Procedure** boxes are located at the top of the **Code** window.

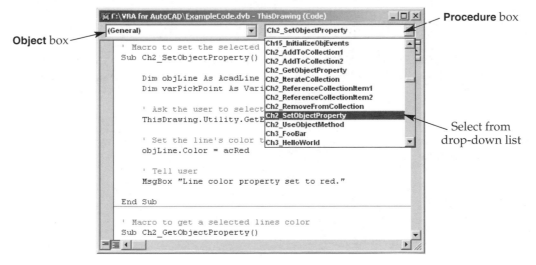

Figure 3-12.
The **Auto List Members** feature provides quick access to the properties and methods for the object or control you are currently referencing.

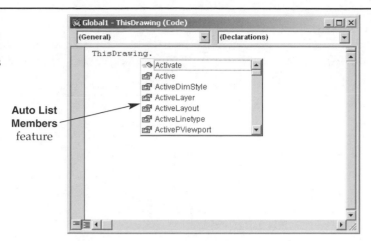

Auto List Members feature

Auto List Members Feature

The **Auto List Members** feature displays, as you type, a list of properties and methods for the object or control you are currently referencing. For example, as soon as the period is entered after typing ThisDrawing, a drop-down list is displayed that contains all of the valid properties and methods for that particular object, **Figure 3-12.** By typing the first couple of characters until a match is found, using the up/down keyboard arrow keys, or using the mouse, you can select the property or method you want. Accept the selected property or method by either entering another period (if another object level is desired) or using the [Tab] or [Enter] key.

To turn this feature off, select **Options...** from the **Tools** pull-down menu in the **Visual Basic Editor**. Then, in the **Editor** tab of the **Options** dialog box, uncheck the **Auto List Members** check box.

Auto Quick Info Feature

The **Auto Quick Info** feature displays information about functions and their arguments as you type. Once the function is recognized by the **Visual Basic Editor**, the **Auto Quick Info** feature is displayed, **Figure 3-13.** Initially, the first argument is bold. As you enter arguments, the next argument becomes bold until all of the required arguments have been entered. Optional arguments are shown inside of square brackets ([ ]).

To turn this feature off, select **Options...** from the **Tools** pull-down menu in the **Visual Basic Editor**. Then, in the **Editor** tab of the **Options** dialog box, uncheck the **Auto Quick Info** check box.

Figure 3-13.
The **Auto Quick Info** feature displays information about functions and their arguments as you type.

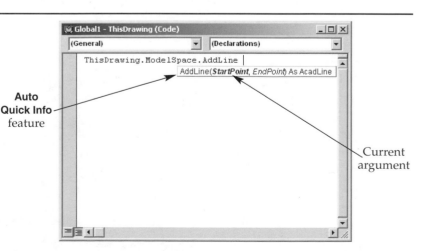

Auto Quick Info feature

Current argument

Professional Tip

The **Auto Quick Info** feature only works for variables that are "early bound." Early binding is discussed in Chapter 1.

Auto Syntax Check Feature

The **Auto Syntax Check** feature checks your code for syntax errors as you type. If an error is detected, the offending code is changed to red and a dialog box is displayed. The dialog box displays the error and suggests corrections, as seen in **Figure 3-14.**

To turn this feature off, select **Options...** from the **Tools** pull-down menu in the **Visual Basic Editor**. Then, in the **Editor** tab of the **Options** dialog box, uncheck the **Auto Syntax Check** check box.

Professional Tip

VBA automatically corrects the case (uppercase or lowercase) of any VBA keywords and "early bound" variables. This means you can type in all lowercase or all uppercase and your code will be corrected automatically—a great time-saver. However, autocorrect does not correct misspelled words.

Figure 3-14.
The **Auto Syntax Check** feature displays a warning when incorrect syntax is detected as you type.

Incorrect syntax

Suggested correction

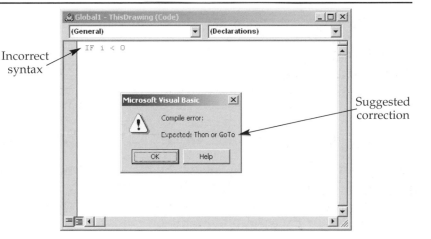

Visual Basic Editor

- The **Visual Basic Editor** is referred to as an Integrated Development Environment (IDE).
- An IDE is a multifeatured software environment that facilitates writing programs by providing various, user-friendly tools.
- The **Project Explorer** window helps you to navigate around a project's different components.
- The **Properties** window allows you to manage the properties of different program objects.
- The debug windows—**Immediate**, **Locals**, **Watch**—allow you to inspect the values of variables and expressions at program run time.
- The **Code** window is where program code is entered.
- The **Object** and **Procedure** boxes are used to navigate the code contained in the **Code** window.
- The **Visual Basic Editor** contains many automated error-checking and error-correcting features that help make writing error-free programs faster and easier.

VBA Project Structure

A VBA project in AutoCAD consists of one or more of the following components:

- An AutoCAD **ThisDrawing** object (default component)
- Forms (dialog boxes)
- Standard modules
- Class modules

By default, every VBA project for AutoCAD contains at least an AutoCAD **ThisDrawing** object. The other components must be inserted into your project via the **Insert** pull-down menu in the **Visual Basic Editor**.

The **Project Explorer** window helps you navigate between the various components of a project. As you insert new components into a project, they are displayed in their respective folder in the **Project Explorer**. **Figure 3-15** shows all of the forms and modules contained in the ExampleCode.dvb project supplied with the book.

Figure 3-15.
These are the forms and modules contained in the ExampleCode.dvb project.

Figure 3-16.
Every VBA project for
AutoCAD contains
the **ThisDrawing**
object.

Program code can reside in as many components as needed. The location of the code depends on the nature of the program. Each of the four components has unique qualities that are explained in detail in the following sections.

ThisDrawing Object

As mentioned previously, every VBA project contains an AutoCAD object called **ThisDrawing**, as shown in **Figure 3-16**. **ThisDrawing** is actually just an alias for the **Application.ActiveDocument** object that refers to the current drawing. Any **Sub** that is created in the **ThisDrawing** object and declared **Public** is automatically available as a macro in AutoCAD. Because of this, the **ThisDrawing** object is the quickest and easiest place to start writing code.

Forms

As mentioned in Chapter 2, a VBA form is a graphic user interface that is very similar to the dialog boxes that you can create using AutoCAD's Dialog Control Language (DCL). However, forms are *much* easier to create using VBA than dialog boxes are to create using DCL.

Forms are added to a project by selecting **UserForm** from the **Insert** pull-down menu in the **Visual Basic Editor**. When a form is added to a project, it is displayed under the Forms folder in the **Project Explorer** with a default name, such as UserForm1, as shown in **Figure 3-17A**. A form is inserted into a project as a blank "slate" in the **Object** window, as seen in **Figure 3-17B**. The selected component in the **Object** window is surrounded by a shaded frame with handles or grips.

Figure 3-17.
A—A form is added to the project that has the default name UserForm1. B—A blank form in the **Object** window.

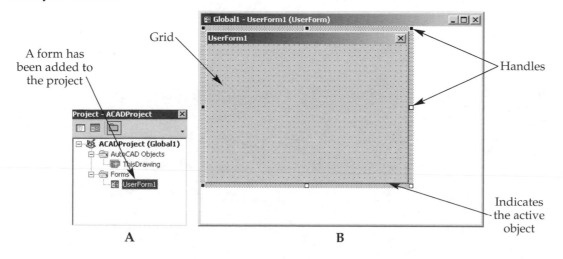

A

B

There are a number of tools and features available to help you create the interface (form) you desire. To start, a form can be resized using standard Windows drag methods. Simply make the form the size you need by dragging one of the handles. The form's background color, title, and other properties can be changed using the **Properties** window. For example, to rename the form to a unique, descriptive name, first select the form in the **Project Explorer**. Then, edit the (Name) property in the **Properties** window by deleting the default name and typing a new one, as shown in **Figure 3-18.** Form names are typically prefixed with frm to help identify them.

In addition, the **Visual Basic Editor** provides a toolbox with all of the different controls you may need on your form. The floating **Toolbox** window contains a number of standard controls including list boxes, text boxes, option buttons, and images. See **Figure 3-19.** To add a control, simply drag the control from the **Toolbox** and drop it directly onto the form. Then, move and resize the control on the form. There is a grid displayed on the form that allows you to "snap" controls into place, which helps aligned controls on a form.

Most of the code that "drives" the form and its controls is added to the project automatically when a form or control is added to a project. However, as mentioned in Chapter 2, forms rely on event-driven programming. All of the possible event procedures are automatically added to your program, but you have to add the code. For instance, every form has an **Initialize** procedure that is run when the form is first loaded. Simply select the **Initialize** procedure from the **Procedure** list box on the top right of the **Code** window and place the code you want to run within that procedure, as shown in **Figure 3-20.**

There are many other event procedures associated with forms and controls. Chapter 14 provides an example of VBA programming using forms.

Figure 3-18.
The default form name—UserForm1—has been changed to frmMyMacros.

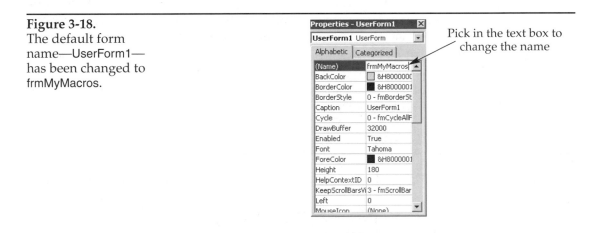

Pick in the text box to change the name

Figure 3-19.
The form controls toolbox contains a number of standard controls that can be dragged and dropped onto a form.

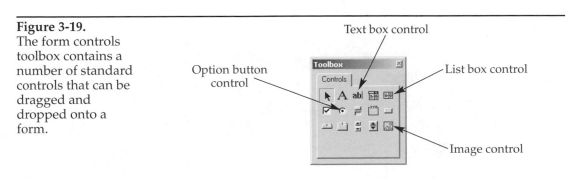

Text box control

Option button control

List box control

Image control

Figure 3-20.
Add the code you want to run to the default **Initialize** procedure for a form.

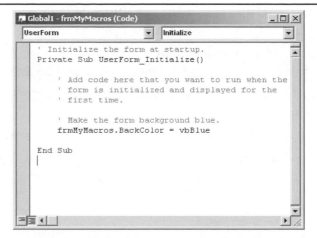

```
' Initialize the form at startup.
Private Sub UserForm_Initialize()

    ' Add code here that you want to run when the
    ' form is initialized and displayed for the
    ' first time.

    ' Make the form background blue.
    frmMyMacros.BackColor = vbBlue

End Sub
```

Standard Modules

Standard modules are used to locate generic code that can be shared with the rest of your program. **Public Sub** procedures located in a module are considered macros in AutoCAD, similar to the **Public Sub** procedures located in **ThisDrawing**. The difference is that code contained in a module can also be accessed from any other component in a project, specifically if they declared **Public** in scope.

Modules are typically used as "helper" procedures that might be used by one or more macros, but do not necessarily need to be AutoCAD macros themselves. A common programming technique is to locate all of your AutoCAD macros in the **ThisDrawing** object and then locate any other supporting procedures in a separate module or modules.

To add a code module to a project, select **Module** from the **Insert** pull-down menu in the **Visual Basic Editor**. The modules in a project are displayed under the Modules folder in the **Project Explorer**. See **Figure 3-21A.** When a module is added, it is given a default name, such as Module1.

To rename a module, first select it in the **Project Explorer**. Then, edit the (Name) property in the **Properties** window by deleting the default name and typing a new one, as shown in **Figure 3-21B.** The module name is now modMyMacros. Module names are typically prefixed with mod to help identify them.

Figure 3-21.
A—The modules in a project are displayed under the Modules folder in the **Project Explorer**.
B—The module name has been changed from the default to modMyMacros.

A module has been added to the project

Pick in the text box to change the name

A   B

Class Modules

Class modules are reserved for your own custom objects. Custom objects are defined as classes in VBA. Defining custom objects and classes is an advanced topic that is beyond the scope of this text. Consult a comprehensive VB or VBA programming text for specific information regarding custom objects and classes.

Importing and Exporting Project Components

Forms, modules, and class modules can be imported to or exported from a project. The file types associated with these components are:

- FRM for forms.
- BAS for modules.
- CLS for class modules.

To export a project component, select it in the **Project Explorer**. Then, select **Export File...** from the **File** menu in the **Visual Basic Editor** or press the [Ctrl][E] key combination. The **Export File** dialog box is displayed. **Figure 3-22** shows the frmMyMacros form being exported to the file frmMyMacros.frm. Notice that the **Save as type:** drop-down list defaults to the file type associated with the component being exported. Name the file in the **File name:** text box, navigate to the folder where you want to store the file, and pick the **Save** button.

To import a project component, select **Import File...** from the **File** pull-down menu in the **Visual Basic Editor** or press the [Ctrl][M] key combination. The **Import File** dialog box is displayed. By default, the FRM, BAS, and CLS files in the current folder are displayed. However, you can select a specific file type from the **Files of type:** drop-down list. Navigate to the folder where the file is saved, select the file you wish to import, and pick the **Open** button. The file is added to the appropriate component folder in the **Project Explorer** based on the file type.

> **Caution**
>
> You cannot import a project component that has the same name as a component of the same type in the current project. For example, if the current project has a form named frmMyMacros, you cannot import a form named frmMyMacros.

Figure 3-22.
Exporting the frmMyMacros form.

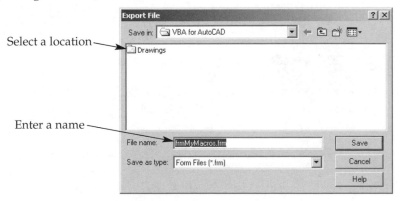

Figure 3-23.
The **Macros** dialog box with the ExampleCode.dvb project loaded.

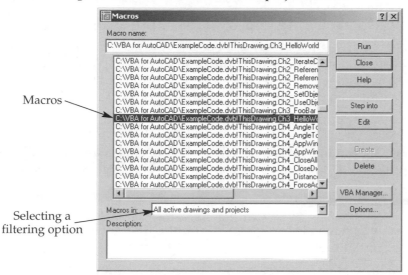

Macros →

Selecting a
filtering option →

Running VBA Macros

As explained earlier, an AutoCAD macro is simply a **Public Sub** located in either **ThisDrawing** or a standard module within a VBA project. To run a macro in AutoCAD, select **Macros...** from the **Macros** cascading menu in the AutoCAD **Tools** pull-down menu, type VBARUN at the AutoCAD command line, or press the [Alt][F8] key combination. The **Macros** dialog box is displayed. **Figure 3-23** shows the **Macros** dialog box for a drawing with the ExampleCode.dvb project loaded.

Macro Dialog Box

The list box in the middle of the **Macros** dialog box shows the available macros. Using the **Macros in:** drop-down list, you can filter the macros that are listed using one of the following categories:

- All drawings and projects.
- All drawings.
- All projects.
- Any individual drawing currently open in AutoCAD.
- Any individual project currently loaded in AutoCAD.

To select a macro, highlight its name in the list box. The name is then listed in the **Macro name:** text box at the top of the dialog box. If a description is provided for the macro, it appears in the **Description:** text box at the bottom of the **Macros** dialog box. Also, the buttons along the right side of the dialog box are enabled.

To run the selected macro, simply pick the **Run** button. The dialog box is closed and the macro runs. To close the **Macros** dialog box without running the macro, pick the **Close** button.

Picking the **Step Into** button displays the **Visual Basic Editor** and begins execution of the selected macro. Execution pauses at the first executable line of code to allow for debugging. Program debugging is discussed in detail in the next section.

Picking the **Edit** button displays the selected macro in the **Visual Basic Editor**. This allows you to edit the macro.

The **Delete** button is used to delete the selected macro from the project. Picking the **VBA Manager** button opens the **VBA Manager** dialog box.

Creating a New Macro Using the Macros Dialog Box

You can create a new macro by first entering a name in the **Macro name:** text box and then picking the **Create** button. If no project file or drawing is specified for the new macro, the **Select Project** dialog box is displayed. Select a project or drawing and pick **OK**. The **Visual Basic Editor** is displayed with an empty procedure for the new macro.

Macro Options

Picking the **Options...** button in the **Macros** dialog box opens the **Options** dialog box, **Figure 3-24.** Using this dialog box, you can set different VBA options for the current AutoCAD session.

The **Enable auto embedding** option automatically creates an embedded VBA project for all drawings when you open the drawing. This option is off by default. To turn the option on, check the check box.

The **Allow Break on errors** option allows VBA to enter break mode when an error is encountered. *Break mode* is a temporary suspension of program execution in the development environment. In break mode, you can examine, debug, reset, step through, or continue program execution. This option is on by default.

The **Enable macro virus protection** option enables the virus protection mechanism for VBA macros. The virus protection mechanism displays a built-in warning message whenever you open a drawing that contains macros, as described earlier. This option is on by default. If you disabled the option by unchecking the **Always ask before opening projects with macros** check box in the "macro virus" dialog box described earlier, you can turn the option back on by checking the **Enable macro virus protection** check box in the **Options** dialog box.

Figure 3-24.
The **Options** dialog box for setting various VBA options.

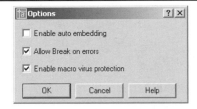

Let's Review...

VBA Project Structure and Running VBA Macros

- **ThisDrawing** is an alias for **Application.ActiveDocument**, which refers to the current drawing.
- A VBA form is a graphic user interface similar to an AutoCAD DCL dialog box, but much easier to create and program.
- A toolbox is provided as part of the **Visual Basic Editor** that contains all of the standard form controls, such as list boxes, text boxes, and option buttons.
- Forms and controls can be located and sized using standard Windows methods.
- Standard and basic modules are used to locate generic code that can be shared throughout a project.
- Class modules are used to create custom objects.
- Forms and modules can be exported from a project as a file.

Debugging VBA Projects

One of the biggest advantages of VBA is that it provides real-time debugging capabilities. *Program debugging* is the act of examining your code while a program is running so that you can isolate and fix "bugs," or errors, as they occur. The term "bug," as it relates to programming errors, was supposedly coined in the 1940s by the mother of computing, Grace Murray Hopper, when she discovered a squashed moth between the contacts of an electromechanical relay on a Harvard Mark II mainframe computer, which was preventing the relay from fully closing. Although VBA does not provide any tools for finding squashed insects, it does allow you to:

- Dynamically observe variable and expression values during program execution.
- Edit and test code during program execution.
- Start and stop program execution at any time.
- Trace code execution.
- Set and clear program breakpoints.

These features are invaluable in helping you find and fix run-time errors. These tools can also be used to optimize your code, even when no errors exist.

Debug Windows

Before examining the "how to" of program debugging, the different debug windows in the VBA IDE—the **Visual Basic Editor**—and how they are used need to be explained. The **Immediate** window, **Locals** window, **Watches** window, and watch expressions are described in the next sections.

Immediate Window

The **Immediate** window displays information resulting from debugging statements in your code or from commands typed directly into the window. It allows you to test lines of code by simply entering the code in the window. It is even possible to set or reset program variables on the fly using the **Immediate** window. To display the **Immediate** window in the **Visual Basic Editor**, select **Immediate Window** from the **View** pull-down menu or press the [Ctrl][G] key combination. See **Figure 3-25.**

Locals Window

The **Locals** window automatically displays all of the declared variables in the current procedure and their values. To open the **Locals** window in the **Visual Basic Editor**, select **Locals Window** from the **View** pull-down menu. See **Figure 3-26.** In this example, all of the local variables that exist in the Ch03_HelloWorld macro located in the ExampleCode.dvb project are displayed along with their current value and data type.

It is possible to double-click in the **Value** column and change the value of a variable, if desired. However, data types *cannot* be changed.

Figure 3-25.
The **Immediate** window displays information resulting from debugging statements or commands typed into the window.

Figure 3-26.
The **Locals** window automatically displays all of the declared variables in the current procedure and their values.

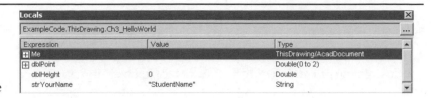

Watches Window and Watch Expressions

Watch expressions are user-defined expressions that enable you to observe the behavior of a variable or expression. The **Watches** window displays any defined watch expressions along with their value, data type, and context. See **Figure 3-27.** In this example, the variables *dblHeight, dblPoint,* and *strYourName* were added as watch expressions, so information for those variables is displayed. The **Watches** window appears automatically when watch expressions are defined for the project. However, it can be displayed manually in the **Visual Basic Editor** by selecting **Watch Window** from the **View** menu.

You can edit the value of a watch expression directly in the **Watches** window, just as you can edit values in the **Immediate** window and **Locals** window described earlier. To remove a watch expression, simply highlight it in the **Watches** window and press the [Delete] key.

You can add a watch expression by selecting **Add Watch...** from the **Debug** pull-down menu in the **Visual Basic Editor** or right-clicking in the **Code** window and selecting **Add Watch...** from the shortcut menu. The **Add Watch** dialog box is displayed, **Figure 3-28.** This dialog box has three sections:

- **Expression**. The **Expression:** text box is where you enter the expression or variable to watch. If any code is selected in the **Code** window when the **Add Watch** dialog box is opened, the **Visual Basic Editor** assumes this is to be added as a watch expression.

Figure 3-27.
The **Watches** window displays any defined watch expressions along with their value, data type, and context.

Figure 3-28.
The **Add Watch** dialog box is used to define a watch expression.

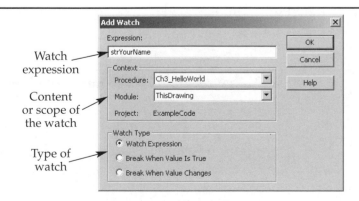

Watch expression

Content or scope of the watch

Type of watch

VBA for AutoCAD

Figure 3-29.
The **Run** pull-down
menu in the **Visual
Basic Editor**
contains commands
used to control the
current mode.

- **Context**. The **Context** area is used to define the scope, or context, in which you wish to watch the expression. You can limit the scope to a particular procedure or module. Variable scope is explained in Chapter 1.
- **Watch Type**. The **Watch Type** area contains three option buttons that determine how the program behaves when the watch expression is encountered. For example, you can elect to enter break mode if the watch is true or if its value changes.

Starting and Stopping Code Execution

The VBA development environment has three different distinct states:

- **Design mode.** When no code is running; when you are adding code.
- **Run mode.** Code is running.
- **Break mode.** Code execution is stopped before the program end; sometimes referred to as "debug mode."

Obviously, most of your time spent in the VBA IDE will be in design mode. *Design mode* is the mode in which you create and edit your code. The *run mode* and *break mode* are where program debugging occurs. The **Run** pull-down menu in the **Visual Basic Editor** contains commands used to control the current mode, **Figure 3-29.**

To run your code, select **Run Macro** from the **Run** pull-down menu or press the [F5] key. Once program execution is started, it may stop for one of the following reasons:

- An untrapped error occurs.
- A trapped run-time error occurs and the **Break on All Errors** option is selected. This option is located in the **General** tab of the **Options** dialog box that is opened by selecting **Options...** from the **Tools** pull-down menu in the **Visual Basic Editor**.
- A breakpoint is encountered. Breakpoints are discussed later in this chapter.
- Execution is halted manually.
- A watch expression is encountered that is set to break if its value changes or is true.

To halt execution manually and switch to break (debug) mode, select **Break** from the **Run** pull-down menu or press the [Ctrl][Break] key combination. In debug mode, you can use all of the debug and inquiry tools described in the previous sections.

For example, if the **Break on All Errors** option is on and you try to run the Ch03_FooBar macro located in the ExampleCode.dvb project, the error shown in **Figure 3-30A** is displayed. Selecting the **Debug** button in this dialog box places you in the **Visual Basic Editor** in debug mode at the line of code where the error occurred, **Figure 3-30B.** The line of code where the error occurred is also highlighted. You can now use the tools described in the previous sections to try to determine the problem. In this case, the error occurred because the file name specified is invalid. The control characters that are assigned to the *strYourName* variable (!@#$%^&*) cannot be used to create the file name during the "save as" process.

Figure 3-30.
A—Code execution stopped because the **Break on All Errors** option is on. The error is displayed. B— Selecting the **Debug** button places you in the **Visual Basic Editor** in debug mode at the line of code where the error occurred.

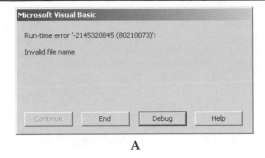

A

Indicates the line with the error

Code containing the error

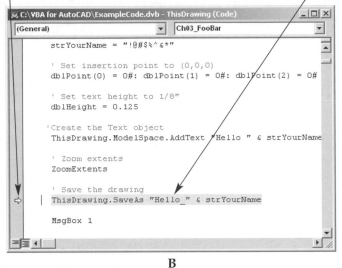

B

Stepping through Your Code

The easiest way to debug your code is to step through it manually. This way you can execute each line of code as needed and figure out exactly what is going on. There are three commands in the **Debug** pull-down menu in the **Visual Basic Editor** that are available in debug mode for stepping through code:

- **Step Into**. This command executes one line of code at a time starting at the beginning of a procedure. It will "step into" any procedure that is called and execute the first line. You can also use the [F8] key to execute this command.
- **Step Over**. This command is similar to **Step Into**, but it will execute any procedure call as a single unit and continue to the next line in the current procedure. You can also use the [Shift][F8] key combination to execute this command.
- **Step Out**. This command executes the remaining lines of a function in which the current execution point lies. The next statement displayed is the statement following the procedure call. You can also use the [Ctrl][Shift][F8] key combination to execute this command.

There is one other command in the **Debug** pull-down menu for stepping through code, but it only works in design mode. The **Run to Cursor** command will start your code and run all of the lines from the beginning of the procedure to the line of code where your cursor is located. The [Ctrl][F8] key combination can also be used to execute this command.

When you step through your code using any of the methods described above, execution stops and you are placed in debug mode with the current line of code highlighted. In **Figure 3-31A,** the **Step Into** command is used to begin execution of the

Figure 3-31.
A—Beginning code execution using the **Step Into** option.
B—Stepping through code using the **Step Into** option.

A

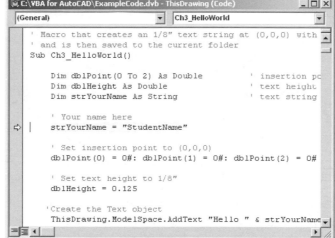

B

Ch03_HelloWorld macro at the first line. Subsequent use of the **Step Into** command highlights the next line of code in the procedure as shown in **Figure 3-31B.** Execution of the highlighted line of code does not occur until execution resumes and the line is no longer highlighted.

Setting and Clearing Breakpoints

Breakpoints are probably one of the handiest debugging features in VBA. Using breakpoints, you can suspend execution at a specific statement in a procedure. In this way, you can isolate where you might think there is a potential for errors in the program or examine the value of a specific variable or expression.

Setting breakpoints is easy. Simply locate the cursor on the line of code on which you wish to stop program execution. Then, do one of the following:

- Select **Toggle Breakpoint** from the **Debug** pull-down menu in the **Visual Basic Editor**.
- Press the [F9] key.
- Pick in the margin bar to the left of the line of code in the **Code** window.

Figure 3-32.
Using a breakpoint to stop code execution.

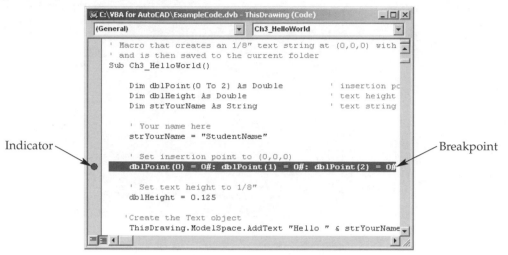

Once you have set the breakpoint, the line of code is highlighted in the breakpoint color and a small circle appears in the margin bar next to the line, as shown in **Figure 3-32.** Now, any time you run this procedure, execution will stop at this line. After examining any variables or expressions, you can then continue program execution using any of the methods previously discussed.

To remove a breakpoint, locate the cursor on the line of code that contains the break-point. Then, since the breakpoint is a toggle, use any of the methods explained above for adding a breakpoint. The breakpoint is turned off.

You can also clear all breakpoints in the project at one time. Select **Clear All Breakpoints** from the **Debug** pull-down menu or press the [Ctrl][Shift][F9] key combination. All breakpoints are removed, or toggled off.

By default, the breakpoint color is dark red. However, you can change this color to suit your needs. Select **Options...** from the **Tools** pull-down menu in the **Visual Basic Editor** to display the **Options** dialog box. Then, select the **Editor Format** tab. See **Figure 3-33.** In the **Code Colors** list box, select **Breakpoint Text**. Then, you can change the appearance by selecting a color from the **Foreground:**, **Background:**, and **Indicator:** drop-down lists. You can also change the font and point size using the options on the right side of the tab. When done, pick the **OK** button to apply the changes.

Figure 3-33.
Changing the color in which breakpoints are displayed.

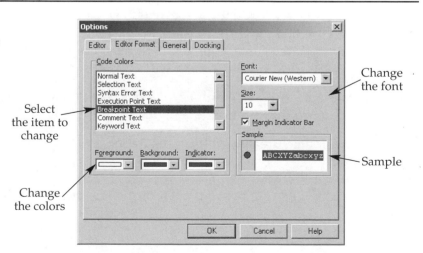

Exercise 3-2

1. Load the ExampleCode.dvb sample VBA project that comes with the book.
2. Navigate to the ThisDrawing module in the **Project Explorer** window. Double-click on it to make it current.
3. Navigate to the Ch03_HelloWorld **Sub** in the code window using the **Procedure** box located at the top of the code window.
4. Change the line of code:
    strYourName = "StudentName"
    to code that sets the variable to your name:
    strYourName = "Elvis"
5. Save the ExampleCode project and exit the **Visual Basic Editor**.
6. Run the Ch03_HelloWorld macro.

AutoCAD VBA Commands

There are a number of AutoCAD commands available that allow you to perform some of the VBA functionality described in this chapter.

*   The **VBAMAN** command displays the **VBA Manager**, which provides options for viewing, creating, loading, unloading, embedding, and extracting projects.
*   The **VBALOAD** command is used to load a VBA project into the current AutoCAD session.
*   The **VBAUNLOAD** command unloads a VBA project from the current AutoCAD session.
*   The **VBAIDE** command displays the **Visual Basic Editor**, or Integrated Development Environment (IDE).
*   The **VBARUN** command displays the **Macros** dialog box, in which you can select and run a VBA macro. The **-VBARUN** command is a command-line only command that allows you to run a VBA macro.
*   The **VBASTMT** command is used to execute a VBA statement on the AutoCAD command line, which allows you to quickly test a line of code.

The **-VBARUN** command suppresses the **Macros** dialog box. This allows the macro name to be entered at the command line:

Command: **-vbarun**
Macro name: **Ch03_HelloWorld**

Even better, if you throw in a little AutoLISP code, you can avoid all user interaction:

Command: **(command "-vbarun" "Ch03_HelloWorld")**

If you are a real power programmer, you can even eliminate the AutoLISP **(command)** function entirely, and go straight to the Visual LISP **(vl-vbarun)** function:

Command: **(vl-vbarun "Ch03_HelloWorld")**

You can use this code to run VBA macros from within your AutoLISP programs! The best part is that when you use the **(vl-vbarun)** function, the "macro virus" warning dialog box is suppressed, even if the **Enable macro virus protection** check box is checked in the **Options** dialog box.

Let's Review...

Debugging

- The VBA IDE provides real-time debugging capabilities that allow you to debug a project when it is running.
- The **Immediate** window allows you to test lines of code on the fly.
- The **Locals** window automatically displays all of the declared variables in the current procedure and their values.
- The **Watches** window displays user-defined watch expressions and their value, data type, and context.
- The VBA development environment has three different distinct states— design mode, run mode, and break mode.
- It is possible to step over, into, or out of code to help in debugging a project.
- Breakpoints can be used to suspend execution of code at a specific statement in a procedure.
- There are a number of VBA-specific AutoCAD commands that can be used to load/unload a VBA project, run a macro, or even evaluate a VBA statement on the command line.

Chapter Test

Answer the following questions on a separate sheet of paper.

1. What is a VBA *project?*
2. How do you create an AutoCAD macro?
3. What is the main AutoCAD tool used to create and manage VBA projects?
4. What are two ways you can make a VBA project load automatically each time a drawing is opened?
5. Define *IDE.*
6. Which tool in the **Visual Basic Editor** helps you to navigate through a VBA project?
7. Which tool in the **Visual Basic Editor** allows you change the properties of a form or control?
8. Which option allows you to take advantage of the automated error checking and automated error correcting features found in the **Visual Basic Editor**?
9. List the four components that can make up a VBA project.
10. Describe the AutoCAD **ThisDrawing** object.
11. What is a VBA *form?*
12. What is a VBA *control* and how is it used?
13. Describe a standard VBA module and why it would be used.
14. What is a VBA *class module?*
15. List the three program components that can be imported or exported from a VBA project along with each component's three character file extension.
16. What two methods can be used to run a VBA macro in AutoCAD?
17. Which AutoCAD command can be used to evaluate a single line of VBA code on the AutoCAD command line?
18. Which AutoCAD command can be used to run a VBA macro from within an AutoLISP program?

Programming Problems

Create the macros described below. All macros should be created in the **ThisDrawing** module of your MyMacros.dvb project. Run and test each macro.

1. Create a macro named p03_AcadColor using the code created for the AcadColor **Sub** in Problem 1-1.
2. Create a macro named p03_DisplayColorName that calls the **Function** ColorName from Problem 1-2 with the integer 3 as its argument value. Display the color name returned from the function in a VBA message box.
3. Add the error handler named ErrorHandler created in Problem 1-4 to the p03_DisplayColorName macro created in Problem 3-2. Make sure to add all the necessary code to implement it. Refer to the Error Handling section of Chapter 1 for any assistance. Once the error handler is implemented, change the integer argument for the **ColorName** function from 3 to –999.
4. Create a macro named p03_ChangeLayer using the code created for the ChangeLayer **Sub** in Problem 2-1.
5. Create a macro named p03_MoveObject using the code created for the MoveObject **Sub** in Problem 2-2.
6. Create a macro named p03_ChangeRadius using the code created for the ChangeRadius **Sub** in Problem 2-3.
7. Create a macro named p03_MirrorText using the code created for the MirrorText **Sub** in Problem 2-4.

The code examples in this chapter are supplied on the Student CD. A—First, open the **Open VBA Project** dialog box by selecting **Load Project...** from the **Macro** cascading menu in AutoCAD's **Tools** pull-down menu. B—Next, select the project Example Code.dvb and pick the **Open** button. C—Finally, display the **Macros** dialog box by picking **Macros...** from the **Macro** cascading menu in AutoCAD's **Tools** pull-down menu. Then, select the macro you wish to run and pick the **Run** button.

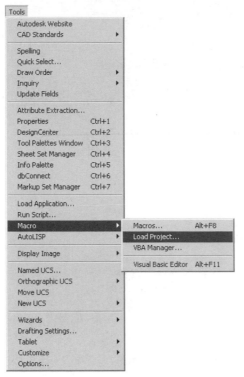

A

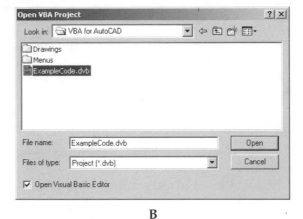

B

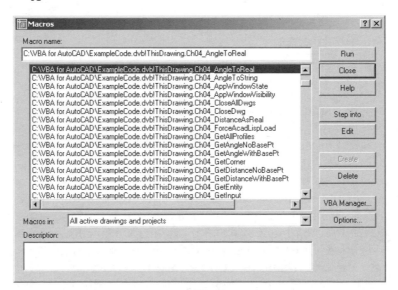

C

CHAPTER 4

Getting Started

Learning Objectives

After completing this chapter, you will be able to create VBA macros that:

- Control the size, position, and visibility of the AutoCAD application window.
- Set and retrieve all of AutoCAD's options and settings.
- Create new AutoCAD drawings.
- Open existing AutoCAD drawings.
- Save AutoCAD drawings.
- Save AutoCAD drawings to a previous release of AutoCAD.
- Set and retrieve AutoCAD system variables.
- Purge an AutoCAD drawing.
- Prompt the AutoCAD user.
- Get information from the AutoCAD user.

Getting Started

Now that you have been introduced to VBA, the AutoCAD object model, and the VBA Integrated Development Environment (IDE), it is time to put all that knowledge to good use programming for AutoCAD. As you have seen, the AutoCAD object model has various different objects, properties, and methods. The easiest way to explore and understand them all is to "take it from the top," the top object that is.

Controlling the AutoCAD Application Window

The top-level object is the AutoCAD **Application**, or root, object. In addition to being the link to other ActiveX Automation applications, the **Application** object also contains unique properties that control the appearance of the AutoCAD window. These properties include the size and position of the AutoCAD window, the state (minimized/maximized) of the window, and whether or not the window is visible.

Minimizing and Maximizing the AutoCAD Window

The **WindowState** property is used to minimize, maximize, or set the AutoCAD window to be normal size. This property can be set as follows.

```
Sub Ch04_AppWindowState()

    ' Minimize window.
    ThisDrawing.Application.WindowState = acMin
    MsgBox "AutoCAD window minimized."

    ' Maximize window.
    ThisDrawing.Application.WindowState = acMax
    MsgBox "AutoCAD window maximized."

    ' Set to normal size.
    ThisDrawing.Application.WindowState = acNorm
    MsgBox "AutoCAD window normal size."

End Sub
```

The ac constants used above are another example of AutoCAD constants. Their values are:

```
acNorm = 1
acMin = 2
acMax = 3
```

Once again, it is evident that using the constants supplied by AutoCAD makes the code much easier to understand.

Controlling the Size and Position of the AutoCAD Window

Sometimes, it may be necessary to control the size of the AutoCAD window and where it is located on the screen. This can be accomplished by setting the following **Application** properties:

```
Sub Ch04_ResizeAppWindow()

    ' Set window to normal size first because the width and height
    ' cannot be set if the window is maximized.
    ThisDrawing.Application.WindowState = acNorm

    ' Set window width and height
    ThisDrawing.Application.Width = 800
    ThisDrawing.Application.Height = 600

    ' Set the upper-left corner
    ThisDrawing.Application.WindowTop = 0
    ThisDrawing.Application.WindowLeft = 0

End Sub
```

This code will resize the AutoCAD window to be 800 pixels × 600 pixels and locate it at the top-left corner of the screen. The window position is always measured from the top-left corner of the computer screen in pixels.

Making the AutoCAD Window Invisible

The **Visible** property controls the visibility of the AutoCAD window. The window can be made visible or invisible as follows.

```
Sub Ch04_AppWindowVisibility()

    ' Make AutoCAD invisible.
    ThisDrawing.Application.Visible = False
    MsgBox "AutoCAD is invisible."

    ' Make AutoCAD visible.
    ThisDrawing.Application.Visible = True
    MsgBox "AutoCAD is visible."

End Sub
```

Specifying the AutoCAD window to be invisible allows you to run a task in the background without AutoCAD being visible on screen or minimized on the task bar.

Professional Tip

A minimized application appears on the task bar. An invisible application does not appear on the task bar.

Setting AutoCAD Options

The **Options** dialog box is displayed in AutoCAD by selecting **Options...** from the **Tools** pull-down menu or right-clicking in the drawing area and selecting **Options...** from the shortcut menu. The **Options** dialog is shown in **Figure 4-1.** All of the AutoCAD options that can be set in the **Options** dialog box can be controlled using VBA.

All settings in the **Options** dialog box have been "objectified" in VBA as the **Preferences** object, including the tabs. In fact, each tab is a subobject of the **Preferences** object. Any option that can be set by the user in AutoCAD can be set using VBA. The **Preferences** object can be referenced as follows.

```
Sub Ch04_GetPreferences()

    Dim objPref As AcadPreferences

    ' Get the Preferences object.
    Set objPref = ThisDrawing.Application.Preferences

End Sub
```

Caution

The **Preferences** object only contains options that are stored in the registry. Options that reside in the drawing are accessed using the **DatabasePreferences** object, which is discussed later in this chapter.

Figure 4-1.
The AutoCAD
Options dialog box.
All of the options
that can be set in
this dialog box can
be set using VBA.

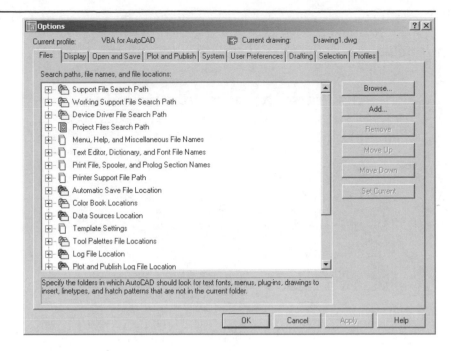

Preferences.Files Object

The **Preferences.Files** object contains all of the options from the **Files** tab in the **Options** dialog box. It is typically accessed using the **Files** property of the **Preferences** object:

```
Sub Ch04_GetPreferenceFiles()

    Dim objPrefFiles As AcadPreferencesFiles

    ' Get the Preferences Files object.
    Set objPrefFiles = ThisDrawing.Application.Preferences.Files

End Sub
```

Once you obtain a reference to the **Preferences.Files** object, you can then set or retrieve any of its properties. For instance, the following code adds the folder C:\MyFonts to the AutoCAD search path:

```
Sub Ch04_SetSupportPath()

    Dim objPrefFiles As AcadPreferencesFiles
    Dim strSupportPath As String

    ' Get the Preferences Files object.
    Set objPrefFiles = ThisDrawing.Application.Preferences.Files

    ' Get the current support path.
    strSupportPath = objPrefFiles.SupportPath

    ' Show the user the current path.
    MsgBox "Current support path:" & vbLf & vbLf & strSupportPath

    ' Add your path to the current path and set the SupportPath property.
    objPrefFiles.SupportPath = strSupportPath & ";C:\MyFonts"

    ' Show the user the new path.
    MsgBox "New support path:" & vbLf & vbLf & strSupportPath & _
        ";C:\MyFonts"

End Sub
```

must have semi-colon (handwritten annotation)

Do not forget to include the semicolon when adding the folder to the path, as shown in the second to last line of code. The semicolon is used to separate folders for all of the **Preference.Files** object path settings.

Professional Tip

The AutoCAD support file search path determines how AutoCAD support files are located. Support files include text fonts, menus, projects, hatch patterns, linetype definitions, and so on. The folders in the support file search path are checked for the various support files in the order in which they appear in the path. Once a support file is located in the path, all of the other folder locations specified are disregarded. This means that if you have multiple copies of a support file with the same name, the first one found via the search path will be used.

Some of the properties associated with the **Preference.Files** object are file based. The following code changes the alternate font file to C:\Program Files\AutoCAD 2005\ Fonts\Romans.shx:

```
Sub Ch04_SetAltFontFile()

    Dim objPrefFiles As AcadPreferencesFiles
    Dim strNewAltFontFile As String

    ' Get the Preferences Files object.
    Set objPrefFiles = ThisDrawing.Application.Preferences.Files

    ' Specify the font file name.
    strNewAltFontFile = " C:\Program Files\AutoCAD 2005\Fonts\Romans.shx "

    ' Set the alternate font file property.
    objPrefFiles.AltFontFile = strNewAltFontFile

    ' Tell the user.
    MsgBox "Alternate font file now set to: " & strNewAltFontFile

End Sub
```

The **Preferences.Files** object also has two methods—**GetProjectFilePath** and **SetProjectFilePath**. These methods are used to retrieve and set the project file path that is used to resolve project external reference (xref) files. Consult *AutoCAD and Its Applications—Basics* published by The Goodheart-Willcox Company or AutoCAD's online documentation for more information about external reference files and project-based xref search paths.

The **GetProjectFilePath** method retrieves a project file path. Its signature is:

ReturnVal = objPrefFiles.GetProjectFilePath (*ProjectName*)

where *ProjectName* is a **String** that is the name of the project for which you wish to determine the path and *ReturnVal* is a **String** that is the project file path.

The **SetProjectFilePath** method sets a project file path. It signature is:

objPrefFiles.SetProjectFilePath *ProjectName, ProjectPath*

where *ProjectName* is a **String** that is the name of the project for which you wish to change the path and *ProjectPath* is a **String** that is the new project path.

For example, suppose you want to add the folder C:\My Xrefs to the current project path. The following code retrieves the current project path and then adds the new folder to the path. A project must be defined for this macro to work.

```
Sub Ch04_ProjectPath()

    Dim objPrefFiles As AcadPreferencesFiles
    Dim strProjName As Variant
    Dim strProjPath As String
    Dim strNewProjPath As String

    ' Get the Preferences Files object.
    Set objPrefFiles = ThisDrawing.Application.Preferences.Files

    ' Get the current project name from the PROJECTNAME system variable.
    strProjName = ThisDrawing.GetVariable("PROJECTNAME")

    ' If the project name was used then proceed; otherwise do nothing.
    If strProjName <> "" Then

        ' Tell the user.
        MsgBox "Adding the folder C:\My Xrefs to the " & strProjName & _
            " project."

        ' Get the current path.
        strProjPath = objPrefFiles.GetProjectFilePath(strProjName)

        ' Create the new path.
        strNewProjPath = strProjPath & ";C:\My Xrefs"

        ' Set the new path.
        objPrefFiles.SetProjectFilePath strProjName, strNewProjPath

    Else

        ' No project current.
        MsgBox "No project currently set."

    End If

End Sub
```

In addition to the methods shown in this section, there are several properties of the **Preferences.Files** object. These are shown in **Figure 4-2.**

Professional Tip

Notice that the code above first checks to see if a project is current by checking the **PROJECTNAME** system variable. A drawing must first be associated with a project in order to use the project's associated path.

Figure 4-2.
Properties of the **Preferences.Files** object.

Property	Description
Application	**Application** object.
AltFontFile	Name of the alternate font file.
AltTabletMenuFile	Alternate tablet menu file.
AutoSavePath	Automatic save folder.
ColorBookPath	Color book path.
ConfigFile	Configuration file.
CustomDictionary	Custom dictionary file.
DefaultInternetURL	Default Internet URL.
DriversPath	Device drivers folder.
FontFileMap	Font file mapping file.
HelpFilePath	Help file folder.
LogFilePath	AutoCAD log file folder.
MainDictionary	Spell checking dictionary file.
MenuFile	Main AutoCAD menu file.
PageSetupOverridesTemplateFile	Default template for page setup overrides.
PlotLogFilePath	Path of the plot log file.
PostScriptPrologFile	Postscript prolog section name.
PrinterConfigPath	Printer configuration file path.
PrinterDescPath	Printer description file path.
PrinterStyleSheetPath	Printer style sheet file path.
PrintFile	Alternate plot file name.
PrintSpoolerPath	Print spool file folder.
PrintSpoolExecutable	Print spool application name.
QNewTemplateFile	Default template file for the **QNEW** command.
SupportPath	AutoCAD support file search path.
TempFilePath	Temporary file folder.
TemplateDWGPath	Drawing template folder.
TempXRefPath	Temporary xref file folder.
TextEditor	Text editor application name.
TextureMapPath	Texture map file path.
ToolPalettePath	Tool palette path.
WorkspacePath	Database workspace file.

Preferences.Display Object

The **Preferences.Display** object contains all of the options from the **Display** tab in the **Options** dialog box. It is typically accessed using the **Display** property of the **Preferences** object:

```
Sub Ch04_GetPreferenceDisplay()

    Dim objPrefDisplay As AcadPreferencesDisplay

    ' Get the Preferences Display object.
    Set objPrefDisplay = ThisDrawing.Application.Preferences.Display

End Sub
```

Once you obtain a reference to the **Preferences.Display** object, you can then set or retrieve any of its properties. In Chapter 2, you were introduced to how the cursor size can be controlled via the **Preferences.Display** object. In the following example, the model space background color is set to red using the **Preferences.Display** object.

```
Sub Ch04_SetBackgroundColor()

    Dim objPrefDisplay As AcadPreferencesDisplay

    ' Get the Preferences Display object.
    Set objPrefDisplay = ThisDrawing.Application.Preferences.Display

    ' Change the model space background color to red.
    objPrefDisplay.GraphicsWinModelBackgrndColor = vbRed

End Sub
```

It is as simple as that. In this example, vbRed is a Visual Basic constant of the type **OLE_COLOR**. These constants can be used to specify colors for various window-type objects on the screen. The other **OLE_COLOR** constants are shown in **Figure 4-3.**

It is also possible to control the display of scroll bars at the right side and bottom of the AutoCAD drawing window. The following code toggles the scroll bars on and off:

```
Sub Ch04_ToggleScrollBars()

    Dim objPrefDisplay As AcadPreferencesDisplay

    ' Get the Preferences Display object.
    Set objPrefDisplay = ThisDrawing.Application.Preferences.Display

    ' Toggle the scroll bars on or off, depending on the current setting.
    If objPrefDisplay.DisplayScrollBars Then

        objPrefDisplay.DisplayScrollBars = False

        ' Tell the user.
        MsgBox "Scroll bars turned off."

    Else
        objPrefDisplay.DisplayScrollBars = True

        ' Tell the user.
        MsgBox "Scroll bars turned on."

    End If

End Sub
```

There are other properties of the **Display** object. These are shown in **Figure 4-4.**

Figure 4-3.
The **OLE_COLOR** constants.

Constant	AutoCAD color
vbBlack	Black
vbRed	Red
vbYellow	Yellow
vbGreen	Green
vbCyan	Cyan
vbBlue	Blue
vbMagenta	Magenta

Figure 4-4.
The properties of the **Display** object.

Property	Description
Application	**Application** object.
AutoTrackingVecColor	Auto tracking vector color.
CursorSize	Cursor size.
DisplayLayoutTabs	Layout tab display.
DisplayScreenMenu	Screen menu display.
DisplayScrollBars	Scroll bar display toggle.
DockedVisibleLines	Number of text lines in command window.
GraphicsWinLayoutBackgrndColor	Background color of layouts.
GraphicsWinModelBackgrndColor	Background color of model space view.
HistoryLines	Number of text lines stored in history.
ImageFrameHighlight	Raster image frame display toggle.
LayoutCreateViewport	Automatic layout viewport toggle.
LayoutCrosshairColor	Layout crosshair color.
LayoutDisplayMargins	Layout margin display toggle.
LayoutDisplayPaper	Layout paper display toggle.
LayoutDisplayPaperShadow	Layout paper shadow toggle.
LayoutShowPlotSetup	Automatic layout plot setup toggle.
MaxAutoCADWindow	Start AutoCAD in full screen toggle.
ModelCrosshairColor	Model space crosshair color.
ShowRasterImage	Display raster image pan/zoom toggle.
TextFontSize	Font size for new text.
TextFont	Font type for new text.
TextFontStyle	Font style for new text.
TextWinBackgrndColor	Text window background color.
TextWinTextColor	Text window text color.
TrueColorImages	True color/palletized color toggle.
XRefFadeIntensity	Controls dimming intensity of xrefs.

Preferences.OpenSave Object

The **Preferences.OpenSave** object contains all of the options from the **Open and Save** tab in the **Options** dialog box. It is typically accessed using the **OpenSave** property of the **Preferences** object:

```
Sub Ch04_GetPreferenceOpenSave()

    Dim objPrefOpenSave As AcadPreferencesOpenSave

    ' Get the Preferences OpenSave object.
    Set objPrefOpenSave = ThisDrawing.Application.Preferences.OpenSave

End Sub
```

Once you obtain a reference to the **Preferences.OpenSave** object, you can then set or retrieve any of its properties. For instance, the following code sets the automatic save interval to 15 minutes:

```
Sub Ch04_SetAutoSave()

    Dim objPrefOpenSave As AcadPreferencesOpenSave

    ' Get the Preferences OpenSave object.
    Set objPrefOpenSave = ThisDrawing.Application.Preferences.OpenSave

    ' Set the save interval to be every 15 minutes.
    objPrefOpenSave.AutoSaveInterval = 15

End Sub
```

The **AutoSaveInterval** property can be set between 0 and 600 minutes. Setting the **AutoSaveInterval** property to 0 turns the automatic save feature off.

You can control the AutoCAD version in which drawings are saved by setting the **SaveAsType** property. The following code sets AutoCAD to save in Release 2000 format.

```
Sub Ch04_SetSaveAsType()

    Dim objPrefOpenSave As AcadPreferencesOpenSave

    ' Get the Preferences OpenSave object.
    Set objPrefOpenSave = ThisDrawing.Application.Preferences.OpenSave

    ' Set the save type to Release 2000.
    objPrefOpenSave.SaveAsType = ac2000_dwg

End Sub
```

In the above code, ac2000_dwg is an AutoCAD **acSaveAsType** constant. The other **acSaveAsType** constants and their values are shown in **Figure 4-5.** The other properties of the **OpenSave** object are shown in **Figure 4-6.**

Figure 4-5.
The **acSaveAsType** constants and their values.

Constant	Description
acR12_DXF	AutoCAD Release12/LT2 DXF.
ac2000_dwg	AutoCAD Release 2000 DWG.
ac2000_dxf	AutoCAD Release 2000 DXF.
ac2000_Template	AutoCAD 2000 drawing template file.
ac2004_dwg	AutoCAD 2004 DWG.
ac2004_dxf	AutoCAD 2004 DXF.
ac2004_Template	AutoCAD 2004 drawing template file.
acNative	The current drawing release format.
acUnknown	Unknown or invalid.

Figure 4-6.
The properties of the **OpenSave** object.

Property	Description
Application	**Application** object.
AutoAudit	Automatic audit on **DXFIN** toggle.
AutoSaveInterval	Automatic save interval.
CreateBackup	Automatic backup file creation toggle.
DemandLoadARXApp	Controls demand loading of ARX applications.
FullCRCValidation	Automatic CRC validation toggle.
IncrementalSavePercent	Percentage of wasted space allowed in drawing.
LogFileOn	AutoCAD log file toggle.
MRUNumber	Number of recently used files on file menu.
ProxyImage	Controls the display of proxy images.
SaveAsType	Drawing type to save drawing.
SavePreviewThumbnail	Save BMP preview toggle.
ShowProxyDialogBox	Display proxy dialog box toggle.
TempFileExtension	Temporary file extension.
XRefDemandLoad	Controls demand loading of xrefs.

Preferences.Output Object

The **Preferences.Output** object contains all of the options from the **Plot and Publish** tab in the **Options** dialog box. It is typically accessed using the **Output** property of the **Preferences** object:

```
Sub Ch04_GetPreferenceOutput()

    Dim objPrefOutput As AcadPreferencesOutput

    ' Get the Preferences Output object.
    Set objPrefOutput = ThisDrawing.Application.Preferences.Output

End Sub
```

Once you obtain a reference to the **Preferences.Output** object, you can then set or retrieve any of its properties. For instance, the following code sets the default output device for new drawings to DWF ePlot PC3. This printer/plotter configuration is used to save AutoCAD drawings in DWF format for publishing on the Internet.

```
Sub Ch04_SetOutputDevice()

    Dim objPrefOutput As AcadPreferencesOutput

    ' Get the Preferences Output object.
    Set objPrefOutput = ThisDrawing.Application.Preferences.Output

    ' Set the default output device to the ePlot driver.
    objPrefOutput.DefaultOutputDevice = "DWF6 ePlot.pc3"

End Sub
```

Figure 4-7.
The properties of **Output** object.

Property	Description
Application	**Application** object.
AutomaticPlotLog	Specifies whether or not to automatically save a plot log.
ContinuousPlotLog	Specifies whether or not to save a continuous plot log.
DefaultOutputDevice	Default output device.
DefaultPlotToFilePath	Default path for drawings plotted to file.
DefaultPlotStyleForLayer	Default plot style for Layer 0 for new drawings.
DefaultPlotStyleForObjects	Default plot style for newly created objects.
OLEQuality	Plot quality of OLE objects.
PlotLegacy	Toggles the legacy plot script.
PlotPolicy	Plot style name policy for new drawings.
PrinterPaperSizeAlert	Toggles the nonstandard paper size alert.
PrinterSpoolAlert	Controls the print spooler alert.
UseLastPlotSettings	Applies the plot settings of the last successful plot.

The **DefaultOutputDevice** property can be set to any configured plot device or any valid PC3 file in the plotter configuration path. For example, to set AutoCAD to use the last successful plot settings for new drawings, simply set the **UseLastPlotSettings** property to **True**:

```
Sub Ch04_UseLastPlotSettings()

    Dim objPrefOutput As AcadPreferencesOutput

    ' Get the Preferences Output object.
    Set objPrefOutput = ThisDrawing.Application.Preferences.Output

    'Use the last successful plot settings.
    objPrefOutput.UseLastPlotSettings = True

End Sub
```

There are other properties of **Output** object. These are shown in **Figure 4-7.**

Preferences.System Object

The **Preferences.System** object contains all of the options from the **System** tab in the **Options** dialog box. It is typically accessed using the **System** property of the **Preferences** object:

```
Sub Ch04_GetPreferenceSystem()

    Dim objPrefSystem As AcadPreferencesSystem

    ' Get the Preferences System object.
    Set objPrefSystem = ThisDrawing.Application.Preferences.System

End Sub
```

Once you obtain a reference to the **Preferences.System** object, you can then set or retrieve any of its properties. For instance, AutoCAD has a multiple document interface (MDI) that allows more than one drawing to be open at a time. By default, the acaddoc.lsp file is loaded each time a new or existing drawing is opened. However, the acad.lsp file is only loaded once when AutoCAD is launched. To force the acad.lsp file to load each time a drawing is opened, you can use the following code:

```
Sub Ch04_ForceAcadLispLoad()

    Dim objPrefSystem As AcadPreferencesSystem

    ' Get the Preferences System object.
    Set objPrefSystem = ThisDrawing.Application.Preferences.System

    ' Load ACAD.LSP for every drawing.
    objPrefSystem.LoadAcadLspInAllDocuments = True

End Sub
```

If for some reason you need to run AutoCAD in a single document interface (SDI), which AutoCAD had through Release 14, you can set the **SingleDocumentMode** property to **True**:

```
Sub Ch04_SetSDIMode()

    Dim objPrefSystem As AcadPreferencesSystem

    ' Get the Preferences System object.
    Set objPrefSystem = ThisDrawing.Application.Preferences.System

    ' Run AutoCAD in SDI mode.
    objPrefSystem.SingleDocumentMode = True

End Sub
```

There are other properties of the **System** object. These are shown in **Figure 4-8.**

Figure 4-8.
The properties of the **System** object.

Property	Description
Application	**Application** object.
BeepOnError	Toggles the alarm beep on error.
DisplayOLEScale	Toggles the display of the OLE scaling dialog box.
EnableStartupDialog	Toggles the display of the startup dialog box.
LoadAcadLspInAllDocuments	Specifies if the acad.lsp file is loaded for each drawing.
ShowWarningMessages	Toggles the display of the warning message dialog box.
SingleDocumentMode	Determines if AutoCAD runs in SDI or MDI mode.
StoreSQLIndex	Toggles the **Store SQL index in drawing** option.
TablesReadOnly	Toggles the read-only mode of database tables.

Preferences.User Object

The **Preferences.User** object contains all of the options from the **User Preferences** tab in the **Options** dialog box. It is typically accessed using the **User** property of the **Preferences** object:

```
Sub Ch04_GetPreferenceUser()

    Dim objPrefUser As AcadPreferencesUser

    ' Get the Preferences User object.
    Set objPrefUser = ThisDrawing.Application.Preferences.User

End Sub
```

Once you obtain a reference to the **Preferences.User** object, you can then set or retrieve any of its properties. For instance, the **ADCInsertUnitsDefaultSource** property can be used to specify which units to automatically use when inserting a block via the AutoCAD **DesignCenter**. An even more powerful application of the **ADCInsertUnitsDefaultSource** property is to use it in conjunction with the **ADCInsertUnitsDefaultTarget** property. By setting the target units to a different value than the source units, AutoCAD will automatically scale a block from one unit system to another when it is inserted. The following code sets the insert source units to inches and the insert target units to feet:

```
Sub Ch04_SetADCUnits()

    Dim objPrefUser As AcadPreferencesUser

    ' Get the Preferences User object.
    Set objPrefUser = ThisDrawing.Application.Preferences.User

    ' Set the ADC default source insert units to inches.
    objPrefUser.ADCInsertUnitsDefaultSource = acInsertUnitsInches

    ' Set the ADC default target insert units to feet.
    objPrefUser.ADCInsertUnitsDefaultTarget = acInsertUnitsFeet

End Sub
```

Now, when a block is inserted using AutoCAD **DesignCenter**, it is automatically scaled up by a ratio of 12:1, which is the ratio between inches and feet. This is very handy when coordinating architectural and civil disciplines that often work in inches and feet, respectively.

In the above example, **acInsertUnitsInches** and **acInsertUnitsFeet** are both AutoCAD **acInsertUnits** constants. The other **acInsertUnits** constants are shown in **Figure 4-9.**

There are other properties of the **User** object. These are shown in **Figure 4-10.**

Figure 4-9.
The **acInsertUnits** constants.

Constant	Unit
acInsertUnitsUnitless	No units
acInsertUnitsInches	Inches
acInsertUnitsFeet	Feet
acInsertUnitsMiles	Miles
acInsertUnitsMillimeters	Millimeters
acInsertUnitsCentimeters	Centimeters
acInsertUnitsMeters	Meters
acInsertUnitsKilometers	Kilometers
acInsertUnitsMicroinches	Microinches
acInsertUnitsMils	Mils
acInsertUnitsYards	Yards
acInsertUnitsAngstroms	Angstroms
acInsertUnitsNanometers	Nanometers
acInsertUnitsMicrons	Microns
acInsertUnitsDecimeters	Decimeters
acInsertUnitsDecameters	Decameters
acInsertUnitsHectometers	Hectometers
acInsertUnitsGigameters	Gigameters
acInsertUnitsAstronomicalUnits	Astronomical units
acInsertUnitsLightYears	Light years
acInsertUnitsParsecs	Parsecs

Figure 4-10.
The properties of the **User** object.

Property	Description
Application	**Application** object.
ADCInsertUnitsDefaultSource	Default **DesignCenter** source insert units.
ADCInsertUnitsDefaultTarget	Default **DesignCenter** target insert units.
HyperlinkDisplayCursor	Toggles the display of the hyperlink cursor and menu.
HyperlinkDisplayTooltip	Toggles the display of the hyperlink tooltip.
KeyboardAccelerator	Windows/AutoCAD classic keyboard.
KeyboardPriority	Controls the input of coordinate data.
SCMCommandMode	Controls the right-click functionality of the command mode.
SCMDefaultMode	Controls the right-click functionality of the default mode.
SCMEditMode	Controls the right-click functionality of the edit mode.
SCMTimeMode	Controls the time sensitive right-click behavior.
SCMTimeValue	Controls the duration of time for a right-click to display the shortcut menu.
ShortCutMenuDisplay	Toggles the display of the right-click shortcut menu.

Preferences.Drafting Object

The **Preferences.Drafting** object contains all of the options from the **Drafting** tab in the **Options** dialog box. It is typically accessed using the **Drafting** property of the **Preferences** object:

```
Sub Ch04_GetPreferenceDrafting()

    Dim objPrefDrafting As AcadPreferencesDrafting

    ' Get the Preferences Drafting object.
    Set objPrefDrafting = ThisDrawing.Application.Preferences.Drafting

End Sub
```

Once you obtain a reference to the **Preferences.Drafting** object, you can then set or retrieve any of its properties. For instance, all of the AutoSnap features can be controlled via the **Drafting** object. The following code toggles the AutoSnap marker on and off:

```
Sub Ch04_ToggleAutoSnapMarker()

    Dim objPrefDrafting As AcadPreferencesDrafting

    ' Get the Preferences Drafting object.
    Set objPrefDrafting = ThisDrawing.Application.Preferences.Drafting

    ' Toggle the AutoSnap marker.
    If objPrefDrafting.AutoSnapMarker Then

        objPrefDrafting.AutoSnapMarker = False

        ' Tell the user.
        MsgBox "AutoSnap marker turned off."

    Else

        objPrefDrafting.AutoSnapMarker = True

        ' Tell the user.
        MsgBox "AutoSnap marker turned on."

    End If

End Sub
```

You can also control the size of the AutoSnap marker. The **AutoSnapMarkerSize** property is used to set the size. The AutoSnap marker size is represented in pixels and must be an integer value between 1 and 20:

```
Sub Ch04_SetAutoMarkerSize()

    Dim objPrefDrafting As AcadPreferencesDrafting

    ' Get the Preferences Drafting object.
    Set objPrefDrafting = ThisDrawing.Application.Preferences.Drafting

    ' Change the AutoSnapMarker size.
    objPrefDrafting.AutoSnapMarkerSize = 10

End Sub
```

There are other properties of the **Drafting** object. These are shown in **Figure 4-11.**

Figure 4-11.
The properties of the **Drafting** object.

Property	Description
Application	**Application** object.
AlignmentPointAcquisition	Controls how alignment points are acquired.
AutoSnapAperture	Toggles the display of the AutoSnap aperture.
AutoSnapApertureSize	Controls the AutoSnap aperture size.
AutoSnapMagnet	Toggles the AutoSnap magnet.
AutoSnapMarker	Toggles the AutoSnap marker.
AutoSnapMarkerColor	Controls the AutoSnap marker color.
AutoSnapMarkerSize	Controls the AutoSnap marker size.
AutoSnapToolTip	Toggles the display of the AutoSnap tooltip.
AutoTrackToolTip	Toggles the display of the AutoTrack tooltip.
FullScreenTrackingVector	Toggles the display of the full-screen tracking vector.
PolarTrackingVector	Toggles the display of the polar tracking vector.

Preferences.Selection Object

The **Preferences.Selection** object contains all of the options from the **Selection** tab in the **Options** dialog box. It is typically accessed using the **Selection** property of the **Preferences** object:

```
Sub Ch04_GetPreferenceSelection()

    Dim objPrefSelection As AcadPreferencesSelection

    ' Get the Preferences Selection object.
    Set objPrefSelection = ThisDrawing.Application.Preferences.Selection

End Sub
```

Once you obtain a reference to the **Preferences.Selection** object, you can then set or retrieve any of its properties. For instance, the following code enables the noun/verb selection process:

```
Sub Ch04_SetNounVerb()

    Dim objPrefSelection As AcadPreferencesSelection

    ' Get the Preferences Selection object.
    Set objPrefSelection = ThisDrawing.Application.Preferences.Selection

    ' Enable noun/verb selection.
    objPrefSelection.PickFirst = True

End Sub
```

Setting the **PickFirst** property to **True** allows the user to select objects before issuing a command. Setting the **PickFirst** property to **False** forces the user to issue a command *before* any objects are selected.

Figure 4-12.
The properties of the **Selection** object.

Property	Description
Application	**Application** object.
DisplayGrips	Toggles the display of grips.
DisplayGripsWithinBlocks	Toggles the display of grips within blocks.
GripColorColorSelected	Controls the color of selected grips.
GripColorColorUnSelected	Controls the color of unselected grips.
GripSize	Controls grip size.
PickAdd	Toggles using the [Shift] key to add to a selection set.
PickAuto	Toggles automatic window selection
PickBoxSize	Controls the pickbox size.
PickDrag	Toggles the selection window drag.
PickFirst	Toggles noun/verb selection.
PickGroup	Toggles group selection.

The size of the pickbox used to select objects can be controlled by setting the **PickBox** property. The pickbox size is represented in pixels and must be an integer value between 1 and 50:

```
Sub Ch04_SetPickBoxSize()

    Dim objPrefSelection As AcadPreferencesSelection

    ' Get the Preferences Selection object.
    Set objPrefSelection = ThisDrawing.Application.Preferences.Selection

    ' Set the pickbox size to 25 pixels.
    objPrefSelection.PickBoxSize = 25

End Sub
```

There are other properties of the **Selection** object. These are shown in **Figure 4-12.**

Preferences.Profiles Object

The **Preferences.Profiles** object contains all of the options from the **Profiles** tab in the **Options** dialog box. It is typically accessed using the **Profiles** property of the **Preferences** object:

```
Sub Ch04_GetPreferenceProfiles()

    Dim objPrefProfiles As AcadPreferencesProfiles

    ' Get the Preferences Profiles object.
    Set objPrefProfiles = ThisDrawing.Application.Preferences.Profiles

End Sub
```

Once you obtain a reference to the **Preferences.Profiles** object, you can then set or retrieve any of its properties or methods. Other than the generic **Application** property shared by all objects, the **Preferences.Profiles** object consists of only one property—**ActiveProfile**. The rest of its interface is composed entirely of methods.

The **ActiveProfile** property controls the current AutoCAD profile. The following code sets the current profile to VBA for AutoCAD:

```
Sub Ch04_SetActiveProfile()

    Dim objPrefProfiles As AcadPreferencesProfiles

    ' Get the Preferences Profiles object.
    Set objPrefProfiles = ThisDrawing.Application.Preferences.Profiles

    ' Set the active profile to "VBA for AutoCAD."
    objPrefProfiles.ActiveProfile = "VBA for AutoCAD"

End Sub
```

 Caution   Trying to set a profile active that does not exist in AutoCAD will generate a run-time error.

Using the **GetAllProfileNames** method, it is possible to first check if a profile exists before setting it active. The signature for the **GetAllProfileNames** method is:

objPrefProfiles.GetAllProfileNames (*ProfileNames*)

where *ProfileNames* is a **Variant** that is a string array of the available profile names.

The following code retrieves all of the available profile names and displays them in a VBA message box:

```
Sub Ch04_GetAllProfiles()

    Dim objPrefProfiles As AcadPreferencesProfiles
    Dim varProfileNames As Variant
    Dim varName As Variant
    Dim strProfiles As String

    ' Get the Preferences Profiles object.
    Set objPrefProfiles = ThisDrawing.Application.Preferences.Profiles

    ' Get all of the available profiles.
    objPrefProfiles.GetAllProfileNames varProfileNames

    ' Initialize string.
    strProfiles = ""

    ' Iterate all profiles.
    For Each varName In varProfileNames
        strProfiles = strProfiles & varName & vbCrLf
    Next

    ' Display the profiles to the user.
    MsgBox "Available profiles: " & vbCrLf & vbCrLf & strProfiles

End Sub
```

If a profile does not exist in the current drawing and it has been previously exported to an ARG file, the profile can be imported using the **ImportProfile** method. The signature for the **ImportProfile** method is:

objPrefProfiles.ImportProfile *Profile, RegFile, IncludePathInfo*

where *Profile* is a **String** that is the name of the profile to import. *RegFile* is a **String** that is the registry file. The file must have an .arg extension. *IncludePathInfo* is a **Boolean** where **True** means the path information in the registry file will be preserved and **False** means the path information in the registry file will not be preserved.

The following code imports the profile VBA for AutoCAD.arg:

```
Sub Ch04_ImportProfile()

    Dim objPrefProfiles As AcadPreferencesProfiles

    ' Get the Preferences Profiles object.
    Set objPrefProfiles = ThisDrawing.Application.Preferences.Profiles

    ' Import the ARG file for the "VBA for AutoCAD" profile.
    objPrefProfiles.ImportProfile "VBA for AutoCAD", _
        "C:\VBA for AutoCAD\VBA for AutoCAD.ARG", True

End Sub
```

Once the profile is imported, the profile can then be set active using the **ActiveProfile** property, as explained above. *Sub Ch04 _ SetActive Profile ( )*

page 129

There are other methods of the **Profiles** object. A partial list is shown in **Figure 4-13.**

Figure 4-13.
A partial list of the methods of the **Profiles** object.

Method	Description
CopyProfile	Copies a specified profile.
DeleteProfile	Deletes a specified profile.
ExportProfile	Exports a specified profile.
GetAllProfileNames	Gets all available profiles.
ImportProfile	Imports a specified profile.
RenameProfile	Renames a specified profile.
ResetProfile	Resets a specified profile.

Refer to the AutoCAD online documentation *ActiveX and VBA Reference* for a complete description of the **Profiles** object's methods and their signatures.

- You can control the size, position, and visibility of the AutoCAD window via the **Application** object properties.
- Every object in the AutoCAD object model has an **Application** property that references the top-level **Application** object.
- The **Application.Preferences.Files** object can be used to control the settings found in the **Files** tab of AutoCAD's **Options** dialog box.
- The **Application.Preferences.Display** object can be used to control the settings found in the **Display** tab of AutoCAD's **Options** dialog box.
- The **Application.Preferences.OpenSave** object can be used to control the settings found in the **Open and Save** tab of AutoCAD's **Options** dialog box.
- The **Application.Preferences.Output** object can be used to control the settings found in the **Plotting** tab of AutoCAD's **Options** dialog box.
- The **Application.Preferences.System** object can be used to control the settings found in the **System** tab of AutoCAD's **Options** dialog box.
- The **Application.Preferences.User** object can be used to control the settings found in the **User Preferences** tab of AutoCAD's **Options** dialog box.
- The **Application.Preferences.Drafting** object can be used to control the settings found in the **Drafting** tab of AutoCAD's **Options** dialog box.
- The **Application.Preferences.Selection** object can be used to control the settings found in the **Selection** tab of AutoCAD's **Options** dialog box.
- The **Application.Preferences.Profiles** object can be used to control the settings found in the **Profiles** tab of AutoCAD's **Options** dialog box.

Exercise 4-1

Create the macros described below. All macros should be created in the **ThisDrawing** module of your MyMacros.dvb project created in Chapter 3. Provide all necessary error checking and control. Run and test each macro.

1. Create a macro named ex04_ZoomExtents that zooms the current viewport to the drawing extents.
2. Create a macro named ex04_SearchPath that adds the folder C:\VBA for AutoCAD to the beginning of the AutoCAD search path.
3. Create a macro named ex04_BackOn that turns on the creation of backup files (BAK) when a drawing is saved.
4. Create a macro named ex04_NoRightClick that makes the right-click mouse button issue an [Enter] instead of displaying a shortcut menu.
5. Create a macro named ex04_ExportProfile that creates a profile named VBA for AutoCAD and then exports it to a file named C:\VBA for AutoCAD\VBA.arg.

Opening, Closing, and Saving AutoCAD Drawings

VBA provides a number of methods that emulate the file operations found in AutoCAD. There are methods to open, close, and save drawings. These methods work similar to their AutoCAD command counterparts.

Opening a New or Existing Drawing

When AutoCAD is set up for a multiple document interface (MDI), a drawing is automatically added to the AutoCAD **Documents** collection object when it is opened. The **Documents** collection object is used to manage all of the open drawings.

Add Method

To open a new drawing, simply add it to the **Documents** collection using the **Add** method. The signature for the **Add** method when used with the **Documents** collection is:

```
Documents.Add
```

The following code adds a new, unnamed drawing to the **Documents** collection and makes it the current drawing:

```
Sub Ch04_OpenNewDwg()

    ' Open a new drawing.
    ThisDrawing.Application.Documents.Add

End Sub
```

Because the new drawing is now current, it also becomes the **ThisDrawing** object. Any reference to the **ThisDrawing** object in the AutoCAD object model now points to the new drawing.

Open Method

The **Open** method opens an existing drawing. Its signature is:

```
Documents.Open DwgName [, ReadOnly]
```

where *DwgName* is a **String** with the full path and file name of the drawing to open. *ReadOnly* is an optional **Boolean**, where **True** opens the drawing as read-only and **False** (default) opens the drawing as read-write.

The following code opens an existing drawing and adds it to the **Documents** collection:

```
Sub Ch04_OpenExistDwg()

    Dim strDwgName As String

    ' Specify the drawing name.
    strDwgName = "C:\VBA for AutoCAD\Drawings\Office.dwg"

    ' Make sure the drawing exists and open it if found; otherwise, tell the user.
    If Dir(strDwgName) <> "" Then
        ThisDrawing.Application.Documents.Open strDwgName
    Else
        MsgBox "File " & strDwgName & " does not exist."
    End If

End Sub
```

This code will open the drawing C:\VBA for AutoCAD\Drawings\Office.dwg and make it current, but only if the drawing exists. The VBA **Dir** function used in this example allows you to check whether a file exists before trying to open it, thus avoiding any run-time errors.

Professional Tip

Because all of the open drawings are stored in a collection, it is easy to use normal VBA techniques to iterate the collection. For example, the following code displays the names of all the drawings that are currently open:

```
Sub Ch04_ListOpenDwgs()

    Dim objDoc As AcadDocument

    ' Display the names of all the open drawings in a
    message box.
    For Each objDoc In Documents
        MsgBox objDoc.Name & " is open."
    Next

End Sub
```

Closing a Drawing

When you are done working in a drawing and no longer need to use it, good practice dictates that you close the drawing. Closing a drawing clears system resources and prevents any accidental changes to the drawing.

A **Document** object's **Close** method closes a drawing. Its signature is as follows:

Document.Close [*SaveChanges*] [, *DwgName*]

SaveChanges is an optional **Boolean**, where **True** (default) saves the drawing and **False** does not save the drawing. *DwgName* is an optional **String**, which is the name to assign to the drawing when saved. If there are no changes to the drawing, the *SaveChanges* and *DwgName* arguments are ignored.

The following code closes the current drawing using the default options:

```
Sub Ch04_CloseDwg()

    ' Close the current drawing.
    ThisDrawing.Close

End Sub
```

It is as easy as that. If you want to close all of the open drawings, you can simply iterate through the **Documents** collection:

```
Sub Ch04_CloseAllDwgs()

    Dim objDoc As AcadDocument

    ' Close all of the open drawings.
    For Each objDoc In Documents
        objDoc.Close
    Next

End Sub
```

Saving a Drawing

Occasionally, it is necessary to save a drawing to preserve any changes or updates made by your project. You can either save or save as.

Save Method

A **Document** object's **Save** method saves a drawing. The signature for the **Save** method when used with the **Document** object is:

Document.Save

The following code saves a drawing to the current file name:

```
Sub Ch04_SaveDwg()

    ' Save the drawing.
    ThisDrawing.Save

End Sub
```

The **Save** method works the same as issuing the **SAVE** command at the AutoCAD command line. A drawing should be saved at least once with a file name before using the **Save** method. Otherwise, the drawing is saved as Drawing#.dwg in the current working folder.

SaveAs Method

The **SaveAs** method can be used to save a new drawing to a specific file name, rename a drawing, or even save a drawing to another version of AutoCAD. Its signature is:

Document.SaveAs *DwgName* [, *FileType*]

where *DwgName* is a **String** that is the full path and file name of drawing. *FileType* is the **acSaveAsType** enum. See **Figure 4-14.** Its use is optional.

Figure 4-14.
The **acSaveAsType** enum settings.

Enum	Description
AcR12_dxf	AutoCAD Release 12 DXF
ac2000_dwg	AutoCAD 2000 DWG
ac2000_dxf	AutoCAD Release 2000 DXF
ac2000_Template	AutoCAD 2000 Template File DWT
ac2004_dwg	AutoCAD 2004 DWG
ac2004_dxf	AutoCAD 2004 DXF
ac2004_Template	AutoCAD 2004 Template File DWT
acNative	The current drawing release format.

The following code saves the current drawing to the file named VBA.dwg in Release 2000 format.

```
Sub Ch04_SaveAsDwg()

    ' Save the drawing in Release 2000 format.
    ThisDrawing.SaveAs "C:\VBA for AutoCAD\Drawings\VBA.dwg", ac2000_dwg

End Sub
```

When the optional *FileType* argument is not specified, the default file type is ac2004_dwg, the current release of AutoCAD.

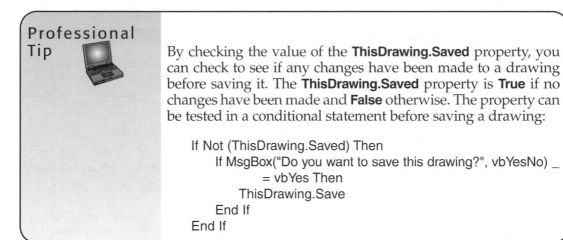

Professional Tip

By checking the value of the **ThisDrawing.Saved** property, you can check to see if any changes have been made to a drawing before saving it. The **ThisDrawing.Saved** property is **True** if no changes have been made and **False** otherwise. The property can be tested in a conditional statement before saving a drawing:

```
If Not (ThisDrawing.Saved) Then
    If MsgBox("Do you want to save this drawing?", vbYesNo) _
                = vbYes Then
            ThisDrawing.Save
    End If
End If
```

Managing the Current AutoCAD Drawing

When programming for AutoCAD, it is very important to be able to manage and control the current drawing environment. The drawing's environment and its current settings determine how the drawing interacts with your macros and, most importantly, the user when a macro is run.

Setting and Retrieving System Variables

Setting and retrieving AutoCAD system variables allow direct control over the drawing environment. If you have programmed with AutoLISP, you have more than likely had to manage system variables. System variables allow you to control things like whether a dialog box is displayed for commands and file operations, whether attributes are automatically requested, and so on. In short, system variables can affect the nature of your whole macro. Fortunately, it is as easy to control system variables in VBA as it is using AutoLISP.

SetVariable Method

The **SetVariable** method changes the value of any AutoCAD system variable that is not read-only. Its signature is:

    ThisDrawing.SetVariable *Name, Value*

where *Name* is a **String** that is the name of the system variable to set and *Value* is a **Variant** that is the new value for the system variable.

For example, the following code sets the **CMDDIA** system variable to 0, which disables certain command-based dialog boxes:

```
Sub Ch04_SetSystemVariable()

    ' Turn off the command dialog variable.
    ThisDrawing.SetVariable "CMDDIA", 0

End Sub
```

> **Caution**
>
> When setting system variables, AutoCAD may require integers, real, or text values. Passing the wrong data type will generate a run-time error.

GetVariable Method

The **GetVariable** method retrieves the value of any AutoCAD system variable. Its signature is:

ReturnVal = ThisDrawing.GetVariable (*VarName*)

where *VarName* is a **String** that is the name of the system variable for which you wish to retrieve the current value and *ReturnVal* is a **Variant** that is the current value of the system variable.

The following code retrieves the value of the **FILLMODE** system variable and displays it in a message box:

```
Sub Ch04_GetSystemVariable()

    Dim varData As Variant

    ' Get the value of the FILLMODE system variable.
    varData = ThisDrawing.GetVariable("FILLMODE")

    MsgBox "Fillmode " & " = " & varData

End Sub
```

> **Professional Tip**
>
>
>
> Notice in the above code that the variable **varData** is declared as a variant. An AutoCAD system variable may be a number of different data types. For this reason, the **GetVariable** method may return different data types, depending on the system variable being queried. A variant data type allows any data type to be returned.

Setting Database Preferences

The options that are stored in the registry are set and retrieved via the **Preferences** object. *Database preferences* represent all of the options in the **Options** dialog box that reside in the drawing, not in the system registry. The options that are stored in the drawing are accessed via the **ThisDrawing.Preferences** object:

```
Sub Ch04_SetDbPreferences()

    ' Turn on solid fill.
    ThisDrawing.Preferences.SolidFill = True

End Sub
```

This code turns on the fill option for multilines, hatches, solids, and wide polylines in the current drawing. The value of the **SolidFill** property is stored in the **FILLMODE** system variable. In fact, most database preferences have corresponding system variables.

There are other properties of the **DatabasePreferences** object. These are shown in **Figure 4-15.**

Figure 4-15.
The properties of the **DatabasePreferences** object.

Property	Description
AllowLongSymbolNames	Toggles the ability to use long symbol names.
Application	**Application** object.
ContourlinesPerSurface	Sets the number of contour lines per surface.
DisplaySilhouette	Toggles the display of silhouette curves.
Lineweight	Sets the default lineweight.
LineweightDisplay	Toggles the display of lineweights.
MaxActiveViewports	Sets the maximum number of active viewports.
ObjectSortByPlotting	Toggles object sort by plotting order.
ObjectSortByPSOutput	Toggles object sort by PostScript order.
ObjectSortByRedraws	Toggles object sort by redraw order.
ObjectSortByRegens	Toggles object sort by regeneration order.
ObjectSortBySelection	Toggles object sort by selection order.
ObjectSortBySnap	Toggles object sort by object snap order.
OLELaunch	Toggles the launch of an OLE object's parent application.
RenderSmoothness	Controls the smoothness of rendered images.
SegmentPerPolyline	Sets the number of segments used for polyline curves.
SolidFill	Toggles the display of fills.
TextFrameDisplay	Toggles the display of text frames.
XrefEdit	Toggles the in place editing of xrefs.
XRefLayerVisibility	Toggles the visibility of xref layers.

Regenerating a Drawing

It is sometimes necessary to regenerate a drawing so that all of the drawing objects are displayed correctly and at the correct resolution. The **Regen** method regenerates either the active viewport or all viewports. When a drawing is regenerated, all of the graphic information is recalculated.

The signature for the **Regen** method is:

    ThisDrawing.Regen *Viewport*

Viewport is an **Integer** where **acActiveViewport** regenerates the active viewport and **acAllViewports** regenerates all viewports.

The following code regenerates all of the viewports in the current drawing:

```
Sub Ch04_RegenAllViewPorts()

    ' Regenerate all of the viewports.
    ThisDrawing.Regen acAllViewports

End Sub
```

The following code regenerates the current viewport only:

```
Sub Ch04_RegenCurrentViewPort()

    ' Regenerate the current viewport.
    ThisDrawing.Regen acActiveViewport

End Sub
```

Purging a Drawing

From time to time, it is necessary to purge a drawing to rid it of any unreferenced objects that still reside in memory. This reduces the drawing size by permanently eliminating unused named objects like layers, text styles, line styles, blocks, and so on.

The **PurgeAll** method purges all unreferenced objects from the drawing. Its signature is:

    ThisDrawing.PurgeAll

The following code purges all of the unreferenced objects in the current drawing:

```
Sub Ch04_Purgeall()

    ' Purge everything.
    ThisDrawing.PurgeAll

End Sub
```

Unlike the **PURGE** command, there is no way to individually purge unreferenced objects. When using VBA, it is all or none.

- When a drawing is opened, it is automatically added to the AutoCAD **Documents** collection object and becomes the current **ThisDrawing** object.
- The VBA **Dir** function allows you to check if a file or folder exists.
- The **ThisDrawing.SaveAs** method can be used to save drawings to an earlier version of AutoCAD, a Drawing Exchange Format file (DXF), or an AutoCAD template file (DWT).
- The **ThisDrawing.Saved** property can be checked to determine whether or not a drawing has been saved.
- The **ThisDrawing.SetVariable** and the **ThisDrawing.GetVariable** methods set and retrieve AutoCAD system variables, respectively.
- The **ThisDrawing.Preferences** object properties control settings that are stored in the drawing and not in the registry.
- The **ThisDrawing.Regen** method can be used to regenerate either the current viewport or all viewports.
- The **ThisDrawing.PurgeAll** method purges all unreferenced, named objects from a drawing.

Exercise 4-2

Create the macros described below. All macros should be created in the **ThisDrawing** module of your MyMacros.dvb project. Provide all necessary error checking and control. Run and test each macro.

1. Create a macro named ex04_NewDWG that creates a new drawing and saves it as C:\VBA for AutoCAD\Drawings\ex04-01.dwg.
2. Create a macro named ex04_DXFOut that opens C:\VBA for AutoCAD\ Drawings\ex04-01.dwg and saves it as a DXF file in AutoCAD Release 12 format.
3. Create a macro named ex04_ObjectSnaps that sets the current AutoCAD object snaps to endpoint, midpoint, center, and quadrant. *Hint:* Object snap settings can be controlled using the **OSMODE** system variable.
4. Create a macro named ex04_NoXrefEdit that makes the current drawing unable to be opened or edited using the AutoCAD **REFEDIT** command.

Interacting with the User

In order to create dynamic, interactive programs, you must communicate with the user. The interaction can vary from displaying a message on the AutoCAD command line to requesting input that is used later by your project. Fortunately, the AutoCAD object model includes the **Utility** object that provides most of the same user interaction functionality found in the AutoLISP programming language. The AutoLISP **PROMPT** function and all of the popular AutoLISP **GET** functions have been emulated in VBA. Even the ability to initialize user input found in the AutoLISP **INITGET** function has been included!

Prompting the User

At the most basic level of communication is the "prompt." A *prompt* is a static form of communication that simply tells the user something. No input is required.

The **Utility** object's **Prompt** method displays a specified text string at the AutoCAD command line. Its signature is:

ThisDrawing.Utility.Prompt *Message*

where *Message* is a **String** that is the text to display on the command line.

The following code displays Hello World! at the command line:

```
Sub Ch04_PromptUser()

    ' Prompt the user.
    ThisDrawing.Utility.Prompt "Hello World!"

End Sub
```

Getting User Input

Many projects require that the user input data. This can range from answering a simple yes or no question, like Do you wish to continue?, to inputting complex data values. Requesting and processing information from the user adds another level of complexity to a project. All of the data entered by the user must be verified before being used by your project to ensure the data type is correct and the data are within the range of possible values. Remember the old computer adage "garbage in, garbage out!"

Luckily, much of this data validity checking has been automated. Just like their AutoLISP counterparts, the **Utility** object's "get" methods limit the data that a user can enter to the required data type. The "get" methods will not accept incorrect data types at run time. If an incorrect data type is entered, the specified user prompt is repeated until the correct data type is entered.

GetString Method

The **GetString** method gets a string of text from the user. Its signature is:

ReturnVal = ThisDrawing.Utility.GetString(*HasSpaces*, [*Prompt*])

HasSpaces is a **Boolean**, where **True** means the return string can have spaces and **False** means the return string cannot have spaces. If the *HasSpaces* argument is set to **True**, the user input string may contain spaces and must be terminated with a carriage return. If the *HasSpaces* argument is set to **False,** no spaces are allowed and either a space or a carriage return will terminate the input string. *Prompt* is a **Variant** string and is the text used to prompt user. Its use is optional. *ReturnVal* is a **String** and is the string returned from the user.

The following code gets a string of text, which can contain spaces, from the user and then displays the string in a message box:

```
Sub Ch04_GetString()

    Dim strReturn As String

    ' Get a string of text from the user. Blank spaces are allowed.
    strReturn = ThisDrawing.Utility.GetString(True, "Enter text: ")

    ' Display.
    MsgBox "String entered: " & strReturn

End Sub
```

This code prompts the user to Enter text: on the AutoCAD command line and, if the response is valid, returns the text in the *strReturn* variable. If the response is invalid, an error message is generated and the Enter text: prompt is repeated until a valid response is entered.

GetInteger Method

The **GetInteger** method gets an integer from the user. Its signature is:

ReturnVal = ThisDrawing.Utility.GetInteger([*Prompt*])

where *Prompt* is a **Variant** string that is the text used to prompt the user. Its use is optional. *ReturnVal* is an **Integer** that is the integer returned from the user.

The following code gets an integer value from the user and displays the integer in a message box:

```
Sub Ch04_GetInteger()

    Dim intReturn As Integer

    ' Get an integer from the user.
    intReturn = ThisDrawing.Utility.GetInteger("Enter an integer: ")

    ' Display.
    MsgBox "Integer entered: " & intReturn

End Sub
```

This code prompts the user to Enter an integer: at the AutoCAD command line and, if the response is valid, returns the integer in the *intReturn* variable. If the response is invalid, an error message is generated and the Enter an integer: prompt is repeated until a valid response is entered.

GetReal Method

The **GetReal** method gets a real number from the user. Its signature is:

ReturnVal = ThisDrawing.Utility.GetReal([*Prompt*])

where *Prompt* is a **Variant** string that is the text used to prompt the user. Its use is optional. *ReturnVal* is a **Double** data type that is the real value returned from the user.

The following code gets a real value from the user and displays the value in a message box:

```
Sub Ch04_GetReal()

    Dim dblReturn As Double

    ' Get a real value from the user.
    dblReturn = ThisDrawing.Utility.GetReal("Enter a real value: ")

    ' Display.
    MsgBox "Real value entered: " & dblReturn

End Sub
```

This code prompts the user to Enter a real value: at the AutoCAD command line and, if the response is valid, returns the real value in the *dblReturn* variable. If the response is invalid, an error message is generated and the Enter a real value: prompt is repeated until a valid response is entered.

GetAngle Method

The **GetAngle** method gets a specified angle from the user. Its signature is:

ReturnVal = ThisDrawing.Utility.GetAngle([*Point*], [*Prompt*])

where *Point* is an optional **Variant** that is an AutoCAD point value. If included, it is used as the angle base point on the screen. *Prompt* is an optional **Variant** string that is the text used to prompt the user. *ReturnVal* is a **Double** data type that is the angle specified in radians.

The angular value can be entered at the keyboard or it can be determined by two pick points on the screen. The angle value is *always* returned in radians.

If the *Point* argument is included, that point is used as the angle base point on the screen. A rubberband line is displayed in the drawing area from the base point to the cursor. The user only needs to pick a second point to determine the angle.

The following code gets an angle from the user without a base point specified:

```
Sub Ch04_GetAngleNoBasePt()

    Dim dblReturn As Double

    ' Get an angle from the user—Do NOT specify the base point.
    dblReturn = ThisDrawing.Utility.GetAngle(, "Enter an angle: ")

    ' Display.
    MsgBox "The angle entered was " & dblReturn

End Sub
```

Notice that the *Point* argument has been omitted. The user can either enter the desired angle at the keyboard or pick two points on the screen. The following code gets an angle from the user with a base point specified:

```
Sub Ch04_GetAngleWithBasePt()

    Dim dblReturn As Double
    Dim dblBasePt(0 To 2) As Double

    ' Specify the base point.
    dblBasePt(0) = 0#: dblBasePt(1) = 0#: dblBasePt(2) = 0#

    ' Get an angle from the user.
    dblReturn = ThisDrawing.Utility.GetAngle(dblBasePt, "Enter an angle: ")

    ' Display.
    MsgBox "The angle entered was " & dblReturn

End Sub
```

This code prompts the user to Enter an angle: and a rubberband line appears from the base point specified in the *dblBasePt* argument (0, 0, 0) to the cursor. The user can then pick the second point on the screen to determine the angle. Note in the above code that the autocorrect feature of the **Visual Basic Editor** automatically replaces the decimal point and trailing 0 with # when 0.0 is entered (0.0 becomes 0#).

The **GetAngle** method always takes into account the current AutoCAD base angle setting. The default base angle is east, or three o'clock. This means that zero degrees is to the right with all angles measured counterclockwise. The base angle can be set to any direction by changing the **ANGBASE** system variable or in the **Direction Control** dialog box accessed through the **Drawing Units** dialog box.

GetPoint Method

The **GetPoint** method gets an AutoCAD point from the user. Its signature is:

ReturnVal = ThisDrawing.Utility.GetPoint([*Point*], [*Prompt*])

where *Point* is an optional **Variant** that is an AutoCAD point value. *Prompt* is an optional **Variant** string that is the text used to prompt the user. *ReturnVal* is a **Variant** three-element array of **Double** data types that is an AutoCAD point in the world coordinate system (WCS).

The AutoCAD point value can be entered at the keyboard by entering a coordinate in the format of the current units or by picking a point on the screen. If the *Point* argument is provided, AutoCAD draws a rubberband line from that point to the current crosshair position. This provides the user with visual feedback as to where the cursor is relative to the first point.

The following code gets a point from the user without a start point specified:

```
Sub Ch04_GetPointNoBasePt()

    Dim varReturn As Variant

    ' Get a point from the user—Do NOT specify the start point.
    varReturn = ThisDrawing.Utility.GetPoint(, "Enter a point: ")

    ' Display.
    MsgBox "The point entered was " & varReturn(0) & "," _
        & varReturn(1) & "," & varReturn(2)

End Sub
```

Notice that the *Point* argument has been omitted. The user can either enter the desired coordinate value at the keyboard or pick a point on the screen.

The following code gets a point from the user by specifying a start point:

```
Sub Ch04_GetPointWithBasePt()

    Dim varReturn As Variant
    Dim dblStartPt(0 To 2) As Double

    ' Specify start point.
    dblStartPt(0) = 0#: dblStartPt(1) = 0#: dblStartPt(2) = 0#

    ' Get a point from the user.
    varReturn = ThisDrawing.Utility.GetPoint(dblStartPt, "Enter a point: ")

    ' Display.
    MsgBox "The point entered was " & varReturn(0) & "," _
        & varReturn(1) & "," & varReturn(2)

End Sub
```

This code prompts the user to Enter a point: with a rubberband line from the point specified in the *dblStartPt* argument (0, 0, 0). The user only has to pick the point on the screen.

GetCorner Method

The **GetCorner** method gets the corner point of a rectangle by drawing a dynamically sized rectangle from the specified *Point* argument value to the current crosshair position on the screen. The signature of the **GetCorner** method is:

ReturnVal = ThisDrawing.Utility.GetCorner(*Point*, [*Prompt*])

where *Point* is a **Variant** that is an AutoCAD point value of the rectangle's first corner. *Prompt* is a **Variant** string that is the text used to prompt the user. Its use is optional. *ReturnVal* is a **Variant** three-element array of **Double** data types that is the AutoCAD point value of the rectangle's second corner in the world coordinate system (WCS).

The second corner's point value can be entered at the keyboard in the format of the current drawing units or can be picked on the screen. AutoCAD draws a rubberband rectangle from *Point* to the current crosshairs position. The following code gets a corner point from the user:

```
Sub Ch04_GetCorner()

    Dim varReturn As Variant
    Dim dblStartPt(0 To 2) As Double

    ' Specify the start point.
    dblStartPt(0) = 0#: dblStartPt(1) = 0#: dblStartPt(2) = 0#

    ' Get a rectangle corner point from the user.
    varReturn = ThisDrawing.Utility.GetCorner(dblStartPt, _
        "Enter other corner: ")

    ' Display.
    MsgBox "The point entered was " & varReturn(0) & "," _
        & varReturn(1) & "," & varReturn(2)

End Sub
```

GetDistance Method

The **GetDistance** method gets a specified distance, in current linear units, from the user. The signature for the **GetDistance** method is:

ReturnVal = ThisDrawing.Utility.GetDistance([*Point*], [*Prompt*])

where *Point* is an optional **Variant** that is an AutoCAD point value for the first endpoint of the distance to be measured. *Prompt* is an optional **Variant** string that is the text used to prompt user. *ReturnVal* is a **Double** data type that is the distance in the current linear units.

The distance can be entered at the keyboard by entering a number in the current units format. The user can also set the distance by specifying two locations on the screen. If the *Point* argument is provided, AutoCAD draws a rubberband line from *Point* to the current crosshair position. The following code gets a distance value from the user without specifying a starting point:

```
Sub Ch04_GetDistanceNoBasePt()

    Dim dblReturn As Double

    ' Get a distance from the user—Do NOT specify the start point.
    dblReturn = ThisDrawing.Utility.GetDistance(, "Enter a distance: ")

    ' Display.
    MsgBox "The distance entered was " & dblReturn

End Sub
```

Notice that the *Point* argument is omitted. The user can either enter the desired distance at the keyboard or pick two points on the screen.

The following code gets a distance value from the user with a base point specified:

```
Sub Ch04_GetDistanceWithBasePt()

    Dim dblReturn As Double
    Dim dblStartPt(0 To 2) As Double

    ' Specify the start point.
    dblStartPt(0) = 0#: dblStartPt(1) = 0#: dblStartPt(2) = 0#

    ' Get a distance from user.
    dblReturn = ThisDrawing.Utility.GetDistance(dblStartPt, "Enter a point: ")

    ' Display.
    MsgBox "The distance entered was " & dblReturn

End Sub
```

This code prompts the user to Enter a point: and a rubberband line is displayed from the point specified in the *dblStartPt* argument (0, 0, 0). The user can then pick another point on the screen to define the distance.

GetOrientation Method

The **GetOrientation** method gets a specified angle from the user, similar to the **GetAngle** method discussed earlier. However, **GetOrientation** ignores the current base angle setting stored in the AutoCAD **ANGBASE** system variable. The angle returned is always relative to the default AutoCAD base angle, which is zero degrees to the right, or three o'clock.

The signature for the **GetOrientation** method is:

ReturnVal = ThisDrawing.Utility.GetOrientation([*Point*], [*Prompt*])

where *Point* is an optional **Variant** that is an AutoCAD point value. If included, it is used as the angle base point on the screen. *Prompt* is an optional **Variant** string that is the text used to prompt the user. *ReturnVal* is a **Double** data type that is the angle specified in radians.

The angular value can be entered at the keyboard or it can be determined by pick points on the screen. If the *Point* argument is included, it is used as the angle base point on the screen, the user only needs to pick a second point to determine the angle. The angles value is always returned in radians.

The following code gets an angle from the user without specifying a start point, or angle base:

```
Sub Ch04_GetOrientNoBasePt()

    Dim dblReturn As Double

    ' Get an angle from the user—Do NOT specify the base point.
    dblReturn = ThisDrawing.Utility.GetOrientation(, "Enter an angle: ")

    ' Display.
    MsgBox "The angle entered was " & dblReturn

End Sub
```

Notice that the *Point* argument has been omitted. The user can either enter the desired angle at the keyboard or pick two points on the screen.

The following code gets an angle from the user with a base point specified:

```
Sub Ch04_GetOrientWithBasePt()

    Dim dblReturn As Double
    Dim dblBasePt(0 To 2) As Double

    ' Specify the base point.
    dblBasePt(0) = 0#: dblBasePt(1) = 0#: dblBasePt(2) = 0#

    ' Get an angle from the user.
    dblReturn = ThisDrawing.Utility.GetOrientation(dblBasePt, "Enter an" & _
        " angle: ")

    ' Display.
    MsgBox "The angle entered was " & dblReturn

End Sub
```

This code prompts the user to Enter an angle: with a rubberband line from the base point specified in the *dblBasePt* argument (0, 0, 0). The user can then pick the second point on the screen to determine the angle.

GetEntity Method

The **GetEntity** method gets an AutoCAD drawing object, or entity, interactively by allowing the user to select the entity on the graphics screen. Its signature is:

    ThisDrawing.Utility.GetEntity *Object*, *PickedPoint*, [*Prompt*]

where *Object* is an **Object** that is returned, which is the AutoCAD drawing object. *PickedPoint* is a **Variant** that is returned, which is the selected AutoCAD point. *Prompt* is a **Variant** string that is the text used to prompt the user. Its use is optional.

The first two arguments (*Object* and *PickedPoint*) are returned by the method. No values are passed to the method in these arguments when they are called in your project. Instead, they are used as placeholders for values returned by the **GetEntity** method. If an entity is picked, the selected object is returned in the *Object* argument and the point used to select the object is returned in the *PickedPoint* argument.

The following code gets an AutoCAD drawing object:

```
Sub Ch04_GetEntity()

    Dim objReturn As AcadObject
    Dim varPickPt As Variant

    ' Get a drawing object.
    ThisDrawing.Utility.GetEntity objReturn, varPickPt, "Select an object: "

    ' Display.
    MsgBox "Object type selected: " & objReturn.ObjectName

End Sub
```

This code prompts the user to Select an object:. If a valid entity is picked, the selected drawing object and the pick point coordinate value used to select the entity are returned in their respective arguments. If the pick point is not on an entity the method fails and a run-time error is generated. Handling user input errors is discussed later in the chapter.

GetSubEntity Method

The **GetSubEntity** method gets an AutoCAD drawing subobject, or subentity, interactively by allowing the user to select the nested entity on the graphics screen. A *subentity* is an entity that is part of a larger complex object, such as a block or an xref. The **GetSubEntity** method disregards the top-level entity that lies under the user pick point and returns information about the subentity. The signature for the **GetEntity** method is:

ThisDrawing.Utility.GetSubEntity *Object*, *PickedPoint*, *TransMatrix*, *SubObjIds* [, *Prompt*]

where *Object* is an **Object** that is returned, which is the AutoCAD drawing entity. *PickedPoint* is a **Variant** that is returned, which is the selected AutoCAD point. *TransMatrix* is a **Variant** that is returned as a 4×4 array of **Double** data types. It is the subentity's translation matrix. *SubObjIds* is a **Variant** that is returned as an array of **Long** data types. It is an array of object IDs for any nested entities in the selected entity. *Prompt* is a **Variant** string that is the text used to prompt the user. Its use is optional.

The first four arguments (*Object*, *PickedPoint*, *TransMatrix*, and *SubObjIds*) are returned by the method. No values are passed to the method in these arguments when they are called in your project. Instead, they are used as placeholders for values returned by the **GetSubEntity** method. If an entity is picked, the selected object is returned in the *Object* argument and the point used to select the object is returned in the *PickedPoint* argument. The subentity's translation matrix is returned in the *TransMatrix* argument and, if there are any further nested subentities, their object IDs are returned in the *SubObjIds* argument.

The following code gets a subentity:

```
Sub Ch04_GetSubEntity()

    Dim objReturn As AcadObject
    Dim varPickPt As Variant
    Dim varTranMat As Variant
    Dim varSubObjIds As Variant

    ' Get a drawing subobject.
    ThisDrawing.Utility.GetSubEntity objReturn, varPickPt, varTranMat, _
        varSubObjIds, "Select a nested object: "

    ' Display.
    MsgBox "Object type selected: " & objReturn.ObjectName

End Sub
```

This code prompts the user to Select a nested object: at the AutoCAD command line. If a valid entity is picked, the selected subentity, the pick point, the subentity's transformation matrix, and any subentities that belong to the selected subentity are returned in their respective arguments. If the pick point is not on a subentity, the method fails and a run-time error is generated. Handling user input errors is discussed later in the chapter.

> **Caution** Both the **GetEntity** and **GetSubEntity** methods can retrieve an entity even if it is not visible on the screen or if it is on a frozen layer.

Initializing User Input

There are many different things that a user can enter at the keyboard in response to a request for input from a project. Trying to predict and test all of the possible values is about as easy as winning the lottery. However, as luck would have it, the **Utility** object provides a method—**InitializeUserInput**—that allows you to initialize what a user can enter and how certain "get" methods behave.

InitializeUserInput Method

The **InitializeUserInput** method restricts what the user can enter in response to most of the "get" input methods described so far. Its signature is:

ThisDrawing.Utility.InitializeUserInput *BitFlag*, [*Keyword*]

where *BitFlag* is an **Integer** that determines the action. To set more than one action at a time, add the values together in any combination. Refer to **Figure 4-16.** *Keyword* is a **Variant** array of **String** data types, which are the keywords that the following user-input method recognizes. Its use is optional.

The *BitFlag* argument controls the behavior of the following "get" method, while the *Keyword* argument limits text input to a specified string of text. Keywords are explained in detail in the next section.

Figure 4-16.
Bitflag integers for the **InitializeUserInput** method.

Bitflag	Action
1	Disallows null input. This prevents the user from responding to the request by entering only [Enter] or a space.
2	Disallows input of zero (0). This prevents the user from responding to the request by entering 0.
4	Disallows negative values. This prevents the user from responding to the request by entering a negative value.
8	Does not check drawing limits, even if the **LIMCHECK** system variable is on. This enables the user to enter a point outside the current drawing limits. This condition applies to the next user-input function even if the AutoCAD **LIMCHECK** system variable is currently set.
16	Not currently used.
32	Uses dashed lines when drawing rubberband lines or boxes. This causes the rubberband line or box that AutoCAD displays to be dashed instead of solid, for those methods that let the user specify a point by selecting a location on the graphics screen. If the **POPUPS** system variable is 0, AutoCAD ignores this bit.
64	Ignores the Z coordinate of 3D points (**GetDistance** method only).This option ensures the function returns a 2D distance.
128	Allows arbitrary input—whatever the user types.

The **InitializeUserInput** method is very similar to the AutoLISP **initget** function. Just as the **initget** function must precede the **getx** AutoLISP function you want to initialize, the **InitializeUserInput** method must precede the "get" method you wish to initialize.

AutoLISP vs. VBA

The following code initializes the **GetInteger** method so that a null input is not allowed:

```
Sub Ch04_InitializeInput1()

    Dim intReturn As Integer

    ' Initialize the GetInteger method so null input is not allowed.
    ThisDrawing.Utility.InitializeUserInput 1

    ' Get an integer from the user.
    intReturn = ThisDrawing.Utility.GetInteger("Enter an integer: ")

    ' Display.
    MsgBox "Integer entered: " & intReturn

End Sub
```

This code initializes the **GetInteger** method so that the user is required to enter something at the Enter an integer: prompt. If the user presses the [Enter] key or the space bar, an error message is generated and the Enter an integer: prompt is repeated until a valid response is entered.

If you want further control over what can be entered, simply add up the bit flags you want and specify the sum as the *BitFlag* argument. For instance, the following code will disallow null input and negative values for the **GetInteger** method:

```
Sub Ch04_InitializeInput2()

    Dim intReturn As Integer

    ' Initialize the GetInteger method so null input and negative
    ' values are not allowed.
    ThisDrawing.Utility.InitializeUserInput 5

    ' Get an integer from the user.
    intReturn = ThisDrawing.Utility.GetInteger("Enter an integer: ")

    ' Display.
    MsgBox "The integer entered was " & intReturn

End Sub
```

The *BitFlag* argument in this example is set to 5, or 1 + 4. If a null or negative value is entered by the user, an error message is generated and the Enter an integer: prompt is repeated until a valid response is entered.

Caution The **InitializeUserInput** method works in conjunction with all of the "get" methods *except* **GetString**. When text string input is desired with initialized input, use the **GetKeyword** method discussed in the next section.

GetKeyword Method

The **GetKeyword** method is used in conjunction with the **InitializeUserInput** method to get a specific text string "keyword" from the user. The signature of the **GetKeyword** method is:

ReturnVal = ThisDrawing.Utility.GetKeyword([*Prompt*])

where *Prompt* is a **Variant** string that is the text used to prompt user. Its use is optional. *ReturnVal* is a **String** that is the keyword string returned from the user.

Like the other "get" methods, the **GetKeyword** method is called in your project after the **InitializeUserInput** method. The **GetKeyword** method is very similar to the **GetString** method in that it returns a text string. The only difference is that the returned text string is determined by the *Keyword* argument of the **InitializeUserInput** method. The *Keyword* argument is a text string that contains one or more keywords separated by spaces. Any text string returned by the **GetKeyword** method is limited to one of those keywords.

For instance, the following code disallows null input and initializes the valid keywords as Line, Circle, and Arc:

```
Sub Ch04_GetKeyWord1()

    Dim strKeyWord As String

    ' Initialize the GetKeyword method with the keywords
    ' Line, Circle, and Arc. Also, disable null input.
    ThisDrawing.Utility.InitializeUserInput 1, "Line Circle Arc"

    ' Get the keyword from the user.
    strKeyWord = ThisDrawing.Utility.GetKeyword _
        ("Enter a keyword [Line/Circle/Arc]: ")

    ' Display.
    MsgBox "Keyword entered: " & strKeyWord

End Sub
```

In the above code, the keyword string argument is initialized to Line Circle Arc. This means the user can only enter Line, Circle, or Arc in response to the Enter a keyword [Line/Circle/Arc]: prompt or an error message is generated and the prompt is repeated.

Notice in the example above that the keywords Line, Circle, and Arc each contain an uppercase character. Uppercase characters have a special property in the *Keyword* argument; they indicate a keyword abbreviation. Abbreviations allow the user to enter only the first one or two characters of a keyword and the whole keyword is returned. In the previous example, the user can enter an L for Line, C for Circle, or A for Arc and the complete keyword is returned. The user can enter lowercase, uppercase, or a mix of both in response to the prompt; the keyword is always returned exactly as it was specified via the **InitializeUserInput** method.

Now, let's see how keywords can be applied in the real world. The following code is an example of a classic Yes-No condition:

```
Sub Ch04_GetKeyWord2()

    Dim strKeyWord As String

    ' Initialize the GetKeyword method with the keywords
    ' Yes and No, and disable null input.
    ThisDrawing.Utility.InitializeUserInput 1, "Yes No"

    ' See if the user wants the project to continue.
    strKeyWord = ThisDrawing.Utility.GetKeyword _
        ("Do you wish to continue? [Yes/No]: ")

    ' If the user does not want to continue, exit the sub.
    If strKeyWord = "No" Then
        Exit Sub
    Else
        MsgBox "Program continuing..."
    End If

End Sub
```

This code requires that the user enter Y or Yes in response to the Do you wish to continue? [Yes/No]: prompt in order for the project to continue. If the user enters N or No, the project exits.

Why should the user have to type anything? It is always good programming practice to provide the user a default value. The following code is basically the same as above, but now if the user wants to answer No in response to the Do you wish to continue? [Yes/No] <No>: prompt, they can simply press [Enter]:

```
Sub Ch04_GetKeyWord3()

    Dim strKeyWord As String

    ' Initialize the GetKeyword method with the keywords
    ' Yes and No, but this time allow null input.
    ThisDrawing.Utility.InitializeUserInput 0, "Yes No"

    ' See if the user wants the macro to continue. Default to No.
    strKeyWord = ThisDrawing.Utility.GetKeyword _
        ("Do you wish to continue? [Yes/No] <No>: ")

    ' If the user does not want to continue, exit the Sub.
    If strKeyWord = "No" Or strKeyWord = "" Then
        Exit Sub
    Else
        MsgBox "Program continuing..."
    End If

End Sub
```

This code checks the value returned by the **GetKeyword** method and exits the macro if *strKeyword* is set to No or is an empty string. In order to allow the user to enter a carriage return the **InitializeUserInput** method's *BitFlag* argument is set to 0.

Professional Tip

Default values are indicated in AutoCAD by enclosing the default value in less than (<) and greater than (>) brackets:

```
strKeyWord = ThisDrawing.Utility.GetKeyword _
    ("Enter a keyword [Line/Circle/Arc] <Arc>: ")
```

GetInput Method

The **GetInput** method allows you to use the **InitializeUserInput** keyword functionality with the other "get" methods discussed earlier (**GetInteger**, **GetReal**, **GetPoint**, etc.). The signature of the **GetInput** method is:

ReturnVal = ThisDrawing.Utility.GetInput ()

where *ReturnVal* is a **String** that is the keyword returned from the user.

Using the **GetInput** method involves doing a little error checking first. If keywords are used with any of the "get" methods other than the **GetKeyword** method, a run-time error is generated. You must check the **Err** object's **Description** property for its value after a call to the "get" method you are using. If the error description returned is User input is a keyword, you can then call the **GetInput** method and retrieve the keyword.

In order to call the **GetInput** method after a run-time error, you must use the **On Error Resume Next** error handling statement. Remember, when the **On Error Resume Next** error handler is used, run-time errors are ignored and control is passed to the next line in your project. See Chapter 1 for more information about error handling.

The following is an example of using keywords with the **GetInteger** method:

```
Sub Ch04_GetInput()

    Dim strColor As String
    Dim intColor As Integer

    ' Initialize the GetKeyword method with keywords for
    ' the first seven AutoCAD colors and set the bit flag
    ' to limit input to positive, nonzero values.
    ThisDrawing.Utility.InitializeUserInput 6, _
        "Red Yellow Green Cyan Blue Magenta White"

    ' Set the error handler to resume on the next line if there is an error.
    On Error Resume Next

    ' Get the value entered by the user.
    intColor = ThisDrawing.Utility.GetInteger("Enter color name or number: ")

    ' If the error description matches "User input is a keyword," get the keyword
    ' using the GetInput method and clear the Err object. Otherwise convert
    ' the integer input to a String value for display in message box.
    If Err.Description = "User input is a keyword" Then
        strColor = ThisDrawing.Utility.GetInput()
        Err.Clear
    Else
        strColor = intColor
    End If

    ' Display the result.
    MsgBox "Color entered: " & strColor

End Sub
```

This code allows the user to enter any color's integer value or the string value of the first seven AutoCAD colors. Of course, there is some more error checking that could be done. Can you think of what invalid input a user can still enter using the code above?

User Interaction

- The **ThisDrawing.Utility** object provides most of the same interactive user functions found in AutoLISP.
- The **ThisDrawing.Utility.Prompt** method displays a text string on the AutoCAD command line.
- The **ThisDrawing.Utility.GetString** method gets a text string from the user.
- The **ThisDrawing.Utility.GetInteger** method gets an integer from the user.
- The **ThisDrawing.Utility.GetReal** method gets a real number from the user.
- The **ThisDrawing.Utility.GetAngle** method gets an angle from the user.
- The **ThisDrawing.Utility.GetPoint** method gets an AutoCAD coordinate point value from the user.
- The **ThisDrawing.Utility.GetCorner** method gets the corner point of a rectangle dynamically using AutoCAD's rubberband box feature.
- The **ThisDrawing.Utility.GetDistance** method gets a distance from the user via either keyboard entry or points picked on the screen.
- The **ThisDrawing.Utility.GetOrientation** method gets an angle from the user, similar to the **ThisDrawing.Utility.GetAngle** method, but the angle returned is always relative to the AutoCAD default base angle of zero degrees to the right, or three o'clock.
- The **ThisDrawing.Utility.GetEntity** method gets an AutoCAD drawing object by allowing the user to select the entity on the screen.
- The **ThisDrawing.Utility.GetSubEntity** method gets an AutoCAD drawing subobject by allowing the user to select the nested entity on the screen.
- The **ThisDrawing.Utility.InitializeUserInput** method restricts what the user can enter in response to most of the **ThisDrawing.Utility** "get" input methods.
- The **ThisDrawing.Utility.GetKeyword** method is used in conjunction with the **InitializeUserInput** method to get a specific text string "keyword" from the user.
- The **ThisDrawing.Utility.GetInput** method allows you to use the **InitializeUserInput** keyword functionality with other **ThisDrawing.Utility** "get" methods besides the **GetKeyword** method.

Exercise 4-3

Create the macros described below. All macros should be created in the **ThisDrawing** module of your MyMacros.dvb project. Provide all necessary error checking and control. Run and test each macro.

1. Create a macro named ex04_Blipmode that allows the user to view and then change the AutoCAD **BLIPMODE** system variable.
2. Create a macro named ex04_SetProfile that allows a user to make a profile current based on a list of the available profiles.
3. Create a macro named ex04_ObjProperties that prompts the user to select an AutoCAD entity and then displays the entity's layer, color, and linetype properties.
4. Create a macro named ex04_PurgeAndQuit that prompts a user if they want to quit AutoCAD and, if so, purges all unreferenced objects in all open drawings, saves each drawing, and then exits AutoCAD. This process should not require any user interaction after the user indicates the desire to quit.

Miscellaneous Utility Methods

There are a number of other, miscellaneous "helper" methods for the **Utility** object. Most of these methods are conversion functions for data types and unit formats. The following sections explain these helper methods in detail.

AngleToReal Method

The **AngleToReal** method converts an angle stored as a **String** to a real number, or **Double** data type. Its signature is:

ReturnVal = ThisDrawing.Utility.AngleToReal(*Angle*, *Units*)

where *Angle* is a **String** that is the angle to convert. *Units* is the **acAngleUnits** enum. See **Figure 4-17.** *ReturnVal* is a **Double** that is the converted angle.

For example, the following code converts an angle stored as a **String** data type to a **Double** data type in the units specified, radians in this case:

```
Sub Ch04_AngleToReal()

    Dim strAngle As String
    Dim dblRadians As Double

    ' Convert an angle given in degrees to radians.
    strAngle = "45"
    dblRadians = ThisDrawing.Utility.AngleToReal(strAngle, acDegrees)
    MsgBox "45 degrees = " & dblRadians & " radians."

    ' Convert the angle given in degrees/minutes/seconds to radians.
    strAngle = "45d0'0"""
    dblRadians = ThisDrawing.Utility.AngleToReal(strAngle, acDegreeMinuteSeconds)
    MsgBox "45 degrees, 0 minutes, 0 seconds = " & dblRadians & " radians."

    ' Convert the angle given in gradians unit to radians.
    strAngle = "50"
    dblRadians = ThisDrawing.Utility.AngleToReal(strAngle, acGrads)
    MsgBox "50 grads = " & dblRadians & " radians."

    ' Convert the angle given in radians unit to radians.
    strAngle = "0.7853979"
    dblRadians = ThisDrawing.Utility.AngleToReal(strAngle, acRadians)
    MsgBox "0.7853979 radians = " & dblRadians & " radians."

End Sub
```

Figure 4-17.
The **acAngleUnits** enum settings.

Constant	Units Converted To
acDegrees	Degrees
acDegreeMinuteSeconds	Degrees/minutes/seconds
acGrads	Gradians
acRadians	Radians

AngleToString Method

The **AngleToString** method converts a radian angle stored as a real number, or **Double** data type, to a **String**. Its signature is:

ReturnVal = ThisDrawing.Utility.AngleToString(*Angle, Units, Precision*)

where *Angle* is a **Double** data type that is the angle to convert, in radians. *Units* is the **acAngleUnits** enum. See **Figure 4-17.** *Precision* is an **Integer** that is the angle precision, in decimal places (0–8). *ReturnVal* is a **String** that is the converted angle.

For example, the following code converts a 45° angle stored in radians as a **Double** data type to a **String** data type in the units specified:

```
Sub Ch04_AngleToString()

    Dim dblRadians As Double
    Dim intPrecision As Long
    Dim strAngle As String

    ' Default radians to 0.7853979 or 45 degrees.
    dblRadians = 0.7853979

    ' Set the decimal places to 4.
    intPrecision = 4

    ' Convert radians to degrees.
    strAngle = ThisDrawing.Utility.AngleToString(dblRadians, acDegrees, intPrecision)
    MsgBox "0.7853979 radians = " & strAngle

    ' Convert radians to degrees/minutes/seconds.
    strAngle = ThisDrawing.Utility.AngleToString(dblRadians, acDegreeMinuteSeconds, _
        intPrecision)
    MsgBox "0.7853979 radians = " & strAngle

    ' Convert radians to gradians.
    strAngle = ThisDrawing.Utility.AngleToString(dblRadians, acGrads, intPrecision)
    MsgBox "0.7853979 radians = " & strAngle

    ' Convert radians to radians.
    strAngle = ThisDrawing.Utility.AngleToString(dblRadians, acRadians, intPrecision)
    MsgBox "0.7853979 radians = " & strAngle

End Sub
```

DistanceToReal Method

The **DistanceToReal** method converts a distance stored as a **String** to a real number, or **Double** data type. The signature of the **DistanceToReal** method is:

ReturnVal = ThisDrawing.Utility.DistanceToReal(*Dist, Units*)

where *Dist* is a **String** data type that is the distance to convert. *Units* is the **acUnits** enum. See **Figure 4-18.** *ReturnVal* is a **Double** data type that is the converted distance.

Figure 4-18.
The **acUnits** enum
settings.

Constant	Units Converted To
acDefaultUnits	Default units
acScientific	Scientific units
acDecimal	Decimal units
acEngineering	Engineering units
acArchitectural	Architectural units
acFractional	Fractional units

For example, the following code converts a distance value from a **String** data type to a **Double** data type in the units specified:

```
Sub Ch04_DistanceAsReal()

    Dim strDistOld As String
    Dim dblDistNew As Double

    ' Convert scientific units to decimal.
    strDistOld = "12.55E+01"
    dblDistNew = ThisDrawing.Utility.DistanceToReal(strDistOld, acScientific)
    MsgBox "12.55E+01 = " & dblDistNew

    ' Convert decimal units to decimal.
    strDistOld = "125.5"
    dblDistNew = ThisDrawing.Utility.DistanceToReal(strDistOld, acDecimal)
    MsgBox "125.5 = " & dblDistNew

    ' Convert engineering units to decimal.
    strDistOld = "10'-5.5"""
    dblDistNew = ThisDrawing.Utility.DistanceToReal(strDistOld, acEngineering)
    MsgBox "10'-5.5"" = " & dblDistNew

    ' Convert architectural units to decimal.
    strDistOld = "10'-5 1/2"""
    dblDistNew = ThisDrawing.Utility.DistanceToReal(strDistOld, acArchitectural)
    MsgBox "10'-5 1/2"" = " & dblDistNew

    ' Convert fractional units to decimal.
    strDistOld = "125 1/2"""
    dblDistNew = ThisDrawing.Utility.DistanceToReal(strDistOld, acArchitectural)
    MsgBox "125 1/2"" = " & dblDistNew

End Sub
```

PolarPoint Method

The **PolarPoint** method gets a coordinate point value at a specified angle and distance from a given point. The signature of the **PolarPoint** method is:

ReturnVal = ThisDrawing.Utility.PolarPoint(*Point, Angle, Distance*)

where *Point* is a **Variant** that is the coordinate point from which the second point is located. *Angle* is a **Double** that is the angle, in radians, that the second point is from the first. *Distance* is a **Double** that is the distance, in current units, that the second point is from the first. *ReturnVal* is a **Variant** three-element array of double data types that is the second coordinate point in the world coordinate system (WCS).

For example, the following code gets the point that is 2″ from the drawing origin (0,0,0) at an angle of 45°:

```
Sub Ch04_PolarPoint()

    Dim varPoint As Variant
    Dim dblBasePt(0 To 2) As Double
    Dim dblAngle As Double
    Dim dblDistance As Double

    ' Set the base point at 0,0,0.
    dblBasePt(0) = 0#: dblBasePt(1) = 0#: dblBasePt(2) = 0#

    ' Set the angle to 45 degrees.
    dblAngle = 0.7853979

    ' Set the distance.
    dblDistance = 2#

    ' Get the polar point.
    varPoint = ThisDrawing.Utility.PolarPoint(dblBasePt, dblAngle, dblDistance)

    ' Show the user.
    MsgBox "Polar point @ 45 degrees - 2"" long from 0,0,0 = " & vbCrLf & _
        varPoint(0) & "," & varPoint(1) & ", 0.0"

End Sub
```

RealToString Method

The **RealToString** method converts a real number, or **Double** data type, to a **String**. The signature of the **RealToString** method is:

ReturnVal = ThisDrawing.Utility.RealToString(*Number*, *Units*, *Precision*)

where *Number* is a **Double** that is the number to convert. *Units* is the **acUnits** enum. See **Figure 4-19.** *Precision* is an **Integer** that is the precision of the converted number, in decimal places (0–8). *ReturnVal* is a **String** that is the number.

Figure 4-19.
The **acUnits** enum settings.

Constant	Converted Units
acDefaultUnits	Default units
acScientific	Scientific units
acDecimal	Decimal units
acEngineering	Engineering units
acArchitectural	Architectural units
acFractional	Fractional units

For example, the following code converts a **Double** data type to a **String** in the units specified:

```
Sub Ch04_RealToString()

    Dim dblDistOld As Double
    Dim strDistNew As String
    Dim intPrecision As Integer

    ' Set the default decimal distance to 12.5.
    dblDistOld = 12.5

    ' Set the number decimal places to four.
    intPrecision = 6

    ' Convert a real value to scientific format.
    strDistNew = ThisDrawing.Utility.RealToString(dblDistOld, acScientific, intPrecision)
    MsgBox "12.5 in scientific format = " & strDistNew

    ' Convert a real value to decimal format.
    strDistNew = ThisDrawing.Utility.RealToString(dblDistOld, acDecimal, intPrecision)
    MsgBox "12.5 in decimal format = " & strDistNew

    ' Convert a real value to engineering format.
    strDistNew = ThisDrawing.Utility.RealToString(dblDistOld, acEngineering, intPrecision)
    MsgBox "12.5 in engineering format = " & strDistNew

    ' Convert a real value to architectural format.
    strDistNew = ThisDrawing.Utility.RealToString(dblDistOld, acArchitectural, intPrecision)
    MsgBox "12.5 in architectural format = " & strDistNew

    ' Convert a real value to fractional format.
    strDistNew = ThisDrawing.Utility.RealToString(dblDistOld, acFractional, intPrecision)
    MsgBox "12.5 in fractional format = " & strDistNew

End Sub
```

Executing AutoCAD Commands

Sometimes, for a variety of reasons, you might want to access and run commands directly at the AutoCAD command line from within a VBA macro. In AutoLISP, this is achieved using the **(command)** function. In VBA, the same functionality is provided via the **SendCommand** method.

The **SendCommand** method executes AutoCAD commands by sending the string specified to the AutoCAD command line where it is executed. Its signature is:

ThisDrawing.SendCommand(*Command*)

where *Command* is a **String** that is the AutoCAD command to execute.

The command string consists of the command and its arguments in the exact order expected by the command. A blank space or a carriage return (**vbCr**) is the equivalent to issuing [Enter] at the command line.

For example, the following code uses AutoCAD commands to draw a circle with a 2″ radius centered at (0,0,0) and then zoom extents:

```
Sub Ch04_SendCommand()

    ' Create a circle with a 2" radius at 0,0,0.
    ThisDrawing.SendCommand "_Circle" & vbCr & "0,0,0" & vbCr & "2" & vbCr

    ' Zoom extents.
    ThisDrawing.SendCommand "_Zoom" & vbCr & "e" & vbCr

End Sub
```

AutoLISP vs. VBA

Invoking the VBA **SendCommand** method without an argument is invalid. In AutoLISP, the **(command)** function can be invoked without an argument.

Let's Review...

Miscellaneous Methods and Executing AutoCAD Commands

- The **AngleToReal** method converts an angle stored as a **String** data type to a **Double** data type.
- The **AngleToString** method converts a radian angle stored as a **Double** data type to a **String** data type.
- The **DistanceToReal** method converts a distance stored as a **String** data type to a **Double** data type.
- The **PolarPoint** method gets a coordinate point value at a specified angle and distance from a given point.
- The **RealToString** method converts a **Double** data type to a **String** data type.
- The **SendCommand** method can be used to execute an AutoCAD command.

Chapter Test

Write your answers on a separate sheet of paper.

1. What is the top level AutoCAD ActiveX object?
2. What is the easiest way to access the top level AutoCAD object in your code?
3. Which AutoCAD object controls and maintains most of the settings found in the AutoCAD **Options** dialog box?
4. Which AutoCAD object is used to control and maintain all of the settings that are stored in a drawing?
5. List the AutoCAD **Preferences** object and property that is used to specify the automatic save folder in AutoCAD.
6. Which AutoCAD **Preferences** object and property controls the AutoCAD version for saved drawings?

7. List all of the possible file types and AutoCAD versions in which a drawing can be saved in AutoCAD 2005 using VBA.
8. Which AutoCAD **Preferences** object and property controls the current AutoCAD profile?
9. What is the VBA function that allows you to check if a file exists?
10. How can you determine if a drawing has been saved or not using VBA?
11. Why must the value returned from the **ThisDrawing.GetVariable** method be a VBA **Variant** data type?
12. Which AutoCAD object contains VBA versions of most of the AutoLISP "get" functions?
13. List all of the VBA "get" methods along with a brief description.
14. Provide a brief description of the VBA **InitializeUserInput** method and how it is used.
15. What is the name of the VBA method that allows you to execute an AutoCAD command on the command line?

Programming Problems

Create the macros described below. All macros should be created in the **ThisDrawing** module of your MyMacros.dvb project. Provide all necessary error checking and error control. Run and test each macro.

1. Create a macro named p04_SetProfile that imports the profile created for #5 in Exercise 4-1 as VBA for AutoCAD and sets it current. After importing the profile, set the following options:
   - Turn off the display **Page Setup** dialog when creating a new layout.
   - Turn off the automatic creation of viewport when creating a new layout.
   - Turn off demand loading of xrefs.
   - Turn on the display of the polar tracking vector.
   - Turn on implied windowing.

   Export the updated profile to VBA.arg.
2. Create a macro named p04_DWGSetup that creates a new drawing with the following settings:
   - Architectural units.
   - Degrees/mins/seconds angle measurement.
   - Limits at (0,0,0) for the bottom left and (136'-0", 88'-0") for the top right.
   - Grid and snap spacing at 12".

   Save drawing as C:\VBA for AutoCAD\Drawings\p04-02.dwg. *Hint:* Most drawing settings can be controlled via AutoCAD's system variables.
3. Create a macro named p04_ChangeLayer that prompts the user to select any type of entity in a drawing and then changes that entity's layer property to a new user-defined layer name.
4. Create a macro named p04_MoveObject that prompts the user to select any type of entity and moves that entity to a new user-defined point.
5. Create a macro named p04_ChangeRadius that prompts the user to select a circle and changes its radius to a user-defined value.
6. Create a macro named p04_MirrorText that prompts the user to select a string of single-line text and mirrors it about a user-defined axis.

The code examples in this chapter are supplied on the Student CD. A—First, open the **Open VBA Project** dialog box by selecting **Load Project...** from the **Macro** cascading menu in AutoCAD's **Tools** pull-down menu. B—Next, select the project Example Code.dvb and pick the **Open** button. C—Finally, display the **Macros** dialog box by picking **Macros...** from the **Macro** cascading menu in AutoCAD's **Tools** pull-down menu. Then, select the macro you wish to run and pick the **Run** button.

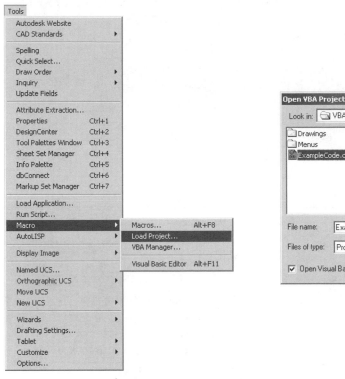

A

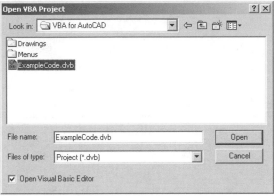

B

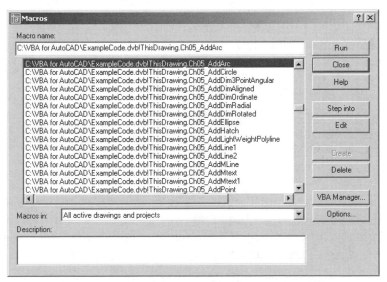

C

CHAPTER 5

Creating AutoCAD Entities

Learning Objectives

After completing this chapter, you will be able to create VBA macros that:

- Draw linear entities, such as lines, polylines, splines, multilines, and construction lines.
- Draw circular entities, such as circles, arcs, and ellipses.
- Draw text objects (single-line and multiline text).
- Draw dimensions.
- Draw points, solids, and hatches.

The AutoCAD object model includes methods for creating all of the graphic entities that exist in an AutoCAD drawing. In fact, using VBA to create AutoCAD entities is almost as simple as using the AutoCAD drawing editor to create entities. You simply add the desired entity to a drawing using one of the various "add" methods. Once you add the entity to a drawing, it becomes an object in VBA with properties and methods, as explained in Chapter 2.

Professional Tip
To avoid confusion with VBA *objects,* the graphic elements in a drawing are called *entities* in this book. Entities include such elements as lines, circles, polylines, text, and so on.

Model Space vs. Paper Space

Entities in an AutoCAD drawing can exist in either model space or paper space. *Model space* is the 3D drawing environment typically used for drawing the "model," or 3D representation of your design. Model space contains most of the text and line work that makes up a drawing. *Paper space* is the 2D environment used for creating multiscaled layouts of the model space information for plotting purposes. A paper space layout usually consists of a title block and one or more views, called viewports, of the model space information.

The concept of having two distinct drawing environments, or spaces, also exists in the AutoCAD object model. When an entity is added to a drawing, it can be added to either the **ModelSpace** collection or the **PaperSpace** collection. Objects added to the **ModelSpace** collection reside in model space in the drawing. Objects added to the **PaperSpace** collection reside in paper space in the drawing.

There is one other top-level collection—the **Block** collection, which is where named blocks are created. In fact, both model space and paper space are represented as blocks in the AutoCAD object model. If you think about it, a *block* is simply a named collection of AutoCAD objects. Model space and paper space are the same things, only they have reserved names.

Let's look again at the AutoCAD object model and how the AutoCAD drawing objects are organized. Refer to **Figure 5-1.** Notice how all of the drawing objects in the AutoCAD object model branch off of either the **ModelSpace** or **PaperSpace** collection. Because of this relationship, you must explicitly specify which collection an object should be part of when it is added to the drawing. The syntax for referencing either collection is:

```
' Get a reference to the model space collection.
ThisDrawing.ModelSpace
```

```
' Get a reference to the paper space collection.
ThisDrawing.PaperSpace
```

Each of these object collections includes unique "add" methods for every AutoCAD drawing entity. The following sections explain how to use these "add" methods to create basic AutoCAD entities.

Professional Tip
Creating and managing viewports for both model space and paper space are discussed in detail in Chapter 10. Named blocks and the **Block** collection are discussed in Chapter 11. Paper space layout management is discussed in Chapter 12.

Creating Linear Objects

AutoCAD has a number of different types of linear objects. The **Line** object is a simple object defined by a start point and an endpoint. There are also complex linear objects, like the **Polyline** object and the **Spline** object, that consist of multiple points, known as vertices. The following sections explain how to add all of the different types of linear objects to a drawing using VBA and the AutoCAD object model.

Line Object

The **AddLine** method creates a line. Its signature is:

Object = Space.AddLine(*StartPoint, EndPoint*)

where *Object* is the **Line** object. *Space* is the **ModelSpace** or **PaperSpace** collection. *StartPoint* is a **Variant** that is a three-element array of **Double** data types defining the start point of the line. *EndPoint* is a **Variant** that is a three-element array of **Double** data types defining the endpoint of the line.

The following code creates a line in model space from the point (0,0,0) to (2,2,0). Refer to **Figure 5-2.**

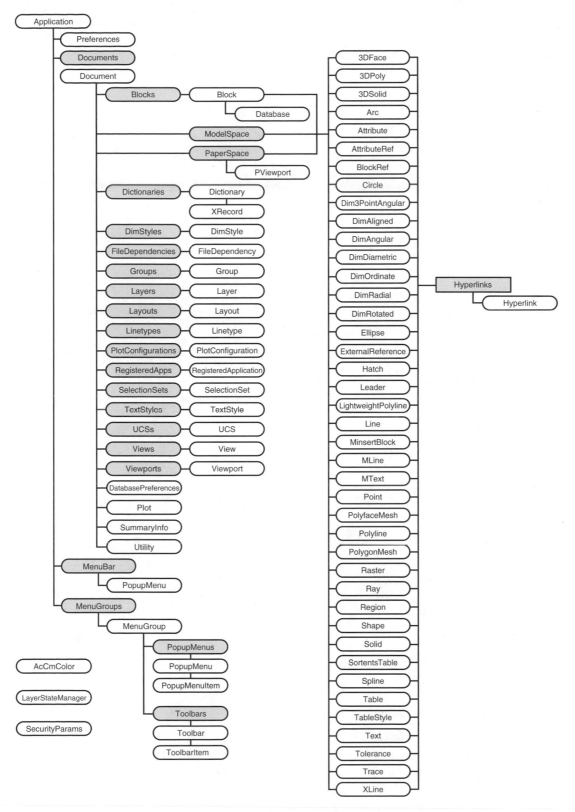

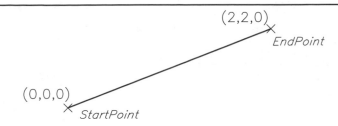

Figure 5-2.
Creating a line
object.

(2,2,0)
EndPoint

(0,0,0)
StartPoint

```
' Add a line in model space.
Sub Ch05_AddLine1()

    Dim objLine As AcadLine
    Dim dblStartPt(0 To 2) As Double
    Dim dblEndPt(0 To 2) As Double

    ' Set the start point.
    dblStartPt (0) = 0.0
    dblStartPt (1) = 0.0
    dblStartPt (2) = 0.0

    ' Set the endpoint.
    dblEndPt (0) = 2.0
    dblEndPt (1) = 2.0
    dblEndPt (2) = 0.0

    ' Create the line in model space.
    Set objLine = ThisDrawing.ModelSpace.AddLine(dblStartPt, dblEndPt)

    ' Update the object so it is sure to appear.
    objLine.Update

End Sub
```

Notice that the last line of code calls the **Line** object's **Update** method. Calling this method ensures that the line actually appears in the drawing. Sometimes, objects do not appear until either the object is updated or the drawing is regenerated. Remember, the code to regenerate all of the drawing viewports is:

```
' Regenerate all viewports in the drawing.
ThisDrawing.Regen acAllViewports
```

When you create a drawing object, more often than not you are going to want to interact with the user. In the Ch05_AddLine1 macro above, the coordinate points are specified in the macro. Typically, however, you will want to prompt the user for coordinate point values:

```
Sub Ch05_AddLine2()

    Dim objLine As AcadLine
    Dim varStartPt As Variant
    Dim varEndPt As Variant

    ' Get points from the user.
    varStartPt = ThisDrawing.Utility.GetPoint(, vbCrLf & "Start point: ")
    varEndPt = ThisDrawing.Utility.GetPoint(varStartPt, vbCrLf & "End point: ")

    ' Create the line in model space.
    Set objLine = ThisDrawing.ModelSpace.AddLine(varStartPt, varEndPt)

    ' Update the object so it is sure to appear.
    objLine.Update

End Sub
```

LightweightPolyline Object

The **AddLightweightPolyline** method creates an optimized, lightweight polyline. This is the default type of polyline drawn by AutoCAD. The signature of the **AddLightweightPolyline** method is:

Object = Space.AddLightweightPolyline(*VerticesList*)

where *Object* is the **LightweightPolyline** object. *Space* is the **ModelSpace** or **PaperSpace** collection. *VerticesList* is a **Variant** array of **Double** data types that is the vertices of the polyline represented by their X and Y coordinates. The Z coordinate is unnecessary because lightweight polylines exist as 2D objects only.

The following code prompts the user for polyline coordinate points. To end coordinate entry, the user presses the [Enter] key. Then, the macro creates a lightweight polyline in model space based on the points entered. Refer to **Figure 5-3.**

```
Sub Ch05_AddLightweightPolyline()

    Dim objLWPline As AcadLWPolyline
    Dim dblPoints() As Double
    Dim intCounter As Integer
    Dim varPoint As Variant

    ' Initialize the counter.
    intCounter = 0

    ' Turn off errors.
    On Error Resume Next

    ' Get the first point.
    varPoint = ThisDrawing.Utility.GetPoint(, vbCrLf & "Start point: ")

    ' Continue to select points until the user presses [Enter].
    While Err.Number = 0
        ' Redimension the array.
        ReDim Preserve dblPoints(intCounter + 1)
        ' Get X.
        dblPoints(intCounter) = varPoint(0)
        ' Get Y.
        dblPoints(intCounter + 1) = varPoint(1)

        ' Get the next point.
        varPoint = ThisDrawing.Utility.GetPoint(varPoint, vbCrLf & "Next point: ")

        ' Advance the counter by two for both points.
        intCounter = intCounter + 2
    Wend

    ' Clear the error.
    Err.Clear

    ' Draw the lightweight polyline.
    Set objLWPline = ThisDrawing.ModelSpace.AddLightweightPolyline(dblPoints)

    ' Update the object so it is sure to appear.
    objLWPline.Update

End Sub
```

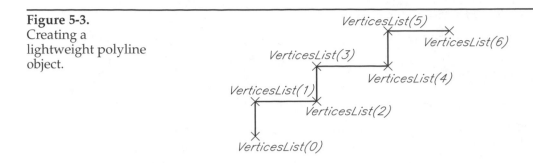

Figure 5-3.
Creating a lightweight polyline object.

Closely examine the error control in the code on the previous page. Notice that built-in VBA error control is turned off via the On Error Resume Next statement at the beginning of the macro. This gives you the ability to prompt the user for an infinite number of points via a **While** loop until the [Enter] key is pressed. Pressing [Enter] in response to the **GetPoint** method generates an error and the **Err.Number** property is no longer set to 0. Make sure to clear the error using the **Err.Clear** method after you exit the loop so **Err.Number** is reset to 0!

Polyline Object

The **AddPolyline** method creates an old-format polyline that is not optimized. Vertex information for old-format polylines is stored as individual subentities, thus consuming more memory. The Z coordinate information is also included in the list of vertices, unlike the list of vertices for a lightweight polyline. The signature for the **AddPolyline** method is:

   Object = Space.AddPolyline(*VerticesList*)

where *Object* is the **Polyline** object. *Space* is the **ModelSpace** or **PaperSpace** collection. *VerticesList* is a **Variant** array of **Double** data types that is the polyline vertices. You *must* include the Z coordinate values.

The following code prompts the user for polyline coordinate points. To end coordinate entry, the user presses the [Enter] key. Then, the macro creates an old-format polyline in model space based on the points entered. Refer to **Figure 5-4.**

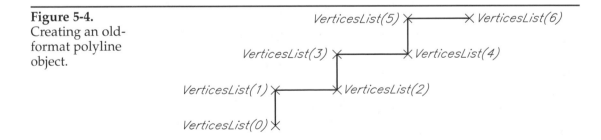

Figure 5-4.
Creating an old-format polyline object.

```
Sub Ch05_AddPolyline()

    Dim objPline As AcadPolyline
    Dim dblPoints() As Double
    Dim intCounter As Integer
    Dim varPoint As Variant

    ' Initialize the counter.
    intCounter = 0

    ' Turn off errors.
    On Error Resume Next

    ' Get the first point.
    varPoint = ThisDrawing.Utility.GetPoint(, vbCrLf & "Start point: ")

    ' Continue to select points until the user presses [Enter].
    While Err.Number = 0
        ' Redimension the array.
        ReDim Preserve dblPoints(intCounter + 2)
        ' Get X.
        dblPoints(intCounter) = varPoint(0)
        ' Get Y.
        dblPoints(intCounter + 1) = varPoint(1)
        ' Get Z.
        dblPoints(intCounter + 2) = varPoint(2)

        ' Get the next point.
        varPoint = ThisDrawing.Utility.GetPoint(varPoint, vbCrLf & "Next point: ")

        ' Advance the counter.
        intCounter = intCounter + 3
    Wend

    ' Clear the error.
    Err.Clear

    ' Draw the old-format polyline.
    Set objPline = ThisDrawing.ModelSpace.AddPolyline(dblPoints)

    ' Update the object so it is sure to appear.
    objPline.Update

End Sub
```

Notice that the *dblPoints* variable in the above macro is redimensioned with an extra element (+ 2) to account for the Z coordinate.

Spline Object

The **AddSpline** method creates a spline. Its signature is:

Object = Space.AddSpline(*PointsArray, StartTangent, EndTangent*)

where *Object* is the **Spline** object. *Space* is the **ModelSpace** or **PaperSpace** collection. *PointsArray* is a **Variant** array of **Double** data types that is the spline curve points represented by their X, Y and Z coordinates. *StartTangent* is a **Variant** three-element array of **Double** data types that is a vector specifying the tangency of the spline curve at the first point. *EndTangent* is a **Variant** three-element array of **Double** data types that is a vector specifying the tangency of the spline curve at the endpoint.

The following code prompts the user for spline fit points until the [Enter] key is pressed. The user is then prompted for the spline start and end tangent points. Finally, a spline is created in model space based on the information entered. Refer to **Figure 5-5.**

Figure 5-5.
Creating a spline object.

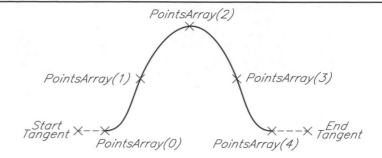

```
Sub Ch05_AddSpline()

    Dim objSpline As AcadSpline
    Dim dblFitPts() As Double
    Dim intCounter As Integer
    Dim varTanPt1 As Variant
    Dim varTanPt2 As Variant
    Dim varFitPt As Variant

    ' Initialize the counter.
    intCounter = 0

    ' Turn off errors.
    On Error Resume Next

    ' Get the first fit point.
    varFitPt = ThisDrawing.Utility.GetPoint(, vbCrLf & "First point: ")

    ' Continue to select points until the user presses [Enter].
    While Err.Number = 0
        ' Redimension the array.
        ReDim Preserve dblFitPts(intCounter + 2)
        ' Get X.
        dblFitPts(intCounter) = varFitPt(0)
        ' Get Y.
        dblFitPts(intCounter + 1) = varFitPt(1)
        ' Get Z.
        dblFitPts(intCounter + 2) = varFitPt(2)

        ' Get the next point.
        varFitPt = ThisDrawing.Utility.GetPoint(varFitPt, vbCrLf & "Next point: ")

        ' Advance counter.
        intCounter = intCounter + 3
    Wend

    ' Clear the error.
    Err.Clear

    ' Get the start tangent point.
    varTanPt1 = ThisDrawing.Utility.GetPoint(, vbCrLf & "Start tangent point: ")

    ' Get the end tangent point.
    varTanPt2 = ThisDrawing.Utility.GetPoint(, vbCrLf & "End tangent point: ")

    ' Create the spline.
    Set objSpline = ThisDrawing.ModelSpace.AddSpline(dblFitPts, varTanPt1, _
        varTanPt2)

    ' Update the object so it is sure to appear.
    objSpline.Update

End Sub
```

This macro uses the same error control technique as the polyline macros described earlier. The user can enter as many points as needed to define the spline. When the user presses the [Enter] key, an error is generated and the **While...Wend** loop is exited.

Mline Object

The **AddMLine** method creates a multiline. Its signature is:

Object = Space.AddMLine(*VertexList*)

where *Object* is the **MLine** object. *Space* is the **ModelSpace** or **PaperSpace** collection. *VertexList* is a **Variant** array of **Double** data types that is the vertices for the multiline represented by their X, Y, and Z coordinates.

The following code prompts the user for coordinate points of the multiline until the [Enter] key is pressed. Then, a multiline is created in model space based on the points entered. Refer to **Figure 5-6.**

```
Sub Ch05_AddMLine()

    Dim objMline As AcadMline
    Dim dblPoints() As Double
    Dim intCounter As Integer
    Dim varPoint As Variant

    ' Initialize the counter.
    intCounter = 0

    ' Turn off errors.
    On Error Resume Next

    ' Get the first point.
    varPoint = ThisDrawing.Utility.GetPoint(, vbCrLf & "Start point: ")

    ' Continue to select points until the user presses [Enter].
    While Err.Number = 0
        ' Redimension the array.
        ReDim Preserve dblPoints(intCounter + 2)
        ' Get X.
        dblPoints(intCounter) = varPoint(0)
        ' Get Y.
        dblPoints(intCounter + 1) = varPoint(1)
        ' Get Z.
        dblPoints(intCounter + 2) = varPoint(2)

        ' Get the next point.
        varPoint = ThisDrawing.Utility.GetPoint(varPoint, vbCrLf & "Next point: ")

        ' Advance the counter.
        intCounter = intCounter + 3
    Wend

    ' Clear the error.
    Err.Clear

    ' Create the mline.
    Set objMline = ThisDrawing.ModelSpace.AddMLine(dblPoints)

    ' Update the object so it is sure to appear.
    objMline.Update

End Sub
```

Figure 5-6.
Creating a multiline
object.

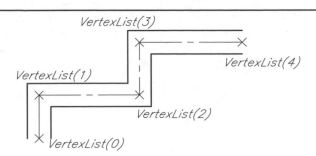

The multiline drawn with the code on the previous page is created using the current multiline style. To specify a style, all you need to do is set the **CMLSTYLE** system variable to the desired style before using the **AddMLine** method:

```
' Set the current multiline style to ROAD.
ThisDrawing.SetVariable "CMLSTYLE", "ROAD"
```

Of course, the ROAD multiline style has to exist and be loaded into the drawing beforehand. Unfortunately, there is currently no way to load a multiline via the AutoCAD object model. The ROAD multiline style must be loaded via the **Linetype Manager** in AutoCAD.

Xline Object

The **AddXLine** method creates a construction line (xline). Xlines extend infinitely in both directions, yet they do not affect AutoCAD's **Zoom Extents** command. They are typically used for orthographic projection when drafting. Using VBA, xlines are defined using two points supplied as separate arguments to the method. The signature for the **AddXLine** method is:

Object = Space.AddXLine(*LocatePt, ThruPt*)

where *Object* is the **XLine** object. *Space* is the **ModelSpace** or **PaperSpace** collection. *LocatePt* is a **Variant** three-element array of **Double** data types that is the xline location point. *ThruPt* is a **Variant** three-element array of **Double** data types that is the xline "through" point.

The following code creates a xline in model space using two points supplied by the user. Refer to **Figure 5-7.**

Figure 5-7.
Creating a
construction line
(xline) object.

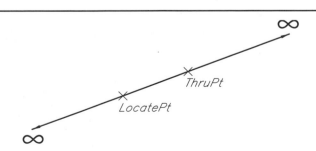

```
Sub Ch05_AddXLine()

    Dim objXline As AcadXline
    Dim varLocPt As Variant
    Dim varThruPt As Variant

    ' Get the points from the user.
    varLocPt = ThisDrawing.Utility.GetPoint(, vbCrLf & "Location point: ")
    varThruPt = ThisDrawing.Utility.GetPoint(varLocPt, vbCrLf & "Through point: ")

    ' Create the construction line in model space.
    Set objXline = ThisDrawing.ModelSpace.AddXLine(varLocPt, varThruPt)

    ' Update the object so it is sure to appear.
    objXline.Update

End Sub
```

Ray Object

The **AddRay** method creates a ray. Rays are similar to xlines, except that they extend infinitely in one direction only. Like xlines, rays do not affect AutoCAD's **Zoom Extents** command and are typically used for orthographic projection. Rays are defined using two points supplied as separate arguments to the method. The signature for the **AddRay** method is:

Object = Space.AddRay(*LocatePt, ThruPt*)

where *Object* is the **Ray** object. *Space* the **ModelSpace** or **PaperSpace** collection. *LocatePt* is a **Variant** three-element array of **Double** data types that is the ray location point. *ThruPt* is a **Variant** three-element array of **Double** data types that is the ray "through" point.

The following code creates a ray in model space using two points supplied by the user. Refer to **Figure 5-8**.

```
Sub Ch05_AddRay()

    Dim objRay As AcadRay
    Dim varStartPt As Variant
    Dim varThruPt As Variant

    ' Get points from the user.
    varStartPt = ThisDrawing.Utility.GetPoint(, vbCrLf & "Start point: ")
    varThruPt = ThisDrawing.Utility.GetPoint(varStartPt, vbCrLf & "Through point: ")

    ' Create the construction line in model space.
    Set objRay = ThisDrawing.ModelSpace.AddRay(varStartPt, varThruPt)

    ' Update the object so it is sure to appear.
    objRay.Update

End Sub
```

Figure 5-8.
Creating a ray
object.

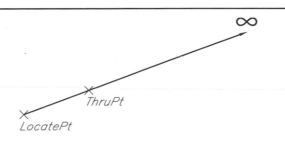

Exercise 5-1

Create the macros described below. All macros should be created in the **ThisDrawing** module of your MyMacros.dvb project. Provide all necessary error checking and control. Run and test each macro.

1. Create a macro named ex05_Rectangle that creates a rectangle using individual line segments based on a user-supplied location, width, and height.
2. Create a macro named ex05_RectPoly that creates a rectangle using a lightweight polyline based on a user-supplied location, width, and height.
3. Create a macro named ex05_XlineHor that creates multiple horizontal construction lines using location points input by the user. The macro should end when the user presses the [Enter] key in place of selecting a point.
4. Create a macro named ex05_XlineVer that creates multiple vertical construction lines using location points input by the user. The macro should end when the user presses the [Enter] key in place of selecting a point.

Creating Circular Objects

There are three different types of circular objects in AutoCAD: **Circle**, **Arc**, and **Ellipse**. The following sections explain how to add all three of the different types of circular objects to a drawing using VBA and the AutoCAD object model.

Circle Object

The **AddCircle** method creates a circle. Its signature is:

Object = *Space*.AddCircle(*CenterPt*, *Radius*)

where *Object* is the **Circle** object. *Space* is the **ModelSpace** or **PaperSpace** collection. *CenterPt* is a **Variant** three-element array of **Double** data types that is the center point of the circle. *Radius* is a **Double** data type that is the radius of the circle.

The following code creates a circle in model space using a center point and radius supplied by the user. The radius must be entered using the keyboard. Refer to **Figure 5-9.**

Figure 5-9.
Creating a circle object.

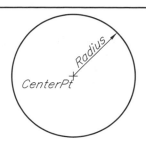

```
Sub Ch05_AddCircle()

    Dim objCircle As AcadCircle
    Dim varCtrPt As Variant
    Dim dblRadius As Double

    ' Get the center point from the user.
    varCtrPt = ThisDrawing.Utility.GetPoint (,vbCrLf & "Center point: ")

    ' Get the radius from the user.
    dblRadius = ThisDrawing.Utility.GetReal(vbCrLf & "Radius: ")

    ' Create the circle.
    Set objCircle = ThisDrawing.ModelSpace.AddCircle(varCtrPt, dblRadius)

    ' Update the object so it is sure to appear.
    objCircle.Update

End Sub
```

Arc Object

The **AddArc** method creates an arc. Its signature is:

Object = *Space*.AddArc(*CenterPt*, *Radius*, *StartAngle*, *EndAngle*)

where *Object* is the **Arc** object. *Space* is the **ModelSpace** or **PaperSpace** collection. *CenterPt* is a **Variant** three-element array of **Double** data types that is the center point of the arc. *Radius* is a **Double** data type that is the radius of the arc. *StartAngle* is a **Double** data type that is the start angle in radians. *EndAngle* is a **Double** data type that is the end angle in radians.

The following code creates an arc in model space using a center point, start angle, end angle, and radius supplied by the user. The radius must be entered using the keyboard, but the other information can be entered using either the keyboard or the mouse. Refer to **Figure 5-10.**

Figure 5-10.
Creating an arc object.

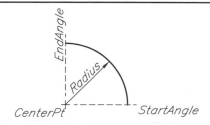

```
Sub Ch05_AddArc()

    Dim objArc As AcadArc
    Dim varCtrPt As Variant
    Dim dblRadius As Double
    Dim dblStartAngle As Double
    Dim dblEndAngle As Double

    ' Get the center point from the user.
    varCtrPt = ThisDrawing.Utility.GetPoint (,vbCrLf & "Center point: ")

    ' Get the start angle from the user.
    dblStartAngle = ThisDrawing.Utility.GetAngle(varCtrPt, vbCrLf & "Start angle: ")

    ' Get the end angle from the user.
    dblEndAngle = ThisDrawing.Utility.GetAngle(varCtrPt, vbCrLf & "End angle: ")

    ' Get the radius from the user.
    dblRadius = ThisDrawing.Utility.GetReal(vbCrLf & "Radius: ")

    ' Create the arc.
    Set objArc = ThisDrawing.ModelSpace.AddArc(varCtrPt, dblRadius, _
        dblStartAngle, dblEndAngle)

    ' Update the object so it is sure to appear.
    objArc.Update

End Sub
```

Ellipse Object

The **AddEllipse** method creates an ellipse. Its signature is:

Object = *Space*.AddEllipse(*Center*, *MajorAxis*, *RadiusRatio*)

where *Object* is the **Ellipse** object. *Space* is the **ModelSpace** or **PaperSpace** collection. *Center* is a **Variant** three-element array of **Double** data types that is the center point of the ellipse. *MajorAxis* is a **Variant Double** data type. It is input-only and the length of the major axis of ellipse. *RadiusRatio* is a **Double** data type that is the major axis-to-minor axis ratio. A ratio of 1.0 creates a circle.

The following code creates an ellipse in model space using a center point, major axis point, and major axis-to-minor axis ratio supplied by the user. Refer to **Figure 5-11.**

Figure 5-11.
Creating an ellipse object.

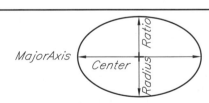

```
Sub Ch05_AddEllipse()

    Dim objEllipse As AcadEllipse
    Dim varCtrPt As Variant
    Dim varAxisPt As Variant
    Dim dblRatio As Double

    ' Get the center point from the user.
    varCtrPt = ThisDrawing.Utility.GetPoint(, vbCrLf & "Center point: ")

    ' Get the axis point from the user.
    varAxisPt = ThisDrawing.Utility.GetPoint(varCtrPt, vbCrLf & "Major axis point: ")

    ' Get the major-to-minor axis ratio.
    dblRatio = ThisDrawing.Utility.GetReal(vbCrLf & "Ratio: ")

    Set objEllipse = ThisDrawing.ModelSpace.AddEllipse(varCtrPt, varAxisPt, _
        dblRatio)

    ' Update the object so it is sure to appear.
    objEllipse.Update

End Sub
```

The options provided to create an ellipse using VBA and the AutoCAD object model are a little different from the options provided using the AutoCAD **ELLIPSE** command. Instead of providing a rotation angle for the ellipse, as you do using the AutoCAD **ELLIPSE** command, you must calculate a ratio between the length of the major and minor axis.

Creating Text Objects

The following sections explain how to add text objects to a drawing using VBA and the AutoCAD object model. There are two types of text in AutoCAD—single line text and multiline text.

Single line text is the "original" type of text in AutoCAD. It is defined by having each line of text treated as a single AutoCAD object.

Multiline text is lines of text in paragraph form that are treated as a single unit, which is defined by a user-defined boundary. Soft returns (line breaks) are entered automatically based on the boundary width, similar to entering text in a text editor. If the boundary definition changes, the line breaks are automatically adjusted accordingly.

Single-Line Text Object

The **AddText** method creates single-line text. Its signature is:

> *Object* = *Space*.AddText(*TextString*, *InsertPoint*, *Height*)

where *Object* is the **Text** object. *Space* is the **ModelSpace** or **PaperSpace** collection. *TextString* is a **String** that is the text string. *InsertPoint* is a **Variant** three-element array of **Double** data types that is the text insertion point. *Height* is a **Double** data type that is the text height.

The following code creates single-line text in model space using a text location point, text height, and text string supplied by the user. Refer to **Figure 5-12.**

Figure 5-12.
Creating a single-
line text object.

SINGLE-LINE TEXT
InsertPoint
Height

```
Sub Ch05_AddText()

    Dim objText As AcadText
    Dim varInsPt As Variant
    Dim dblHeight As Double
    Dim strText As String

    ' Get the text location point from the user.
    varInsPt = ThisDrawing.Utility.GetPoint(, vbCrLf & "Start point: ")

    ' Get the height.
    dblHeight = ThisDrawing.Utility.GetReal(vbCrLf & "Height: ")

    ' Get the text.
    strText = ThisDrawing.Utility.GetString(True, vbCrLf & "Text: ")

    ' Create the text.
    Set objText = ThisDrawing.ModelSpace.AddText(strText, varInsPt, dblHeight)

    ' Update the object so it is sure to appear.
    objText.Update

End Sub
```

Multiline Text Object

The **AddMText** method creates multiline text. Its signature is:

Object = Space.AddMText(*InsertPoint*, *Width*, *Text*)

where *Object* is the **MText** object. *Space* is the **ModelSpace** or **PaperSpace** collection. *InsertPoint* is a **Variant** three-element array of **Double** data types that is the insertion point of the mtext bounding box. *Width* is a **Double** data type that is the width of the mtext bounding box. *Text* is a **String** that is the text string.

The following code creates multiline text in model space using a multiline text boundary box location point, width, and a text string supplied by the user. Refer to **Figure 5-13.**

Figure 5-13.
Creating a multiline
text object.

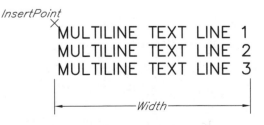
InsertPoint
MULTILINE TEXT LINE 1
MULTILINE TEXT LINE 2
MULTILINE TEXT LINE 3
Width

```
Sub Ch05_AddMtext()

    Dim objMtext As AcadMText
    Dim varInsPt As Variant
    Dim dblWidth As Double
    Dim strText As String

    ' Get the text location point from the user.
    varInsPt = ThisDrawing.Utility.GetPoint(, vbCrLf & "Start point: ")

    ' Get the width.
    dblWidth = ThisDrawing.Utility.GetReal(vbCrLf & "Width: ")

    ' Get the text.
    strText = ThisDrawing.Utility.GetString(True, vbCrLf & "Text: ")

    ' Create the mtext.
    Set objMtext = ThisDrawing.ModelSpace.AddMText(varInsPt, dblWidth, strText)

    ' Update the object so it is sure to appear.
    objMtext.Update

End Sub
```

Professional Tip

The text created in the examples above is created using the current text style. To specify a specific style, all you need to do is set the **TEXTSTYLE** system variable to the desired style before using either of the add text methods described above:

```
' Set the current text style to Architectural.
ThisDrawing.SetVariable "TEXTSTYLE", "Architectural"
```

Similar to the multiline styles discussed earlier, the Architectural text style has to exist in the drawing before it can be set current. Unlike multiline styles, the AutoCAD object model *does* provide a way to create different text styles. Chapter 9 explains how to create new text styles using VBA and the AutoCAD object model. In fact, Chapter 9 shows you how to create text styles *and* set them current via the **TextStyles** object collection without having to mess around setting AutoCAD system variables.

Creating Circular and Text Objects

Let's Review...

- The **AddCircle** method creates a circle.
- The **AddArc** method creates an arc.
- The **AddEllipse** method creates an ellipse.
- The **AddText** method creates single line text.
- The **AddMText** method creates multiline text.

Create the macros described below. All macros should be created in the **ThisDrawing** module of your MyMacros.dvb project. Provide all necessary error checking and control. Run and test each macro.

1. Create a macro named ex05_YinYang that creates a yin yang symbol similar to the one shown below using a user-supplied center point for the symbol and an overall symbol radius.

2. Create a macro named ex05_GridBubble that creates a grid bubble similar to the one shown below that has a 1/2″ diameter circle and 1/4″ high, single line text indicating the grid row or column.

3. Create a macro named ex05_TheBard that creates the following quote from Shakespeare's Hamlet using multiline text with a boundary box that is 6″ wide and an insertion point located by the user.

> To be, or not to be, that is the question:
> Whether 'tis nobler in the mind to suffer
> The slings and arrows of outrageous fortune
> Or to take arms against a sea of troubles,
> And by opposing end them?

Creating Dimension Objects

There are six different types of dimension objects in AutoCAD:

- **Aligned.** A linear dimension between two points.
- **Rotated.** A rotated linear dimension.
- **Angular.** The measure of an angle in angular units, such as radians or degrees.
- **Diametric.** The diameter of a circular object.
- **Radial.** The radius of a circular object.
- **Ordinate.** An arrowless dimension.

The following sections explain how to add all of the different types of dimension objects to a drawing using VBA and the AutoCAD object model.

Aligned Dimension Object

The **AddDimAligned** method creates an aligned dimension. Its signature is:

Object = Space.AddDimAligned(*ExtPoint1, ExtPoint2, DimLocation*)

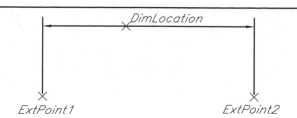

Figure 5-14.
Creating an aligned
dimension object.

where *Object* is the **DimAligned** object. *Space* is the **ModelSpace** or **PaperSpace** collection. *ExtPoint1* is a **Variant** three-element array of **Double** data types that is the endpoint of first extension line. *ExtPoint2* is a **Variant** three-element array of **Double** data types that is the endpoint of second extension line. *DimLocation* is a **Variant** three-element array of **Double** data types that is the dimension location point.

The following code creates an aligned dimension in model space using the two extension line origin points and dimension line location supplied by the user. Refer to **Figure 5-14.**

```
Sub Ch05_AddDimAligned()

    Dim objDim As AcadDimAligned
    Dim varExtPt1 As Variant
    Dim varExtPt2 As Variant
    Dim varLocPt As Variant

    ' Get the first extension line point.
    varExtPt1 = ThisDrawing.Utility.GetPoint(, vbCrLf & "First extension line origin: ")

    ' Get the second extension line point.
    varExtPt2 = ThisDrawing.Utility.GetPoint(, vbCrLf & "Second extension " & _
        "line origin: ")

    ' Get the dimension location.
    varLocPt = ThisDrawing.Utility.GetPoint(, vbCrLf & "Dimension line location: ")

    ' Create the aligned dimension.
    Set objDim = ThisDrawing.ModelSpace.AddDimAligned(varExtPt1, varExtPt2, _
        varLocPt)

    ' Update the object so it is sure to appear.
    objDim.Update

End Sub
```

Rotated Dimension Object

The **AddDimRotated** method creates a rotated dimension. Its signature is:

   Object = Space.AddDimRotated(*ExtPoint1, ExtPoint2, DimLocation, RotateAngle*)

where *Object* is the **DimRotated** object. *Space* is the **ModelSpace** or **PaperSpace** collection. *ExtPoint1* is a **Variant** three-element array of **Double** data types that is the endpoint of first extension line. *ExtPoint2* is a **Variant** three-element array of **Double** data types that is the endpoint of second extension line. *DimLocation* is a **Variant** three-element array of **Double** data types that is the location point of the dimension line. *RotateAngle* is a **Double** data type that is the dimension rotation angle, in radians.

The following code creates a rotated dimension in model space using two extension line origin points, a dimension line location, and a rotation angle supplied by the user. Refer to **Figure 5-15.**

Figure 5-15.
Creating a rotated
dimension object.

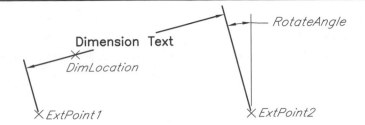

```
Sub Ch05_AddDimRotated()

    Dim objDim As AcadDimRotated
    Dim varExtPt1 As Variant
    Dim varExtPt2 As Variant
    Dim varLocPt As Variant
    Dim dblRotAngle As Double

    ' Get the first extension line point.
    varExtPt1 = ThisDrawing.Utility.GetPoint(, vbCrLf & "First extension line origin: ")

    ' Get the second extension line point.
    varExtPt2 = ThisDrawing.Utility.GetPoint(, vbCrLf & "Second extension " & _
        "line origin: ")

    ' Get the dimension location.
    varLocPt = ThisDrawing.Utility.GetPoint(, vbCrLf & "Dimension line location: ")

    ' Get the rotation angle from the user.
    dblRotAngle = ThisDrawing.Utility.GetAngle(, vbCrLf & "Rotation angle: ")

    ' Create a rotated dimension.
    Set objDim = ThisDrawing.ModelSpace.AddDimRotated(varExtPt1, varExtPt2, _
        varLocPt, dblRotAngle)

    ' Update the object so it is sure to appear.
    objDim.Update

End Sub
```

Three Point Angular Dimension Object

The **AddDim3PointAngular** method creates an angular dimension. Its signature is:

Object = Space.AddDim3PointAngular(*Vertex, EndPoint1, EndPoint2, TextPoint*)

where *Object* is the **Dim3PointAngular** object. *Space* is the **ModelSpace** or **PaperSpace** collection. *Vertex* is a **Variant** three-element array of **Double** data types that is the angle vertex point. *EndPoint1* is a **Variant** three-element array of **Double** data types that is the endpoint of the first line defining the angle. *EndPoint2* is a **Variant** three-element array of **Double** data types that is the endpoint of the second line defining the angle. *TextPoint* is a **Variant** three-element array of **Double** data types that is the location point for the dimension text.

The following code creates an angular dimension in model space using a vertex point, angle endpoints, and a text location supplied by the user. Refer to **Figure 5-16.**

```
Sub Ch05_AddDim3PointAngular ()

    Dim objDim As AcadDim3PointAngular
    Dim varVertexPt As Variant
    Dim varAngPt1 As Variant
    Dim varAngPt2 As Variant
    Dim varLocPt As Variant
```

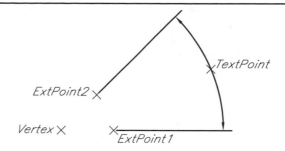

Figure 5-16.
Creating an angular
dimension object.

```
' Get the vertex point.
varVertexPt = ThisDrawing.Utility.GetPoint(, vbCrLf & "Angle vertex: ")

' Get the first angle point.
varAngPt1 = ThisDrawing.Utility.GetPoint(varVertexPt, vbCrLf & "First angle" & _
    " endpoint: ")

' Get the second angle point.
varAngPt2 = ThisDrawing.Utility.GetPoint(varVertexPt, vbCrLf & "Second" & _
    " angle endpoint")

' Get the dimension location.
varLocPt = ThisDrawing.Utility.GetPoint(, vbCrLf & "Dimension line location: ")

' Create the angular dimension.
Set objDim = ThisDrawing.ModelSpace.AddDim3PointAngular(varVertexPt, _
    varAngPt1, varAngPt2, varLocPt)

' Update the object so it is sure to appear.
objDim.Update

End Sub
```

Diametric Dimension Object

The **AddDimDiametric** method creates a diameter dimension. Its signature is:

Object = *Space*.AddDimDiametric(*ChordPoint, FarChordPoint, LdrLength*)

where *Object* is the **DimDiametric** object. *Space* is the **ModelSpace** or **PaperSpace** collection. *ChordPoint* is a **Variant** that is a three-element array of **Double** data types defining the first diameter point and leader line attachment point. *FarChordPoint* is a **Variant** that is a three-element array of **Double** data types defining the second diameter point. *LdrLength* is a **Double** data type that is the length of the leader.

The following code creates a diameter dimension in model space based on two points picked by the user and a leader line length entered by the user. Refer to **Figure 5-17.**

```
Sub Ch05_AddDimDiameter()
```

Figure 5-17.
Creating a diameter
dimension object.

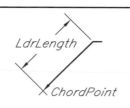

```
Dim objDim As AcadDimDiametric
Dim varPt1 As Variant
Dim varPt2 As Variant
Dim dblLdrLength As Double

' Get the first point.
varPt1 = ThisDrawing.Utility.GetPoint(, vbCrLf & "First point on diameter: ")

' Get the diameter distance.
varPt2 = ThisDrawing.Utility.GetPoint(varPt1, vbCrLf & "Opposite point on diameter: ")

' Get the leader length.
dblLdrLength = ThisDrawing.Utility.GetReal(vbCrLf & "Enter leader length: ")

' Create the diameter dimension in model space.
Set objDim = ThisDrawing.ModelSpace.AddDimDiametric(varPt1, _
    varPt2, dblLdrLength)

' Update the object so it is sure to appear.
objDim.Update

End Sub
```

Radial Dimension Object

The **AddDimRadial** method creates a radial dimension. Its signature is:

Object = *Space*.AddDimRadial(*Center, ChordPoint, LdrLength*)

Object is the **DimRadial** object. *Space* is the **ModelSpace** or **PaperSpace** collection. *Center* is a **Variant** three-element array of **Double** data types that is the center point of the circle or arc to be dimensioned. *ChordPoint* is a **Variant** three-element array of **Double** data types that is the attachment point of the leader line. *LdrLength* is a **Double** data type that is the length of the leader.

The following code creates a radial dimension in model space using a center point, a point defining the radius length, and the leader line length supplied by the user. The leader line length must be entered using the keyboard. Refer to **Figure 5-18.**

Figure 5-18.
Creating a radial
dimension object.

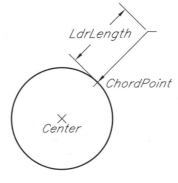

```
Sub Ch05_AddDimRadial()

    Dim objDim As AcadDimRadial
    Dim varCtrPt As Variant
    Dim varRadPt As Variant
    Dim dblLdrLength As Double

    ' Get the center point.
    varCtrPt = ThisDrawing.Utility.GetPoint(, vbCrLf & "Center point: ")

    ' Get the radius point.
    varRadPt = ThisDrawing.Utility.GetPoint(varCtrPt, vbCrLf & "Point on radius: ")

    ' Get the leader length.
    dblLdrLength = ThisDrawing.Utility.GetReal(vbCrLf & "Leader length: ")

    ' Create the radial dimension in model space.
    Set objDim = ThisDrawing.ModelSpace.AddDimRadial(varCtrPt, varRadPt, _
        dblLdrLength)

    ' Update the object so it is sure to appear.
    objDim.Update

End Sub
```

Ordinate Dimension Object

The **AddDimOrdinate** method creates an ordinate, or arrowless, dimension. Its signature is:

$Object = Space$.AddDimOrdinate($DefPoint$, $LdrEndPoint$, X_Axis)

where $Object$ is the **DimOrdinate** object. $Space$ is the **ModelSpace** or **PaperSpace** collection. $DefPoint$ is a **Variant** three-element array of **Double** data types that is the point to dimension. $LdrEndPoint$ is a **Variant** three-element array of **Double** data types that is the attachment point of the leader line. X_Axis is a **Boolean** flag, where **True** creates an ordinate dimension displaying the value for the X axis and **False** creates an ordinate dimension displaying the value for the Y axis.

The following code creates an ordinate dimension in model space using a definition point, a leader location point, and the axis to dimension supplied by the user. Refer to **Figure 5-19**.

Figure 5-19.
Creating an
ordinate dimension
object.

×0,0

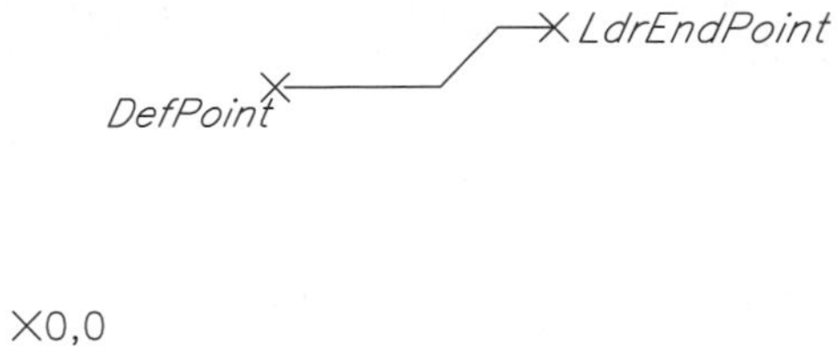

```
Sub Ch05_AddDimOrdinate()

    Dim objDim As AcadDimOrdinate
    Dim varDefPt As Variant
    Dim varLdrPt As Variant
    Dim strKeyWord As String
    Dim blnXaxis As Boolean

    ' Get the definition point.
    varDefPt = ThisDrawing.Utility.GetPoint(, vbCrLf & "Feature location: ")

    ' Get the leader point.
    varLdrPt = ThisDrawing.Utility.GetPoint(varDefPt, vbCrLf & "Leader endpoint: ")

    ' Initialize the GetKeyword method with the keywords "X and Y"
    ' and disable null input.
    ThisDrawing.Utility.InitializeUserInput 1, "X Y"

    ' Determine the axis the user wants to dimension.
    strKeyWord = ThisDrawing.Utility.GetKeyword _
        ("X axis or Y axis? [X/Y]: ")

    ' Set the Boolean flag appropriately.
    If strKeyWord = "X" Then
        blnXaxis = True
    Else
        blnXaxis = False
    End If

    ' Create the ordinate dimension.
    Set objDim = ThisDrawing.ModelSpace.AddDimOrdinate(varDefPt, varLdrPt, _
        blnXaxis)

    ' Update the object so it is sure to appear.
    objDim.Update

End Sub
```

Notice the use of the **GetKeyword** method to get the geometric axis desired by the user. It is simply a variation of the Ch4_GetKeyWord2 code in Chapter 4 that was used to get an answer to a yes/no prompt.

Creating Miscellaneous Objects

There are a few other objects that can be added to a drawing using VBA and the AutoCAD object model. The following sections explain how to add miscellaneous objects such as points, 2D solids, and hatches.

Point Object

The **AddPoint** method creates a point using the current **PDMODE** setting. Its signature is:

Object = Space.AddPoint(*Point*)

where *Object* is the point object. *Space* is the **ModelSpace** or **PaperSpace** collection. *Point* is a **Variant** three-element array of **Double** data types that is the point coordinates.

The following code creates a point in model space using a coordinate location supplied by the user. Refer to **Figure 5-20.** The coordinate location can be entered using the keyboard or the mouse.

Figure 5-20.
Creating a point
object.

Point

```
Sub Ch05_AddPoint()

    Dim objPoint As AcadPoint
    Dim varLocPt As Variant

    ' Get the point location.
    varLocPt = ThisDrawing.Utility.GetPoint(, vbCrLf & "Point location: ")

    ' Create the point.
    Set objPoint = ThisDrawing.ModelSpace.AddPoint(varLocPt)

    ' Update the object so it is sure to appear.
    objPoint.Update

End Sub
```

Solid Object

The **AddSolid** method creates a 2D solid. Its signature is:

> *Object = Space*.AddSolid(*Point1, Point2, Point3, Point4*)

where *Object* is the 2D **Solid** object. *Space* is the **ModelSpace** or **PaperSpace** collection. *Point1* is a **Variant** three-element array of **Double** data types that is the first point of the solid. *Point2* is a **Variant** three-element array of **Double** data types that is the second point of the solid. *Point3* is a **Variant** three-element array of **Double** data types that is the third point of the solid. *Point4* is a **Variant** three-element array of **Double** data types that is the fourth point of the solid.

The following code creates a 2D solid in model space using four coordinate points supplied by the user. Refer to **Figure 5-21.** The coordinate points can be entered using the keyboard, mouse, or a combination of both.

```
Sub Ch05_AddSolid()

    Dim objSolid As AcadSolid
    Dim varPt1 As Variant
    Dim varPt2 As Variant
    Dim varPt3 As Variant
    Dim varPt4 As Variant

    ' Get the points.
    varPt1 = ThisDrawing.Utility.GetPoint(, vbCrLf & "First point: ")
    varPt2 = ThisDrawing.Utility.GetPoint(varPt1, vbCrLf & "Second point: ")
    varPt3 = ThisDrawing.Utility.GetPoint(varPt2, vbCrLf & "Third point: ")
    varPt4 = ThisDrawing.Utility.GetPoint(varPt3, vbCrLf & "Fourth point: ")

    ' Create the solid.
    Set objSolid = ThisDrawing.ModelSpace.AddSolid(varPt1, varPt2, varPt3, _
        varPt4)

    ' Update the object so it is sure to appear.
    objSolid.Update

End Sub
```

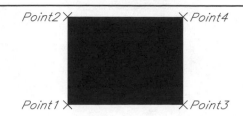

Figure 5-21.
Creating a 2D solid object.

Point2 ✕   ✕ Point4

Point1 ✕   ✕ Point3

Hatch Object

The **AddHatch** method creates a hatch pattern. Its signature is:

Object = *Space*.AddHatch(*PatternType*, *PatternName*, *Associativity*)

where *Object* is the **Hatch** object. *Space* is the **ModelSpace** or **PaperSpace** collection. *PatternType* is the **acPatternType** enum hatch type. See **Figure 5-22.** *PatternName* is a **String** that is the hatch pattern name. *Associativity* is a **Boolean** where **True** creates an associative hatch and **False** creates a nonassociative hatch.

The following code adds an associative hatch pattern to a user-selected object (drawing entity) in model space using the predefined ANSI32 hatch pattern. Refer to **Figure 5-23.**

```
Sub Ch05_AddHatch()

    Dim objHatch As AcadHatch
    Dim strPatternName As String
    Dim intPatternType As Long
    Dim blnAssociativity As Boolean
    Dim objOutLoop(0 To 0) As AcadObject
    Dim varPickPt As Variant

    ' Turn off errors.
    On Error Resume Next

    ' Hatch definition.
    strPatternName = "ANSI32"
    intPatternType = acHatchPatternTypePreDefined
    blnAssociativity = True
```

Figure 5-22.
Pattern types for creating a hatch pattern object.

acPatternType enum	Type of pattern
acHatchPatternTypePredefined	Predefined
acHatchPatternTypeUserDefined	User defined
acHatchPatternTypeCustomDefined	Custom

Figure 5-23.
Creating a hatch pattern object.

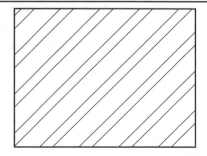

```
' Create the associative Hatch object in model space.
Set objHatch = ThisDrawing.ModelSpace.AddHatch(intPatternType, _
    strPatternName, blnAssociativity)

' Get the object to hatch.
ThisDrawing.Utility.GetEntity objOutLoop(0), varPickPt, "Select object: "

' Make sure the user selected something.
If Err.Number = 0 Then

    ' Append the hatch outer boundary to hatch object.
    objHatch.AppendOuterLoop (objOutLoop)

    ' Evaluate the hatch for display.
    objHatch.Evaluate

    ' Regenerate the drawing.
    ThisDrawing.Regen True

Else

    ' Clear the error.
    Err.Clear

End If

End Sub
```

Caution You must append the outer loop of the **Hatch** object with the **AppendOuterLoop** method in order for the **Hatch** object to be closed and become a valid AutoCAD entity. If you do not immediately close the **Hatch** object using the **AppendOuterLoop** method, AutoCAD may crash.

Creating Dimension and Miscellaneous Objects

Let's Review...

- The **AddDimAligned** method creates an aligned dimension.
- The **AddDimRotated** method creates a rotated dimension.
- The **AddDim3PointAngular** method creates an angular dimension.
- The **AddDimRadial** method creates a radial dimension.
- The **AddDimOrdinate** method creates an ordinate, or arrowless, dimension.
- The **AddPoint** method creates a point.
- The **AddSolid** method creates a 2D solid.
- The **AddHatch** method creates a hatch pattern.

Exercise 5-3

Create the macros described below. All macros should be created in the **ThisDrawing** module of your MyMacros.dvb project. Provide all necessary error checking and control. Run and test each macro.

1. Create a macro named **ex05_Gasket** that creates the gasket shown below. Include all dimensions.

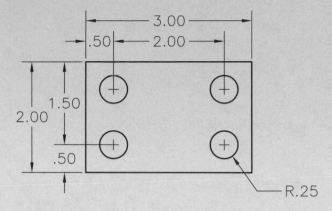

2. Create a macro named **ex05_Chassis** that creates the chassis base shown below. Include all dimensions. All radii are .125".

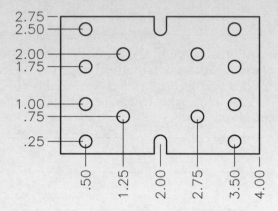

3. Create a macro named **ex05_Logo** that creates the logo shown below. Use the Solid hatch pattern for all filled-in areas.

 ARCHITECTUAL
ENGINEERING
CONSTRUCTION

Chapter Test

Write your answers on a separate sheet of paper.

1. List the two top-level object collections, or environments, to which a new drawing object can be added and show how each is referenced in VBA.
2. What is the name of the shared drawing object method that ensures new objects are visible in the drawing?
3. Why is a Z coordinate value not needed when creating a **LWPolyline** object?
4. What is the name of the "add" method that creates an old-format polyline object?
5. Which two drawing objects are typically used for orthographic projections?
6. When creating a circle using the **AddCircle** method, what information must you provide?
7. Explain how the **AddEllipse** method differs from creating an ellipse in the AutoCAD drawing editor.
8. List and describe the three arguments used with the **AddText** method.
9. List and describe the three arguments used with the **AddMText** method.
10. What is the name of the "add" method that can create both horizontally and vertically aligned dimensions?
11. Which method is used to create a diameter dimension using VBA?
12. How do you control which axis (X or Y) the **AddDimOrdinate** method references when creating an arrowless dimension?
13. What must you do after creating a **Hatch** object in order for it to become a valid AutoCAD object and prevent AutoCAD from crashing?

Programming Problems

Create the macros described below. All macros should be created in the **ThisDrawing** module of your MyMacros.dvb project. Provide all necessary error checking and error control. Run and test each macro.

1. Create a macro named p05_WindowSchedule that creates the window schedule shown below.

WINDOW SCHEDULE					
SYM.	WIDTH	HEIGHT	MATERIAL	TYPE	QUAN.
A	3'-6"	5'-0"	ALUMINUM	DOUBLE HUNG	4
B	2'-6"	4'-0"	ALUMINUM	DOUBLE HUNG	2
C	2'-0"	3'-6"	ALUMINUM	DOUBLE HUNG	2
D	2'-0"	3'-0"	ALUMINUM	DOUBLE HUNG	1
E	3'-0"	2'-0"	WOOD	CASEMENT	1
F	2'-6"	2-0"	WOOD	CASEMENT	1

2. Create a macro named p05_ParaWindow that creates the window drawing shown below based on a user-supplied width and height. Include the width and height dimensions on the final drawing.

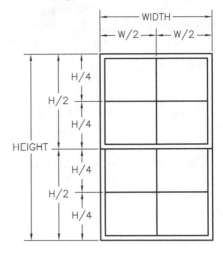

3. Create a macro named p05_BasePlate that creates the base plate shown below. Include all dimensions and the HOLE LAYOUT table.

HOLE LAYOUT			
KEY	SIZE	DEPTH	NO. REQD.
A	⌀.25	THRU	6
B	⌀.125	THRU	4
C	⌀.375	THRU	4
D	R.125	THRU	2

4. Create a macro named p05_DrawCMU that creates a stack of concrete masonry units (CMU) similar to those shown below. The blocks should be based on user-supplied width, height, and joint spacing. The user should also specify the total number of blocks in the stack. Hatch each block with the AR-CONC hatch pattern. *Hint:* The **Hatch** object's **PatternScale** property can be used to control the hatch scale.

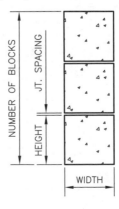

Editing AutoCAD Entities

Learning Objectives

After completing this chapter, you will be able to create VBA macros that:

● Change the color, layer, and linetype properties of an AutoCAD object.
● Change the diameter of a circle.
● Change the height of a text object.
● Edit a text object's string value.
● Perform standard AutoCAD modifying operations using an AutoCAD object's own methods (array, copy, mirror, move, offset, rotate, and scale).
● Highlight an AutoCAD object.
● Explode complex AutoCAD objects, such as polylines and blocks.

Editing AutoCAD Entities

As you saw in Chapter 2, you can edit AutoCAD entities in VBA by using the entity object's own properties and methods. Each AutoCAD object shares general properties and methods that allow you to reproduce most of the editing commands found in the AutoCAD drawing editor. The following sections discuss these shared general properties and methods, plus a few of those that are unique to particular object types.

AutoCAD Drawing Object Properties

In VBA, AutoCAD drawing entities share the general properties of **Color**, **Layer**, **Linetype**, **Normal**, **Thickness**, and **Visibility**. In addition to these shared properties, AutoCAD objects have unique properties that correspond to the type of drawing entity. For instance, in addition to the general properties, a **Circle** object has a **Radius** property and a **Diameter** property, while a **Text** object has a **Height** property and a **StyleName** property. These properties can be managed using traditional AutoCAD selection methods to first obtain the objects you wish to modify. Then, you can set or retrieve the desired properties.

AutoCAD Drawing Object Methods

Just as AutoCAD objects share general properties, as described earlier, AutoCAD objects also share general methods. These methods can be used to modify objects using techniques similar to the "modify" commands available in the AutoCAD drawing editor. With object methods, you can perform such common modifying operations as moving, copying, and mirroring…just about any operation that can be performed by the commands found in the **Modify** pull-down menu in the AutoCAD drawing editor, for that matter. This is evident when you look at some of the modify methods shared by most drawing objects: **ArrayPolar**, **ArrayRectangular**, **Copy**, **Delete**, **Highlight**, **Mirror**, **Mirror3D**, **Move**, **Offset**, **Rotate**, **Rotate3D**, and **ScaleEntity**.

Certain objects have unique methods, just as certain objects have unique properties, based on their object type. For instance, a complex object, like a polyline or block reference, has an **Explode** method that allows you to break up the object into its component subobjects. On the other hand, a hatch object has a **SetPattern** method so that you can set its hatch pattern.

Using object methods to modify objects in AutoCAD is a little more complex than simply setting object properties. Because of the dynamic nature of methods, most methods require one or more arguments with data about the operation being performed. For instance, if you want to move a line, AutoCAD has to know where you want it moved to. To accomplish this, the "from" location and the "to" location are supplied as arguments to the **Move** method. On the other hand, the **Rotate** method requires that you specify a base point and a rotation angle as method arguments, while the **Scale** method needs a base point and a scale factor. How to determine the arguments for a particular method and how they are used is explained in the next section.

Determining an AutoCAD Object's Properties and Methods

The easiest way to determine an AutoCAD object's properties and methods, and how they are used, is to use the AutoCAD object model diagram in the *ActiveX and VBA Reference* guide in the online AutoCAD Developer Documentation. To locate the object model diagram, open the AutoCAD online documentation by selecting **Developer Help** from AutoCAD's **Help** pull-down menu. In the **Contents** tab, select the **ActiveX and VBA Reference** entry. Finally, select **Object Model** on the right-hand side of the screen to display the diagram.

For instance, to find all of the properties and methods for a **Line** object, select the **Line** object in the object model diagram. All of the properties and methods are then displayed along with a description of the object, as shown in **Figure 6-1.**

Figure 6-1.
The properties and methods for an object are listed in the online documentation. Here, the properties and methods for the **Line** object are shown.

Each method and property is hyperlinked to a description and example code. If you pick the **ArrayPolar** method, for example, information about that method and its arguments is displayed, **Figure 6-2A.**

Picking the **Example** link in the upper, right-hand corner displays sample code that utilizes the **ArrayPolar** method, **Figure 6-2B.** The code example shows how the method can be used in a macro. You can even cut and paste from the sample code directly into your own macros. Talk about a time-saver!

Figure 6-2.
A—Picking on an object's method or property displays information about that method or property. Here, a description of the **Line** object's **ArrayPolar** method is displayed. To see sample code for the method, pick **Example**. B—Sample code for the **ArrayPolar** method.

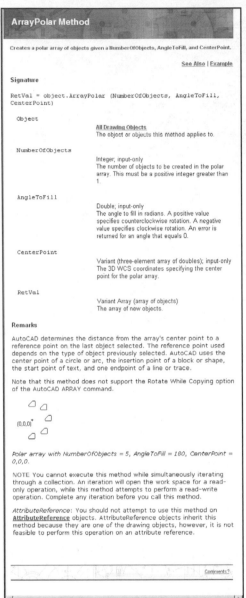

B

A

- Every AutoCAD drawing object shares general properties and methods that allow you to reproduce most of the editing commands found in the AutoCAD drawing editor.
- AutoCAD objects also have unique properties and methods, depending on their object type.
- To easily determine an AutoCAD objects properties and methods, select the object in the AutoCAD object model diagram in the *ActiveX and VBA Reference* guide. This guide is located in the online AutoCAD Developer Documentation.

Editing AutoCAD Objects Using Properties

As explained earlier, modifying an AutoCAD object via its properties is easy. Simply get a reference to the object you wish to modify and then set any of the object's properties using the VBA assignment operator (**=**). A reference can be obtained either by creating a new object or by using one of the traditional AutoCAD selection methods to get a reference to an existing object. The following sections explore how to modify AutoCAD drawing objects via their properties.

Changing an Object's Color

The **Color** property of an object controls the color of the entity in the AutoCAD drawing editor:

```
AcadObject.Color
```

There are 255 colors in the AutoCAD Color Index (ACI). The first seven colors are represented by the following VBA constants:

```
acRed = 1
acYellow = 2
acGreen = 3
acCyan = 4
acBlue = 5
acMagenta = 6
acWhite = 7
```

The following code prompts the user to select an entity in a drawing, displays the entity's current color setting, changes the entity's **Color** property red, and informs the user the color has been changed:

```
Sub Ch06_ChangeColor()

    Dim objSelected As AcadObject
    Dim varPickPt As Variant
    Dim varColor As Variant

    ' Prompt the user to select an entity.
    ThisDrawing.Utility.GetEntity objSelected, varPickPt, "Select object: "

    ' Get entity's color.
        varColor = objSelected.Color

    ' Convert the color.
    If varColor < 7 Then
        varColor = Choose(varColor + 1, "ByBlock", "Red", "Yellow", _
                "Green", "Cyan", "Blue", "Magenta", "White")
    ElseIf varColor = 256 Then
        varColor = "ByLayer"
    End If

    ' Display the current color.
    MsgBox "Current object color: " & varColor

    ' Change entity's color to red.
    objSelected.Color = acRed

    ' Update the object.
    objSelected.Update

    ' Display the new color.
    MsgBox "Object color changed to red."

End Sub
```

Notice the use of the VBA **Choose** function in the above example. The **Choose** function returns a value from a list based on an index value. The signature is:

Choose(*Index*, *Choice_1*, *Choice_2*,…, *Choice_n*)

Index is an **Integer** that is from 1 to the total number of choices. *Choice_n* is a **Variant** that is the value to return. If *Index* is set to 1, then **Choose** returns the first choice in the list. If *Index* is set to 2, the second choice is returned, and so on.

An object's color can be set to assume the **Color** property of the layer it is on by setting the object's **Color** property to 256. This value represents the ByLayer color setting in the ACI. The ByBlock color setting is represented in the AutoCAD Color Index by 0. The ByBlock property is used when creating complex blocks, or symbols, that are made up of multiple nested objects. When the **Color** property of a nested object is set to ByBlock, the object assumes the current color setting in the AutoCAD drawing editor when the block is inserted.

An object's **Linetype** and **Lineweight** property can also be set to ByLayer or ByBlock with similar results. For more information about the special ByLayer and ByBlock properties, consult AutoCAD's online documentation.

Changing an Object's Layer

Layers are the primary means of organizing information in a drawing. Every drawing object should reside on a layer that indicates what type of object it represents. The concept of layers and how layers are used is explained in detail in Chapter 8. Creating layers using VBA and the AutoCAD object model is also described in Chapter 8.

The **Layer** property of an object controls the layer on which the object resides. The signature is:

```
AcadObject.Layer
```

The following code prompts the user to select an object in a drawing and then changes that object's **Layer** property to the WALL layer:

```
Sub Ch06_ChangeLayer()

    Dim objSelected As AcadObject
    Dim varPickPt As Variant

    ' Prompt the user to select an object.
    ThisDrawing.Utility.GetEntity objSelected, varPickPt, "Select object: "

    ' Display the current layer.
    MsgBox "Current object layer: " & objSelected.Layer

    ' Change the object's layer to WALL.
    objSelected.Layer = "WALL"

    ' Update the object.
    objSelected.Update

    ' Display the new layer.
    MsgBox "Object's layer changed to: " & objSelected.Layer

End Sub
```

Caution

When updating an object's **Layer** property, you must be sure the layer name exists or the message box shown in **Figure 6-3** is displayed.

Figure 6-3.
This VBA error
message appears if
you attempt to update
the **Layer** or **Linetype**
property to a layer or
linetype name that
does not exist in the
drawing.

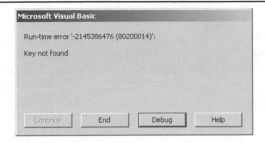

Changing an Object's Linetype

AutoCAD linetypes control the dots, dashes, gaps, and even text that make up a line. The concept of linetypes and how linetypes are used is explained in detail in Chapter 8. Loading linetypes using VBA and the AutoCAD object model is also described in Chapter 8.

The **Linetype** property of an object controls its linetype assignment. The signature is:

    AcadObject.Linetype

The following code prompts the user to select an object in the drawing and then changes the object's **Linetype** property to the HIDDEN linetype:

```
Sub Ch06_ChangeLinetype()

    Dim objSelected As AcadObject
    Dim varPickPt As Variant

    ' Prompt the user to select an object.
    ThisDrawing.Utility.GetEntity objSelected, varPickPt, "Select object: "

    ' Display the current linetype.
    MsgBox "Current object linetype: " & objSelected. Linetype

    ' Change the object's linetype to HIDDEN.
    objSelected.Linetype = "HIDDEN"

    ' Update the object.
    objSelected.Update

    ' Display the new linetype.
    MsgBox "Object's linetype changed to: " & objSelected.Linetype

End Sub
```

 Caution   When updating an object's **Linetype** property, you must be sure the linetype is loaded or the message box shown in **Figure 6-3** is displayed.

Changing the Diameter of a Circle Object

Unlike the general shared properties described in the previous sections, the **Diameter** property of a circle is unique to that object. The **Diameter** property of a **Circle** object controls its size. The signature is:

```
AcDbCircle.Diameter
```

The following code prompts the user to select a circle, displays its current diameter, and then changes the diameter to a user-supplied value, which must be entered using the keyboard. Because the **Diameter** property is unique, it is a good idea to add some error checking to your code that ensures that the user selects the correct object type.

```vb
Sub Ch06_ChangeDiameter()

    Dim objSelected As AcadObject
    Dim varPickPt As Variant
    Dim dblDiameter As Double

    ' Prompt the user to select a circle.
    ThisDrawing.Utility.GetEntity objSelected, varPickPt, "Select circle: "

    ' Make sure the object is a circle.
    If objSelected.ObjectName = "AcDbCircle" Then

        ' Get the circle's current diameter.
        dblDiameter = objSelected.Diameter

        ' Display the current diameter.
        MsgBox "Current circle diameter: " & dblDiameter

        ' Get the new diameter from the user.
        dblDiameter = ThisDrawing.Utility.GetReal(vbCrLf & "Diameter: ")

        ' Change the circle's diameter.
        objSelected.Diameter = dblDiameter

        ' Update the object.
        objSelected.Update

        ' Get the circle's new diameter.
        dblDiameter = objSelected.Diameter

        ' Display the new diameter.
        MsgBox "New circle diameter: " & dblDiameter

    Else

        ' Wrong object type.
        MsgBox "Object is not a circle!"

    End If

End Sub
```

Notice in the code example on the previous page that the **ObjectName** property is first checked to determine if a circle has been selected before the macro tries to update the **Diameter** property. This is done because the **Diameter** property is unique to circular objects. Obviously, trying to change the diameter of an object that is not a circle will result in a runtime error. Unfortunately, there is no complete list of valid object names, but the general rule of thumb is to simply prefix the object name (**Circle**, **Line**, **Text**, etc.) with **AcDb**. For example:

Circle object = **AcDbCircle**

Line object = **AcDbLine**

Text object = **AcDbText**

Changing the Height of a Text Object

The **Height** property of a **Text** object controls the vertical height of the text. Both single-line and multiline text have a **Height** property. The signatures are:

```
AcDbText.Height
or
AcDbMText.Height
```

The following code prompts the user to select text, displays the current text height, and then changes the height to a user-supplied value:

```
Sub Ch06_ChangeTextHeight()

    Dim objSelected As AcadObject
    Dim varPickPt As Variant
    Dim dblTextHeight As Double

    ' Prompt the user to select text.
    ThisDrawing.Utility.GetEntity objSelected, varPickPt, "Select text: "

    ' Make sure the object is single-line or multiline text.
    If objSelected.ObjectName = "AcDbText" or _
        objSelected.ObjectName = "AcDbMText" Then

        ' Get the text's current height.
        dblTextHeight = objSelected.Height

        ' Display the current height.
        MsgBox "Current text height: " & dblTextHeight

        ' Get the new text height from the user.
        dblTextHeight = ThisDrawing.Utility.GetReal(vbCrLf & "Text height: ")

        ' Change the text height.
        objSelected.Height = dblTextHeight

        ' Update the object.
        objSelected.Update

        ' Get the new text height.
        dblTextHeight = objSelected.Height

        ' Display the new text height.
        MsgBox "New text height: " & dblTextHeight
```

```
        Else

            ' Wrong object type.
            MsgBox "Object is not text!"

        End If

    End Sub
```

Notice that this code works for both single-line and multiline text. Both types of text have a height property, so the macro can filter for both text types in the conditional statement that checks to see if the user selected the correct object type.

Changing a Text Object's Text String

The value of a text string is controlled by the **TextString** property. Both single-line text and multiline text have a **TextString** property. The signatures are:

AcDbText.TextString

or

AcDbMText.TextString

The following code prompts the user to select text in a drawing, displays the current text string, and then changes the text to a user-supplied string:

```
Sub Ch06_ChangeTextString()

    Dim objSelected As AcadObject
    Dim varPickPt As Variant
    Dim strTextString As String

    ' Prompt the user to select text.
    ThisDrawing.Utility.GetEntity objSelected, varPickPt, "Select text:"

    ' Make sure the object is single-line or multiline text.
    If objSelected.ObjectName = "AcDbText" or _
        objSelected.ObjectName = "AcDbMText" Then

        ' Get the text's current text string.
        strTextString = objSelected.textString

        ' Display the current string.
        MsgBox "Current text string: " & strTextString

        ' Get the new text string from the user—allow spaces.
        strTextString = ThisDrawing.Utility.GetString(True, vbCrLf & "Text: ")

        ' Change the text string.
        objSelected.textString = strTextString

        ' Update the object.
        objSelected.Update

        ' Get the new text height.
        strTextString = objSelected.textString

        ' Display the new text string.
        MsgBox "New text string: " & strTextString

    Else

        ' Wrong object type.
        MsgBox "Object is not text!"

    End If

End Sub
```

Figure 6-4.
These are a few of the text formatting codes. A complete list can be found in AutoCAD's online documentation.

Format Code	Description
\O...\o	Turns overline on and off.
\L...\l	Turns underline on and off.
\~	Inserts a nonbreaking space.
\\	Inserts a backslash.
\{...\}	Inserts opening and closing braces.
\File name;	Changes to the specified font file.
\Hvalue;	Changes the text height; specified in drawing units.
\Hvaluex;	Changes the text height to a multiple of the current text height.
\S...^...;	Stacks subsequent text at the \, #, or ^ symbol.
\Tvalue;	Adjusts the space between characters.
\Qangle;	Changes the obliquing angle.
\Wvalue;	Changes the width factor.

If you are updating multiline text, you will need to know the formatting codes. There are many codes; a few are shown in **Figure 6-4.** For a complete list of all the multiline text formatting codes, refer to *ActiveX and VBA Reference* in the AutoCAD online documentation.

Let's Review... Editing AutoCAD Objects Using Properties

- The **Color** property of an object controls the display color.
- The **Layer** property of an object controls on which layer the object resides.
- The **Linetype** property of an object controls which linetype is assigned to the object.
- The **Diameter** property of a **Circle** object controls the size of the object.
- The **Height** property of **Text** and **MText** objects controls the text height.
- The **TextString** property of **Text** and **MText** objects stores the text value, or string.

Exercise 6-1

Create the macros described below. All macros should be created in the **ThisDrawing** module of your MyMacros.dvb project. Provide all necessary error checking and control. Run and test each macro.

1. Create a macro named ex06_ChangeProps that prompts a user to select any type of entity in a drawing and change its **Color**, **Layer**, and **Linetype** property to user-supplied values. *1-255* *must already exist*
2. Create a macro named ex06_ScaleText that prompts a user to select a text entity in a drawing and then scales the text height by a factor equal to the value of the current **DIMSCALE** system variable setting.
3. Create a macro named ex06_ReplaceText that prompts a user for a text string and then updates one or more text entities in a drawing that are selected by the user until no text entities are selected.

Editing AutoCAD Objects Using Methods

As mentioned earlier, modifying an AutoCAD object via its methods is little more complicated than modifying an object via its properties. This is because of a method's dynamic nature and the need to typically supply arguments to the method per its signature.

Just like object properties, accessing and using an object's methods require that you first get a reference to the object you wish to modify. This can be done by either creating a new object or by getting a reference to an existing object using one of the traditional AutoCAD selection methods. You can then use any of the object's methods. The following sections explore how to modify AutoCAD drawing objects via their methods.

Arraying an Object

There are two basic types of arrays in AutoCAD—rectangular and polar. A rectangular array is created by copying an object a specified number of times in two or three directions to create rows and columns. A polar array is created by copying an object a specified number of times in a circular manner about a center point.

Rectangular Array

The **ArrayRectangular** method creates a 2D or 3D rectangular array, or matrix, of objects. See **Figure 6-5.** The signature is:

ReturnVal = objSelected.ArrayRectangular (*NumberOfRows,* _
    NumberOfColumns, NumberOfLevels, DistBetweenRows, _
    DistBetweenColumns, DistBetweenLevels)

The selected drawing object is *objSelected. NumberOfRows* is an **Integer** that is the number of rows in the array. *NumberOfColumns* is an **Integer** that is the number of columns in the array. *NumberOfLevels* is an **Integer** that is the number of levels in a 3D array. *DistBetweenRows* is a **Double** data type that is the distance between rows. *DistBetweenColumns* is a **Double** data type that is the distance between columns. *DistBetweenLevels* is a **Double** data type that is the distance between the levels in a 3D array. *ReturnVal* is a **Variant** that is the array of objects.

The following code prompts the user to select an object and then creates a 2D rectangular array based on the number of rows, number of columns, and the distance between them as supplied by the user.

Figure 6-5.
Creating a rectangular array using the **ArrayRectangular** method.

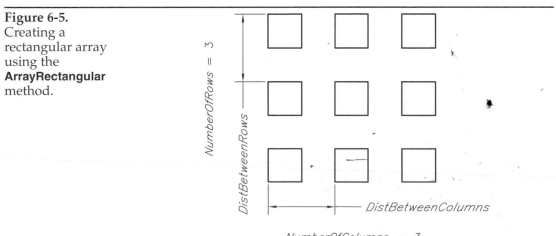

Chapter 6   Editing AutoCAD Entities

```
Sub Ch06_ArrayRectangular()

    Dim objSelected As AcadObject
    Dim varPickPt As Variant
    Dim intRows As Integer
    Dim intColumns As Integer
    Dim intLevels As Integer
    Dim dblRowDistance As Double
    Dim dblColDistance As Double
    Dim dblLevelDistance As Double

    ' Prompt the user to select an object.
    ThisDrawing.Utility.GetEntity objSelected, varPickPt, "Select object: "

    ' Get the number of rows and columns.
    intRows = ThisDrawing.Utility.GetInteger("Rows: ")
    intColumns = ThisDrawing.Utility.GetInteger("Columns: ")
    intLevels = 1

    ' Get the distance between rows and columns.
    dblRowDistance = ThisDrawing.Utility.GetReal("Row distance: ")
    dblColDistance = ThisDrawing.Utility.GetReal("Column distance: ")
    dblLevelDistance = 0.0

    ' Create the array.
    objSelected.ArrayRectangular intRows, intColumns, intLevels, _
        dblRowDistance, dblColDistance, dblLevelDistance

    ' Zoom all.
    ZoomAll

End Sub
```

Polar Array

The **ArrayPolar** method creates a 2D polar array of objects rotated about a center point. See **Figure 6-6.** The signature is:

$$ReturnVal = objSelected.\text{ArrayPolar} (NumberOfObjects, AngleToFill, CenterPt)$$

The selected drawing object is *objSelected*. *NumberOfObjects* is an **Integer** that is the number of objects in the polar array. *AngleToFill* is a **Double** data type that is the angle to fill, in radians. *CenterPt* is a **Variant** that is the center point of the polar array. *ReturnVal* is a **Variant** that is the array of objects.

Figure 6-6.
Creating a polar array using the **ArrayPolar** method.

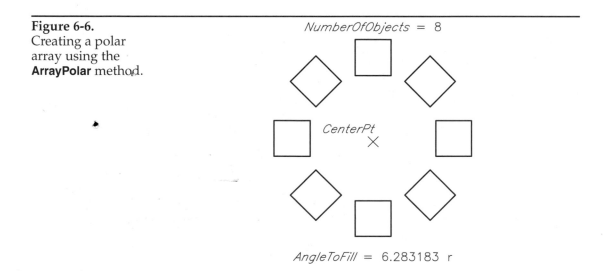

NumberOfObjects = 8

CenterPt

AngleToFill = 6.283183 r

The following code prompts the user to select an object and then creates a 2D polar array based on the user-supplied center point, total number of items, and angle to fill.

```
Sub Ch06_ArrayPolar()

    Dim objSelected As AcadObject
    Dim varPickPt As Variant
    Dim intNumber As Integer
    Dim varCtrPt As Variant
    Dim dblFillAngle As Double

    ' Prompt the user to select an object.
    ThisDrawing.Utility.GetEntity objSelected, varPickPt, "Select object: "

    ' Get the center point.
    varCtrPt = ThisDrawing.Utility.GetPoint(, vbCrLf & "Center point: ")

    ' Get the number of items.
    intNumber = ThisDrawing.Utility.GetInteger("Number of items: ")

    ' Get the angle to fill.
    dblFillAngle = ThisDrawing.Utility.GetReal(vbCrLf & "Angle to fill: ")

    ' Convert to radians.
    dblFillAngle = dblFillAngle * 3.141592 / 180#

    ' Create the polar array.
    objSelected.ArrayPolar intNumber, dblFillAngle, varCtrPt

    ' Zoom all.
    ZoomAll

End Sub
```

Copying an Object

The **Copy** method makes a copy of an object. The signature is:

ReturnVal = objSelected.Copy

The selected drawing object is *objSelected*. *ReturnVal* is the duplicate object.

The following code prompts the user to select an object and then makes a copy of it. Then, the duplicate is moved based on a user-supplied base point and distance.

```
Sub Ch06_CopyObject()

    Dim objSelected As AcadObject
    Dim objCopy As AcadObject
    Dim varPickPt As Variant
    Dim varPt1 As Variant
    Dim varPt2 As Variant

    ' Prompt the user to select an object.
    ThisDrawing.Utility.GetEntity objSelected, varPickPt, "Select object: "

    ' Get the base point.
    varPt1 = ThisDrawing.Utility.GetPoint(, vbCrLf & "Base point: ")

    ' Get the second point.
    varPt2 = ThisDrawing.Utility.GetPoint(varPt1, vbCrLf & "Second point: ")

    ' Copy the object.
    Set objCopy = objSelected.Copy()
```

```
' Move the copied object.
objCopy.Move varPt1, varPt2

' Update the object so it will appear.
objCopy.Update

End Sub
```

Professional Tip

Notice in the code example above that it is necessary to move the newly created object in order to emulate how the AutoCAD **Copy** command works in the drawing editor. The **Move** method is explained in detail later in this chapter.

Deleting an Object

The **Delete** method deletes an object. The signature is:

objSelected.Delete

where *objSelected* is the selected drawing object.

The following code prompts the user to select an object and then deletes it. This macro allows only one object to be deleted.

```
Sub Ch06_DeleteObject()

    Dim objSelected As AcadObject
    Dim varPickPt As Variant

    ' Prompt the user to select an object.
    ThisDrawing.Utility.GetEntity objSelected, varPickPt, "Select object: "

    ' Delete the object.
    objSelected.Delete

End Sub
```

The **Erase** method can also be used to delete an object. The signature is:

objSelected.Erase

where *objSelected* is the selected drawing object.

The following code prompts the user to select an object and then deletes it. Like the above code, this macro allows only one object to be deleted.

```
Sub Ch06_EraseObject()

    Dim objSelected As AcadObject
    Dim varPickPt As Variant

    ' Prompt the user to select an object.
    ThisDrawing.Utility.GetEntity objSelected, varPickPt, "Select object: "

    ' Erase the object.
    objSelected.Erase

End Sub
```

Highlighting an Object

The **Highlight** method highlights an entity so it appears dashed, as if the entity were selected in the AutoCAD drawing editor as part of a selection set. Its use helps you emulate the selection process in the AutoCAD drawing editor by providing visual feedback to the user. You should try to use this method whenever a user selects objects. The signature for the **Highlight** method is:

objSelected.Highlight *HighlightFlag*

where *objSelected* is the selected drawing object. *HighlightFlag* is a **Boolean** where **True** highlights the object and **False** removes the highlight from the object.

The following code prompts the user to select an object and then highlights it. Using the **REGEN** command in AutoCAD removes the highlight.

```
Sub Ch06_Highlight()

    Dim objSelected As AcadObject
    Dim varPickPt As Variant

    ' Prompt the user to select an object.
    ThisDrawing.Utility.GetEntity objSelected, varPickPt, "Select object: "

    ' Highlight the object.
    objSelected.Highlight True

End Sub
```

Mirroring an Object

The **Mirror** method mirrors an object about an axis line. See **Figure 6-7.** The signature is:

ReturnVal = *objSelected*.Mirror(*Point1, Point2*)

where *objSelected* is the selected drawing object. *Point1* is a **Variant** that is the first point of the mirror axis. *Point2* is a **Variant** that is the second point of the mirror axis. *ReturnVal* is the mirrored object.

Figure 6-7.
Using the **Mirror** method to mirror an object.

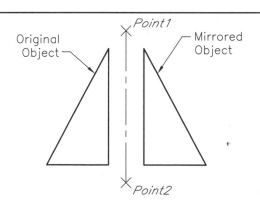

The following code prompts the user to select an object and then mirrors it about an axis line defined by two user-supplied points:

```
Sub Ch06_MirrorObject()

    Dim objSelected As AcadObject
    Dim varPickPt As Variant
    Dim varPt1 As Variant
    Dim varPt2 As Variant

    ' Prompt the user to select an object.
    ThisDrawing.Utility.GetEntity objSelected, varPickPt, "Select object: "

    ' Highlight the object.
    objSelected.Highlight True

    ' Get the first point of the mirror line.
    varPt1 = ThisDrawing.Utility.GetPoint(, vbCrLf & "First point of mirror " & _
        " line: ")

    ' Get the second point of the mirror line.
    varPt2 = ThisDrawing.Utility.GetPoint(varPt1, vbCrLf & "Second" & _
        " mirror line: ")

    ' Mirror the object.
    objSelected.Mirror varPt1, varPt2

    ' Unhighlight the object.
    objSelected.Highlight False

End Sub
```

Moving an Object

The **Move** method moves an object a specified distance. See **Figure 6-8.** The signature is:

objSelected.Move *Point1, Point2*

where *objSelected* is the selected drawing object. *Point1* is a **Variant** that is the base point of displacement. *Point2* is a **Variant** that is the second point of displacement.

The following code prompts the user to select an object and then moves it the distance defined by a user-supplied base point and second point of displacement. Notice the use of the **Highlight** method to show which object is selected.

Figure 6-8.
Using the **Move**
method to move an
object.

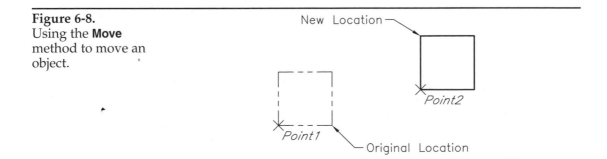

```
Sub Ch06_MoveObject()

    Dim objSelected As AcadObject
    Dim varPickPt As Variant
    Dim varPt1 As Variant
    Dim varPt2 As Variant

    ' Prompt the user to select an object.
    ThisDrawing.Utility.GetEntity objSelected, varPickPt, "Select object: "

    ' Highlight the object.
    objSelected.Highlight True

    ' Get the "from" point.
    varPt1 = ThisDrawing.Utility.GetPoint(, vbCrLf & "Base point: ")

    ' Get the "to" point.
    varPt2 = ThisDrawing.Utility.GetPoint(varPt1, vbCrLf & "Second" & _
        " point of displacement: ")

    ' Move the object.
    objSelected.Move varPt1, varPt2

    ' Unhighlight the object.
    objSelected.Highlight False

End Sub
```

Offsetting an Object

The **Offset** method creates a new object that is offset from an original by a specified distance. See **Figure 6-9.** The signature is:

ReturnVal = objSelected.Offset(*Distance*)

where *objSelected* is the selected drawing object. *Distance* is a **Double** data type that is the distance to offset the object. *ReturnVal* is a **Variant** that is the offset object.

Notice that the **Offset** method does not have a "side to offset" argument. Unlike offsetting an object with the AutoCAD **OFFSET** command, it is possible to specify a negative offset distance when using the **Offset** method. This is how the "side to offset" is determined. However, it is important to note that the "sides" are affected by how the entity is drawn. For example, assume you have drawn a vertical line from top to bottom. Specifying a negative offset distance offsets the line to the left while a positive offset distance offsets the line to the right. However, if the line is drawn from bottom to top, a negative distance offsets the line to the right and positive to the left.

Figure 6-9.
Offsetting an object
using the **Offset**
method.

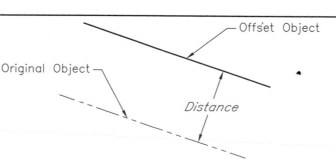

The following code prompts the user for an offset distance and the object to offset. The offset distance must be entered using the keyboard. Then, the object is offset the distance specified.

```
Sub Ch06_OffsetObject()

    Dim objSelected As AcadObject
    Dim varPickPt As Variant
    Dim dblDistance As Double

    ' Get the offset distance.
    dblDistance = ThisDrawing.Utility.GetReal(vbCrLf & "Offset distance: ")

    ' Prompt the user to select an object.
    ThisDrawing.Utility.GetEntity objSelected, varPickPt, "Select object: "

    ' Highlight the object.
    objSelected.Highlight True

    ' Offset the object.
    objSelected.Offset dblDistance

    ' Unhighlight the object.
    objSelected.Highlight False

End Sub
```

Rotating an Object

The **Rotate** method rotates an object around a center point at a specified angle. See **Figure 6-10.** The signature is:

objSelected.Rotate *BasePoint, RotationAngle*

where *objSelected* is the selected drawing object. *BasePoint* is a **Variant** that is the point about which the object is to be rotated. *RotationAngle* is a **Double** data type that is the angle, in radians, the object is to be rotated.

Figure 6-10.
Rotating an object using the **Rotate** method.

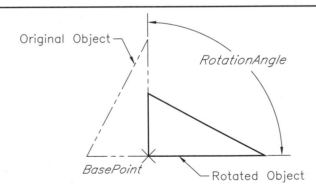

The following code prompts the user to select an object and then rotates it about a user-supplied base point the number of degrees specified by the user:

```
Sub Ch06_RotateObject()

    Dim objSelected As AcadObject
    Dim varPickPt As Variant
    Dim varBasePt As Variant
    Dim dblAngle As Double

    ' Prompt the user to select an object.
    ThisDrawing.Utility.GetEntity objSelected, varPickPt, "Select object: "

    ' Highlight the object.
    objSelected.Highlight True

    ' Get the base point.
    varBasePt = ThisDrawing.Utility.GetPoint(, vbCrLf & "Base point: ")

    ' Get the rotation angle.
    dblAngle = ThisDrawing.Utility.GetReal(vbCrLf & "Rotation angle: ")

    ' Convert to radians.
    dblAngle = dblAngle * 3.141592 / 180#

    ' Rotate the object.
    objSelected.Rotate varBasePt, dblAngle

    ' Unhighlight the object.
    objSelected.Highlight False

End Sub
```

Scaling an Object

The **ScaleEntity** method scales an object by a specified scale factor. See **Figure 6-11.** The signature is:

objSelected.**ScaleEntity** *BasePoint, ScaleFactor*

where *objSelected* is the selected drawing object. *BasePoint* is a **Variant** that is the base point of scaling. *ScaleFactor* is a **Double** data type that is the scale factor.

Figure 6-11.
Using the
ScaleEntity method
to scale an object.

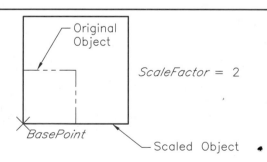

The following code prompts the user to select an object and then scales it by the user-supplied scale factor about a base point supplied by the user:

```
Sub Ch06_ScaleObject()

    Dim objSelected As AcadObject
    Dim varPickPt As Variant
    Dim varBasePt As Variant
    Dim dblScale As Double

    ' Prompt the user to select an object.
    ThisDrawing.Utility.GetEntity objSelected, varPickPt, "Select object: "

    ' Highlight the object.
    objSelected.Highlight True

    ' Get the base point.
    varBasePt = ThisDrawing.Utility.GetPoint(, vbCrLf & "Base point: ")

    ' Get the scale factor.
    dblScale = ThisDrawing.Utility.GetReal(vbCrLf & "Scale factor: ")

    ' Scale the object.
    objSelected.ScaleEntity varBasePt, dblScale

    ' Unhighlight the object.
    objSelected.Highlight False

End Sub
```

Exploding an Object

The **Explode** method explodes complex objects, like polylines or blocks, into their individual subobjects. It returns an array of the exploded objects. The signature is:

ReturnVal = *objSelected*.Explode

where *objSelected* is the selected drawing object. *ReturnVal* is a **Variant** that is the array of exploded objects.

The following code prompts the user to select an object, makes sure it is a complex object, and then explodes it:

```
Sub Ch06_ExplodeObject()

    Dim objSelected As AcadObject
    Dim varPickPt As Variant

    ' Prompt the user to select an object.
    ThisDrawing.Utility.GetEntity objSelected, varPickPt, "Select object: "

    ' Make sure the object is either a polyline or a block.
    If objSelected.ObjectName = "AcDbPolyline" or _
        objSelected.ObjectName = "AcDbBlockReference" Then

        ' Explode the object.
        objSelected.Explode

    Else

        ' Warn if the object is not a complex object.
        MsgBox "Not a complex object. Cannot explode!"

    End If

End Sub
```

Editing AutoCAD Objects Using Methods

- Because of a method's dynamic nature, you typically need to supply arguments to the method per its signature.
- The **ArrayRectangular** method copies an object to create a 2D or 3D rectangular array in rows, columns, and levels (in 3D).
- The **ArrayPolar** method copies an object to create a 2D polar array of objects rotated about a center point.
- The **Copy** method makes a copy of an object.
- Both the **Delete** method and the **Erase** method delete an object.
- The **Highlight** method highlights an object so it appears dashed in the AutoCAD drawing editor.
- The **Mirror** method mirrors an object about a line defined by two points.
- The **Move** method moves an object a specified distance.
- The **Offset** method offsets an object a specified distance.
- The **Rotate** method rotates an object around a center point at a specified angle.
- The **ScaleEntity** method scales an object a specified scale factor.
- The **Explode** method explodes complex objects, like polylines or blocks, into their subobjects.

Exercise 6-2

Create the macros described below. All macros should be created in the **ThisDrawing** module of your MyMacros.dvb project. Provide all necessary error checking and control. Run and test each macro.

1. Create a macro named ex06_GridLayout that can be used to create a grid column layout by prompting the user to select a column in a drawing and then array it based on a user-supplied number of rows and columns and the horizontal and vertical distance between them.

2. Create a macro named ex06_OffsetOnCurLayer that prompts a user to select any type of entity in a drawing and offset it a user-supplied distance. The new, offset entity resides on the currently active layer.

3. Create a macro named ex06_RotateCopy that prompts a user to select any type of entity in a drawing and rotate it a user-supplied angle while maintaining the original copy.

Chapter Test

Write your answers on a separate sheet of paper.

1. List five properties shared by all AutoCAD drawing objects.
2. List five methods shared by all AutoCAD drawing objects.
3. Explain the differences between editing an object using its properties versus editing an object using its methods.
4. What is the easiest way to determine an object's properties and methods and how they are used?
5. Which VBA operator is used to set an object property?
6. Describe how the VBA **Choose** function works.
7. Which AutoCAD Color Index (ACI) number is used to represent the ByLayer color property?
8. Which AutoCAD Color Index (ACI) number is used to represent the ByBlock color property?
9. Explain what it means when an object's **Color** property is set to ByLayer.
10. Explain what it means when an object's **Color** property is set to ByBlock.
11. What must be done before setting an object's **Layer** or **Linetype** property?
12. In which format are angles measured when working with VBA methods?
13. Explain why it is necessary to move an object after copying it using the **Copy** method.
14. List all of the methods that can be used to permanently remove an object from an AutoCAD drawing.
15. What effect does specifying a negative offset distance have when using the **Offset** method?

Programming Problems

Create the macros described below. All macros should be created in the **ThisDrawing** module of your MyMacros.dvb project. Provide all necessary error checking and error control. Run and test each macro.

1. Create a macro named p06_MakeByLayer that prompts a user to select any type of entity in a drawing and then changes the **Color**, **Layer**, and **Linetype** properties of that entity to ByLayer.
2. Create a macro named p06_UpCaseText that prompts a user to select a text entity in a drawing and then converts the entire text string to all uppercase letters. *Hint:* The VBA **UCase** function converts a text string to all uppercase letters.
3. Create a macro named p06_HoleLayout that arrays a circle based on a user-supplied distance and direction, axis center point, and number of circles desired.
4. Create a macro named p06_ChangeDwgScale that prompts the user to select any type of entity in a drawing and then scales that entity based on the current **DIMSCALE** system variable setting using the drawing origin (0,0,0) as the base point.

CHAPTER 7

Selection Sets

Learning Objectives

After completing this chapter, you will be able to create VBA macros that:

- Create a new selection set.
- Add entities to a selection set using the standard AutoCAD selection methods.
- Use selection set filters.
- Reference entities in a selection set.
- Iterate a selection set.
- Remove entities from a selection set.
- Control AutoCAD's selection mode (noun/verb or verb/noun).
- Retrieve an active selection set selected before a command is issued (noun/verb).

Selection Sets

One of the fundamental principles of editing entities in an AutoCAD drawing is that you must be able to select the entities you wish to modify. In AutoCAD, you can select one or more entities and then perform a command on all of the entities as a single unit. This concept is known as creating a *selection set.* There are several ways to create a selection set in AutoCAD. Some of the common entity selection methods include:

- Picking entities one at a time.
- Selecting multiple entities using a rectangular window or crossing selection.
- Selecting multiple entities using a polygonal window or crossing selection.
- Selecting multiple entities using a fence selection.
- Automatically selecting the last entity added to the drawing.
- Automatically selecting *all* of the entities in a drawing.

VBA provides all of these traditional entity selection methods, and then some, via the AutoCAD object model. All of the familiar selection methods that require user interaction are provided, as well as the ability to create selection set filters. Using *selection set filters* you can select multiple entities based on matching properties...with or *without* user interaction!

Many of the methods and functionality described in this chapter closely resemble the selection set functions provided in AutoLISP, in particular the AutoLISP **(ssget)** function and its DXF code filtering mechanisms. Comparisons are provided where applicable.

Using VBA to create selection set filters and all of the other traditional methods of selecting entities in an AutoCAD drawing are explained in detail in the following sections. First, however, we need to examine where selection sets "live" in the AutoCAD object model. You may be a little surprised.

Professional Tip

Refer to *AutoCAD and Its Applications—Basics*, published by The Goodheart-Willcox Co., Inc., or the AutoCAD online documentation for more information about creating selection sets in AutoCAD.

SelectionSets Collection

Selection sets are implemented as **SelectionSet** objects and are maintained in the **SelectionSets** object collection in the AutoCAD object model, **Figure 7-1.** Remember, VBA object collections allow you to organize and process a group of similar entities as a unit, similar to an array. Object collections and their usage are described in detail in Chapter 2.

Because the **SelectionSets** collection is an object collection, it can contain multiple **SelectionSet** objects with unique names. This means that you can manage multiple selection sets at one time using VBA. A **SelectionSet** object can be referenced by using either its unique name or its index in the collection.

The **SelectionSet** object itself is a group of one or more AutoCAD drawing entities that are treated as one unit. It is not a VBA collection in the pure sense of the word, rather it is closer to a VBA array. Accessing and iterating **SelectionSet** objects are discussed a little later in this chapter. But, before we do that, we first have to create a selection set.

Figure 7-1.
The **SelectionSets** collection contains the **SelectionSet** objects.

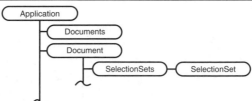

Creating a Selection Set

Unlike AutoLISP, VBA requires that you first create a selection set before you can add any entities to it. This is accomplished by adding a new **SelectionSet** object with a name of your choice to the **SelectionSets** collection. For more information about object collections, see Chapter 2.

To create a selection set, you must add a **SelectionSet** object with a unique name to the **SelectionSets** collection. The **Add** method adds a **SelectionSet** object with the specified name to the **SelectionSets** collection. Its signature is:

objSSet = SelectionSet.Add("*Name*")

where *objSSet* is the **SelectionSet** object and *Name* is a **String** that is the name of the selection set to add.

The following code adds a **SelectionSet** object named SS1 to the current drawing's **SelectionSets** collection:

```
Sub Ch07_CreateSelectionSet()

    Dim objSSet As AcadSelectionSet

    ' Create a new selection set.
    Set objSSet = ThisDrawing.SelectionSets.Add("SS1")

    ' Delete the selection set.
    objSSet.Delete

End Sub
```

Professional Tip

Because each **SelectionSet** object has a unique name, you must either delete it when you are done with it, as shown in the code example above, or you must be sure to use another unique name the next time you create a selection set using VBA. If you do not, you will get the error message shown in **Figure 7-2.**

Figure 7-2.
If you attempt to use a selection set name that already exists, this error message is displayed.

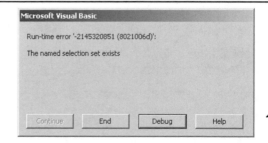

Microsoft Visual Basic

Run-time error '-2145320851 (8021006d)':

The named selection set exists

[Continue]   [End]   [Debug]   [Help]

Creating Selection Sets

- Selecting one or more AutoCAD entities in order to perform an operation on all of them as a single unit is known as creating a selection set.
- VBA provides a number of ways to select entities in a drawing via the AutoCAD object model that are very similar to their AutoLISP counterparts.
- Selection sets are implemented as **SelectionSet** objects, and are maintained in the **SelectionSets** collection in the AutoCAD object model.

Adding Entities to a Selection Set

Once a **SelectionSet** object is created, you can then add entities to it by using one of several methods—**AddItems**, **Select**, **SelectAtPoint**, **SelectByPolygon**, and **SelectOnScreen**. These methods are discussed in the next sections.

AddItems Method

The **AddItems** method allows you to add a predefined array of AutoCAD entities to a **SelectionSet** object. Its signature is:

objSSet.AddItems *Objects*

where *objSSet* is the **SelectionSet** object and *Objects* is a **Variant** that is the array of objects.

The following code adds all of the entities in model space to a selection set by iterating the **ModelSpace** collection:

```
Sub Ch07_AddToSelectionSet()

    Dim objSSet As AcadSelectionSet
    Dim objSelected As AcadObject
    Dim varPickPt As Variant
    Dim objSSetObjs() As AcadEntity
    Dim intCounter As Integer

    ' Create a new selection set.
    Set objSSet = ThisDrawing.SelectionSets.Add("SS1")

    ' Redimension the object array to the number of entities in model space.
    ReDim objSSetObjs(0 To ThisDrawing.ModelSpace.Count - 1)

    ' Step through all entities in model space and add them to the object array.
    For intCounter = 0 To ThisDrawing.ModelSpace.Count - 1

        ' Highlight the entity.
        ThisDrawing.ModelSpace.Item(intCounter).Highlight True

        ' Add the object to the object array.
        Set objSSetObjs(intCounter) = _
            ThisDrawing.ModelSpace.Item(intCounter)

    Next

    ' Add the object array to the selection set.
    objSSet.AddItems objSSetObjs

    ' Delete the selection set.
    ObjSSet.Delete

End Sub
```

Figure 7-3.
The selection types
for the **Select**
method.

Enum	Selection type
acSelectionSetWindow	Window selection.
acSelectionSetCrossing	Crossing selection.
acSelectionSetPrevious	Previous selection set.
acSelectionSetLast	Last object in the drawing.
acSelectionSetAll	All objects in the drawing.

[handwritten annotations: enclosed, touches, entity put in drawing]

Select Method

The **Select** method allows you to select entities in a drawing and add them to a **SelectionSet** object using one of the following AutoCAD selection methods:

- Window selection.
- Crossing selection.
- Previous selection set.
- Last object added to the drawing.
- All entities in drawing.

The signature for the **Select** method is:

objSSet.**Select** *Mode*[, *Point1*][, *Point2*][, *FilterType*][, *FilterData*]

where *objSSet* is the **SelectionSet** object. *Mode* is the **acSelect** enum that determines the selection method used. See **Figure 7-3.** *Point1* is a **Variant** that is the first coordinate point of a window. Its use is optional. *Point2* is a **Variant** that is the second coordinate point of a window. Its use is optional. *FilterType* is an **Integer** that is the DXF group code specifying filter type. Its use is optional. *FilterData* is a **Variant** that is the value to filter. Its use is optional.

The following code adds entities to a **SelectionSet** object based on a user-defined window. Notice the **acSelectionSetWindow** enum specified in the **Mode** argument. The selected entities are highlighted so the user can see which entities are included in the selection set.

```
Sub Ch07_SelectWindow()

    Dim objSSet As AcadSelectionSet
    Dim varPt1 As Variant
    Dim varPt2 As Variant

    ' Create a new selection set.
    Set objSSet = ThisDrawing.SelectionSets.Add("SS1")

    ' Get the first corner.
    varPt1 = ThisDrawing.Utility.GetPoint(, vbCrLf & "First corner: ")

    ' Get the second corner.
    varPt2 = ThisDrawing.Utility.GetCorner(varPt1, vbCrLf & "Opposite" & _
        " corner: ")

    ' Select the entities using a window.
    objSSet.Select acSelectionSetWindow, varPt1, varPt2

    ' Highlight the selection set.
    objSSet.Highlight True

    ' Delete the selection set.
    ObjSSet.Delete

End Sub
```

The following code, on the other hand, adds *all* of the entities in a drawing to a **SelectionSet** object. This is done by specifying the **acSelectionSetAll** enum in the **Mode** argument.

```
Sub Ch07_SelectAll()

    Dim objSSet As AcadSelectionSet

    ' Create a new selection set.
    Set objSSet = ThisDrawing.SelectionSets.Add("SS1")

    ' Select everything in the drawing.
    objSSet.Select acSelectionSetAll

    ' Highlight the selection set.
    objSSet.Highlight True

    ' Delete the selection set.
    ObjSSet.Delete

End Sub
```

Professional Tip

The **acSelectionSetAll** option is commonly used with the optional filter arguments to allow you to select entities in a drawing *without* user interaction based on an entity's properties.

SelectAtPoint Method

The **SelectAtPoint** method selects the last-drawn entity passing through a given point and adds it to a **SelectionSet** object. The signature for the **SelectAtPoint** method is:

objSSet.SelectAtPoint Point[, *FilterType*][, *FilterData*]

where *objSSet* is the **SelectionSet** object. *Point* is a **Variant** that is the coordinate point for the selection. *FilterType* is an **Integer** that is the DXF group code specifying the filter type. Its use is optional. *FilterData* is a **Variant** that is the value to filter. Its use is optional.

The following code adds the last entity drawn that passes through the point 0,0,0 to a **SelectionSet** object:

```
Sub Ch07_SelectAtPoint()

    Dim objSSet As AcadSelectionSet
    Dim dblPoint(0 To 2) As Double

    ' Create a new selection set.
    Set objSSet = ThisDrawing.SelectionSets.Add("SS1")

    ' Set the point to the origin @ 0,0,0.
    dblPoint(0) = 0#
    dblPoint(1) = 0#
    dblPoint(2) = 0#

    ' Select all entities that cross the origin.
    objSSet.SelectAtPoint dblPoint

    ' Highlight the selection set.
    objSSet.Highlight True

    ' Delete the selection set.
    ObjSSet.Delete

End Sub
```

Figure 7-4.
The selection types for the **SelectByPolygon** method.

Enum	Selection type
acSelectionSetFence	Fence selection.
acSelectionSetWindowPolygon	Polygon window selection.
acSelectionSetCrossingPolygon	Polygon crossing selection

SelectByPolygon Method

The **SelectByPolygon** method allows the user to select entities in a drawing using a fence, polygon window, or polygon crossing selection and adds the entities to a **SelectionSet** object. The signature is:

objSSet.SelectByPolygon *Mode, PointsList*[, *FilterType*][, *FilterData*]

where *objSSet* is the **SelectionSet** object. *Mode* is the **acSelect** enum that determines the selection method used. See **Figure 7-4.** *PointList* is a **Variant** that is an array of points defining a fence, window, or crossing boundary. *FilterType* is an **Integer** that is the DXF group code specifying the filter type. Its use is optional. *FilterData* is a **Variant** that is the value to filter. Its use is optional.

The following code adds entities to a **SelectionSet** object via a polygon window that is a predefined triangle. This is done by defining the points that form the triangle and specifying the **acSelectionSetWindowPolygon** enum in the **Mode** argument.

```
Sub Ch07_SelectByPolygon()

    Dim objSSet As AcadSelectionSet
    Dim dblPoints(0 To 8) As Double

    ' Create a new selection set.
    Set objSSet = ThisDrawing.SelectionSets.Add("SS1")

    ' Set the first point to the origin @ 0,0,0.
    dblPoints(0) = 0#
    dblPoints(1) = 0#
    dblPoints(2) = 0#

    ' Set the second point to 2,0,0.
    dblPoints(3) = 2#
    dblPoints(4) = 0#
    dblPoints(5) = 0#

    ' Set the third point to 1,1,0.
    dblPoints(6) = 1#
    dblPoints(7) = 1#
    dblPoints(8) = 0#

    ' Select all entities within the triangular window.
    objSSet.SelectByPolygon acSelectionSetWindowPolygon, dblPoints

    ' Highlight the selection set.
    objSSet.Highlight True

    ' Delete the selection set.
    ObjSSet.Delete

End Sub
```

SelectOnScreen Method

The **SelectOnScreen** method adds entities to a **SelectionSet** object by prompting a user to select entities on the screen. The signature is:

objSSet.SelectOnScreen [*FilterType*][, *FilterData*]

where *objSSet* is the **SelectionSet** object. *FilterType* is an **Integer** that is the DXF group code specifying the filter type. Its use is optional. *FilterData* is a **Variant** that is the value to filter. Its use is optional.

The following code prompts the user to select entities on the screen and adds the selected entities to a **SelectionSet** object. The user can continue selecting entities until the [Enter] key or spacebar is pressed.

```
Sub Ch07_SelectOnScreen()

    Dim objSSet As AcadSelectionSet

    ' Create a new selection set.
    Set objSSet = ThisDrawing.SelectionSets.Add("SS1")

    ' Prompt the user to select entities on screen.
    objSSet.SelectOnScreen

    ' Highlight the selection set.
    objSSet.Highlight True

    ' Delete the selection set.
    ObjSSet.Delete

End Sub
```

The **SelectOnScreen** method is a bit of a sleeper because it actually supports all of the selection methods available in the AutoCAD drawing editor without any additional code. The method simply asks the user to select entities using the standard Select objects: AutoCAD prompt. The user can then choose to use a window, crossing, fence, or any other standard selection method.

Using Selection Set Filters

As mentioned at the beginning of this chapter, selection set filters allow you to select entities based on their properties. In AutoCAD, selection set filters are implemented via the **QSELECT** command. This command is initiated by selecting **Quick Select...** in the **Tools** pull-down menu or typing QSELECT at the Command: prompt. When the **QSELECT** command is initiated, the dialog box shown in **Figure 7-5** is displayed. You can apply the equals (=), not equal to (<>), greater than (>), and less than (<) Boolean logic operators to further filter the selection.

DXF group codes are a numerical system used to represent different AutoCAD drawing entities and their properties. The codes are used to create Drawing eXchange Format (DXF) files from AutoCAD drawings. DXF files are a public, ASCII-text-based file format used to exchange drawing data with different CAD programs. For more information about DXF codes, see *Group Codes in Numerical Order* in the DXF Reference in the AutoCAD Developers Guide.

To create filters in VBA, the first thing you have to do is set up a pair of arrays that are dimensioned to exactly the same size, or number of items. The first array contains **Integer** values that represent the DXF group code numbers. See **Figure 7-6.** The second array contains **Variant** values that represent the value for the corresponding DXF code in the first array. Remember, their array indexes must be exactly the same! The following code selects all of the lines on the WALL layer and adds them to the current selection set:

Figure 7-5.
AutoCAD's **Quick Select** dialog box.

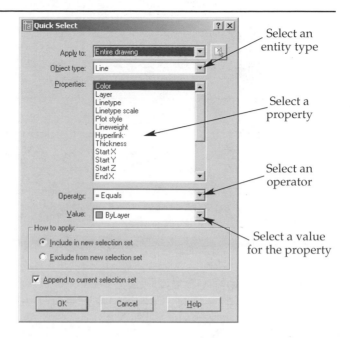

Select an entity type

Select a property

Select an operator

Select a value for the property

Figure 7-6.
Common DXF codes. For a comprehensive list, refer to *Group Codes in Numerical Order* in the AutoCAD online documentation.

DXF Code	Filter Type
0	String; AutoCAD entity type; Examples include: line, circle, text, mtext
6	String; Linetype; Examples include: Continuous Center Dashed Hidden
8	String; Layer; Examples include: 0, Defpoints *LAY*
62	Integer; Color number index; Index range: 1 to 256 (0 = ByBlock, 256 = Bylayer)

2   NAME; Attribute tag, block name,

```
Sub Ch07_SelectFilter()

    Dim objSSet As AcadSelectionSet
    Dim intDxfCode(0 To 1) As Integer
    Dim varDxfValue(0 To 1) As Variant

    ' Create a new selection set.
    Set objSSet = ThisDrawing.SelectionSets.Add("SS1")

    ' Set the entity DXF code to match the line entity type.
    intDxfCode(0) = 0
    varDxfValue(0) = "LINE"

    ' Set the layer DXF code to match the "WALL" layer name.
    intDxfCode(1) = 8
    varDxfValue(1) = "WALL"

    ' Select all lines on the WALL layer.
    objSSet.Select acSelectionSetAll, , , intDxfCode, varDxfValue

    ' Highlight the selection set.
    objSSet.Highlight True

    ' Delete the selection set.
    ObjSSet.Delete

End Sub
```

AutoLISP vs. VBA

Using AutoLISP, the same logic is implemented with the **(ssget)** function and DXF group codes. For example, the following AutoLISP code selects all of the lines on the WALL layer and adds them to the current selection set (just as the VBA code shown on the previous page):

```
(ssget "x" '((0 . "LINE")(8 . "WALL")))
```

In this example, 0 is the DXF code used to represent the object type and 8 is the DXF code used to represent the layer. Luckily, Autodesk implemented a very similar system in VBA. You can use the exact same DXF group code numbers and descriptions. The only difference in VBA is the data type used to store the DXF group code number and the data type used to store the description. The rest is exactly the same!

Let's Review...

Adding Entities to a Selection Set and Using Selection Set Filters

- VBA requires that you first create a **SelectionSet** object before you can add any entities to it.
- The **AddItemsMethod** adds a predefined array of AutoCAD entities to a **SelectionSet** object.
- The **Select** method allows you to select entities in a drawing and add them to a **SelectionSet** object using a window or crossing selection, the previous selection set, or all entities in the drawing.
- The **SelectAtPoint** method selects entities passing through a given point and adds them to a **SelectionSet** object.
- The **SelectByPolygon** method allows you to select entities in a drawing and add them to a **SelectionSet** object using the typical polygon window selection methods available in AutoCAD.
- The **SelectOnScreen** method prompts the user to select entities on the screen and then adds the entities to a **SelectionSet** object.
- The **SelectOnScreen** method supports all of the selection methods available in AutoCAD.
- Selection set filters can be used with any of the **SelectionSet** object's selection methods.

Accessing and Iterating a Selection Set

As mentioned earlier, a **SelectionSet** object is similar to a VBA array in that it is a group of one or more AutoCAD drawing entities that are treated as a unit. Because of this similarity, referencing individual entities in the **SelectionSet** object and iterating a **SelectionSet** object rely on the same techniques.

Referencing a SelectionSet Object

To reference an individual drawing entity in a **SelectionSet** object, simply specify the index number of the entity you wish to retrieve. **SelectionSet** objects are zero based, just like VBA arrays.

The following code returns a reference to the first entity in a selection set, highlights the entity, and changes its color property to red:

```
Sub Ch07_ReferenceSSet()

    Dim objSSet As AcadSelectionSet
    Dim objItem As AcadObject

    ' Create a new selection set.
    Set objSSet = ThisDrawing.SelectionSets.Add("SS1")

    ' Prompt the user to select entities on screen.
    objSSet.SelectOnScreen

    ' Change the color of the first item in the selection set to red.
    Set objItem = objSSet(0)
    objItem.Highlight True
    objItem.Color = acRed
    objItem.Update

    ' Delete the selection set so the same name can be used again.
    objSSet.Delete

End Sub
```

Iterating through a Selection Set

Iterating all of the drawing entities in a selection set can be done using the same techniques used to iterate an array. One of the easiest approaches is to use the VBA **For...Each** loop structure.

The following code prompts the user to create a selection set using the **SelectOnScreen** method. The macro then steps through each entity in the selection set, highlighting each and setting its color property to red:

```
Sub Ch07_IterateSSet()

    Dim objSSet As AcadSelectionSet
    Dim objItem As AcadObject

    ' Create a new selection set.
    Set objSSet = ThisDrawing.SelectionSets.Add("SS1")

    ' Prompt the user to select entities on screen.
    objSSet.SelectOnScreen

    ' Step through the selection set
    ' and change the color of each entity to red.
    For Each objItem In objSSet
        objItem.Highlight True
        objItem.Color = acRed
        objItem.Update
    Next objItem

    ' Delete the selection set so the
    ' same name can be used again.
    objSSet.Delete

End Sub
```

Determining How Many Entities Are in a Selection Set

Sometimes it is necessary to determine how many entities are in a selection set. The **Count** property is used to keep track of how many entities are in a **SelectionSet** object.

The following code prompts the user to create a selection set using the **SelectOnScreen** method, checks the **SelectionSet** object's **Count** property, and then informs the user how many entities were selected:

```
Sub Ch07_CountSSet()

    Dim objSSet As AcadSelectionSet
    Dim objItem As AcadObject

    ' Create a new selection set.
    Set objSSet = ThisDrawing.SelectionSets.Add("SS1")

    ' Prompt the user to select entities on screen.
    objSSet.SelectOnScreen

    ' Determine how many entities have been selected and tell the user.
    If objSSet.Count > 0 Then

        ' Display the number of entities selected.
        MsgBox "The current selection set contains " & objSSet.Count & " entities."

    Else

        ' Nothing selected.
        MsgBox "Nothing selected."

    End If

    ' Delete the selection set so the same
    ' name can be used again.
    objSSet.Delete

End Sub
```

Removing Entities from a Selection Set

There are three different methods that can be used to remove entities from a selection set. These methods are explained in the following sections.

Clear Method

The **Clear** method empties a selection set. This method does not delete the **SelectionSet** object, but the object will no longer contain any drawing entities. The entities that were in the selection set still exist in the AutoCAD drawing, they are just no longer part of the **SelectionSet** object. The signature for the **Clear** method is:

objSSet.Clear

where *objSSet* is the **SelectionSet** object.

The following code prompts the user to create a selection set by selecting entities on screen and then changes the color property of all entities in the selection set to red. The **SelectionSet** object is then cleared and used again. The user is prompted to create a different selection set and then changes the color property of all entities in the selection set to blue.

```
Sub Ch07_ClearSSet()

    Dim objSSet As AcadSelectionSet
    Dim objItem As AcadObject

    ' Create a new selection set.
    Set objSSet = ThisDrawing.SelectionSets.Add("SS1")

    ' Prompt the user to select entities on screen.
    objSSet.SelectOnScreen

    ' Step through the selection set and change
    ' each entity's color to red.
    For Each objItem In objSSet
        objItem.Highlight True
        objItem.Color = acRed
        objItem.Update
    Next objItem

    ' Clear the selection set.
    objSSet.Clear

    ' Use the same SelectionSet object to select more entities.
    objSSet.SelectOnScreen

    ' Step through the selection set and change each entity's color to blue.
    For Each objItem In objSSet
        objItem.Highlight True
        objItem.Color = acBlue
        objItem.Update
    Next objItem

    ' Delete the selection set.
    objSSet.Delete

    ' Regen the drawing.
    ThisDrawing.Regen acActiveViewport

End Sub
```

Erase Method

The **Erase** method clears all entities from a **SelectionSet** object *and* erases those entities from the current drawing. The **SelectionSet** object still exists and can be used again. The signature for the **Erase** method is:

objSSet.Erase

where *objSSet* is the **SelectionSet** object.

The following code prompts the user to create a selection set by picking the entities on screen and then permanently erases all of the selected entities from both the selection set and the current drawing:

```
Sub Ch07_EraseSSet()

    Dim objSSet As AcadSelectionSet
    Dim objItem As AcadObject

    ' Create a new selection set.
    Set objSSet = ThisDrawing.SelectionSets.Add("SS1")

    ' Prompt the user to select entities on screen.
    objSSet.SelectOnScreen

    ' Erase all entities in the selection set.
    objSSet.Erase

    ' Delete the selection set so the
    ' same name can be used again.
    objSSet.Delete

End Sub
```

RemoveItems Method

The **RemoveItems** method removes one or more entities from a selection set. The removed entities still exist in the drawing, but they no longer reside in the **SelectionSet** object. The signature is:

objSSet.RemoveItems *Objects*

where *objSSet* is the **SelectionSet** object and *Objects* is a **Variant** that is an array of the entities to be removed.

The following code prompts the user to create a selection set by picking entities on screen and then highlights all of the selected entities. The user is then prompted to select an entity to remove from the selection set using the **GetEntity** method introduced in Chapter 4. The entity is removed using the **RemoveItems** method and then the color of the remaining entities is changed to red.

```
Sub Ch07_RemoveItems()

    Dim objSSet As AcadSelectionSet
    Dim objRemove(0) As AcadObject
    Dim objItem As AcadObject
    Dim varPickPt As Variant

    ' Create a new selection set.
    Set objSSet = ThisDrawing.SelectionSets.Add("SS1")

    ' Prompt the user to select entities on screen.
    objSSet.SelectOnScreen

    ' Highlight the selection set.
    objSSet.Highlight True

    ' Prompt the user to select an entity to remove from
    ' the selection set and places the entity in an array.
    ThisDrawing.Utility.GetEntity objRemove(0), varPickPt, "Select object to remove: "

    ' Remove the entity from the selection set.
    objSSet.RemoveItems objRemove

    ' Step through the selection set and change each entity's color to red.
    For Each objItem In objSSet
        objItem.Highlight True
        objItem.Color = acRed
        objItem.Update
    Next objItem

    ' Delete the selection set so the same name can be used again.
    objSSet.Delete

    ' Regen the drawing.
    ThisDrawing.Regen acActiveViewport

End Sub
```

Controlling the Selection Mode

When working in the AutoCAD drawing editor, there are two different types of selection modes:

- **Verb-noun.** This is where you enter a command then select the entities to modify.
- **Noun-verb.** In this method, you can first select entities and then enter the modify command.

Basically, "noun" refers to the selected drawing entities, or selection set, and "verb" is the command. The user gets to have it both ways, so to speak. AutoCAD provides everything for everyone, remember?

While great for the user, having two selection modes makes the job of a programmer a little harder. Fortunately, Autodesk has provided some unique ways to deal with both modes in VBA. We have already seen how to work with selection sets using the traditional "verb-noun" selection mode. The next two sections show you how to deal with selection sets via the "noun-verb" selection mode.

PickFirst Property

In Chapter 4, you learned how to control the selection process via the **PickFirst** property found in the **Preferences** object. Just as a refresher, the following code enables the noun-verb selection mode by setting the **PickFirst** property to **True**:

```
ThisDrawing.Application.Preferences.Selection.PickFirst = True
```

The **PickFirst** property and the noun-verb selection mode are enabled by default in AutoCAD.

PickfirstSelectionSet Property

The **PickfirstSelectionSet** property allows you to retrieve an active selection set when the noun-verb selection process is enabled. The best part is that you do not even have to create a new, named **SelectionSet** object first. The object is created for you automatically. A new **SelectionSet** object named **PICKFIRST** is returned regardless of whether or not any entities are selected. All you have to do is check the **PICKFIRST** object's **Count** property. If it is greater than 0, a selection set exists!

The following code gets a selection set via the **PickfirstSelectionSet** property. Then, it determines if anything was selected by checking to see if the selection set's **Count** property is greater than 0. If there are any entities in the selection set, the **SelectionSet** object is iterated and each entity's **Color** property is set to red. Note: Open the **Visual Basic Editor**, select the entity in AutoCAD, switch to the **Visual Basic Editor** ([Alt][Tab]), and then run the macro. Otherwise, the selection set is canceled when the macro is run from inside AutoCAD.

```
Sub Ch07_PickfirstSSet()

    Dim objSSet As AcadSelectionSet
    Dim objItem As AcadObject

    ' Get the current selection set.
    Set objSSet = ThisDrawing.PickfirstSelectionSet

    ' See if anything is selected by checking if the
    ' Count property is greater than 0.
    If objSSet.Count > 0 Then

        ' Step through the selection set and
        ' change each entity's color to red.
        For Each objItem In objSSet
            objItem.Color = acRed
            objItem.Update
        Next objItem

    Else

        ' Tell the user nothing is selected.
        MsgBox "Nothing selected."

    End If

    ' Delete the selection set.
    objSSet.Delete

End Sub
```

VBA has another property called **ActiveSelectionSet** that returns the currently selected objects. However, it will also return objects that are not currently selected (highlighted), but are part of the last selection set used. This property may be an alternative to the **PickfirstSelectionSet** property.

Professional Tip

It is possible to know when a "pick first" selection set changes via the **SelectionChanged** event, which is at the document level. Whenever a user adds or removes an entity from an active selection set the **SelectionChanged** reactor is fired. This allows you to create code that will run when a "pick first" selection set changes. Refer to Chapter 15 for more information about document-level events and reactor-based code.

Accessing and Iterating Selection Sets, Removing Entities from Selection Sets, and Controlling the Selection Mode

Let's Review...

- To reference an individual drawing entity in a **SelectionSet** object, simply specify the index number of the entity you wish to retrieve. This is similar to referencing an item in an array.
- Iterating all of the drawing entities in a selection set can be done using the same techniques used to iterate an array.
- The **Count** property keeps track of how many entities are in a **SelectionSet** object.
- The **Clear** method empties a selection set.
- The **Erase** method erases all entities in a selection set from the current drawing and removes them from the **SelectionSet** object.
- The **RemoveItems** method removes one or more entities from a selection set.
- The **Application.Preferences.Selection.PickFirst** property controls the noun-verb and verb-noun selection processes. If it is set to **True**, noun-verb selection is possible.
- The **ThisDrawing.PickfirstSelectionSet** property allows you to retrieve an active selection set when the noun-verb selection process is enabled.

Chapter Test

Write your answers on a separate sheet of paper.

1. What is a *selection set* and how is it used?
2. List five ways to create a selection set in AutoCAD.
3. How are selection sets implemented in the AutoCAD object model?
4. Why is it important to use a unique name when creating a VBA selection set?
5. Which **SelectionSet** method allows you to select all entities in a drawing?
6. Which **SelectionSet** method supports all of the selection methods available in the AutoCAD drawing editor without any additional code?
7. Explain *selection set filters* and how they are used.
8. List and describe three DXF codes common to all drawing entities.
9. How do you iterate all entities contained within a selection set?
10. Which **SelectionSet** property indicates how many entities are in a selection set?
11. Explain the differences between the **SelectionSet Clear** and **Erase** methods.
12. List the two different selection modes in AutoCAD and describe how each mode works.
13. Which object and property are used to control the different selection modes?
14. What is *always* the name of the selection set stored in the **ThisDrawing.PickfirstSelectionSet** property?

Programming Problems

Create the macros described below. All macros should be created in the **ThisDrawing** module of your MyMacros.dvb project. Provide all necessary error checking and control. Run and test each macro.

1. Create a macro named p07_MakeAllByLayer that changes the **Color**, **Layer**, and **Linetype** properties of *all* entities in a drawing to ByLayer.
2. Create a macro named p07_UpCaseAllText that converts every text string in a drawing to uppercase. *Hint:* The VBA **UCase** function converts a text string to all uppercase letters.
3. Create a macro named p07_ScaleAllText that scales all text in a drawing by the current **DIMSCALE** system variable setting.
4. Create a macro named p07_ChangeAllRads that changes the radius of all circles in a drawing to a user-supplied radius.

CHAPTER 8

Layers and Linetypes

Learning Objectives

After completing this chapter, you will be able to create VBA macros that:

- Reference an existing layer.
- Iterate through all layers in a drawing.
- Create a layer.
- Make a layer current.
- Rename a layer.
- Control layer properties (on/off, freeze/thaw, lock/unlock, color, linetype, and lineweight).
- Delete a layer.
- Reference a loaded linetype description.
- Iterate through all linetypes in a drawing.
- Load a linetype.
- Make a linetype current.
- Rename a linetype.
- Change a linetype's description.
- Set the global linetype scale.
- Set an individual drawing entity's linetype scale.
- Delete a linetype.

Layers

One of the most important properties an AutoCAD drawing entity has is its **Layer** property. Layers are the primary way that drawing entities are organized in an AutoCAD drawing.

The concept of using layers to organize drawing information is based on how drafting was done in the "old days." A process referred to as *pin-board drafting* allowed drafters to overlay multiple drawings created on transparent vellum that had prepunched holes on the edges of the sheet. The drafter aligned the drawings using a series of pins, or pegs, that protruded from the perimeter of the drafting table. This allowed multiple people to work on different aspects of a drawing while coordinating their work with other team members. For instance, an architect might have been working on the architectural features (walls, doors, windows) of a floor plan while the electrical engineer added the electrical wiring and fixtures. At the same time, a structural engineer might have been laying out the structural building grid. The drawing created by each individual would then be overlaid to produce the complete floor plan, as shown in **Figure 8-1.**

In AutoCAD, this concept is emulated by grouping entities on different layers. The layers are usually given descriptive names based on what information they represent in the drawing. For instance, in the example shown in **Figure 8-1** all lines that represent walls might be put on a layer named WALL. Using this technique, you can then isolate and control the following aspects of an entity's appearance:

- Visibility (on/off or freeze/thaw).
- Color.
- Protection (locked/unlocked).
- Linetype.
- Lineweight.
- Plot style.
- Plotted/not plotted.

The major advantage here is that you can use layers to group similar entities, thus recreating in the digital world the pin-based drafting techniques from the "ancient" analog past.

The drawing named Wilhome.dwg located in the AutoCAD sample folder provides a good example of using layers to organize drawing information. First, open the drawing in AutoCAD. Then, display the **Layers Properties Manager** dialog box by picking the **Layer Properties Manager** button on the **Layers** toolbar.

As you can see in **Figure 8-2,** the drawing contains many different layers. Each of these layers contains specific entities in the drawing that relate to what the layer represents, which is usually indicated by the layer name itself. For instance, linework and text that indicate an appliance reside on the AR APPLIANCE layer. In this way, you can control the appearance of all the "appliances" in the drawing by simply setting the different layer properties listed.

Figure 8-1.
AutoCAD layers can be thought of as transparent drawing sheets. When all sheets are overlaid (all layers visible), all entities appear in their correct positions.

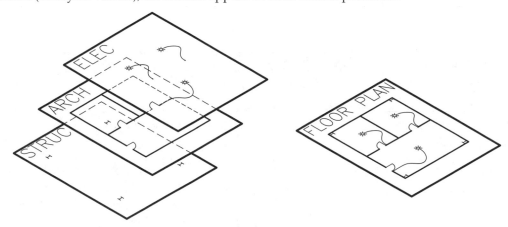

Figure 8-2.
The **Layer Properties Manager** dialog box shows all of the layers in the drawing, in this case the Wilhome.dwg sample supplied with AutoCAD.

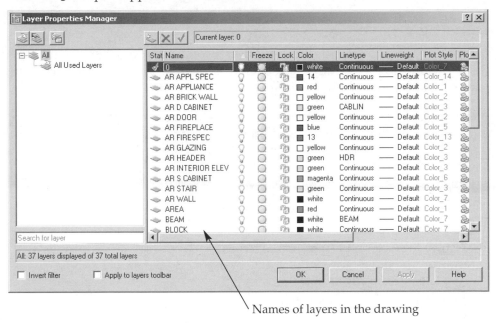

Names of layers in the drawing

Professional Tip

In order to use layers to control the appearance of individual drawing entities, the properties you wish to control must be set to ByLayer. This special property indicates that the entity should rely on the properties of the layer to which it is assigned. The following properties can be set to ByLayer:

- Color
- Linetype
- Lineweight

Setting these properties to anything other than ByLayer is considered overriding the layer properties and is typically discouraged. By default, all three properties are set to ByLayer when an AutoCAD drawing entity is created using an "add" method. See Chapter 5 for more information about creating AutoCAD entities.

Layers Collection

In the AutoCAD object model, each layer in a drawing is represented by a **Layer** object that is part of the drawing's **Layers** collection. Object collections and their usage are discussed in Chapter 2. The following sections show you how to manage a drawing's **Layers** collection and its **Layer** objects so you can:

- Reference an existing layer in a drawing.
- Iterate through all the layers in a drawing.
- Create a new layer.
- Make a layer current.

- Rename a layer.
- Control all of a layer's properties (on/off, freeze/thaw, etc.).
- Delete a layer.

Referencing a Layer

You can get a reference to an existing **Layer** object by either specifying the index number in the **Layers** collection or by specifying the layer name. Specifying the name is the preferred method when working with named objects, like layers.

The following code creates a reference to the WALL **Layer** object in the **Layers** collection and displays the layer's color and linetype to the user:

```
Sub Ch08_GetLayer1()

    Dim objLayer As AcadLayer

    ' Get the WALL layer from the Layers collection.
    Set objLayer = ThisDrawing.Layers.Item("WALL")

    ' Display the Color and Linetype properties.
    MsgBox "The properties for the WALL layer are:" & vbLf & vbLf & _
        "Color: " & objLayer.Color & vbLf & _
        "Linetype: " & objLayer.Linetype

End Sub
```

If the **Layer** object named WALL does not exist, the error message shown in **Figure 8-3** is displayed. The easiest way to deal with this situation is to add some simple error handling code:

```
Sub Ch08_GetLayer2()

    Dim objLayer As AcadLayer

    On Error GoTo NOTFOUND:

    ' Get the WALL layer from the Layers collection.
    Set objLayer = ThisDrawing.Layers.Item("WALL")

    ' Display the Color and Linetype properties.
    MsgBox "The properties for the WALL layer are:" & vbLf & vbLf & _
        "Color: " & objLayer.Color & vbLf & _
        "Linetype: " & objLayer.Linetype

    Exit Sub

NOTFOUND:

    ' The layer WALL does not exist.
    MsgBox "WALL layer not found."

End Sub
```

Figure 8-3.
If the layer name does not exist, this error is generated.

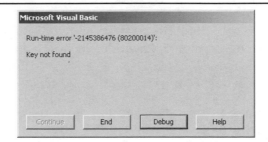

Figure 8-4.
By adding error
checking and
correction, you can
inform the user that the
layer does not exist.
This prevents the user
from seeing a VBA
error message.

Now if the WALL layer is not found, VBA generates the same error, but macro execution jumps to the NOTFOUND code block and displays a message box informing the user the layer was not found. See **Figure 8-4.**

Iterating the Layers Collection

You can step through all of the layers in a drawing by using a **For Each...** loop to iterate the **Layers** collection. This type of approach was first introduced in Chapter 2 and can be used to iterate any of the named symbol table collections.

The following code iterates the **Layers** collection and displays a list of all the layer names in the current drawing:

```
Sub Ch08_IterateLayers()

    Dim strLayers As String
    Dim objLayer As AcadLayer

    ' Initialize string.
    strLayers = ""

    ' Step through all layers in the drawing.
    For Each objLayer In ThisDrawing.Layers
    strLayers = strLayers & objLayer.Name & vbCrLf
    Next

    ' Display the layers to the user.
    MsgBox "Layers defined in current drawing: " & vbCrLf & vbCrLf & _
        strLayers

End Sub
```

Creating a New Layer

To create a new layer using VBA and the AutoCAD object model you simply need to add a new **Layer** object with the desired name to the **Layers** collection. After the object is added, you can get a reference to it using the methods described earlier. Once you have a reference to the new **Layer** object, you can set any of its properties or use any of its methods, as shown in the following sections.

The **Add** method adds a **Layer** object with the specified name to the **Layers** collection. If the layer name exists, it is ignored. The signature for the **Add** method is:

objLayer = Layers.Add(*Name*)

where *objLayer* is the **Layer** object and *Name* is a **String** that is the name of the layer to add.

The following code adds a layer named WALL to the current drawing:

```
Sub Ch08_AddLayer1()

    ' Add the layer WALL to the drawing.
    ThisDrawing.Layers.Add "WALL"

    ' Display to the user.
    MsgBox "Layer WALL added to drawing"

End Sub
```

Remember, if you plan on immediately setting any properties of the new **Layer** object or using any of its methods, you must return a reference to the object at the same time you add it to the collection by using the VBA **Set** statement. The following code adds the layer WALL to the drawing and changes the layer's color to red:

```
Sub Ch08_AddLayer2()

    Dim objLayer As AcadLayer

    ' Add the layer WALL to the Layers collection.
    Set objLayer = ThisDrawing.Layers.Add("WALL")

    ' Display to the user.
    MsgBox "Layer WALL added to drawing"

    ' Set the layer color to red.
    objLayer.Color = acRed

    ' Tell the user.
    MsgBox "WALL layer color set to red."

End Sub
```

Making a Layer Current

To ensure that new entities drawn in AutoCAD reside on the correct layer, you must first make the layer current. Using VBA, the current layer is controlled via the **ActiveLayer** property of the **ThisDrawing** object. In order to make a layer current, the **ActiveLayer** property must be set to an existing **Layer** object, not just a layer name. This requires first getting a reference to the **Layer** object from the **Layers** collection and then assigning it to the **ActiveLayer** property.

The following code adds the layer WALL to the drawing, gets a reference to the WALL **Layer** object, and then makes that layer current via the **ActiveLayer** property:

```
Sub Ch08_ActiveLayer()

    Dim objLayer As AcadLayer

    ' Add the layer WALL to the drawing.
    Set objLayer = ThisDrawing.Layers.Add("WALL")

    ' Make the layer WALL current.
    ThisDrawing.ActiveLayer = objLayer

    ' Tell the user.
    MsgBox "Layer WALL added to drawing and is now current."

End Sub
```

Renaming a Layer

You can rename a layer by getting a reference to the desired **Layer** object and then simply changing its **Name** property to the new name.

The following code changes a layer's name from WALL to A-WALL. A run-time error is generated if the layer WALL does not exist.

```
Sub Ch08_LayerRename()

    Dim objLayer As AcadLayer

    ' Get the layer WALL from the Layers collection.
    Set objLayer = ThisDrawing.Layers.Item("WALL")

    ' Rename the layer to A-WALL.
    objLayer.Name = "A-WALL"

    ' Tell the user.
    MsgBox "Layer WALL renamed to A-WALL"

End Sub
```

Layer Visibility

Layer visibility in a drawing is controlled by two different aspects of layer management. A layer can be turned on or off. A layer can also be thawed or frozen. Each of these aspects is controlled by a layer property setting in VBA and has a different effect on drawing entities.

Entities on layers that are turned off are not visible in a drawing, but are still included in any drawing display regeneration. The entities can also be selected via the **All** selection method and modified. Turning a layer back on makes entities on that layer reappear instantly.

On the other hand, entities on frozen layers are temporarily removed from any drawing calculations, like display regeneration. They also cannot be accessed via any selection process, including AutoLISP and VBA! Entities on frozen layers are protected from any modify commands.

LayerOn Property

The **LayerOn** property is a **Boolean** switch that controls the on/off visibility of entities on the specified layer. Its value can be set to either **True** (on) or **False** (off).

The following code displays the status of the WALL layer's **LayerOn** property and then toggles it to the opposite setting using the VBA **Not** operator:

```
Sub Ch08_LayerOn()

    Dim objLayer As AcadLayer

    ' Get the layer WALL from the Layers collection.
    Set objLayer = ThisDrawing.Layers.Item("WALL")

    ' Display the current on/off status.
    GoSub SHOWSTATUS

    ' Toggle the on/off property.
    objLayer.LayerOn = Not (objLayer.LayerOn)

    ' Display the new on/off status.
    GoSub SHOWSTATUS

    Exit Sub

' Display the on/off status.
SHOWSTATUS:

    If objLayer.LayerOn Then
        MsgBox "Layer """ & objLayer.Name & """ is now on."
    Else
        MsgBox "Layer """ & objLayer.Name & """ is now off."
    End If

    ' Return to the calling Sub.
    Return

End Sub
```

Notice the use of the **Not** logical operator. This operator returns **True** if a **Boolean** value is **False**, and **False** if a **Boolean** value is **True**. Because of this, the **Not** logical operator can be used to quickly toggle a layer on and off by simply switching the current value of the **Layer** object's **LayerOn** property. If the **LayerOn** property is **True**, the property is set to **False** so the layer is turned off. If the **LayerOn** property is **False**, the property is set to **True** so the layer is turned on.

Professional Tip

The VBA **GoSub...Return** statement branches to and returns from a subroutine within a procedure. This allows you to encapsulate code that is used more than once in a procedure and call it multiple times. In the example above, the SHOWSTATUS code block is called twice to display the current layer on/off status.

Freeze Property

The **Freeze** property is a **Boolean** switch that controls the freeze/thaw visibility of entities on the specified layer, but it also controls whether or not the entities are included in calculations or selection sets. Its value can be set to either **True** (frozen) or **False** (thawed).

The following code displays the status of the WALL layer's **Freeze** property and then toggles it to the opposite setting using the VBA **Not** operator:

```
Sub Ch08_LayerFreeze()

    Dim objLayer As AcadLayer

    ' Get the layer WALL from the Layers collection.
    Set objLayer = ThisDrawing.Layers.Item("WALL")

    ' Display the current freeze/thaw status.
    GoSub SHOWSTATUS

    ' Toggle the freeze/thaw property.
    objLayer.Freeze = Not (objLayer. Freeze)

    ' Display the new freeze/thaw status.
    GoSub SHOWSTATUS

    Exit Sub

' Display the freeze/thaw status.
SHOWSTATUS:

    If objLayer. Freeze Then
        MsgBox "Layer """ & objLayer.Name & """ is now frozen."
    Else
        MsgBox "Layer """ & objLayer.Name & """ is now thawed."
    End If

    ' Return to the calling Sub.
    Return

End Sub
```

If the layer WALL is current, a run-time error is generated because the current layer cannot be frozen.

Locking and Unlocking a Layer

A layer's **Lock** property allows you to protect entities on a specific layer from being modified *without* affecting entity visibility. When a layer is frozen, the entities contained on that layer are not visible. Locking a layer gives you the protection provided by freezing a layer while allowing any entities on the locked layer to be referenced on the screen.

The **Lock** property is a **Boolean** switch that locks or unlocks entities on the specified layer. Its value can be set to either **True** (locked) or **False** (unlocked).

The following code displays the status of the WALL layer's **Lock** property and then toggles it to the opposite setting using the VBA **Not** operator:

```
Sub Ch08_LayerLock()

    Dim objLayer As AcadLayer

    ' Get the layer WALL from the Layers collection.
    Set objLayer = ThisDrawing.Layers.Item("WALL")

    ' Display the current lock/unlock status.
    GoSub SHOWSTATUS

    ' Toggle the lock/unlock property.
    objLayer.Lock = Not (objLayer.Lock)

    ' Display the new lock/unlock status.
    GoSub SHOWSTATUS

    Exit Sub

' Display the lock/unlock status.
SHOWSTATUS:

    If objLayer.Lock Then
        MsgBox "Layer """ & objLayer.Name & """ is now locked."
    Else
        MsgBox "Layer """ & objLayer.Name & """ is now unlocked."
    End If

    ' Return to the calling Sub.
    Return

End Sub
```

Controlling a Layer's Color

A layer's **Color** property controls the color assigned to a layer and, by default, all entities that reside on that layer. Remember, each entity's individual **Color** property must be set to ByLayer in order for the layer to control entity color.

When the layer controls the color of entities, you can use layers to separate different drawing features and even systems. For instance, lines representing architectural features might be drawn on a layer named ARCH that is assigned the color red. On the other hand, lines representing electrical features might be drawn on a layer named ELEC that is assigned the color green. In this way, it is easy to see what each line represents in a drawing. Refer to **Figure 8-1.**

Colors are also used in AutoCAD to control lineweights when a drawing is plotted. This is achieved by mapping each color in a drawing to a particular plotter pen that has a certain line thickness. This mapping is typically managed using color-based plot style tables (CTB) that maintain the relationship between a plotter's pen numbers and the AutoCAD Color Index (ACI). For example:

- ACI number 1 (red) = plotter pen 1.
- ACI number 2 (yellow) = plotter pen 2.
- ACI number 3 (green) = plotter pen 3.

The plotter's "virtual" pens can then be set to print at the specified line thickness. For example:

- Pen 1 = 0.35 mm.
- Pen 2 = 0.50 mm.
- Pen 3 = 0.70 mm.

Therefore, an entity with a yellow display color will be plotted with a 0.50 mm line thickness. Confusing, is it not? This approach is used mostly for the sake of legacy. It is now possible to assign lineweights directly to a layer in AutoCAD and skip all of this mapping. See the section later in this chapter that discusses the **Lineweight** property for more information.

The **Color** property controls which color is assigned to a layer. Remember, there are 255 colors in the ACI, the first seven of which are represented by the following VBA constants:

```
acRed = 1
acYellow = 2
acGreen = 3
acCyan = 4
acBlue = 5
acMagenta = 6
acWhite = 7
```

The following code sets the WALL layer's **Color** property to cyan via the **acCyan** constant:

```
Sub Ch08_LayerColor()

    Dim objLayer As AcadLayer

    ' Get the layer WALL from the Layers collection.
    Set objLayer = ThisDrawing.Layers.Item("WALL")

    ' Change the layer color to cyan.
    objLayer.Color = acCyan

    ' Display the color and linetype properties.
    MsgBox "The properties for the WALL layer are:" & vbLf & vbLf & _
        "Color: " & objLayer.Color & vbLf & _
        "Linetype: " & objLayer.Linetype

End Sub
```

Professional Tip

Color-based plot style tables are only one approach to managing lineweights at plot time; there are other approaches. For more information, refer to the section Create Layouts and Plotting in AutoCAD's online documentation. Using VBA to manage layouts and plotting is discussed in detail in Chapter 12.

Controlling a Layer's Linetype

A layer's **Linetype** property controls which linetype is assigned to the layer. See the section Linetypes later in this chapter for a detailed description of linetypes, including how they are defined and managed in a drawing. A linetype must first be "loaded" into a drawing before it can be assigned. See the section Loading a Linetype later in this chapter to learn how to load a linetype using VBA.

The following code checks to see if the HIDDEN linetype is loaded and, if so, assigns it to the WALL layer's **Linetype** property. If the HIDDEN linetype is not loaded, the line-type is unchanged.

```
Sub Ch08_LayerLinetype()

    Dim objLayer As AcadLayer
    Dim objLinetype As AcadLineType

    ' Get the layer WALL from the Layers collection.
    Set objLayer = ThisDrawing.Layers.Item("WALL")

    ' Check to see if the linetype is loaded before assigning it.
    For Each objLinetype In ThisDrawing.Linetypes

        If StrComp(objLinetype.Name, "HIDDEN", 1) = 0 Then

            ' Change the layer's linetype to HIDDEN.
            objLayer.Linetype = "HIDDEN"

            Exit For

        End If

    Next

    ' Display the color and linetype properties.
    MsgBox "The properties for the WALL layer are:" & vbLf & vbLf & _
        "Color: " & objLayer.Color & vbLf & _
        "Linetype: " & objLayer.Linetype

End Sub
```

Controlling a Layer's Lineweight

Graphic lineweights were introduced to AutoCAD in Release 2000, thus making it possible to assign line thickness to entities that are visible on the screen. Prior to the advent of lineweights in AutoCAD, line thickness was controlled only at plot time by mapping an entity's color to a plotter pen thickness using a variety of means. See Chapter 12 for detailed information about plotting with VBA.

Now, you can assign a line thickness to an individual drawing entity via the **Properties** window in the AutoCAD drawing editor. A line thickness can also be assigned to a layer using the **Lineweight** dialog box shown in **Figure 8-5,** which is accessed through the **Layer Properties Manager**. Then, any drawing entity that has its lineweight assigned "by layer" will inherit the lineweight of the layer on which the entity resides.

The VBA **Lineweight** property controls the lineweight assigned to a layer. By default, a layer's lineweight is set to Default. This simply means that lines and circles appear at the default constant thickness of 0.025 mm. This thickness is displayed as approximately one pixel in model space, if AutoCAD is set to display lineweights, and plots at the thinnest lineweight available on the specified plotting device.

Using VBA, the **Lineweight** property can only be set using values that are in increments of hundredths of a millimeter. Autodesk provides the VBA constants shown in **Figure 8-6** to help facilitate the process.

Figure 8-5.
The **Lineweight Settings** dialog box.

Select a lineweight for the layer

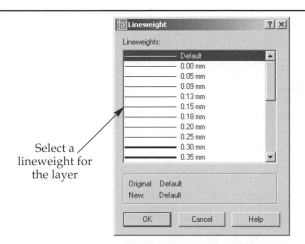

Figure 8-6.
The VBA lineweight constants.

VBA Constant	Lineweight
acLnWtByLwDefault	Default
acLnWtByLayer	ByLayer
acLnWtByBlock	ByBlock
acLnWt000	0.00 mm
acLnWt005	0.05 mm
acLnWt009	0.09 mm
acLnWt013	0.13 mm
acLnWt015	0.15 mm
acLnWt018	0.18 mm
acLnWt020	0.20 mm
acLnWt025	0.25 mm
acLnWt030	0.30 mm
acLnWt035	0.35 mm
acLnWt040	0.40 mm
acLnWt050	0.50 mm
acLnWt053	0.53 mm
acLnWt060	0.60 mm
acLnWt070	0.70 mm
acLnWt080	0.80 mm
acLnWt090	0.90 mm
acLnWt100	1.00 mm
acLnWt106	1.06 mm
acLnWt120	1.20 mm
acLnWt140	1.40 mm
acLnWt158	1.58 mm
acLnWt200	2.00 mm
acLnWt211	2.11 mm

The following code changes the WALL layer's **Lineweight** property to 0.70 millimeters thick:

```
Sub Ch08_LayerLineweight()

    Dim objLayer As AcadLayer

    ' Get the layer WALL from the Layers collection.
    Set objLayer = ThisDrawing.Layers.Item("WALL")

    ' Change the layer lineweight to 0.70 mm.
    objLayer.Lineweight = acLnWt070

    ' Tell the user.
    MsgBox "The lineweight for the WALL layer is now 0.70 mm."

End Sub
```

Professional Tip

Lineweight display is off by default in a drawing. In order to see graphic lineweights on screen, you must turn on the lineweight display in the drawing. The following code turns the **LineweightDisplay** property on via the drawing's database preferences:

```
' Turn on graphic lineweights.
ThisDrawing.Preferences.LineweightDisplay = True
```

See the section Setting Database Preferences in Chapter 4 for more information about managing database preferences.

Deleting a Layer

It is possible to delete a layer from a drawing's **Layers** collection, as seen in Chapter 2 in the section Adding and Removing Objects from Object Collections, as long as the following criteria are met:

- Layer is not current.
- Layer is not Layer 0.
- Layer is not xref dependent.
- Layer does not contain any entities.
- Layer is not referenced by a block definition.

Basically, a layer can only be deleted if it is empty and not referenced by anything in the drawing.

The **Delete** method deletes a **Layer** object from the **Layers** collection as long as the criteria outlined above is met. The signature is:

objLayer.Delete

where *objLayer* is the **Layer** object.

The following code deletes the layer WALL from the current drawing, if the criteria are met, and then tells you whether or not it was successful:

```
Sub Ch08_DeleteLayer()

    Dim objLayer As AcadLayer

    ' Disable errors.
    On Error Resume Next

    ' Get the layer WALL from the Layers collection.
    Set objLayer = ThisDrawing.Layers.Item("WALL")

    ' Delete the layer.
    objLayer.Delete

    ' Tell the user what happened.
    If Err.Number = 0 Then
        MsgBox "WALL layer deleted."
    Else
        MsgBox "Cannot delete WALL layer."
        Err.Clear
    End If

End Sub
```

The code example above is interesting for its use of error control. Rather than check to see if the layer WALL is referenced, the VBA error control is disabled and the code tries to delete the layer. If an error is generated, then the macro knows the layer is referenced and the user can be informed.

Layers and the Layer Collection Let's Review...

- Each layer in a drawing is represented by a **Layer** object that is part of the drawing's **Layers** collection.
- A reference to an existing **Layer** is obtained by specifying the layer name in the **Layers** collection.
- You can step through all of the layers in a drawing by using a **For Each...** loop to iterate the **Layers** collection.
- A new layer is created by adding a new **Layer** object with the desired name to the **Layers** collection.
- To make a layer current, the **ThisDrawing.ActiveLayer** property must be set to reference an existing **Layer** object.
- A layer can be renamed by changing the **Layer** object's **Name** property.
- The **LayerOn** property controls the on/off status of a layer.
- The **Freeze** property controls the freeze/thaw status of a layer.
- The **Lock** property controls the lock/unlock status of a layer.
- The **Color** property determines the color assigned to a layer.
- The **Linetype** property controls which linetype is assigned to a layer.
- The **Lineweight** property determines the lineweight assigned to a layer.
- The **Delete** method deletes a **Layer** object from the **Layers** collection.

Exercise 8-1

Create the macros described below. All macros should be created in the **ThisDrawing** module of your MyMacros.dvb project. Provide all necessary error checking and error control. Run and test each macro.

1. Create a macro named ex08_MakeLayers that creates seven new layers using the naming convention of your choice.
2. Create a macro named ex08_LayerProps that will set a unique color and lineweight property for each layer created by the ex08_MakeLayers macro.
3. Create a macro named ex08_LockLayers that locks all layers created as part of the ex08_MakeLayers macro.

Linetypes

It is common drafting practice to use unique line patterns, or *linetypes,* to graphically represent different features on a drawing. This practice allows the person reading a drawing to quickly recognize features by identifying the linetype. For instance, a gas line on a utility location plan might look as shown in **Figure 8-7.**

To facilitate this practice, AutoCAD provides a number of predefined linetypes that can be assigned directly to a drawing entity or, preferably, to the layer on which the entities are drawn. These linetype definitions are maintained in the file acad.lin located in the AutoCAD \Support folder. This ASCII text file defines the dots, dashes, gaps, and even special text strings and shapes that compose each linetype. These existing linetype definitions can be customized using a typical text editor. New linetype definitions can also be created using a text editor. Refer to the AutoCAD online documentation for more information on creating custom linetypes.

Except for the Continuous linetype, a linetype must be loaded into a drawing in order to be assigned to a property. Continuous is the default, solid linetype that is assigned to every drawing entity and to every layer when they are first created. Linetypes are loaded in the AutoCAD drawing editor using the **Load or Reload Linetypes** dialog box shown in **Figure 8-8.**

Figure 8-7.
This linetype is used to represent a gas line on a utility plan.

——— GAS ——— GAS ———

Figure 8-8.
The **Load Linetypes** dialog box is used in the AutoCAD drawing editor to load linetypes into a drawing.

Select a linetype to load

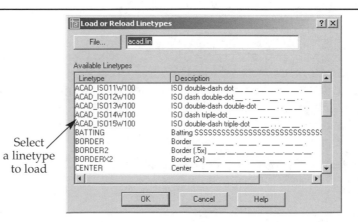

Like layers, linetypes are considered a named symbol table in AutoLISP terminology. In addition, just like layers, the linetype symbol table is stored as an object collection in VBA. The **Linetypes** collection and linetype management are explained in the following sections.

Linetypes Collection

Each linetype in a drawing is represented by a **Linetype** object that is part of a drawing's **Linetypes** collection. Object collections and their usage are discussed in Chapter 2. The following sections show you how to manage a drawing's **Linetypes** collection and its **Linetype** objects so you can:

- Reference an existing linetype in a drawing.
- Iterate through all of the linetypes in a drawing.
- Load a linetype.
- Make a linetype current.
- Rename a linetype.
- Change a linetype's description.
- Scale a linetype.
- Delete a linetype.

Referencing a Linetype

You can get a reference to an existing **Linetype** object by either specifying the index number in the **Linetypes** collection or by specifying the linetype name. Specifying the name is the preferred method when working with named objects, like linetypes.

The following code creates a reference to the HIDDEN **Linetype** object in the **Linetypes** collection and displays the linetypes name and description to the user. See **Figure 8-9A.**

```
Sub Ch08_GetLinetype()

    Dim objLinetype As AcadLineType

    ' Error means the linetype is not loaded.
    On Error GoTo NOTLOADED

    ' Get the HIDDEN linetype from the Linetypes collection.
    Set objLinetype = ThisDrawing.Linetypes.Item("HIDDEN")

    ' Display the name and description.
    MsgBox "The properties for the HIDDEN linetype are:" & vbLf & vbLf & _
        "Name: " & objLinetype.Name & vbLf & _
        "Description: " & objLinetype.Description

    Exit Sub

NOTLOADED:

    ' The linetype is not loaded.
    MsgBox "The HIDDEN linetype is not loaded."

End Sub
```

If the HIDDEN linetype is not loaded, an error is generated and code execution jumps to the NOTLOADED code block, which displays a message box informing the user, **Figure 8-9B.** Also, notice the use of the **Name** and **Description** properties. These are discussed later in this chapter.

Figure 8-9.
A—The user is
informed of the name
and description
properties of the
HIDDEN linetype.
B—If the HIDDEN
linetype is not loaded,
the user is informed
via a VBA message.

A

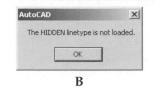

B

Iterating the Linetypes Collection

You can step through all of the linetypes in a drawing by using a **For Each...** loop to iterate the **Linetypes** collection. This approach was first introduced in Chapter 2 and can be used to iterate any of the named symbol table collections.

The following code iterates the **Linetypes** collection and displays a list of all the linetypes loaded in the current drawing:

```
Sub Ch08_IterateLinetypes()

    Dim strLinetypes As String
    Dim objLinetype As AcadLineType

    ' Initialize string.
    strLinetypes = ""

    ' Iterate the Linetypes collection.
    For Each objLinetype In ThisDrawing.Linetypes
        strLinetypes = strLinetypes & objLinetype.Name & vbCrLf
    Next

    ' Display the linetypes to the user.
    MsgBox "Linetypes in drawing: " & vbCrLf & vbCrLf & strLinetypes
End Sub
```

Loading a Linetype

As mentioned earlier, in order to use a particular linetype, that linetype must first be loaded into the current drawing. Linetype definitions are stored in the following AutoCAD support files:

- acad.lin (linetypes for drawings in US Customary units).
- acadiso.lin (linetypes for drawings in metric units).

Both of these files are located in the AutoCAD \Support folder. Therefore, they can be located using VBA via the AutoCAD support file search path. See the section Preferences.Files Object in Chapter 4 for more information regarding the AutoCAD search path.

The **Load** method references a linetype in a specified linetype definition file and adds it as a **Linetype** object to the drawing's **Linetypes** collection. In other words, it "loads" the linetype into the drawing. The signature for the **Load** method is:

objLinetype = Linetypes.Load(*Name*, *FileName*)

where *objLinetype* is the **Linetype** object. *Name* is a **String** that is the name of the linetype to add. *FileName* is a **String** that is the name of linetype file that contains the linetype definition.

The following code loads the CENTER linetype from the file acad.lin:

```
Sub Ch08_LoadLinetype()

    Dim strLinetype As String
    Dim objLinetype As AcadLineType
    Dim blnLoaded As Boolean

    ' Initialize variables.
    strLinetype = "CENTER"
    blnLoaded = False

    ' Check to see if the linetype is loaded.
    For Each objLinetype In ThisDrawing.Linetypes
        If objLinetype.Name = strLinetype Then
            blnLoaded = True
            Exit For
        End If
    Next

    ' Load the linetype if it was not already in the drawing.
    If Not blnLoaded Then
        ThisDrawing.Linetypes.Load strLinetype, "acad.lin"
        MsgBox "Linetype " & strLinetype & " loaded successfully."
    Else
        MsgBox "Linetype " & strLinetype & " already loaded."
    End If

End Sub
```

Notice that the code first checks to see if the linetype is already loaded in the drawing by iterating the **Linetypes** collection. If the linetype is located, the **Boolean** variable *blnLoaded* is set to **True** and the loop is exited. If the linetype is not located, the **Load** method is used to load it from the acad.lin file. Remember that the full path to the file is not necessary if the file is located in the AutoCAD search path.

Making a Linetype Current

If you want AutoCAD to create new drawing entities with a linetype property other than the default ByLayer, you must first make the linetype current. Using VBA, the current linetype in an AutoCAD drawing is controlled via the **ActiveLinetype** property of the **ThisDrawing** object. Remember, however, that the practice of assigning linetypes "by entity" rather than "by layer" is typically discouraged.

In order to make a linetype current, the **ActiveLinetype** property must be set to an existing **Linetype** *object*, not just to a linetype name. This requires first getting a reference to the **Linetype** object from the **Linetypes** collection. Then, the **Linetype** object can be assigned to the **ActiveLinetype** property.

The following code gets a reference to the CENTER **Linetype** object and then makes it the current linetype via the **ActiveLinetype** property:

```
Sub Ch08_ActiveLinetype()

    Dim strLinetype As String
    Dim objLinetype As AcadLineType
    Dim blnLoaded As Boolean

    ' Initialize variables.
    strLinetype = "CENTER"
    blnLoaded = False

    ' Check to see if the linetype is loaded.
    For Each objLinetype In ThisDrawing.Linetypes
        If objLinetype.Name = strLinetype Then
            blnLoaded = True
            Exit For
        End If
    Next

    ' Load the linetype if it was not already in the drawing.
    If Not blnLoaded Then
        ThisDrawing.Linetypes.Load strLinetype, "acad.lin"
        ' Get the linetype that was just loaded.
        Set objLinetype = ThisDrawing.Linetypes(strLinetype)
        MsgBox "Linetype " & strLinetype & " loaded successfully."
    Else
        MsgBox "Linetype " & strLinetype & " already loaded."
    End If

    ' Make the linetype current.
    ThisDrawing.ActiveLinetype = objLinetype

    ' Tell the user.
    MsgBox "Linetype " & objLinetype.Name & " is now current."

End Sub
```

In this example, the code first checks to see if the CENTER linetype is loaded into the drawing. If it is not, the linetype is loaded from the acad.lin file. Then, the linetype is set to be the current linetype. If you try to set the **ActiveLinetype** property to a linetype that is not loaded, the error shown in **Figure 8-10** is generated.

Figure 8-10.
If the linetype is not loaded, this error is generated.

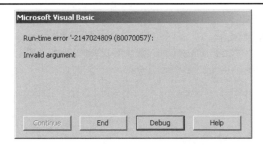

Renaming a Linetype

You can rename a linetype. To do so, first get a reference to the desired **Linetype** object. Then, simply change its **Name** property to the new name.

The following code changes a linetype's name from CENTER to NEW-CENTER:

```
Sub Ch08_LinetypeRename()

    Dim objLinetype As AcadLineType

    ' Turn off errors.
    On Error Resume Next

    ' Get the linetype CENTER from the Linetypes collection.
    Set objLinetype = ThisDrawing.Linetypes.Item("CENTER")

    If Err.Number = 0 Then
        ' Rename the linetype to NEW-CENTER.
        objLinetype.Name = "NEW-CENTER"
        ' Tell the user.
        MsgBox "Linetype CENTER renamed to NEW-CENTER"
    Else
        ' The linetype CENTER was found.
        MsgBox "The linetype CENTER was not found."
    End If

End Sub
```

In this example, VBA error control is turned off so that an error is generated if the linetype is not loaded in the drawing. The **Err** object's **Number** property is checked immediately after trying to reference the named object. If the **Number** property is not set to 0, the linetype was not found. You can use this approach to check for the existence of any of the named symbol table objects.

Changing a Linetype's Description

The linetype's description identifies the linetype and its usage. It also provides an approximation of what the linetype looks like. The description can be seen in the **Description** column of the **Linetype Manager** dialog box, as shown in **Figure 8-11.**

Figure 8-11.
The **Linetype Manager** dialog box is used in the AutoCAD drawing editor to manage linetypes in the drawing. Notice the description of each linetype.

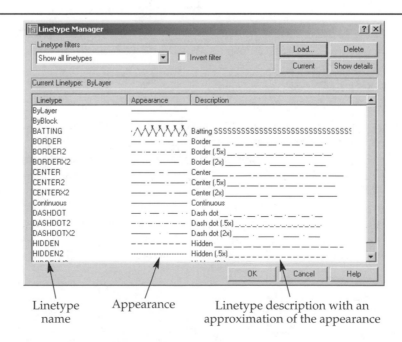

Linetype name   Appearance   Linetype description with an approximation of the appearance

---

The **Description** property controls the text-based description of the linetype. It is initially set when the linetype is loaded from the LIN definition file because the description is part of the linetype definition. For instance, the entry for the CENTER linetype in the acad.lin file looks like:

```
*CENTER,Center ____ _ ____ _ ____ _ ____ _ ____ _ ____
A,1.25,-.25,.25,-.25
```

The linetype description is the item in the first line that appears after the comma.

The following code changes the default description for the CENTER linetype:

```
Sub Ch08_LinetypeDescription()

    Dim objLinetype As AcadLineType

    ' Turn off errors.
    On Error Resume Next

    ' Get the linetype CENTER from the Linetypes collection.
    Set objLinetype = ThisDrawing.Linetypes.Item("CENTER")

    If Err.Number = 0 Then
        ' Change the linetype description.
        objLinetype.Description = "--- -- --- Left of Center --- -- ---"
        ' Tell the user.
        MsgBox "Linetype CENTER description changed."
    Else
        ' The linetype CENTER was not found.
        MsgBox "The linetype CENTER was not found."
    End If

End Sub
```

Professional Tip

When you change the linetype description via code, you are doing so in the drawing, not in the LIN file. Therefore, if the linetype is unloaded and then reloaded, the description will revert to what is in the LIN file.

Linetype Scale

There is another factor that affects a linetype's appearance in a drawing...the scale. All of the linetype definitions in the LIN files are based on a scale of 1:1. This means that when your drawing scale is 1:1, a 1/8" long dash in a line appears as exactly 1/8" long. If the drawing scale is different than 1:1, the dash will appear either larger or smaller than its original definition, depending on the drawing scale factor.

AutoCAD provides both global and local control over the scale factor applied to a linetype. The global linetype scale setting affects the linetype scale of *all* linework in a drawing. The local linetype scale affects individual entities. They are directly related to each other, as you will see in the next sections.

Figure 8-12.
In this example, the global linetype scale is set to 1 (top). However, the local linetype scale on the bottom line is set to 0.5. Notice the difference in the display of the two lines.

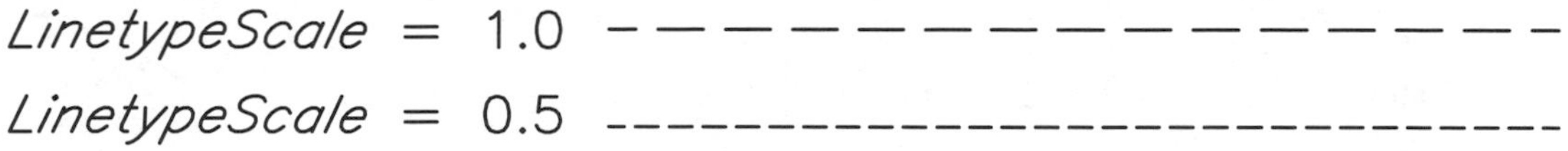

LinetypeScale = 1.0 ────────────────────

LinetypeScale = 0.5 ──────────────────────────

Drawing Scale Factor

The drawing scale factor is a multiplier that is used to scale annotation features—text, dimensions, linetypes—so that they plot at the correct size. For instance, if the plot scale is set to 1/4″ = 1′-0″, the drawing will be scaled down to 1/48 of its actual size when it is plotted. To accommodate this shrinkage, drawing features such as linetypes, dimensions, and text sizes must be scaled up by the inverse of the plot scale. This inverse value is considered the *drawing scale factor.* For example, the plot scale of 1/4″ = 1′-0″ reduces to 1/48, so the drawing scale factor is the inverse, or 48.

Setting the Global Linetype Scale

The global linetype scale is controlled by AutoCAD's **LTSCALE** system variable. As you saw in Chapter 4, in VBA you set system variables using the **ThisDrawing** object's **SetVariable** method. The following code sets the **LTSCALE** system variable to 48:

```
' Set the linetype scale to 48.
ThisDrawing.SetVariable "LTSCALE", 48
```

Now *all* lines in the drawing have their linetype definition scaled up by a factor of 48.

Setting an Individual Object's Linetype Scale

What if you do not want all of the linetypes in your drawing to be scaled exactly the same? There is always that oddball situation. Fortunately, AutoCAD provides the ability to set the linetype scale at the local level via an entity's **LinetypeScale** property.

Object.LinetypeScale

The **LinetypeScale** property is unique in that it is actually a scale factor of the global linetype scale (**LTSCALE**) discussed in the previous section. It is a scale factor of the scale factor! For example, if the global linetype scale is set to 48, you can set an entity's individual (local) **LinetypeScale** property to 0.5 and the drawing entity will appear to have a linetype scale of 24, as shown in **Figure 8-12.** This gives you the ability to refine the linetype appearance of individual entities without affecting everything in the drawing.

The following code prompts the user to select a drawing entity, displays the current local linetype scale setting, and then changes the local linetype scale to 0.5 (or half of the global linetype scale).

```
Sub Ch08_ChangeLinetypeScale()

    Dim objSelected As AcadObject
    Dim varPickPt As Variant

    ' Prompt the user to select an entity.
    ThisDrawing.Utility.GetEntity objSelected, varPickPt, "Select object: "

    ' Display the current linetype scale.
    MsgBox "Current object linetype scale: " & objSelected.LinetypeScale

    ' Change the entity's linetype scale to 0.5.
    objSelected.LinetypeScale = 0.5

    ' Update the entity.
    objSelected.Update

    ' Display the new linetype scale.
    MsgBox "Object's linetype scale changed to: " & _
        objSelected.LinetypeScale

End Sub
```

Deleting a Linetype

The **Delete** method deletes a **Linetype** object from the **Linetypes** collection. A linetype can be deleted from a drawing's **Linetypes** collection as long as the linetype:

- Is not ByLayer, ByBlock, or Continuous.
- Is not current.
- Is not xref dependent.
- Does not have any entities that use it.
- Is not referenced by a block definition.

The signature for the **Delete** method is:

objLinetype.Delete

where *objLinetype* is the **Linetype** object.

The following code tries to delete the linetype CENTER from the current drawing and then informs the user if it was successful:

```
Sub Ch08_DeleteLinetype()

    Dim objLinetype As AcadLineType

    ' Disable errors.
    On Error Resume Next

    ' Get the linetype CENTER from the Linetypes collection.
    Set objLinetype = ThisDrawing.Linetypes.Item("CENTER")

    ' Delete the linetype.
    objLinetype.Delete

    ' Tell the user what happened.
    If Err.Number = 0 Then
        MsgBox "CENTER linetype deleted."
    Else
        MsgBox " Cannot delete CENTER linetype. "
        Err.Clear
    End If

End Sub
```

sub Ch08_LoadLinetype()

Exercise 8-2

Create the macros described below. All macros should be created in the **ThisDrawing** module of your MyMacros.dvb project. Provide all necessary error checking and control. Run and test each macro.

1. Create a macro named ex08_LoadLinetypes that loads seven linetype definitions of your choice from the acad.lin file.
2. Create a macro named ex08_LayerLinetypes that associates the linetypes loaded via the ex08_LoadLinetypes macro with the layers created by the ex08_MakeLayers macro in #1 in Exercise 8-1.
3. Create a macro named ex08_HideLine that prompts the user to select any type of entity in a drawing and changes its linetype to HIDDEN and its local linetype scale to 0.5.

sub Ch08_LayerLinetype()

Linetypes and the Linetypes Collection

Let's Review...

- Each linetype in a drawing is represented by a **Linetype** object that is part of a drawing's **Linetypes** collection.
- You get a reference to a loaded **Linetype** by specifying the linetype name in the **Linetypes** collection.
- You can step through all of the linetypes in a drawing by using a **For Each...** loop to iterate the **Linetypes** collection.
- The **Load** method references a linetype from a specified linetype definition file and adds it to the drawing's **Linetypes** collection.
- To make a linetype current, the **ThisDrawing.ActiveLinetype** property must be set to reference an existing **Linetype** object.
- You can rename a linetype by changing the **Linetype** object's **Name** property.
- The **Description** property controls the description of the linetype.
- The global linetype scale is controlled by the **LTSCALE** system variable and can be set using the **ThisDrawing** object's **SetVariable** method.
- You control the linetype scale at the entity, or local, level via an entity's **LinetypeScale** property.
- The **Delete** method deletes a **Linetype** object from the **Linetypes** collection.

Chapter Test

Write your answers on a separate sheet of paper.
1. Explain what *layers* are and why they are used in AutoCAD.
2. Why is it preferred to set an entity's color, linetype, and lineweight property to ByLayer?
3. To ensure that new entities are drawn on the correct layer, what must you first do?
4. Explain the difference between turning a layer off and freezing a layer.
5. Describe how the **GoSub...Return** statement works and why you might want to use it in your code.
6. Why might you want to lock a layer rather than freeze it?
7. List two reasons why colors are used in an AutoCAD drawing.
8. Describe what an AutoCAD *linetype* is and how it is used.
9. What is the default lineweight, in millimeters, of an AutoCAD entity?
10. How is the on-screen visibility of lineweights controlled?
11. What are the names of the two linetypes definition files that come with AutoCAD?
12. What is *linetype scale* and how is it calculated?
13. Explain the two different ways to control a linetype's scale in AutoCAD.

Programming Problems

Create the macros described below. All macros should be created in the **ThisDrawing** module of your MyMacros.dvb project. Provide all necessary error checking and control. Run and test each macro.

1. Update the macro p04_DWGSetup created in Problem 4-2 so that it creates the layers listed below with the properties indicated. Save the updated macro as p08_DWGSetup.

Layer Name	Color	Linetype	Lineweight
Center	Red	CENTER	0.25 mm
Dimension	Yellow	Continuous	0.35 mm
Hidden	Green	HIDDEN	0.25 mm
Object	Cyan	Continuous	0.50 mm
Phantom	Blue	PHANTOM	0.25 mm
Text	Magenta	Continuous	0.50 mm

2. Create a macro named p08_LayerFreezePick that prompts the user to pick an entity and then freezes the layer on which it resides.
3. Create a macro named p08_LockXrefs that locks all layers that are part of any xrefed drawing(s). *Hint:* The VBA **Like** operator can be used to perform wild card string matching.
4. Create a macro named p08_DemoLayer that renames every layer and linetype in a drawing so each has the prefix Demo-.

CHAPTER 9

Text and Dimension Styles

Learning Objectives

After completing this chapter, you will be able to create VBA macros that:

- Reference an existing text style.
- Iterate the text styles in a drawing.
- Create a text style.
- Make a text style current.
- Rename a text style.
- Specify a text style's associated font.
- Control a text style's height.
- Set a text style's oblique angle.
- Make a text style display backward or upside down.
- Delete a text style.
- Reference an existing dimension style.
- Iterate the dimension styles in a drawing.
- Create a new dimension style.
- Make a dimension style current.
- Rename a dimension style.
- Create dimension overrides.
- Save dimension overrides to a dimension style.
- Delete a dimension style.

Text Styles

All text in an AutoCAD drawing is associated with a text style. The *text style* defines how the text looks in a drawing by controlling the:

- Font
- Height
- Effects (oblique angle, width, etc.)

Using text styles to control the appearance of text allows you to manage similar text entities as a single unit. When a text style is set current, any new text that is created is automatically formatted to match that text style.

Figure 9-1.
Different text styles
are often used so that
various elements of a
drawing can be easily
recognized.

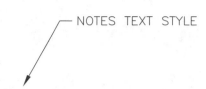

TITLES TEXT STYLE

NOTES TEXT STYLE

Figure 9-2.
The **Text Style** dialog box is used to create a new text style in the AutoCAD drawing editor.

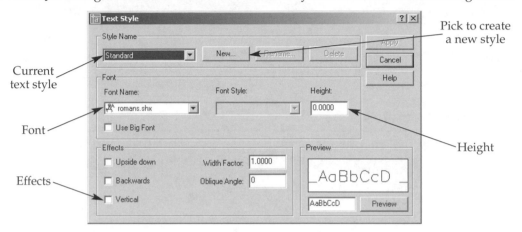

Many companies establish standard text styles so that they can properly control the appearance of text in their drawings. For instance, you might group notes and leader text under one text style called NOTES, while title text might be assigned a text style named TITLES. Using this approach, different heights and fonts can be specified for each type of text, as shown in **Figure 9-1.**

Every new AutoCAD drawing has the STANDARD text style already defined. Custom text styles have to be added to the drawing. In the AutoCAD drawing editor, new text styles are added via the **Text Style** dialog box shown in **Figure 9-2.**

Text styles are yet another example of a symbol table in AutoCAD. Because of this, text styles are also implemented as an object collection in VBA. The **TextStyles** collection and text style management are explained in the following sections.

TextStyles Collection

Each text style in a drawing is represented by a **TextStyle** object that is part of the drawing's **TextStyles** collection. Object collections and their usage are discussed in Chapter 2. The following sections show you how to manage a drawing's **TextStyles** collection and its **TextStyle** objects so you can:

- Reference an existing text style in a drawing.
- Step through all the text styles in a drawing.
- Create a new text style.
- Make a text style current.
- Rename a text style.

Figure 9-3.
The height and font
of the text style
STANDARD are
displayed to the
user.

- Control the text style font.
- Control the text style height.
- Control the text style obliquing angle.
- Control the text style generation flag.
- Delete a text style.

Referencing a Text Style

You can get a reference to an existing **TextStyle** object by either specifying the index number in the **TextStyles** collection or by specifying the text style name. Specifying the name is the preferred method when working with named objects, like text styles.

The following code creates a reference to the STANDARD **TextStyle** object in the **TextStyles** collection and then displays the text style's height and font to the user. See **Figure 9-3.**

```
Sub Ch09_GetTextstyle()

    Dim objTextstyle As AcadTextStyle

    ' Get the Standard text style from the TextStyles collection.
    Set objTextstyle = ThisDrawing.TextStyles.Item("STANDARD")

    ' Display the height and font properties.
    MsgBox "The properties for the Standard text style are:" & vbLf & vbLf & _
        "Height: " & objTextstyle.Height & vbLf & _
        "Font: " & objTextstyle.fontFile

End Sub
```

Iterating the TextStyles Collection

You can step through all of the text styles in a drawing by utilizing a **For Each...** loop to iterate the **TextStyles** collection. This approach was first introduced in Chapter 2 and can be used to iterate any of the named symbol table collections.

The following code iterates the **TextStyles** collection and displays a list of all of the text styles in the current drawing. See **Figure 9-4.**

```
Sub Ch09_IterateTextstyles()

    Dim strTextstyles As String
    Dim objTextstyle As AcadTextStyle

    ' Initialize string.
    strTextstyles = ""

    ' Step through all text styles in the drawing.
    For Each objTextstyle In ThisDrawing.TextStyles
        strTextstyles = strTextstyles & objTextstyle.Name & vbCrLf
    Next

    ' Display the text styles to the user.
    MsgBox "Text styles in the drawing: " & vbCrLf & vbCrLf & strTextstyles

End Sub
```

Figure 9-4.
The text styles in the
drawing are displayed
to the user.

Creating a New Text Style

To create a new text style using VBA and the AutoCAD object model you simply need to add a new **TextStyle** object with the desired name to the **TextStyles** collection. Once the object is added, you can get a reference to it using the methods described in previous chapters. After you have a reference to the new **TextStyle** object, you can set any of its properties or use any of its methods.

The **Add** method adds a **TextStyle** object with the specified name to the **TextStyles** collection. The signature is:

objTextstyle = TextStyles.Add(*Name*)

where *objTextstyle* is the **TextStyle** object. *Name* is a **String** that is the name of text style to add.

The following code adds a text style named Romans to the current drawing:

```
Sub Ch09_AddTextstyle()

    ' Add the text style Romans to the drawing.
    ThisDrawing.TextStyles.Add "Romans"

    ' Display to the user.
    MsgBox "Text style Romans added to drawing."

End Sub
```

The new **TextStyle** object is added using the properties of the current text style. Setting a text style current is explained in the next section.

Making a Text Style Current

To ensure that new text added to an AutoCAD drawing is the correct text style, you must first make the text style current. Using VBA, the current text style is controlled via the **ActiveTextStyle** property of the **ThisDrawing** object. In order to make a text style current, the property must be set to an existing **TextStyle** object, *not* just a text style name. This requires first getting a reference to the **TextStyle** object from the **TextStyles** collection and then assigning the object to the **ActiveTextStyle** property.

The following code adds the text style Romans to the drawing, gets a reference to the **TextStyle** object, and then makes Romans the current text style via the **ActiveTextStyle** property. See **Figure 9-5.**

Figure 9-5.
The text style
Romans is added to
the drawing and
made current.

```
Sub Ch09_ActiveTextstyle()

    Dim objTextstyle As AcadTextStyle

    ' Add the text style Romans to drawing.
    Set objTextstyle = ThisDrawing.TextStyles.Add("Romans")

    ' Make the Textstyle Romans current.
    ThisDrawing.ActiveTextStyle = objTextstyle

    ' Tell the user.
    MsgBox "Text style Romans added to drawing and is now current."

End Sub
```

Managing Text Style Fonts

The font file associated with a text style controls the appearance of text in the drawing. Font files define the shapes of the text characters that make up each character set. In AutoCAD, you can use either TrueType fonts or SHX fonts. TrueType fonts are the scaleable fonts used by most Windows applications. SHX fonts are compiled AutoCAD shape files that typically reside in AutoCAD's \Fonts folder. The **TextStyle** object's **FontFile** property controls which font file is associated with the text style.

The following code displays the font associated with the current text style and then tries to change it to romans.shx, if that font file exists. If the romans.shx font file is *not* found, the code changes the font to simplex.shx.

```
Sub Ch09_FontFile()

    Dim objTextStyle As AcadTextStyle
    Dim strCurFontFile As String
    Dim strNewFontFile As String

    ' Get the current text style.
    Set objTextStyle = ThisDrawing.ActiveTextStyle

    ' Get the current FontFile value.
    strCurFontFile = objTextStyle.fontFile

    ' Display.
    MsgBox "The current text style's font file is set to: " & strCurFontFile

    ' Specify the new font file.
    strNewFontFile = "c:\Program Files\AutoCAD 2005\Fonts\Romans.shx"

    ' Check to see if the font file exists before changing.
    ' If the font file is not found, change to the Simplex font.
    If Dir(strNewFontFile) <> "" Then
        objTextStyle.fontFile = strNewFontFile
    Else
        objTextStyle.fontFile = "Simplex"
    End If

    MsgBox "The current text style's font file has been changed to: " & _
            objTextStyle.fontFile

End Sub
```

Setting the Text Style Height

The height of text located in model space on an AutoCAD drawing is dependent on the final scale at which the drawing will be plotted. For instance, text that you want to appear 1/8″ high on a drawing with a plot scale or viewport scale of 1/4″ = 1′-0″ must have its height multiplied by the inverse of the scale factor. The inverse of the scale 1/4″ = 1′-0″ is 48. The formula for calculating the text height is:

Final Plotted Height × Dwg Scale Factor = Text Height in Model Space

Plugging in the numbers results in a text height of 6″:

0.125″ × 48 = 6″ Text Height

There are two ways you can assign a text height in AutoCAD. A text height can be assigned directly to a text object, as seen in Chapter 6, or via the text style. Using a text style to control the height of text is preferred from a management standpoint because it centralizes control in one place. The **TextStyle** object's **Height** property controls the text height associated with a text style.

The following code displays the height of the current text style and then updates it to a user-supplied height:

```
Sub Ch09_SetTextHeight()

    Dim objTextStyle As AcadTextStyle
    Dim dblTextHeight As Double

    ' Get the current text style.
    Set objTextStyle = ThisDrawing.ActiveTextStyle

    ' Get the current text height.
    dblTextHeight = objTextStyle.Height

    ' Display the current height.
    MsgBox "Current text style height: " & dblTextHeight, vbInformation, _
        "Ch09_SetTextHeight"

    ' Get the new text height from the user.
    dblTextHeight = ThisDrawing.Utility.GetReal(vbCrLf & _
        "New text style height: ")

    ' Change the text style height.
    objTextStyle.Height = dblTextHeight

End Sub
```

Setting the Text Style Obliquing Angle

The *obliquing angle* of a text style determines the forward or backward slant of the text. It is a way of creating italic type. The obliquing angle is input as an angular offset from vertical (90 degrees) and can be between –85 degrees and 85 degrees. A positive obliquing angle slants text to the right. A negative obliquing angle slants text to the left. See **Figure 9-6**. The **TextStyle** object's **ObliqueAngle** property controls the obliquing angle associated with the text style.

Figure 9-6.
The obliquing angle can be used to create italicized text.

NO OBLIQUING ANGLE
POSITIVE OBLIQUING ANGLE
NEGATIVE OBLIQUING ANGLE

The following code displays the oblique angle of the current text style and then updates it to a user-supplied angle:

```
Sub Ch09_SetTextObliqueAngle()

    Dim objTextStyle As AcadTextStyle
    Dim dblObliqueAngle As Double

    ' Get the current text style.
    Set objTextStyle = ThisDrawing.ActiveTextStyle

    ' Get the current obliquing angle.
    dblObliqueAngle = objTextStyle.ObliqueAngle

    ' Convert radians to degrees.
    dblObliqueAngle = dblObliqueAngle * (180 / 3.141592)

    ' Display the current obliquing angle in degrees.
    MsgBox "Current text style oblique angle: " & dblObliqueAngle, _
        vbInformation, "Ch09_SetTextObliqueAngle"

    ' Get the new obliquing angle from the user.
    dblObliqueAngle = ThisDrawing.Utility.GetReal(vbCrLf & _
        "New text style oblique angle: ")

    ' Convert the user-supplied degrees to radians.
    dblObliqueAngle = dblObliqueAngle * (3.141592 / 180)

    ' Change the text style.
    objTextStyle.ObliqueAngle = dblObliqueAngle

End Sub
```

Notice that the current angle is displayed to the user in degrees by first converting the radian value to degrees. Remember, VBA angles are in radians. Also, notice that the user enters the new angle in degrees, which is then converted to radians.

Setting the Text Style Generation Flag

The *text generation flag* of the text style is used to make the text display backward, upside down, or both. See **Figure 9-7.** The **TextStyle** object's **TextGenerationFlag** property controls these effects and is set using the AutoCAD constants:

acTextFlagBackward = Display text backward
acTextFlagUpsideDown = Display text upside down
0 = Normal text

To make the text display both backward and upside down, you can add the two constants together by specifying **acTextFlagBackward + acTextFlagUpsideDown** when the **TextGenerationFlag** property is assigned.

Figure 9-7.
The text style generation flag is used to create text that is backward, upside down, or both.

NO EFFECT

BACKWARD

UPSIDE DOWN

BOTH EFFECTS

The following code displays the text generation flag of the current text style and then changes it to upside down:

```
Sub Ch09_TextGenerationFlag()

    Dim objTextStyle As AcadTextStyle
    Dim dblObliqueAngle As Double

    ' Get the current text style.
    Set objTextStyle = ThisDrawing.ActiveTextStyle

    ' Display the generation flag.
    MsgBox "Current text generation flag: " & _
        objTextStyle.TextGenerationFlag

    ' Change the text generation flag to upside down.
    objTextStyle.TextGenerationFlag = acTextFlagUpsideDown

    ' Tell the user.
    MsgBox "Text generation flag is set to upside down."

End Sub
```

Professional Tip "Vertical" text generation is not available using VBA and the current AutoCAD object model.

Deleting a Text Style

It is possible to delete a text style from a drawing's **TextStyles** collection, as seen in the section Adding Objects to and Removing Objects from Object Collections in Chapter 2. However, the text style must not:

- Be the current text style.
- Be the text style STANDARD.
- Be xref dependent.
- Have any entities that use it.
- Be referenced by a block definition.

The **Delete** method is used to delete a **TextStyle** object from the **TextStyles** collection as long as the criteria outlined above are met. The signature for the **Delete** method is:

objTextStyle.Delete

where *objTextStyle* is the **TextStyle** object to delete.

The following code tries to delete the ROMANS_125 linetype from the current drawing and then tells the user whether or not it succeeded:

```
Sub Ch09_DeleteTextStyle()

    Dim objTextStyle As AcadTextStyle

    ' Disable errors.
    On Error Resume Next

    ' Get the text style ROMANS_125 from the TextStyles collection.
    Set objTextStyle = ThisDrawing.TextStyles.Item("ROMANS_125")

    ' Delete the text style.
    objTextStyle.Delete

    ' Tell the user what happened.
    If Err.Number = 0 Then
        MsgBox "ROMANS_125 text style deleted."
    Else
        MsgBox "Cannot delete ROMANS_125 text style."
        Err.Clear
    End If

End Sub
```

Text Styles and the Text Styles Collection

Let's Review...

- Each text style in a drawing is represented by a **TextStyle** object that is part of the drawing's **TextStyles** collection.
- You get a reference to an existing **TextStyle** by specifying the text style name in the **TextStyles** collection.
- You can step through all of the text styles in a drawing by using a **For Each...** loop to iterate the **TextStyles** collection.
- A new text style is created by adding a new **TextStyle** object with the desired name to the **TextStyles** collection.
- To make a text style current, the **ThisDrawing.ActiveTextStyle** property must be set to reference an existing **TextStyle** object.
- The **FontFile** property controls the font associated with a text style.
- The **Height** property controls the text height associated with a text style.
- The **ObliqueAngle** property controls the obliquing angle associated with a text style.
- The **TextGenerationFlag** property controls whether text is displayed normally, backward, or upside down.
- The **Delete** method deletes a **TextStyle** object from the **TextStyles** collection.

Create the macros described below. All macros should be created in the **ThisDrawing** module of your MyMacros.dvb project. Provide all necessary error checking and control. Run and test each macro.
1. Create a macro named ex09_MakeTextStyles that creates five text styles using the naming convention of your choice.
2. Create a macro named ex09_TextStyleFonts that associates a unique font with each text style created by the ex09_MakeTextStyles macro.
3. Create a macro named ex09_IsoTextStyles that creates two isometric text styles with unique names. One text style should have an obliquing angle of 30 degrees, while the other should have obliquing angle of −30 degrees.

Dimension Styles

Dimensions are some of the most complex entities in an AutoCAD drawing…probably the most important, too! Without dimensions, a printed drawing is pretty much worthless. It is impossible to build something if you do not know what size to make the product.

Every industry has a different way of displaying dimensions. Even some countries have certain dimension styles. There are national dimension standards and groups dedicated to the cause. A classic example of differing styles is dimensioning an architectural drawing compared to dimensioning a mechanical drawing. For instance, a horizontal dimension in a mechanical drawing might look like the one shown in **Figure 9-8A.** The same dimension in an architectural drawing might look like the one shown in **Figure 9-8B.** Mechanical dimension lines typically have arrowheads, whereas architectural dimension lines typically have tick marks. Architectural dimension values are displayed in feet and fractional inches (in the US), while mechanical values are decimal inches.

There are over 50 system variables in AutoCAD related to dimensioning that control everything from the arrow type to the length of extension lines. Fortunately, AutoCAD provides dimension styles to help manage all of these different settings.

Named *dimension styles* allow you to group dimensions based on how they appear in the drawing. In the example above, you might create two dimension styles—one named Architectural and one named Mechanical—to manage their different settings. Like text

Figure 9-8.
A—This is a typical dimension style for a mechanical drawing. B—This is a typical dimension style for an architectural drawing.

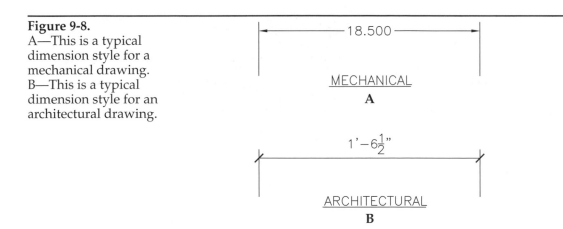

styles, managing dimensions through dimension styles allows you more control over your drawing. If a standard is revised, you only need to change a style and everything in the drawing is updated accordingly.

The default dimension style is STANDARD and is part of every new drawing. In the AutoCAD drawing editor, the settings of a dimension style are managed using the **Modify Dimension Style** dialog box, **Figure 9-9.** As you can see, there are many different options available. Typically, multiple dimension styles are created to manage all of the different settings. The desired style is set current using the **Dimension Style Manager** dialog box before creating a dimension, **Figure 9-10.**

Dimension styles are still another example of a symbol table in AutoCAD. Because of this, dimension styles are also implemented as an object collection in VBA. The **DimStyles** collection and dimension style management are explained in the following sections.

Figure 9-9.
In the AutoCAD drawing editor, the **Modify Dimension Style** dialog box is used to manage the settings for a dimension style.

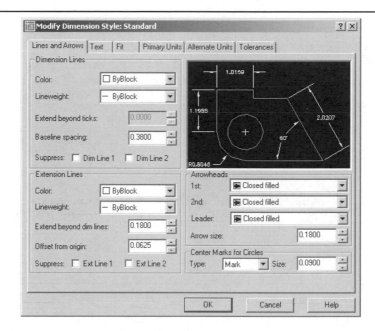

Figure 9-10.
In the AutoCAD drawing editor, the **Dimension Style Manager** dialog box is used to manage dimension styles and set a style current.

Select a style

Pick to make current

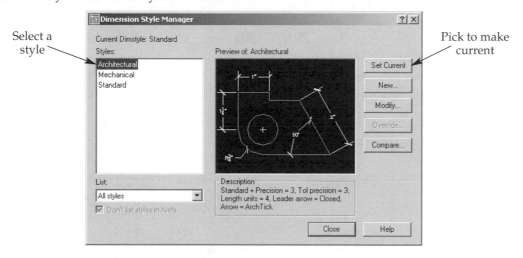

DimStyles Collection

Each dimension style in a drawing is represented by a **DimStyle** object that is part of the drawing's **DimStyles** collection. Object collections and their usage are discussed in Chapter 2. The following sections show you how to manage a drawing's **DimStyles** collection and its **DimStyle** objects so you can:

- Reference an existing dimension style in a drawing.
- Step through all the dimension styles in a drawing.
- Create a new dimension style.
- Make a dimension style current.
- Rename a dimension style.
- Set and retrieve a dimension style's font.
- Delete a dimension style.

Referencing a Dimension Style

You can get a reference to an existing **DimStyle** object by either specifying the index number in the **DimStyles** collection or the dimension style name. Specifying the name is the preferred method when working with named objects, like dimension styles.

The following code creates a reference to the STANDARD **DimStyle** object in the **DimStyles** collection:

```
Sub Ch09_GetDimstyle()

    Dim objDimstyle As AcadDimStyle

    ' Get the DimStyle STANDARD from the DimStyles collection.
    Set objDimstyle = ThisDrawing.DimStyles.Item("STANDARD")

End Sub
```

Professional Tip

Surprisingly, the **DimStyle** object has limited functionality. Its only property is the **Name** property. All dimension style settings must be managed using the dimension override technique explained later in this chapter.

Iterating the DimStyles Collection

You can step through all of the dimension styles in a drawing by using a **For Each...** loop to iterate the **DimStyles** collection. This approach was first introduced in Chapter 2 and can be used to iterate any of the named symbol table collections.

The following code iterates the **DimStyles** collection and displays a list of all the dimension styles in the current drawing. See **Figure 9-11.**

Figure 9-11.
The dimension styles in the current drawing are displayed to the user.

```
Sub Ch09_IterateDimstyles()

    Dim strDimstyles As String
    Dim objDimstyle As AcadDimStyle

    ' Initialize string.
    strDimstyles = ""

    ' Step through all dimension styles in the drawing.
    For Each objDimstyle In ThisDrawing.DimStyles
        strDimstyles = strDimstyles & objDimstyle.Name & vbCrLf
    Next

    ' Display the dimension styles to the user.
    MsgBox "Dimension styles in the drawing: " & vbCrLf & vbCrLf & strDimstyles

End Sub
```

Creating a New Dimension Style

Creating a new dimension style using VBA and the AutoCAD object model is a little more complicated than simply adding a new **DimStyle** object with the desired name to the **DimStyles** collection. When you add a new **DimStyle** object, it is added with only the default AutoCAD dimension settings and nothing more. Management of all of the other dimension settings is controlled via overrides of the dimensioning system variables and by using the **CopyFrom** method, as explained later in this chapter.

The **Add** method adds a **DimStyle** object with the specified name to the **DimStyles** collection with the default AutoCAD settings. The signature is:

objDimstyle = DimStyles.Add(*Name*)

where *objDimstyle* is the **DimStyle** object and *Name* is a **String** that is the name of the dimension style to add.

The following code adds a dimension style named Architectural to the current drawing and informs the user. See **Figure 9-12.**

```
Sub Ch09_AddDimstyle()

    ' Add the dimension style Architectural to the drawing.
    ThisDrawing.DimStyles.Add ("Architectural")

    ' Tell the user.
    MsgBox "Dimension style Architectural was added to the drawing."

End Sub
```

Figure 9-12.
The dimension style
Architectural is added
to the drawing.

Making a Dimension Style Current

New dimensions added to an AutoCAD drawing are created using the current dimension style. Using VBA, the current dimension style is controlled via the **ActiveDimStyle** property of the **ThisDrawing** object. To make a dimension style current, the **ActiveDimStyle** property must be set to an existing **DimStyle** object, not just a dimension style name. This requires first getting a reference to the **DimStyle** object from the **DimStyles** collection. Then, the object can be assigned to the **ActiveDimStyle** property.

The following code adds the dimension style Architectural to the drawing, gets a reference to the Architectural **DimStyle** object, and then makes Architectural the current dimension style via the **ActiveDimStyle** property:

```
Sub Ch09_ActiveDimstyle()

    Dim objDimstyle As AcadDimStyle

    ' Add the dimension style Architectural to the drawing.
    Set objDimstyle = ThisDrawing.DimStyles.Add("Architectural")

    ' Make the dimension style Architectural current.
    ThisDrawing.ActiveDimStyle = objDimstyle

    ' Tell the user.
    MsgBox "Dimension style Architectural was added to the drawing and is now current."
End Sub
```

Renaming a Dimension Style

The **DimStyle** object's **Name** property controls the dimension style name. To rename a dimension style, get a reference to the desired **DimStyle** object and then simply change its **Name** property to the new name.

The following code changes the name of the Architectural dimension style to Mechanical:

```
Sub Ch09_DimstyleRename()

    Dim objDimstyle As AcadDimStyle

    ' Get the dimension style Architectural from the DimStyles collection.
    Set objDimstyle = ThisDrawing.DimStyles.Item("Architectural")

    ' Rename the dimension style to Mechanical.
    objDimstyle.Name = "Mechanical"

    ' Tell the user.
    MsgBox "Dimension style Architectural was renamed to Mechanical."
End Sub
```

Overriding a Dimension Style Setting

As mentioned earlier, the only way to control a dimension style's settings and appearance using VBA is via AutoCAD's dimensioning system variables. This is referred to as setting a *dimension override* because you are altering aspects of the dimension style, but not actually changing the settings of the style. When an override of a dimension style is created, it appears in the **Dimension Style Manager** as shown in **Figure 9-13.** Dimension overrides are applied to the current dimension style and only affect new dimensions that are created in the drawing. Existing dimensions are unaffected unless they are manually updated.

There are over 50 system variables that can be used to override a dimension style. These variables all share the prefix DIM. Refer to AutoCAD's online documentation for a complete list of dimensioning system variables.

Figure 9-13.
Dimension overrides are displayed in the **Dimension Style Manager** dialog box.

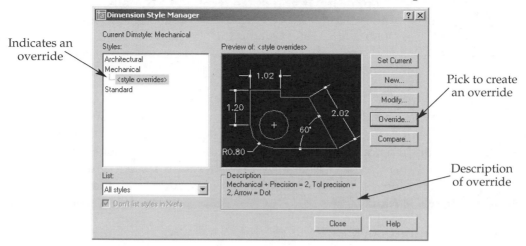

Indicates an override

Pick to create an override

Description of override

Setting Dimensioning System Variables

Remember from Chapter 4 that system variables are part of the **ThisDrawing** object. The **SetVariable** method is used to change the value of any system variable, including the dimensioning system variables.

The following code creates a dimension override by changing the dimension line arrowheads. This is done by setting the AutoCAD **DIMBLK** system variable to Oblique. See **Figure 9-14.**

```
Sub Ch09_SetDimVariable()

    ' Change arrowheads to oblique by setting the DIMBLK variable.
    ThisDrawing.SetVariable "DIMBLK", "Oblique"

    ' Tell the user.
    MsgBox "Dimension arrowheads changed to oblique."

End Sub
```

Figure 9-14.
A—The arrowhead style has been changed to create a dimension override. B—In the **Dimension Style Manager**, the override is indicated and a description of the override can be seen.

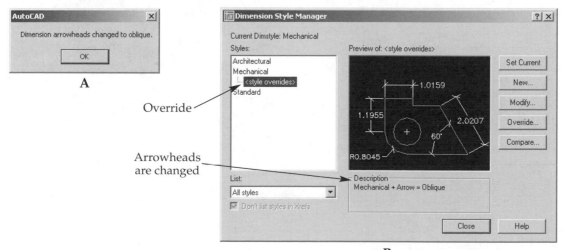

Override

Arrowheads are changed

A

B

Saving Dimension Overrides to a Dimension Style

It is possible to save all dimension overrides to a specific dimension style. This is done by copying all of the current dimension variable settings to the desired style. The **CopyFrom** method copies the dimension settings from another dimension entity, a dimension style, or even the current drawing. This allows you to create a dimension style with unique settings, thus providing a way around the limitations of the **Add** method discussed earlier.

The signature for the **CopyFrom** method is:

objDimStyle.CopyFrom *SourceObject*

where *objDimStyle* is the **DimStyle** object that will receive the copied settings. *SourceObject* is from where the settings are copied. It can be a **Document** object, **DimStyle** object, or **Dimension** object.

The following code creates and saves a dimension override. First, the dimension style Mechanical is created, if it does not already exist, and set current. Then, the override is created by changing the arrowhead style (**DIMBLK**) to Oblique. Finally, the override is saved by copying all of the dimension overrides from the current drawing to the dimension style Mechanical using the **CopyFrom** method. See **Figure 9-15.**

Figure 9-15.
A—The user is informed that the dimension style Mechanical has been created. B—The dimension override has been saved to the style Mechanical. Note that no overrides are indicated, but the arrowhead style has been changed.

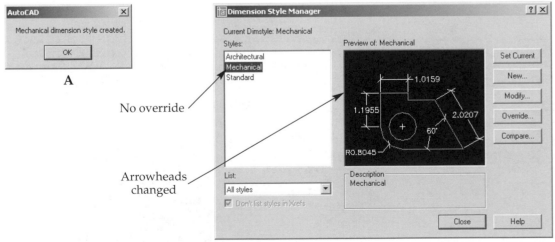

```
Sub Ch09_UpdateDimStyle()

    Dim objDimstyle As AcadDimStyle

    ' Turn off errors.
    On Error Resume Next

    ' Get the dimension style Mechanical from the
    ' DimStyles collection if it exists.
    Set objDimstyle = ThisDrawing.DimStyles.Item("Mechanical")

    ' If the dimension style Mechanical does not exist then add it.
    If Err.Number <> 0 Then
        Set objDimstyle = ThisDrawing.DimStyles.Add("Mechanical")
        Err.Clear
    End If

    ' Make the dimension style current.
    ThisDrawing.ActiveDimStyle = objDimstyle

    ' Change arrowheads to oblique by setting the DIMBLK variable.
    ThisDrawing.SetVariable "DIMBLK", "Oblique"

    ' Copy the overrides set in the drawing.
    objDimstyle.CopyFrom ThisDrawing

    ' Tell the user.
    MsgBox "Mechanical dimension style created."

End Sub
```

Deleting a Dimension Style

It is possible to delete a dimension style from a drawing's **DimStyles** collection, as seen in the section Adding Objects to and Removing Objects from Object Collections in Chapter 2. However, the dimension style must not:

- Be the current dimension style.
- Be the STANDARD dimension style.
- Be xref dependent.
- Have any entities that use it.
- Be referenced by a block definition.

The **Delete** method is used to delete a **DimStyle** object from the **DimStyles** collection as long as the criteria outlined above are met. The signature for the **Delete** method is:

objDimStyle.Delete

where *objDimStyle* is the **DimStyle** object to delete.

The following code tries to delete the Mechanical dimension style from the current drawing and then tells the user whether or not it succeeded:

```
Sub Ch09_DeleteDimStyle()

    Dim objDimStyle As AcadDimStyle

    ' Disable errors.
    On Error Resume Next

    ' Get the dimension style Mechanical from the DimStyles collection.
    Set objDimStyle = ThisDrawing.DimStyles.Item("Mechanical")

    ' Delete the dimension style.
    objDimStyle.Delete

    ' Tell the user what happened.
    If Err.Number = 0 Then
        MsgBox "The  dimension style Mechanical was deleted."
    Else
        MsgBox "Cannot delete the dimension style Mechanical."
        Err.Clear
    End If

End Sub
```

Let's Review...

Dimension Styles and the DimStyles Collection

- Each dimension style in a drawing is represented by a **DimStyle** object that is part of the drawing's **DimStyles** collection.
- You get a reference to an existing **DimStyle** by specifying the dimension style name in the **DimStyles** collection.
- You can step through all of the dimension styles in a drawing by using a **For Each...** loop to iterate the **DimStyles** collection.
- A new dimension style is created by adding a new **DimStyle** object with the desired name to the **DimStyles** collection.
- To make a dimension style current, the **ThisDrawing.ActiveDimStyle** property must be set to reference an existing **DimStyle** object.
- A dimension style can be renamed by changing the **DimStyle** object's **Name** property.
- Dimension overrides are created by setting dimensioning system variables with the **ThisDrawing** object's **SetVariable** method.
- The **CopyFrom** method copies dimension settings from another dimension entity, a dimension style, or the current drawing and can be used to save dimension overrides to a dimension style.

Create the macros described below. All macros should be created in the **ThisDrawing** module of your MyMacros.dvb project. Provide all necessary error checking and control. Run and test each macro. Refer to AutoCAD's online documentation for a complete list of dimensioning system variables.

1. Create a macro named ex09_MakeDimStyles that creates five new dimension styles. Use the naming convention of your choice for the style names.
2. Create a macro named ex09_DimStyleText that associates the five text styles created by the ex09_MakeTextStyles macro from #1 in Exercise 9-1 with the five dimension styles created by the ex09_MakeDimStyles macro.
3. Create a macro named ex09_DimStyleUnits that associates five different unit settings with the five dimension styles created by the ex09_MakeDimStyles macro.

Chapter Test

Write your answers on a separate sheet of paper.

1. Explain *text styles* and why they are used in AutoCAD.
2. List three text properties that can be controlled using text styles.
3. Which text style is contained in every AutoCAD drawing?
4. Explain the difference between a TrueType (TTF) font and an AutoCAD (SHX) font.
5. What are the advantages of using AutoCAD's support file search path to locate fonts?
6. How is text height typically calculated when the text is drawn in model space?
7. Which text property can be used to create italicize text?
8. List the two constants used to set the **TextGenerationFlag** property.
9. Explain *dimension styles* and why they are used in AutoCAD.
10. What is a *dimension override?*
11. What happens to any dimension overrides whenever the current dimension style is changed?
12. How are dimension overrides saved using VBA?

Programming Problems

Create the macros described below. All macros should be created in the **ThisDrawing** module of your MyMacros.dvb project. Provide all necessary error checking and control. Run and test each macro.

1. Update the macro p08_DWGSetup created from Problem 8-1 so that it creates the text styles listed below with the properties indicated. Save the updated macro as p09_DWGSetup.

Style Name	Font	Height
ROMANS_125	romans.shx	.125"
ROMANS_25	romans.shx	.250"
ROMAND_125	romand.shx	.125"
ROMAND_25	romand.shx	.250"
TITLE_25	arial.ttf	.250"
TITLE_5	arial.ttf	.500"

2. Create a macro named p09_MakeDimStyles that creates the dimension styles listed below with the properties indicated.

Style Name	Arrowheads	Arrowhead Size	Text Height
ARCHITECTURAL	Oblique	.125″	.125″
CIVIL	None	—	.125″
MECHANICAL	Closed Filled	.15″	.125″

Style Name	Vertical Text Placement	Text Alignment	Units	Measurement Scale
ARCHITECTURAL	Above	Aligned	Architectural	—
CIVIL	Above	Aligned	Decimal	.083333
MECHANICAL	Centered	Horizontal	Decimal	—

3. Create a macro named p09_FixFont that iterates all text styles in a drawing and changes any TrueType font reference to the standard simplex.shx font.
4. Create a macro named p09_ChangeDWGScale that changes the scale of a drawing to a user-specified scale factor by updating the:
   A. Dimension scale for all dimension styles.
   B. Text height for all text styles not set to 0″.
   C. Height of all text entities in the drawing.
   D. Global linetype scale factor.
   Hint: Perform a zoom extents and regenerate the drawing after all steps are complete.

CHAPTER 10

Views and Viewports

Learning Objectives

After completing this chapter, you will be able to create VBA macros that:

- Reference a named view.
- Iterate all named views in a drawing.
- Create a named view.
- Make a named view current.
- Rename a named view.
- Delete a named view.
- Control the active drawing environment (model space/paper space).
- Reference a model space viewport.
- Iterate all model space viewports in a drawing.
- Create a model space viewport.
- Make a model space viewport current.
- Split a model space viewport.
- Rename a model space viewport.
- Delete a model space viewport.
- Create a paper space viewport.
- Make a paper space viewport current.
- Set a paper space viewport scale.
- Delete a paper space viewport.

Named Views

It is possible to create multiple named views in an AutoCAD drawing. A *named view* is a rectangular area of the drawing, defined by the user, that can be redisplayed later. Recalling named views eliminates the need to pan and zoom to areas of a drawing that are frequently viewed. Using named views presents many advantages in several applications, including:

- Plotting.
- Drawing navigation.
- 3D constructions.

Figure 10-1.
In the AutoCAD drawing editor, the **View** dialog box is used to create new named views.

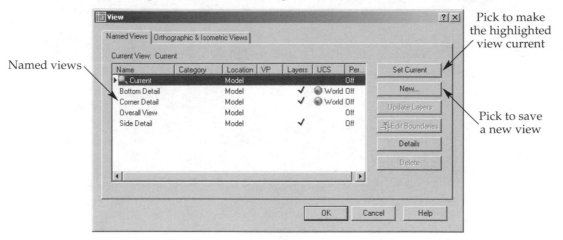

It is possible to specify a named view when plotting a drawing. Plotting is discussed in detail in Chapter 12. Most of the other advantages are related to being more efficient and productive when navigating in a drawing. Using named views, it is possible to work on the overall drawing and rely on named views to quickly zoom in to do detail work. You can also set up multiple views for working in 3D to make it easier to work on all sides of a model. Named views are created in the AutoCAD drawing editor using the **View** dialog box shown in **Figure 10-1.**

Named views are implemented as an object collection in VBA. The **Views** collection and named view management are explained in the following sections.

Views Collection

Each named view in a drawing is represented by a **View** object that is part of the drawing's **Views** collection. Object collections and their usage are discussed in Chapter 2. The following sections show you how to manage a drawing's **Views** collection and its **View** objects so you can:

- Reference an existing named view in a drawing.
- Iterate the named views in a drawing.
- Create a named view.
- Make a named view current.
- Rename a named view.
- Delete a named view.

Referencing a Named View

You can get a reference to an existing **View** object by either specifying the index number in the **Views** collection or by specifying the view name. Specifying the name is the preferred method when working with named objects, like views.

The following code creates a reference to the **View** object named VIEW1 in the **Views** collection and then displays the height and width of the view to the user:

```
Sub Ch10_GetView()

    Dim objView As AcadView

    ' Turn off errors.
    On Error Resume Next

    ' Get the view from the Views collection.
    Set objView = ThisDrawing.Views.Item("VIEW1")

    If Err.Number = 0 Then
        ' Display the height and width properties.
        MsgBox "The properties for the view ""View1"" are:" & vbLf & vbLf & _
            "Height: " & objView.Height & vbLf & _
            "Width: " & objView.Width

    Else
        ' No view exists.
        MsgBox "View not found."
        Err.Clear
    End If

End Sub
```

Iterating the Views Collection

You can step through all of the named views in a drawing by utilizing a **For Each...** loop to iterate the **Views** collection. This approach was first introduced in Chapter 2 and can be used to iterate any of the named symbol table collections.

The following code iterates the **Views** collection and displays a list of all of the named views in the current drawing. See **Figure 10-2.**

```
Sub Ch10_IterateViews()

    Dim strViews As String
    Dim objView As AcadView

    ' Initialize string.
    strViews = ""

    ' Step through all views in the drawing.
    For Each objView In ThisDrawing.Views
        strViews = strViews & objView.Name & vbCrLf
    Next

    ' Display the views to the user.
    MsgBox "Named views in the drawing: " & vbCrLf & vbCrLf & strViews

End Sub
```

Figure 10-2.
The named views in the drawing are displayed to the user.

Creating a New Named View

To create a new named view using VBA and the AutoCAD object model you simply need to add a new **View** object with the desired name to the **Views** collection. After the view is added, you can get a reference to the object using the methods described in earlier chapters. Once you have a reference to the new **View** object, you can set any of its properties or use any of its methods.

The **Add** method adds a **View** object to the **Views** collection. The signature is:

objView = Views.Add(*Name*)

where *objView* is the **View** object and *Name* is a **String** that is the name of the view to add.

The following code adds a view named View1 to the current drawing:

```
Sub Ch10_AddView()

    ' Add the view to the drawing.
    ThisDrawing.Views.Add "View1"

    ' Display to the user.
    MsgBox "Named view ""View1"" added to drawing."

End Sub
```

Professional Tip

The **Add** method uses the current display to create the new view. It is not possible to set the width and height with this method. The desired display should be set prior to calling the **Add** method.

Making a Named View Current

As you will see in the sections Model Space Viewports and Paper Space Viewports later in this chapter, it is possible to have multiple viewports in a drawing. Therefore, it is necessary to indicate which viewport to use whenever you make a named view current. This is most easily accomplished by recalling a saved named view in the active viewport using the **SetView** method. This method actually belongs to the **Viewport** object type examined later in this chapter, but is discussed here for the sake of clarity.

The signature for the **SetView** method is:

objViewport.SetView *objView*

where *objViewport* is the **Viewport** object and *objView* is the **View** object.

The following code makes the saved view named VIEW1 current:

```
Sub Ch10_SetView()

    Dim objView As AcadView
    Dim objViewport As AcadViewport

    ' Get the view from the Views collection.
    Set objView = ThisDrawing.Views.Item("VIEW1")

    ' Get the current active viewport.
    Set objViewport = ThisDrawing.ActiveViewport

    ' Set the view in the viewport.
    ThisDrawing.ActiveViewport.SetView objView
    ThisDrawing.ActiveViewport = objViewport

    ' Regen the drawing.
    ThisDrawing.Regen True

End Sub
```

Renaming a Named View

You can rename a view. This is done by getting a reference to the desired **View** object and then simply changing the object's **Name** property to the new name.

The following code changes the name of VIEW1 to VIEW2. See **Figure 10-3.**

```
Sub Ch10_ViewRename()

    Dim objView As AcadView

    ' Get VIEW1 from the Views collection.
    Set objView = ThisDrawing.Views.Item("VIEW1")

    ' Rename to VIEW2.
    objView.Name = "VIEW2"

    ' Tell the user.
    MsgBox "Named view ""VIEW1"" renamed to ""VIEW2"""

End Sub
```

Figure 10-3.
The named view
View1 is renamed to
View2.

Deleting a Named View

It is possible to delete a named view from a drawing's **Views** collection, as seen in the section Adding Objects to and Removing Objects from Object Collections in Chapter 2. The **Delete** method deletes a **View** object from the **Views** collection. The signature is:

objView.Delete

where *objView* is the **View** object to delete.

The following code deletes the named view VIEW1 from the current drawing:

```
Sub Ch10_ViewDelete()

    Dim objView As AcadView

    ' Get VIEW1 from the Views collection.
    Set objView = ThisDrawing.Views.Item("VIEW1")

    ' Delete the view.
    objView.Delete

    ' Tell the user.
    MsgBox "Named view ""VIEW1"" deleted."

End Sub
```

Let's Review...

Named Views and the Views Collection

- Each named view in a drawing is represented by a **View** object that is part of the drawing's **Views** collection.
- You get a reference to an existing **View** by specifying the view name in the **Views** collection.
- You can step through all of the named views in a drawing by utilizing a **For Each...** loop to iterate the **Views** collection.
- A new named view can be created by adding a new **View** object with the desired name to the **Views** collection.
- The **Viewport** object's **SetView** method recalls a saved named view.
- You can rename a view by changing the **View** object's **Name** property.
- The **Delete** method deletes a **View** object from the **Views** collection.

Exercise 10-1

Create the macros described below. All macros should be created in the **ThisDrawing** module of your MyMacros.dvb project. Provide all necessary error checking and control. Run and test each macro.
1. Create a macro named ex10_MakeViews that creates four different user-defined named views. *Hint:* The VBA **ZoomPickWindow** method zooms the current viewport to a window defined by two pick points.
2. Create a macro named ex10_CycleViews that cycles through all of the views in a drawing allowing the user to select which view to display.

Viewports

Viewports allow you to display multiple views of a drawing at the same time. How viewports look and behave depends on whether model space or paper space is active. The concepts of model space and paper space are introduced in Chapter 5. Just to review, model space is the 3D environment where your drawing, or model, is created and edited. Paper space is the 2D environment where layouts of the model space drawing information are created for plotting purposes.

The **ThisDrawing.ActiveSpace** property controls which drawing environment is active. It can be used to check which environment is active or to switch from one environment to the other.

The following code checks to see which drawing environment is active and informs the user:

```
' Determine if model space or paper space is active.
Sub Ch10_CheckActiveSpace()

    ' Check to see if model space is active.
    If ThisDrawing.ActiveSpace = acModelSpace Then
        MsgBox "Model space is active!"
    ' Check to see if paper space is active.
    ElseIf ThisDrawing.ActiveSpace = acPaperSpace Then
        MsgBox "Paper space is active!"
    End If

End Sub
```

As you can see in the code example above, AutoCAD provides two constants to make your job easier and your code more readable when checking which environment is active:

- **acModelSpace** for model space.
- **acPaperSpace** for paper space.

You can switch the drawing environment between model space and paper space by setting the **ThisDrawing.ActiveSpace** property to the desired constant:

```
' Switch the drawing environment between
' model space and paper space.
Sub Ch10_SwitchActiveSpace()

    ' If model space is active, switch to paper space.
    If ThisDrawing.ActiveSpace = acModelSpace Then
        ThisDrawing.ActiveSpace = acPaperSpace
    ' Paper space is active; switch to model space.
    Else
        ThisDrawing.ActiveSpace = acModelSpace
    End If

End Sub
```

Model Space Viewports

Model space viewports allow you to split up the graphics screen into multiple, adjacent, rectangular views. Because of this, AutoCAD refers to model space viewports as *tiled viewports.* The analogy is that model space viewports are similar to rectangular floor tiles because they must be aligned directly next to each other.

Model space viewports are commonly used in 3D drawing to allow you to see multiple sides of a 3D model at the same time. A popular approach is to create four viewports that provide the top view, front view, side view, and an isometric view. See **Figure 10-4.**

In the AutoCAD drawing editor, both model space and paper space viewports are created using the **Viewports** dialog box. Which options are displayed in the dialog depend on the current drawing environment (model space or paper space). If model space is active when the dialog box is opened, the dialog box looks like **Figure 10-5.**

When you are working in model space, it is possible to save a viewport configuration to a specific name so that it can be recalled later. This makes the configurations named objects, just like layers, linetypes, etc. Because of this, viewport configurations are also implemented as object collections in VBA. The model space **Viewports** collection and model space viewport management are discussed in the following sections.

Figure 10-4.
In a typical model space viewport configuration, the top, left, front, and an isometric view are displayed.

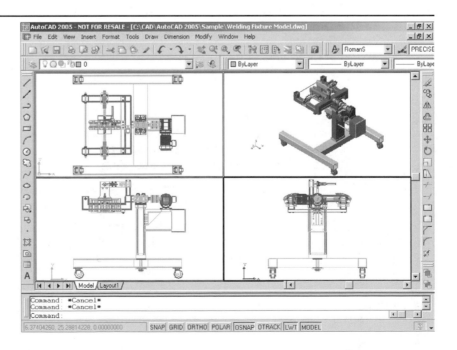

Figure 10-5.
The **Viewports** dialog box provides these options when opened from model space.

Predefined
configurations

Preview

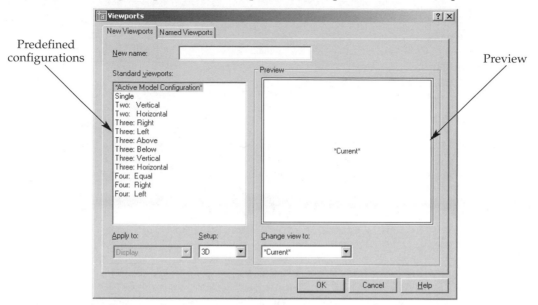

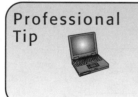

Professional Tip

A VBA **Viewport** object is a model space viewport configuration. However, in the AutoCAD drawing editor, a model space viewport is part of a viewport configuration. This can be confusing, so be sure to understand the terminology.

Model Space Viewports Collection

Each named viewport configuration in a drawing is represented by a **Viewport** object that is part of the drawing's **Viewports** collection. Object collections and their usage are discussed in Chapter 2. The following sections show you how to manage a drawing's **Viewports** collection and its **Viewport** objects so you can:

- Reference an existing viewport configuration in a drawing.
- Iterate the viewport configurations in a drawing.
- Create a named viewport configuration.
- Make a named viewport configuration current.
- Rename a named viewport configuration.
- Delete a named viewport configuration.

Referencing a Model Space Viewport

You can get a reference to an existing **Viewport** object (viewport configuration) by either specifying the index number in the **Viewports** collection or by specifying the viewport name. Specifying the name is the preferred method when working with named objects, like viewport configurations.

The following code creates a reference to the VIEWPORT1 **Viewport** object in the **Viewports** collection and displays the viewport's height and width. See **Figure 10-6.**

Figure 10-6.
A—The viewport's
height and width are
displayed to the user.
B—If the viewport is
not found, this
message box appears.

A   B

```
Sub Ch10_GetViewport()

    Dim objViewport As AcadViewport

    ' Turn off errors.
    On Error Resume Next

    ' Get the viewport configuration from the Viewports collection.
    Set objViewport = ThisDrawing.Viewports.Item("Viewport1")

    If Err.Number = 0 Then
        ' Display the height and width properties.
        MsgBox "The properties for ""Viewport1"" are:" & vbLf & vbLf & _
            "Height: " & objViewport.Height & vbLf & _
            "Width: " & objViewport.Width
    Else
        ' The viewport configuration does not exist.
        MsgBox "Viewport not found."
        Err.Clear
    End If

End Sub
```

Iterating the Model Space Viewports Collection

You can step through all of the viewport configurations in a drawing by using a **For Each...** loop to iterate the **Viewports** collection. This approach was first introduced in Chapter 2 and can be used to iterate any of the named symbol table collections.

The following code iterates the **Viewports** collection and displays a list of all the viewport configurations in the current drawing:

```
Sub Ch10_IterateViewports()

    Dim strViewports As String
    Dim objViewport As AcadViewport

    ' Initialize string.
    strViewports = ""

    ' Step through all of the viewport configurations in the drawing.
    For Each objViewport In ThisDrawing.Viewports
        strViewports = strViewports & objViewport.Name & vbCrLf
    Next

    ' Display the viewport configurations to the user.
    MsgBox "Named viewports in the drawing: " & vbCrLf & vbCrLf & strViewports

End Sub
```

Creating a New Model Space Viewport

To create a new viewport configuration using VBA and the AutoCAD object model, you simply need to add a new **Viewport** object with the desired name to the **Viewports** collection. After the object is added, you can get a reference to it using the methods described earlier. Once you have a reference to the new **Viewport** object, you can set any of its properties or use any of its methods.

The **Add** method adds a **Viewport** object to the **Viewports** collection. The signature is:

objViewport = Viewports.Add(*Name*)

where *objViewport* is the **Viewport** object and *Name* is a **String** that is the name of the viewport configuration to add.

The following code adds a viewport configuration named VIEWPORT1 to the current drawing:

```
Sub Ch10_AddViewport()

    ' Add the viewport configuration to the drawing.
    ThisDrawing.Viewports.Add "Viewport1"

    ' Display to the user.
    MsgBox "Named viewport configuration ""Viewport1"" added to the drawing."

End Sub
```

Professional Tip

The **Add** method creates a viewport configuration consisting of a single viewport. To create a viewport configuration with multiple viewports, it is necessary to split a single viewport using the **Split** method discussed later in this chapter.

Making a Model Space Viewport Active

The current viewport configuration is controlled via the **ActiveViewport** property of the **ThisDrawing** object. In order to make a viewport configuration current, the **ActiveViewport** property must be set to an existing **Viewport** object, not just a viewport configuration name. This requires first getting a reference to the **Viewport** object from the **Viewports** collection and then assigning the object to the **ActiveViewport** property.

The following code gets a reference to the VIEWPORT1 **Viewport** object and then makes it the current viewport configuration via the **ActiveViewport** property:

```
Sub Ch10_ActiveViewport()

    Dim objViewport As AcadViewport

    ' Get the viewport configuration from the Viewports collection.
    Set objViewport = ThisDrawing.Viewports.Item("Viewport1")

    ' Make the viewport configuration active.
    ThisDrawing.ActiveViewport = objViewport

    ' Regen the drawing.
    ThisDrawing.Regen True

End Sub
```

Splitting a Model Space Viewport

As seen earlier, when you create a new viewport configuration using the **Add** method, only one viewport is created. If you want to create a viewport configuration with more than one viewport, you must use the **Split** method. This method allows you to split a viewport configuration into multiple viewports using most of the same options found in the **Viewports** dialog box in the AutoCAD drawing editor. The signature for the **Split** method is:

objViewport.Split *Number*

where *objViewport* is the **Viewport** object and *Number* is an AutoCAD **Constant**, as shown in **Figure 10-7**.

The following code splits the current model space viewport configuration into four equal viewports:

```
Sub Ch10_SplitViewport()

    Dim objViewport As AcadViewport

    ' Get the active viewport.
    Set objViewport = ThisDrawing.ActiveViewport

    ' Split the viewport configuration into four new viewports.
    objViewport.Split acViewport4

    ' Reset the active viewport so the changes appear.
    ThisDrawing.ActiveViewport = objViewport

    ' Tell the user.
    MsgBox "Current viewport configuration split into four windows."

End Sub
```

Figure 10-7.
AutoCAD viewport constants for use in VBA.

Constant	Description
acViewport2Horizontal	Two equally sized horizontal viewports.
acViewport2Vertical	Two equally sized vertical viewports.
acViewport3Left	Three viewports with the large viewport on the left.
acViewport3Right	Three viewports with the large viewport on the right.
acViewport3Horizontal	Three equally sized horizontal viewports.
acViewport3Vertical	Three equally sized vertical viewports.
acViewport3Above	Three viewports with the large viewport on top.
acViewport3Below	Three viewports with the large viewport on bottom.
acViewport4	Four equally sized viewports.

Deleting a Model Space Viewport

It is possible to delete a named viewport configuration from a drawing's **Viewports** collection. However, this is not accomplished using the **Delete** method that has been discussed so far with the other named object collections. Instead, the special **DeleteConfiguration** method is used to delete a **Viewport** object from the **Viewports** collection. The signature for the **DeleteConfiguration** method is:

objViewports.DeleteConfiguration *Name*

where *objViewports* is the **Viewports** collection and *Name* is a **String** that is the name of the viewport configuration to delete.

The following code deletes the named viewport configuration VIEWPORT1 from the current drawing:

```
Sub Ch10_ViewportDeleteConfig()

    ' Delete the viewport configuration.
    ThisDrawing.Viewports.DeleteConfiguration ("Viewport1")

    ' Tell the user.
    MsgBox "Named Viewport ""Viewport1"" deleted."

End Sub
```

Unlike the generic **Delete** method used with most of the other named object collections, the **DeleteConfiguration** method does not require you to first get a reference to the **Viewport** object you wish to delete. You can delete it by name!

Model Space Viewports — Let's Review...

- How viewports look and behave depends on whether you are in model space or paper space.
- The **ThisDrawing.ActiveSpace** property controls which drawing environment is active—model space or paper space.
- Model space viewports are called tiled viewports because they must be adjacent to each other, cannot overlap, and cannot have space between them, similar to a tile pattern.
- Each named viewport configuration in a drawing is represented by a **Viewport** object that is part of the drawing's **Viewports** collection.
- You get a reference to an existing viewport configuration by specifying the viewport name in the **Viewports** collection.
- You can step through all of the viewport configurations in a drawing by utilizing a **For Each...** loop to iterate the **Viewports** collection.
- A new viewport configuration can be created by adding a new **Viewport** object with the desired name to the **Viewports** collection.
- To make a viewport configuration current, the **ThisDrawing.ActiveViewport** property must be set to reference an existing **Viewport** object.
- The **Split** method allows you to split a **Viewport** object into multiple viewports.
- You can rename a viewport configuration by changing a **Viewport** object's **Name** property.
- The **DeleteConfiguration** method is used to delete a **Viewport** object from the **Viewports** collection.

Write a macro named ex10_4MspaceViews that creates four model space view-ports, which display the top, front, right, and an isometric view. The macro should be created in the **ThisDrawing** module of your MyMacros.dvb project. Provide all necessary error checking and control. Run and test the macro. *Hint:* The **VPOINT** system variable can be used to set the view display point.

Paper Space Viewports

Paper space viewports are a bit different from model space viewports. Unlike model space viewports, paper space viewports do not have to be adjacent to each other. They can also be moved and resized, just like regular AutoCAD drawing entities. Because of this, paper space viewports are referred to as *floating viewports.*

A good analogy is to think of paper space viewports as holes in the 2D paper space layout that allow you to view the model space information below. Each "cutout" can display a different scale view of the model space info, as shown in **Figure 10-8.** In this example, three viewports have been "cut" in the paper space layout: a 1/8" = 1'-0" overall view of the floor plan and two 1 1/2" = 1'-0" enlarged detail views. You can create as many viewports as you need up to a maximum of 64 (the maximum **MAXACTVP** system variable setting).

Figure 10-9 shows a good example of utilizing paper space viewports. By using paper space viewports, two enlarged views—of the stairwell and the kitchen—have been included with an overall view of the floor plan that is at a smaller scale. All views are of the same model space information, but at different scales with different layer properties. Layer visibility can be controlled in each floating viewport so that different drawing information can be displayed. Paper space viewports can also be moved and resized, just like regular AutoCAD entities such as lines and circles. They do not even have to be rectangular. Paper space viewports can be polygonal, circular, or almost any other closed entity.

Figure 10-8.
Paper space viewports can be thought of as "holes" through which you can view the model space construction.

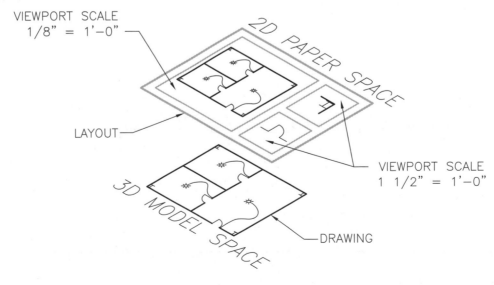

Figure 10-9.
This drawing makes good use of three paper space viewports. Each viewport shows a different view of the drawing.

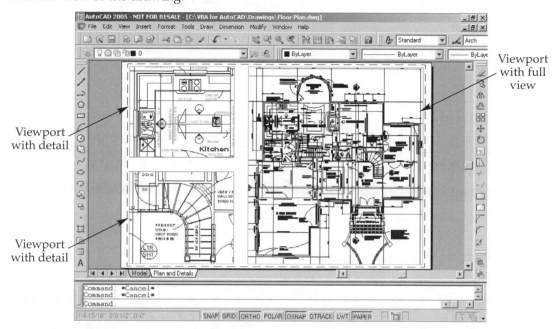

Viewport with full view

Viewport with detail

Viewport with detail

In the AutoCAD drawing editor, paper space viewports are created using the **Viewports** dialog box shown in **Figure 10-10.** Notice that the dialog box is slightly different from the dialog displayed when model space is active. The command is the same, but the dialog box contains different options. The obvious difference is that it is possible to set the spacing between viewports using the **Viewport Spacing:** text box.

Paper space viewports are treated as just another drawing entity in AutoCAD. Therefore, there is no need to have a separate paper space viewport collection. Paper space viewports are represented as **PViewport** objects and are part of the **PaperSpace** collection. Refer to the AutoCAD object model shown in **Figure 10-11.** Creating and referencing paper space viewports are explained in the following sections.

Figure 10-10.
The **Viewports** dialog box provides these options when opened from paper space.

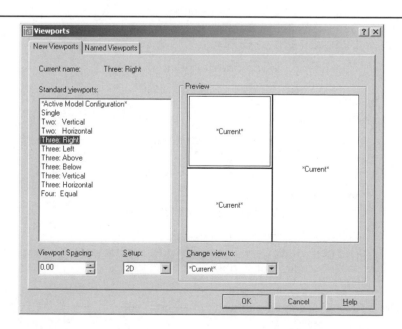

Figure 10-11.
Paper space viewports
are represented as
PViewport objects in
AutoCAD's object
model.

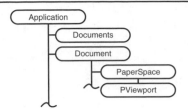

> **Professional Tip**
>
> Unfortunately, it is not possible to create polygonal or circular paper space viewports using VBA at this time. Currently, only rectangular viewports can be created using VBA. Polygonal and circular paper space viewports must be created in the AutoCAD drawing editor.

Creating a New Paper Space Viewport

The **AddPViewport** method adds a new **PViewport** object to the **PaperSpace** collection. Unlike creating a model space viewport, when you create a paper space viewport you must specify its location, width, and height. These properties are included when you add a new **PViewport** object to the **PaperSpace** collection using the **AddPViewport** method. The signature for the **AddPViewport** method is:

objPViewport = PaperSpace.AddPViewport(*CenterPt*, *Width*, *Height*)

where *objPViewport* is the **PViewport** object. *CenterPt* is a **Variant** three-element array of **Double** data types that represents the center point of the viewport. *Width* is a **Double** data type that is the width of the viewport. *Height* is a **Double** data type that is the height of the viewport.

The following code creates a 34″ × 23″ paper space viewport that is centered at the point (17.3,11.77). It is intended to be used with a 36″ × 24″ D-size sheet.

```
Sub Ch10_AddPViewport()

    Dim objPViewport As AcadPViewport
    Dim dblCtrPt(0 To 2) As Double
    Dim dblWidth As Double
    Dim dblHeight As Double

    ' Define the viewport center point.
    dblCtrPt(0) = 17.75
    dblCtrPt(1) = 11.25
    dblCtrPt(2) = 0

    ' Define the viewport width and height.
    dblWidth = 34
    dblHeight = 22

    ' Switch to paper space.
    ThisDrawing.ActiveSpace = acPaperSpace

    ' Create the paper space viewport.
    Set objPViewport = ThisDrawing.PaperSpace.AddPViewport(dblCtrPt, _
        dblWidth, dblHeight)

    ' Regen the viewports.
    ThisDrawing.Regen acAllViewports

End Sub
```

This code centers a 22″ × 34″ viewport on a 36″ × 24″ D-size sheet. But why the odd center point location, you might wonder? This is because the origin of the coordinate system in paper space is based on the printable area of the layout. The printable area is represented by a dashed line on the layout.

Professional Tip

Remember that a paper space viewport is treated like any of the other typical drawing entities in AutoCAD and, as such, has the same general properties, including layer, linetype, and color. Once you have a reference to **PViewport** object, you can set any of these properties using the same techniques shown in Chapter 6.

Making a Paper Space Viewport Active

The current, or active, paper space viewport is controlled via the **ActiveViewport** property of the **ThisDrawing** object. In order to make a paper space viewport current, the property must be set to an existing **PViewport** object.

The following code creates a 34″ × 22″ paper space viewport that is centered at the point (17.75,11.25), makes it current, and then sets the viewport scale factor to 1/4″ = 1′-0″:

```
Sub Ch10_ActivePViewport()

    Dim objPViewport As AcadPViewport
    Dim dblCtrPt(0 To 2) As Double
    Dim dblWidth As Double
    Dim dblHeight As Double

    ' Define the viewport center point.
    dblCtrPt(0) = 17.75
    dblCtrPt(1) = 11.25
    dblCtrPt(2) = 0

    ' Define the viewport width and height.
    dblWidth = 34
    dblHeight = 22

    ' Switch to paper space.
    ThisDrawing.ActiveSpace = acPaperSpace

    ' Create the paper space viewport.
    Set objPViewport = ThisDrawing.PaperSpace.AddPViewport(dblCtrPt, _
        dblWidth, dblHeight)

    ' Turn the viewport display on.
    objPViewport.Display (True)

    ' Switch to model space.
    ThisDrawing.MSpace = True

    ' Make the viewport active.
    ThisDrawing.ActivePViewport = objPViewport

    ' Zoom extents.
    ZoomExtents

    ' Set the viewport scale to 1/4"=1'-0".
    objPViewport.StandardScale = acVp1_4in_1ft

End Sub
```

The **ThisDrawing.MSpace** property is the equivalent of both the **MSPACE** and **PSPACE** commands in the AutoCAD drawing editor. Setting **ThisDrawing.Mspace** to **True** is the same as using the **MSPACE** command, while setting **ThisDrawing.Mspace** to **False** is the same as using the **PSPACE** command.

Caution

You *must* turn the display on by setting the **Display** property to **True** before switching to model space or a run-time error will be generated.

Setting a Paper Space Viewport Scale

The code example in the last section shows you how to set the scale factor for a paper space viewport to 1/4" = 1'-0". This is done by setting the **StandardScale** property of the **PViewport** object to the AutoCAD scale constant **acVp1_4in_1ft**. AutoCAD provides the standard scale constants shown in **Figure 10-12**.

The following code prompts the user to select a paper space viewport and then sets the viewport to a user-defined scale:

```
Sub Ch10_ScalePViewport()

    Dim objSelected As AcadObject
    Dim varPickPt As Variant
    Dim dblScaleFactor As Double

    ' Switch to paper space.
    ThisDrawing.ActiveSpace = acPaperSpace

    ' Prompt the user to select a floating viewport.
    ThisDrawing.Utility.GetEntity objSelected, varPickPt, "Select a viewport: "

    ' Make sure the entity is a viewport.
    If objSelected.ObjectName = "AcDbViewport" Then

        ' Get the current viewport scale.
        dblScaleFactor = objSelected.CustomScale

        ' Display the current viewport scale.
        MsgBox "Current viewport scale: " & dblScaleFactor

        ' Get the new scale from the user.
        dblScaleFactor = ThisDrawing.Utility.GetReal(vbCrLf & "New scale: ")

        ' Set the standard scale to "custom."
        objSelected.StandardScale = acVpCustomScale

        ' Set the custom scale.
        objSelected.CustomScale = dblScaleFactor

    Else

        ' No viewport was selected.
        MsgBox "No viewport selected."

    End If

End Sub
```

Figure 10-12.
AutoCAD viewport
scale constants for
use in VBA.

Constant	Scale
acVpScaleToFit	Scale to fit
acVpCustomScale	Custom
acVp1_128in_1ft	1/128″= 1′
acVp1_64in_1ft	1/64″= 1′
acVp1_32in_1ft	1/32″= 1′
acVp1_16in_1ft	1/16″= 1′
acVp3_32in_1ft	3/32″= 1′
acVp1_8in_1ft	1/8″ = 1′
acVp3_16in_1ft	3/16″= 1′
acVp1_4in_1ft	1/4″ = 1′
acVp3_8in_1ft	3/8″ = 1′
acVp1_2in_1ft	1/2″ = 1′
acVp3_4in_1ft	3/4″ = 1′
acVp1in_1ft	1″= 1′
acVp3in_1ft	3″= 1′
acVp6in_1ft	6″= 1′
acVp1ft_1ft	1′= 1′
acVp1_1	1:1
acVp1_2	1:2
acVp1_4	1:4
acVp1_8	1:8
acVp1_10	1:10
acVp1_16	1:16
acVp1_20	1:20
acVp1_30	1:30
acVp1_40	1:40
acVp1_50	1:50
acVp1_100	1:100
acVp2_1 2	1
acVp4_1	4:1
acVp8_1	8:1
acVp10_1	10:1
acVp100_1	100:1

Professional Tip

The **acVpCustomScale** constant allows you to set a custom scale, although it is a two-step process. First, you must set the **StandardScale** property to the **acVpCustomScale** constant and then you can set the **CustomScale** property to the desired custom scale. This is shown in the above code.

Deleting a Paper Space Viewport

As stated earlier, a paper space viewport is treated like any other regular AutoCAD drawing entity that is part of the **PaperSpace** collection. Therefore, you can delete a paper space viewport using the **Delete** method introduced in Chapter 6. Just as a refresher, the signature for the **Delete** method is:

objSelected.Delete

where *objSelected* is the selected paper space viewport to delete.

The following code prompts the user to select a paper space viewport and then deletes it. Note that the code does not switch to paper space, so you should be in paper space when the macro is run.

```
Sub Ch10_DeletePViewport()

    Dim objSelected As AcadObject
    Dim varPickPt As Variant

    ' Prompt the user to select the floating viewport.
    ThisDrawing.Utility.GetEntity objSelected, varPickPt, _
        "Select paper space viewport to delete: "

    ' Delete the viewport.
    objSelected.Delete

End Sub
```

Let's Review... Paper Space Viewports

- Paper space viewports are called floating viewports because they do not have to abut each other in a tile type pattern; they can have space between them.
- Paper space viewports are represented as **PViewport** objects and are part of the **PaperSpace** collection.
- The **AddPViewport** method adds a new **PViewport** object with the specified center point, width, and height to the **PaperSpace** collection.
- To make a paper space viewport current, the **ThisDrawing.ActiveViewport** property must be set to reference an existing **PViewport** object.
- The **ThisDrawing.MSpace** property is the equivalent of both the **MSPACE** and **PSPACE** commands in the AutoCAD drawing editor.
- You set the scale factor for a paper space viewport by setting its **StandardScale** property to one of the AutoCAD scale constants. Custom scales are also allowed.
- The **Delete** method deletes a **PViewport** object from the **PaperSpace** collection.

Exercise 10-3

Write a macro named ex10_4PspaceViews that creates four paper space viewports of equal size with user-defined spacing and scale factors. The macro should be created in the **ThisDrawing** module of your MyMacros.dvb project. Provide all necessary error checking and control. Run and test each macro. *Hint:* The drawing **LIMITS** setting can be used to determine the viewport size.

Chapter Test

Write your answers on a separate sheet of paper.
1. Explain *named views* and how they are used in AutoCAD.
2. List three advantages of using named views in AutoCAD.
3. Which VBA method is used to recall a saved named view?
4. Which VBA property controls whether model space or paper space is active?
5. Explain the differences between *model space viewports* and *paper space viewports*.
6. How do you create multiple tiled viewports in model space using VBA?
7. List three advantages of using paper space viewports.
8. Which VBA object represents paper space viewports in the AutoCAD object model?
9. List five methods provided by the **PViewport** object.
10. Which **ThisDrawing** object property allows you to toggle between model space and paper space when working in paper space?
11. Which **PViewport** property is used to set a standard paper space viewport scale?
12. Which **PViewport** property is used to set a custom paper space viewport scale?
13. What must you do prior to setting a custom paper space viewport scale?

Programming Problems

Create the macros described below. All macros should be created in the **ThisDrawing** module of your MyMacros.dvb project. Provide all necessary error checking and control. Run and test each macro.

1. Create a macro named p10_CreatePlotView that iterates all open drawings, thaws all layers, zooms to the drawing extents, creates a view named PLOT, and then saves the drawing to a new name consisting of the original name with the prefix PLOT-. For example, drawing1.dwg becomes PLOT-drawing1.dwg.
2. Create a macro named p10_MVSetupMS that sets up a drawing in model space, similar to AutoCAD's **MVSETUP** command, based on the following user-supplied information:
   A. Units.
   B. Scale factor.
   C. Limits.
   D. Number of viewports and viewport configuration.
   Hint: Use the scale factor to calculate the limits, set the linetype scale, and set the dimension scale.
3. Create a macro named p10_MakeDtlSht that creates a detail sheet with multiple viewports in paper space based on the following user-supplied information:
   A. Number of details (viewports).
   B. Overall rectangular area to fill based on two pick points.
   C. Spacing between viewports.
   D. Scale for all viewports.
   Hint: Create all viewports on a layer named VIEWPORT that is set not to plot.

The code examples in this chapter are supplied on the Student CD. A—First, open the **Open VBA Project** dialog box by selecting **Load Project...** from the **Macro** cascading menu in AutoCAD's **Tools** pull-down menu. B—Next, select the project Example Code.dvb and pick the **Open** button. C—Finally, display the **Macros** dialog box by picking **Macros...** from the **Macro** cascading menu in AutoCAD's **Tools** pull-down menu. Then, select the macro you wish to run and pick the **Run** button.

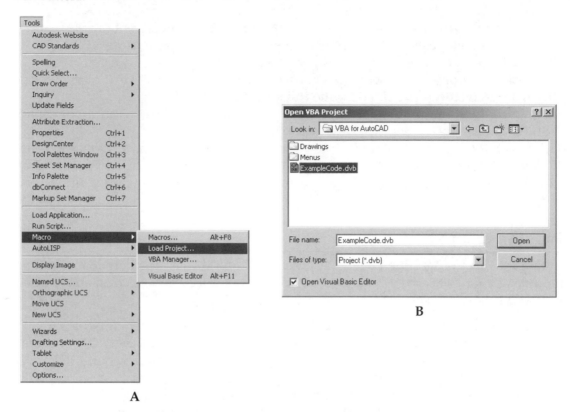

A

B

C

CHAPTER 11

Blocks, Block Attributes, and Xrefs

Learning Objectives

After completing this chapter, you will be able to create VBA macros that:

- Reference a block definition.
- Iterate all block definitions in a drawing.
- Create a block definition.
- Rename a block definition.
- Delete a block definition.
- Insert a block.
- Retrieve a block insert.
- Explode a block insert.
- Delete a block insert.
- Write a block to disk.
- Create block attributes.
- Insert a block containing attributes.
- Retrieve a block containing attributes.
- Attach an xref.
- Detach an xref.
- Unload an xref.
- Reload an xref.
- Bind an xref.

Blocks

A *block* is a named collection of one or more AutoCAD drawing entities. The entities within a block are treated as a single object. Blocks allow you to reuse drawing content within the same drawing or across multiple drawings.

Blocks can be made up of all of the standard AutoCAD entities, including lines, circles, and text. In fact, a special dynamic text type called a block attribute can be defined so that text in a block can be updated. Block attributes are a very powerful feature and discussed later in this chapter. Some of the advantages of using blocks include:

- Reuse of drawing content.
- Creation of symbol libraries.

- Use of attributes for annotation and information extraction.
- Reduction of drawing size.

AutoCAD includes a number of sample symbol libraries in the \Sample\DesignCenter folder that is installed with AutoCAD. The examples in this chapter make use of these sample files. **DesignCenter** is AutoCAD's multipurpose drawing management tool. If the **DesignCenter** sample files are not installed, insert the AutoCAD installation CD and choose the Install option. Select the Add or Remove Features option and make sure the Program Files\Sample\DesignCenter Samples feature is highlighted. Finally, pick the Next button to initiate the installation. Once the installation is complete, exit the installation program.

Using **DesignCenter**, you can view the blocks defined in the Basic Electronics.dwg sample drawing file, as shown in **Figure 11-1,** by highlighting Blocks in the drawing's tree. A list is displayed, including previews, of the blocks that are defined in the Basic Electronics.dwg. Using **DesignCenter** it is possible to drag and drop blocks, like the block Generator-AC shown in **Figure 11-2,** directly into a drawing.

It is also possible to "write" a block defined in a drawing to a separate drawing file. This allows the block to be shared across multiple drawings. In the AutoCAD drawing editor, blocks are created using the **Block Definition** dialog box shown in **Figure 11-3.** When a block is defined, it is necessary to include a base point. The base point of the block is placed at the point of insertion specified when the block is inserted into a drawing. It is also possible to include an icon, description, and even a hyperlink to a web page.

When a block is inserted into a drawing, it actually references the original block definition and becomes a **BlockReference** object in VBA, better known as an "insert" in AutoCAD. The **BlockReference** object stores only the following information:

- Name.
- Insertion point.
- X, Y, and Z scale.
- Rotation.

Figure 11-1.
Viewing blocks in a drawing using **DesignCenter**.

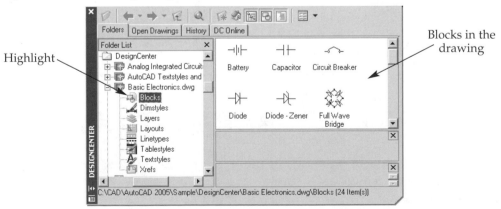

Figure 11-2.
The Generator-AC block contained within the Basic Electronics drawing.

Figure 11-3.
In the AutoCAD
drawing editor, the
Block Definition
dialog box is used
to create a block.

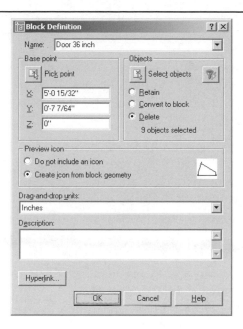

This is evident when a block is inserted using the **Insert** dialog box in the AutoCAD drawing editor, as shown in **Figure 11-4.**

Everything else that affects the blocks appearance (lines, circles, text, object properties, etc.) is derived from the centralized block definition that is stored in what is commonly known as the *block table.* This provides two benefits:

- Less use of memory resources.
- The ability to update/redefine a block definition in one location and affect all instances of the block in the drawing.

In VBA, the block table is represented as an object collection. The **Blocks** collection and block management are explained in the following sections.

Figure 11-4.
In the AutoCAD drawing editor, the **Insert** dialog box is used to insert a block. The **BlockReference** object stores the information shown here.

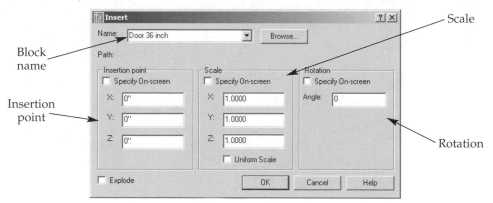

Each block in a drawing is represented by a **Block** object that is part of the drawing's **Blocks** collection. Object collections and their usage are discussed in Chapter 2. The following sections show you how to manage a drawing's **Blocks** collection and its **Block** objects so you can:

- Reference an existing block definition in a drawing.
- Iterate all of the block definitions in a drawing.
- Create a new block definition.
- Rename a block definition.
- Delete a block definition.

Referencing a Block Definition

You can get a reference to an existing **Block** object by either specifying the index number in the **Blocks** collection or by specifying the block name. Specifying the name is the preferred method when working with named objects, like blocks.

The following code creates a reference to the Generator-AC **Block** object in the **Blocks** collection and displays how many subentities the block contains. See **Figure 11-5.**

```
Sub Ch11_GetBlockDef()

    Dim objBlock As AcadBlock

    ' Go to NOTFOUND if an error occurs.
    On Error GoTo NOTFOUND:

    ' Get the "Generator-AC" block definition from the Blocks collection.
    Set objBlock = ThisDrawing.Blocks.Item("Generator - AC")

    ' Display how many subentities make up the block.
    MsgBox "The block Generator-AC contains " & objBlock.Count & _
        " subentities."

    Exit Sub

NOTFOUND:

    ' "Generator-AC" block definition does not exist.
    MsgBox "The block Generator-AC was not found."

End Sub
```

If the Generator-AC block is not found, the message box shown in **Figure 11-5B** is displayed.

Figure 11-5.
A—The user is informed that the Generator-AC block has been inserted.
B—The user is informed if the block is not found.

A

B

Iterating the Blocks Collection

You can step through all of the blocks in a drawing by using a **For Each...** loop to iterate the **Blocks** collection. This approach was first introduced in Chapter 2 and can be used to iterate any of the named symbol table collections.

The following code iterates the **Blocks** collection and displays a list of all the blocks defined in the current drawing:

```
Sub Ch11_IterateBlockDefs()

    Dim strBlocks As String
    Dim objBlockRef As AcadBlock

    ' Initialize string.
    strBlocks = ""

    ' Step through all of the blocks in the drawing.
    For Each objBlockRef In ThisDrawing.Blocks
        strBlocks = strBlocks & objBlockRef.Name & vbCrLf
    Next

    ' Display the blocks to the user.
    MsgBox "Blocks defined in drawing: " & vbCrLf & vbCrLf & strBlocks

End Sub
```

Creating a New Block

To create a new block using VBA and the AutoCAD object model you simply need to add a new **Block** object with the desired name to the **Blocks** collection. Once a new **Block** object is created, you can add drawing objects to it using the same methods used to add drawing objects to the **ModelSpace** and **PaperSpace** collection, as described in Chapter 5.

Professional Tip

Remember from Chapter 5 that model space and paper space are represented as named collections in VBA. The only difference between them and the named block objects described in this chapter is that their names are reserved. You *cannot* create a new block object named **ModelSpace** or **PaperSpace**!

The **Add** method adds a **Block** object with the specified name to the **Blocks** collection. The signature for the **Add** method is:

objBlock = Blocks.Add(*BasePt*, *Name*)

where *objBlock* is the **Block** object. *BasePt* is a **Variant** that is a three-element array of **Double** data types. It is the block base point. *Name* is a **String** that is the name of the block to add.

The following code adds a block named MyBlock to the current drawing. The block consists of three circles and an arc.

```
Sub Ch11_AddBlockDef()

    Dim objBlock As AcadBlock
    Dim dblBasePt(0 To 2) As Double
    Dim dblCenterPt(0 To 2) As Double
    Dim dblRadius As Double

    ' Define the base point of the block.
    dblBasePt(0) = 0
    dblBasePt(1) = 0
    dblBasePt(2) = 0

    ' Add an empty block definition.
    Set objBlock = ThisDrawing.Blocks.Add(dblBasePt, "MyBlock")

    ' Add a circle to the block.
    dblCenterPt(0) = 0
    dblCenterPt(1) = 0
    dblCenterPt(2) = 0
    dblRadius = 1

    objBlock.AddCircle dblCenterPt, dblRadius

    ' Add another circle to the block.
    dblCenterPt(0) = -0.375
    dblCenterPt(1) = 0.375
    dblCenterPt(2) = 0
    dblRadius = 0.125

    objBlock.AddCircle dblCenterPt, dblRadius

    ' Add yet another circle to the block.
    dblCenterPt(0) = 0.375
    dblCenterPt(1) = 0.375
    dblCenterPt(2) = 0
    dblRadius = 0.125

    objBlock.AddCircle dblCenterPt, dblRadius

    ' Add an arc to the block.
    dblCenterPt(0) = 0
    dblCenterPt(1) = 0
    dblCenterPt(2) = 0
    dblRadius = 0.75

    objBlock.AddArc dblCenterPt, dblRadius, 3.14159, 0

    ' Tell the user that the block has been defined.
    MsgBox "Block named ""MyBlock"" has been defined in the drawing."

End Sub
```

Renaming a Block

The **Block** object's **Name** property controls the block name. You can rename a block by getting a reference to the desired **Block** object and then simply changing its **Name** property to the new name.

The following code changes the name of the block MyBlock to YourBlock:

```
Sub Ch11_BlockRename()

    Dim objBlock As AcadBlock

    ' Go to NOTFOUND if an error occurs.
    On Error GoTo NOTFOUND:

    ' Get the "MyBlock" block definition from the Blocks collection.
    Set objBlock = ThisDrawing.Blocks.Item("MyBlock")

    ' Change the name.
    objBlock.Name = "YourBlock"

    ' Tell the user.
    MsgBox """MyBlock"" block renamed to ""YourBlock""."

    Exit Sub

NOTFOUND:

    ' "MyBlock" block definition does not exist.
    MsgBox """MyBlock"" not found."

End Sub
```

Deleting a Block   ~~Reference~~ definition

It is possible to delete a block from a drawing's **Blocks** collection, as seen in the section Adding Objects to and Removing Objects from Object Collections in Chapter 2, as long as the following criteria are met:

- Block is not inserted in the drawing.
- Block is not xref dependent.

The **Delete** method will delete a **Block** object from the **Blocks** collection. The signature is:

objBlock.Delete

where *objBlock* is the **Block** object to delete.

The following code deletes the block named YourBlock from the current drawing:

```vba
Sub Ch11_DeleteBlock()

    Dim objBlock As AcadBlock

    ' Disable errors.
    On Error Resume Next

    ' Get the block definition "YourBlock" from the Blocks collection.
    Set objBlock = ThisDrawing.Blocks.Item("YourBlock")

    ' Delete the block.
    objBlock.Delete

    ' Tell the user what happened.
    If Err.Number = 0 Then
        MsgBox "The block definition ""YourBlock"" was deleted."
    Else
        MsgBox "Cannot delete the block definition ""YourBlock""."
        Err.Clear
    End If

End Sub
```

Inserting a Block

As explained earlier, a block reference is the graphic representation of the information stored in the block definition. The **BlockReference** object stores only the block name, insertion point, scale factors, and rotation factor.

The **InsertBlock** method inserts a named block definition as a **BlockReference** object at a specified insertion point, scale, and rotation. If successful, it returns a reference to the newly created **BlockReference** object. The signature for the **InsertBlock** method is:

objBlockRef = *Space*.InsertBlock(*InsertPt, Name, XScale, YScale, ZScale, _
    Rotation*)

where *objBlockRef* is the **BlockReference** object. *Space* is the **ModelSpace** or **PaperSpace** collection. *InsertPt* is a **Variant** three-element array of **Double** data types that is the insertion point. *Name* is a **String** that is the block name. *XScale*, *YScale*, and *ZScale* are **Double** data types that are the scale factor on the respective axes. *Rotation* is a **Double** data type that is the rotation angle, in radians.

The following code creates a block definition named MyBlock and then inserts it at 0,0,0 with a scale of 1.0 and a rotation angle of 0°:

```vba
Sub Ch11_InsertBlock()

    Dim objBlock As AcadBlock
    Dim dblBasePt(0 To 2) As Double
    Dim dblCenterPt(0 To 2) As Double
    Dim dblInsertPt(0 To 2) As Double
    Dim dblRadius As Double

    ' Define the base point of the block.
    dblBasePt(0) = 0
    dblBasePt(1) = 0
    dblBasePt(2) = 0

    ' Add an empty block definition.
    Set objBlock = ThisDrawing.Blocks.Add(dblBasePt, "MyBlock")
```

```
' Add a circle to the block.
dblCenterPt(0) = 0
dblCenterPt(1) = 0
dblCenterPt(2) = 0
dblRadius = 1

objBlock.AddCircle dblCenterPt, dblRadius

' Add another circle to the block.
dblCenterPt(0) = -0.375
dblCenterPt(1) = 0.375
dblCenterPt(2) = 0
dblRadius = 0.125

objBlock.AddCircle dblCenterPt, dblRadius

' Add yet another circle to the block.
dblCenterPt(0) = 0.375
dblCenterPt(1) = 0.375
dblCenterPt(2) = 0
dblRadius = 0.125

objBlock.AddCircle dblCenterPt, dblRadius

' Add an arc to the block.
dblCenterPt(0) = 0
dblCenterPt(1) = 0
dblCenterPt(2) = 0
dblRadius = 0.75

objBlock.AddArc dblCenterPt, dblRadius, 3.14159, 0

' Insert the block at 0,0,0.
dblInsertPt(0) = 0
dblInsertPt(1) = 0
dblInsertPt(2) = 0

ThisDrawing.ModelSpace.InsertBlock dblInsertPt, "MyBlock", 1#, 1#, 1#, 0

' Zoom extents.
ZoomExtents

End Sub
```

Blocks and the Blocks Collection   Let's Review...

- Each block definition in a drawing is represented by a **Block** object that is part of the drawing's **Blocks** collection.
- You get a reference to an existing **Block** by specifying the block name in the **Blocks** collection.
- You can step through all of the block definitions in a drawing by using a **For Each...** loop to iterate the **Blocks** collection.
- A new block definition is created by adding a new **Block** object with the desired name to the **Blocks** collection.
- A block definition is renamed by changing a **Block** object's **Name** property.
- The **Delete** method deletes a **Block** object from the **Blocks** collection.
- The **InsertBlock** method inserts a named block definition as a **BlockReference** object at a specified insertion point, scale, and rotation.

Manipulating Block References

As noted earlier, a block definition becomes a block reference after it has been inserted into a drawing. It is common practice to have multiple references of a single block definition in a drawing. This approach is often promoted because it reduces drawing size and makes drawings easier to update because information is centrally located. Managing and manipulating block references is discussed in the following sections.

Retrieving a Block Insert

Because a block is a named object, it is possible to retrieve multiple instances of a block using selection set filters. Using selection set filters and the "select all" selection option, you can select all instances of a named block without any user interaction. This is achieved using the 0 and 2 DXF group codes, where group code 0 represents the object type and group code 2 represents the object name. Using these two DXF codes, you can create a selection set of all of the **INSERT** object types with the name MyBlock. The following code gets all instances of the block MyBlock and reports the total number found.

```
Sub Ch11_GetInsert()

    Dim objSSet As AcadSelectionSet
    Dim intDxfCode(0 To 1) As Integer
    Dim varDxfValue(0 To 1) As Variant

    ' Create a new selection set.
    Set objSSet = ThisDrawing.SelectionSets.Add("SS1")

    ' Set the entity DXF code to match the Insert entity type.
    intDxfCode(0) = 0
    varDxfValue(0) = "INSERT"

    ' Set the entity name DXF code to match the block name MyBlock.
    intDxfCode(1) = 2
    varDxfValue(1) = "MyBlock"

    ' Get all instances of "MyBlock" in the drawing.
    objSSet.Select acSelectionSetAll, , , intDxfCode, varDxfValue

    ' Tell the user how many instances were found, if any.
    If objSSet.Count > 0 Then
        MsgBox objSSet.Count & _
            " copy(s) of ""MyBlock"" insert found in this drawing."
    Else
        MsgBox """MyBlock"" not found in drawing."
    End If

    ' Delete the selection set.
    objSSet.Delete

End Sub
```

<table>
<tr><td>**Professional Tip**</td><td>For more information about selection set filters, see the section Using Selection Set Filters in Chapter 7. For more information about DXF codes, see the entry Group Codes in Numerical Order in the DXF Reference in the AutoCAD Developers Guide.</td></tr>
</table>

Exploding a Block

Because a block is a complex object comprised of one or more entities, it is possible to "explode" it back into its individual subentities. The **Explode** method was first introduced in Chapter 6 where it was used to explode polylines. The signature for the **Explode** method is:

ReturnVal = objSelected.Explode

where *objSelected* is the selected drawing object and *ReturnVal* is a **Variant** that is an array of the objects in the exploded block.

The following code relies on the selection set filter methods introduced in the previous section to find all instances of the block MyBlock. The selection set is then iterated and all instances of the block are exploded:

```
Sub Ch11_ExplodeInserts()

    Dim objSSet As AcadSelectionSet
    Dim objBlockRef As AcadBlockReference
    Dim intDxfCode(0 To 1) As Integer
    Dim varDxfValue(0 To 1) As Variant
    Dim intCounter As Integer

    ' Create a new selection set.
    Set objSSet = ThisDrawing.SelectionSets.Add("SS1")

    ' Set the entity DXF code to match the Insert entity type.
    intDxfCode(0) = 0
    varDxfValue(0) = "INSERT"

    ' Set the entity name DXF code to match the block name MyBlock.
    intDxfCode(1) = 2
    varDxfValue(1) = "MyBlock"

    ' Get all instances of "MyBlock" in the drawing.
    objSSet.Select acSelectionSetAll, , , intDxfCode, varDxfValue

    ' Explode the blocks, if any are found.
    If objSSet.Count > 0 Then
        For intCounter = 0 To objSSet.Count - 1
            ' Explode.
            objSSet.Item(intCounter).Explode
            ' Delete.
            objSSet.Item(intCounter).Delete
        Next
    Else
        MsgBox "No copies of ""MyBlock"" found in this drawing."
    End If

    ' Delete the selection set.
    objSSet.Delete

End Sub
```

Professional Tip

Notice in the code example above that it is necessary to delete the block insert after it is exploded. This is because a copy of the original insert is maintained even after the block is exploded. If you do not delete the original insert, you end up with an array of exploded subentities *and* the original insert after the block is exploded.

Deleting a Block   Reference

Sometimes it is necessary to delete an instance of a block. This is most easily accomplished via the **Delete** method. The signature for the **Delete** method is:

objSelected.Delete

where *objSelected* is the **BlockRef** object to delete. Note: The block reference (the entity) is deleted, but the block definition is not purged from the drawing.

The following code relies on the selection set filter methods introduced in the previous sections to find all instances of the MyBlock block. The selection set is then iterated and all instances of the block are deleted:

```
Sub Ch11_DeleteInsert()

    Dim objSSet As AcadSelectionSet
    Dim objBlockRef As AcadBlockReference
    Dim intDxfCode(0 To 1) As Integer
    Dim varDxfValue(0 To 1) As Variant
    Dim intCounter As Integer

    ' Create a new selection set.
    Set objSSet = ThisDrawing.SelectionSets.Add("SS1")

    ' Set the entity DXF code to match the Insert entity type.
    intDxfCode(0) = 0
    varDxfValue(0) = "INSERT"

    ' Set the entity name DXF code to match the block name MyBlock.
    intDxfCode(1) = 2
    varDxfValue(1) = "MyBlock"

    ' Get all instances of "MyBlock" in the drawing.
    objSSet.Select acSelectionSetAll, , , intDxfCode, varDxfValue

    ' Delete the blocks, if any are found.
    If objSSet.Count > 0 Then
        For intCounter = 0 To objSSet.Count - 1
            ' Delete the block.
            objSSet.Item(intCounter).Delete
        Next
    Else
        MsgBox "No copies of ""MyBlock"" found in this drawing."
    End If

    ' Delete the selection set.
    objSSet.Delete

End Sub
```

Writing a Block to Disk

In order to share a block definition, so it can be used in multiple drawings, you must first write the definition to disk and create a separate drawing file. The drawing file can then be inserted into multiple drawings using AutoCAD's **INSERT** command. This process is achieved in the AutoCAD drawing editor using the **WBLOCK** command. Using VBA, the "write block" process is accomplished via the **WBlock** method. The signature of the **WBlock** method is:

ThisDrawing.WBlock *FileName, SelectionSet*

where *FileName* is a **String** that is the name of the file to write. *SelectionSet* is the **SelectionSet** object that contains the objects to write to file.

The following code relies on the selection set filter methods introduced in the previous sections to find an instance of the block MyBlock. If the block is found, it is exploded and the subentities are put into a new selection set. The new selection set is then passed to the **WBlock** method where it is written to the file C:\VBA for AutoCAD\Drawings\MyBlock.dwg.

```vba
Sub Ch11_WBlockInsert()

    Dim objSSet1 As AcadSelectionSet
    Dim intDxfCode(0 To 1) As Integer
    Dim varDxfValue(0 To 1) As Variant

    ' Create a new selection set.
    Set objSSet1 = ThisDrawing.SelectionSets.Add("SS1")

    ' Set the entity DXF code to match the Insert entity type.
    intDxfCode(0) = 0
    varDxfValue(0) = "INSERT"

    ' Set the entity name DXF code to match the block name MyBlock.
    intDxfCode(1) = 2
    varDxfValue(1) = "MyBlock"

    ' Get all instances of MyBlock in the drawing.
    objSSet1.Select acSelectionSetAll, , , intDxfCode, varDxfValue

    ' Proceed if the block was found.
    If objSSet1.Count > 0 Then

        Dim varExplodedObjs As Variant
        Dim objSSet2 As AcadSelectionSet

        ' Explode the block and make a new selection set.
        varExplodedObjs = objSSet1.Item(0).Explode

        ' Create a new selection set.
        Set objSSet2 = ThisDrawing.SelectionSets.Add("SS2")

        ' Add the object array to the selection set.
        objSSet2.AddItems varExplodedObjs

        ' Wblock the objects.
        ThisDrawing.WBlock "C:\VBA for AutoCAD\Drawings\MyBlock.dwg", objSSet2

        ' Tell the user.
        MsgBox """MyBlock"" wblocked to file " & _
            """C:\VBA for AutoCAD\Drawings\MyBlock.dwg"""

        ' Erase the objects.
        objSSet2.Erase

        ' Delete the selection set.
        objSSet2.Delete

    Else
        ' Insert not found.
        MsgBox """MyBlock"" not found in drawing."
    End If

    ' Delete the selection set.
    objSSet1.Delete

End Sub
```

- You can retrieve all instances of a block insert, or **BlockRef**, in a drawing using selection set filters with the 0 and 2 DXF codes.
- The **Explode** method will break down a block into its individual subentities.
- The **Delete** method deletes a **BlockRef** object from either the **ModelSpace** or **PaperSpace** collection.
- You must delete a block using its **Delete** method after exploding the block. Otherwise, the original block remains in the drawing after exploding.
- The **WBlock** method writes a selection set of objects to a specified drawing file.

Exercise 11-2

Create the macros described below. All macros should be created in the **ThisDrawing** module of your MyMacros.dvb project. Provide all necessary error checking and control. Run and test each macro.

1. Create a macro named ex11_ExplodeGridBub that explodes all instances of the GRIDBUB block in the drawing C:\VBA for AutoCAD\Drawings\Grid_Plan.dwg created in #1 in Exercise 11-1.
2. Create a macro named ex11_WriteBlock that writes the GRIDBUB block created in #2 in Exercise 11-1 to a drawing file named C:\VBA for AutoCAD\Drawings\GridBub.dwg.

Block Attributes

As mentioned earlier, blocks can be defined with special dynamic text called attributes. *Block attributes* can be updated with different alphanumeric information when the block is inserted or anytime after that. It is even possible to extract the attribute data to an external file or to other Windows applications, such as Microsoft Excel or Access. Two of the benefits of using block attributes are:

- One block definition can be used multiple times with different alphanumeric information. This allows you to increase drawing productivity, reduce drawing memory resources, and more easily maintain drawing standards.
- Attributes make drawings "intelligent" so that you can create schedules, a bill of materials, and parts lists.

Attributes are one of the most powerful features in an AutoCAD drawing because they allow you to create intelligent drawings. For instance, a building facilities manager might create a block that represents a computer with the following attributes:

- Computer manufacturer.
- Computer type.
- Computer ID number.
- Employee assigned to.
- Location.

This block can then be inserted into each office or cubicle on a floor plan with updated information about each computer. The facilities manager can then use the floor plan to maintain a list of equipment and locations by simply extracting the computer block attribute information in the desired format.

Attribute information is defined and referenced in a block using a unique identifier called a *tag.* A tag is similar to a variable in a computer program or a field in a database. It is where the alphanumeric information associated with the block is stored. The tag name is used to identify which attribute values are read during the extraction process. The tags for the computer in the example above might look like those shown in **Figure 11-6.**

Each tag can have a prompt and a default value associated with it. In this way, the user is presented with easy-to-understand prompts, like those shown in **Figure 11-7,** when the block attributes are updated.

An attribute tag also has four different "modes" that determine its behavior:

- **Invisible.** Attribute values do not appear when the block is inserted.
- **Constant.** The attribute has a fixed value.
- **Verify.** The user is prompted to verify the attribute value during insertion.
- **Preset.** The attribute is set to its default value when the block is inserted.

Invisible tags allow you to include information that is important, but does not need to appear on a printed drawing. For instance, the computer block in the example above might have all of the attributes invisible except for the employee number. See **Figure 11-8.** In this way, when the floor layout is printed, only the employee number is shown. The other information contained within the block is only necessary for data extraction.

Figure 11-6.
This block of a computer has five attribute tags.

MANUFACTURER
TYPE
COMP_ID
EMPLOYEE
LOCATION

Figure 11-7.
When the computer block is inserted, the user is prompted for values. Easy-to-understand prompts help the user understand what information is required.

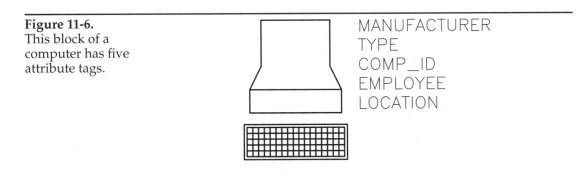

Prompts

| Enter Attributes | ? X |

Block name: Computer

Computer location   1st Floor - SW

Computer ID number   8008

Computer manufacturer   Dell

Employee number   1010

Computer type   P4

| OK | Cancel | Previous | Next | Help |

Figure 11-8.
All of the attribute tags for the computer block are invisible except for the employee number tag.

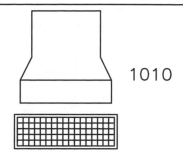

1010

Finally, because an attribute is a text object, it also has the following text properties that control its appearance:

- Justification.
- Text style.
- Height.
- Rotation.

Professional Tip

AutoCAD's **ATTDISP** system variable can be used to override the invisible mode. By default, **ATTDISP** is set to **Normal**. To view all attributes, set **ATTDISP** to **On**.

Creating Block Attributes

Because attributes must be defined as part of a block, they must be added during the block creation process. The **AddAttribute** method is used to create an attribute definition. The signature is:

objAttribute = Space.AddAttribute(*Height, Mode, Prompt, InsertPt, Tag, Value*)

where *objAttribute* is the **Attribute** object. *Space* is the **ModelSpace** or **PaperSpace** collection. *Height* is a **Double** data type that is the text height. *Mode* is the **acAttributeMode** enum. See **Figure 11-9.** *Prompt* is a **String** that is the attribute prompt. *InsertPt* is a **Variant** three-element array of **Double** data types that is the insertion point. *Tag* is a **String** that is the attribute tag. *Value* is a **String** that is the default attribute value.

Figure 11-9.
The five constants you can use to specify the attribute mode.

Constant	Description
acAttributeModeNormal	Current mode of the attribute is maintained.
acAttributeModeInvisible	Attribute value does not appear when the block is inserted.
acAttributeModeConstant	Attribute is given a fixed value.
acAttributeModeVerify	User is prompted to verify the attribute value when the block is inserted.
acAttributeModePreset	When the block is inserted, the attribute is set to its default value.

It is possible to use any combination of the different modes shown in **Figure 11-9.** To specify more than one option, simply add the constants together. For instance, to specify both the invisible and constant modes, enter:

```
acAttributeModeInvisible + acAttributeModeConstant
```

The following code defines a block of a valve in the current drawing. The block name is Valve and the block contains an attribute named SIZE that is used to designate the valve size:

```
Sub Ch11_CreateAttributes()

    Dim objBlock As AcadBlock
    Dim dblBasePt(0 To 2) As Double
    Dim dblStartPt(0 To 2) As Double
    Dim dblEndPt(0 To 2) As Double
    Dim objText As AcadText
    Dim strTextValue As String
    Dim dblTextInsPt(0 To 2) As Double
    Dim dblTextHeight As Double
    Dim objAttribute As AcadAttribute
    Dim dblAttHeight As Double
    Dim intAttMode As Long
    Dim strAttPrompt As String
    Dim dblAttInsPt(0 To 2) As Double
    Dim strAttTag As String
    Dim strAttValue As String

    ' Define the block base point.
    dblBasePt(0) = 0
    dblBasePt(1) = 0
    dblBasePt(2) = 0

    ' Add an empty block definition named Valve.
    Set objBlock = ThisDrawing.Blocks.Add(dblBasePt, "Valve")

    ' Create the linework for the valve.
    ' First line.
    dblStartPt(0) = -0.25
    dblStartPt(1) = -0.125
    dblStartPt(2) = 0
    dblEndPt(0) = 0.25
    dblEndPt(1) = 0.125
    dblEndPt(2) = 0
    objBlock.AddLine dblStartPt, dblEndPt

    ' Second line.
    dblStartPt(0) = -0.25
    dblStartPt(1) = 0.125
    dblStartPt(2) = 0
    dblEndPt(0) = 0.25
    dblEndPt(1) = -0.125
    dblEndPt(2) = 0
    objBlock.AddLine dblStartPt, dblEndPt

    ' Third line.
    dblStartPt(0) = 0.25
    dblStartPt(1) = -0.125
    dblStartPt(2) = 0
    dblEndPt(0) = 0.25
    dblEndPt(1) = 0.125
```

```
    dblEndPt(2) = 0
    objBlock.AddLine dblStartPt, dblEndPt

    ' Fourth line.
    dblStartPt(0) = -0.25
    dblStartPt(1) = -0.125
    dblStartPt(2) = 0
    dblEndPt(0) = -0.25
    dblEndPt(1) = 0.125
    dblEndPt(2) = 0
    objBlock.AddLine dblStartPt, dblEndPt

    ' Text.
    ' Height.
    dblTextHeight = 0.125
    ' Text insertion point.
    dblTextInsPt(0) = 0
    dblTextInsPt(1) = -0.25
    dblTextInsPt(2) = 0
    ' Text value.
    strTextValue = "VALVE"
    Set objText = objBlock.AddText(strTextValue, dblTextInsPt, dblTextHeight)

    ' Set the text justification to middle center.
    objText.Alignment = acAlignmentMiddleCenter
    objText.TextAlignmentPoint = dblTextInsPt

    ' Create the attribute definition.
    ' Height.
    dblAttHeight = 0.125
    ' Attribute mode.
    intAttMode = acAttributeModeNormal
    ' Attribute prompt.
    strAttPrompt = "Size"
    ' Attribute insertion point.
    dblAttInsPt(0) = 0
    dblAttInsPt(1) = -0.5
    dblAttInsPt(2) = 0
    ' Attribute tag.
    strAttTag = "SIZE"
    ' Default attribute value.
    strAttValue = "6"""

    ' Create the attribute definition object on the block.
    Set objAttribute = objBlock.AddAttribute(dblAttHeight, intAttMode, strAttPrompt, _
        dblAttInsPt, strAttTag, strAttValue)

    ' Set the attribute's justification to middle center.
    objAttribute.Alignment = acAlignmentMiddleCenter
    objAttribute.TextAlignmentPoint = dblAttInsPt

    ' Tell the user that the block was created.
    MsgBox "Valve block (Valve) with attributes has been defined in the drawing."

End Sub
```

Creating a block with attributes is only half of the equation. The important part is how the attributes are updated after a block is inserted. The key is to get a reference to the inserted block. This can occur directly after the block is inserted or by using the selection set filters discussed in Chapter 7 to retrieve a block, or blocks, based on the block name. Both approaches are discussed in the following sections.

Inserting a Block with Attributes

Once you have created a block with attributes, it can then be inserted and the attributes can be updated on the fly. The key is to get a reference to a block during the insertion process. Once you have a reference, you can then use the **GetAttributes** method to retrieve and update any of the block's attributes and values, if they exist. The signature is:

varAttributes = BlockRef.GetAttributes()

where *varAttributes* is a **Variant** (an array of **AttributeReference** objects) that is the array of attributes. *BlockRef* is the **BlockRef** object.

The following code defines a block of a valve in the current drawing. The block is named Valve and has an attribute named SIZE that is used to designate the valve size. The code then inserts the block at 0,0,0 and updates the SIZE attribute to 8".

```
Sub Ch11_InsertAttributes()

    Dim objBlock As AcadBlock
    Dim dblBasePt(0 To 2) As Double
    Dim dblStartPt(0 To 2) As Double
    Dim dblEndPt(0 To 2) As Double
    Dim objText As AcadText
    Dim strTextValue As String
    Dim dblTextInsPt(0 To 2) As Double
    Dim dblTextHeight As Double
    Dim objAttribute As AcadAttribute
    Dim dblAttHeight As Double
    Dim intAttMode As Long
    Dim strAttPrompt As String
    Dim dblAttInsPt(0 To 2) As Double
    Dim strAttTag As String
    Dim strAttValue As String
    Dim intCounter As Integer
    Dim dblBlkInsPt(0 To 2) As Double
    Dim objBlockRef As AcadBlockReference
    Dim varAttributes As Variant

    ' Define the block base point.
    dblBasePt(0) = 0
    dblBasePt(1) = 0
    dblBasePt(2) = 0

    ' Add an empty block definition named Valve.
    Set objBlock = ThisDrawing.Blocks.Add(dblBasePt, "Valve")

    ' Create the linework for the valve.
    ' First line.
    dblStartPt(0) = -0.25
    dblStartPt(1) = -0.125
    dblStartPt(2) = 0
    dblEndPt(0) = 0.25
    dblEndPt(1) = 0.125
    dblEndPt(2) = 0
    objBlock.AddLine dblStartPt, dblEndPt

    ' Second line.
    dblStartPt(0) = -0.25
    dblStartPt(1) = 0.125
    dblStartPt(2) = 0
```

```
dblEndPt(0) = 0.25
dblEndPt(1) = -0.125
dblEndPt(2) = 0
objBlock.AddLine dblStartPt, dblEndPt

' Third line.
dblStartPt(0) = 0.25
dblStartPt(1) = -0.125
dblStartPt(2) = 0
dblEndPt(0) = 0.25
dblEndPt(1) = 0.125
dblEndPt(2) = 0
objBlock.AddLine dblStartPt, dblEndPt

' Fourth line.
dblStartPt(0) = -0.25
dblStartPt(1) = -0.125
dblStartPt(2) = 0
dblEndPt(0) = -0.25
dblEndPt(1) = 0.125
dblEndPt(2) = 0
objBlock.AddLine dblStartPt, dblEndPt

' Text.
' Height.
dblTextHeight = 0.125
' Text insertion point.
dblTextInsPt(0) = 0
dblTextInsPt(1) = -0.25
dblTextInsPt(2) = 0
' Text value.
strTextValue = "VALVE"
Set objText = objBlock.AddText(strTextValue, dblTextInsPt, dblTextHeight)

' Set the text justification to middle center.
objText.Alignment = acAlignmentMiddleCenter
objText.TextAlignmentPoint = dblTextInsPt

' Create the attribute definition.
' Height.
dblAttHeight = 0.125
' Attribute mode.
intAttMode = acAttributeModeNormal
' Attribute prompt.
strAttPrompt = "Size"
' Attribute insertion point.
dblAttInsPt(0) = 0
dblAttInsPt(1) = -0.5
dblAttInsPt(2) = 0
' Attribute tag.
strAttTag = "SIZE"
' Default attribute value.
strAttValue = "6"""

' Create the attribute definition object on the block.
Set objAttribute = objBlock.AddAttribute(dblAttHeight, intAttMode, strAttPrompt, _
    dblAttInsPt, strAttTag, strAttValue)

' Set the attribute justification to middle center.
objAttribute.Alignment = acAlignmentMiddleCenter
objAttribute.TextAlignmentPoint = dblAttInsPt
```

```
' Insert the block.
dblBlkInsPt(0) = 0
dblBlkInsPt(1) = 0
dblBlkInsPt(2) = 0

' Get a reference to the block during insertion so the attributes can be retrieved.
Set objBlockRef = ThisDrawing.ModelSpace.InsertBlock(dblBlkInsPt, _
    "Valve", 1, 1, 1, 0)

' Get the attributes for the block reference.
varAttributes = objBlockRef.GetAttributes

' Update the SIZE attribute to 8".
For intCounter = LBound(varAttributes) To UBound(varAttributes)
    If varAttributes(intCounter).TagString = "SIZE" Then
        varAttributes(intCounter).TextString = "8"""
    End If
Next

End Sub
```

Retrieving a Block with Attributes

You can use the **GetAttributes** method to retrieve block attributes anytime after a block is inserted. All you need to do is get a reference to the block. The easiest way to do this is to use the selection set filter methods introduced in Chapter 7. Once a block is retrieved, you can determine if it has attributes via the **HasAttributes** property.

HasAttributes Property

A **BlockRef** object's **HasAttributes** property allows you to determine whether or not a block has attributes associated with it. The **HasAttributes** property is a **Boolean** data type that is set to **True** if the block has attributes and **False** otherwise.

The following code retrieves the block named Valve using a selection set filter. It then checks to see if the block has attributes via the **HasAttributes** property. If so, the attribute tags and their values are displayed in a message box.

```
Sub Ch11_GetAttributes()

    Dim objSSet As AcadSelectionSet
    Dim objBlockRef As AcadBlockReference
    Dim intDxfCode(0 To 1) As Integer
    Dim varDxfValue(0 To 1) As Variant
    Dim intCounter As Integer

    ' Create a new selection set.
    Set objSSet = ThisDrawing.SelectionSets.Add("SS1")

    ' Set the entity DXF code to match the Insert entity type.
    intDxfCode(0) = 0
    varDxfValue(0) = "INSERT"

    ' Set the entity name DXF code to match the block name Valve.
    intDxfCode(1) = 2
    varDxfValue(1) = "Valve"

    ' Get all instances of "Valve" in the drawing.
    objSSet.Select acSelectionSetAll, , , intDxfCode, varDxfValue
```

```
' Get the attributes if the block was found.
If objSSet.Count > 0 Then

    ' Get the attributes for the block reference.
    Dim varAttributes As Variant
    varAttributes = objSSet.Item(0).GetAttributes

    ' Check if the block has attributes and proceed.
    If objSSet.Item(0).HasAttributes Then

        ' Initialize string.
        Dim strAttributes As String
        strAttributes = ""

        ' Display all attribute tags and their values.
        For intCounter = LBound(varAttributes) To UBound(varAttributes)

            strAttributes = strAttributes & " Tag: " & _
                varAttributes(intCounter).TagString & vbCrLf & _
                " Value: " & varAttributes(intCounter).TextString

        Next

        MsgBox "The attributes for the ""Valve"" block are: " & _
        vbCrLf & strAttributes

    End If

Else
    MsgBox """Valve"" not inserted in drawing."
End If

' Delete the selection set.
objSSet.Delete

End Sub
```

GetConstantAttributes Method

Attributes that are created using the **Constant** mode are a little tricky in VBA, not unlike trying to manipulate **Constant** attributes in the AutoCAD drawing editor. The **GetAttributes** method will not retrieve **Constant** attributes. In order to retrieve **Constant** attributes, you must use the **GetConstantAttributes** method. Its signature is:

varAttributes = *BlockRef*.GetConstantAttributes()

where *varAttributes* is a **Variant** that is the array of attributes (an array of **AttributeReference** objects). *BlockRef* is the **BlockRef** object.

The following code defines a block of a valve in the current drawing. The block is named Valve and contains a mixture of attributes and attribute modes, including **Constant**. The code then inserts the block and displays the attribute tags and their values in a message box.

```
Sub Ch11_GetAllAttributes()

    Dim objBlock As AcadBlock
    Dim dblBasePt(0 To 2) As Double
    Dim dblStartPt(0 To 2) As Double
    Dim dblEndPt(0 To 2) As Double
    Dim objAttribute As AcadAttribute
    Dim dblAttHeight As Double
    Dim intAttMode As Long
```

```vba
Dim strAttPrompt As String
Dim dblAttInsPt(0 To 2) As Double
Dim strAttTag As String
Dim strAttValue As String
Dim intCounter As Integer
Dim dblBlkInsPt(0 To 2) As Double
Dim objBlockRef As AcadBlockReference
Dim strAttributes As String
Dim varAttributes As Variant

' Define the block base point.
dblBasePt(0) = 0
dblBasePt(1) = 0
dblBasePt(2) = 0

' Add an empty block definition named Valve.
Set objBlock = ThisDrawing.Blocks.Add(dblBasePt, "Valve")

' Create the linework for the valve.
' First line.
dblStartPt(0) = -0.25
dblStartPt(1) = -0.125
dblStartPt(2) = 0
dblEndPt(0) = 0.25
dblEndPt(1) = 0.125
dblEndPt(2) = 0
objBlock.AddLine dblStartPt, dblEndPt

' Second line.
dblStartPt(0) = -0.25
dblStartPt(1) = 0.125
dblStartPt(2) = 0
dblEndPt(0) = 0.25
dblEndPt(1) = -0.125
dblEndPt(2) = 0
objBlock.AddLine dblStartPt, dblEndPt

' Third line.
dblStartPt(0) = 0.25
dblStartPt(1) = -0.125
dblStartPt(2) = 0
dblEndPt(0) = 0.25
dblEndPt(1) = 0.125
dblEndPt(2) = 0
objBlock.AddLine dblStartPt, dblEndPt

' Fourth line.
dblStartPt(0) = -0.25
dblStartPt(1) = -0.125
dblStartPt(2) = 0
dblEndPt(0) = -0.25
dblEndPt(1) = 0.125
dblEndPt(2) = 0
objBlock.AddLine dblStartPt, dblEndPt

' Create first attribute definition.
' Height.
dblAttHeight = 0.125
' Attribute mode.
intAttMode = acAttributeModeConstant
' Attribute prompt.
```

```
strAttPrompt = "Valve type"
' Attribute insertion point.
dblAttInsPt(0) = 0
dblAttInsPt(1) = -0.25
dblAttInsPt(2) = 0
' Attribute tag.
strAttTag = "TYPE"
' Default attribute value.
strAttValue = "VALVE"

' Create the attribute definition object on the block.
Set objAttribute = objBlock.AddAttribute(dblAttHeight, intAttMode, _
    strAttPrompt, dblAttInsPt, strAttTag, strAttValue)

' Set the attribute justification to middle center.
objAttribute.Alignment = acAlignmentMiddleCenter
objAttribute.TextAlignmentPoint = dblAttInsPt

' Create the second attribute definition.
' Height.
dblAttHeight = 0.125
' Attribute mode.
intAttMode = acAttributeModeInvisible
' Attribute prompt.
strAttPrompt = "Manufacturer"
' Attribute insertion point.
dblAttInsPt(0) = 0
dblAttInsPt(1) = -0.5
dblAttInsPt(2) = 0
' Attribute tag.
strAttTag = "MFR"
' Default attribute value.
strAttValue = "CRANE"

' Create the attribute definition object on the block.
Set objAttribute = objBlock.AddAttribute(dblAttHeight, intAttMode, _
    strAttPrompt, dblAttInsPt, strAttTag, strAttValue)

' Set the attribute justification to middle center.
objAttribute.Alignment = acAlignmentMiddleCenter
'objAttribute.TextAlignmentPoint = dblAttInsPt

' Create the third attribute definition.
' Height.
dblAttHeight = 0.125
' Attribute mode.
intAttMode = acAttributeModeNormal
' Attribute prompt.
strAttPrompt = "Size"
' Attribute insertion point.
dblAttInsPt(0) = 0
dblAttInsPt(1) = -0.75
dblAttInsPt(2) = 0
' Attribute tag.
strAttTag = "SIZE"
' Default attribute value.
strAttValue = "6"""

' Create the attribute definition object on the block.
Set objAttribute = objBlock.AddAttribute(dblAttHeight, intAttMode, _
    strAttPrompt, dblAttInsPt, strAttTag, strAttValue)
```

```
' Set the attribute justification to middle center.
objAttribute.Alignment = acAlignmentMiddleCenter
objAttribute.TextAlignmentPoint = dblAttInsPt

' Insert the block.
dblBlkInsPt(0) = 0
dblBlkInsPt(1) = 0
dblBlkInsPt(2) = 0

' Get a reference to the block so its attributes can be retrieved.
Set objBlockRef = ThisDrawing.ModelSpace.InsertBlock(dblBlkInsPt, _
    "Valve", 1, 1, 1, 0)

' Get the attributes for the block reference.
varAttributes = objBlockRef.GetConstantAttributes

' Initialize string.
strAttributes = ""

' Iterate all constant attributes and create a string.
For intCounter = LBound(varAttributes) To UBound(varAttributes)

    strAttributes = strAttributes & " Tag: " & _
        varAttributes(intCounter).TagString & vbCrLf & _
        " Value: " & varAttributes(intCounter).textString & vbCrLf & vbCrLf

Next

' Show the user the constant attributes.
MsgBox "The constant attribute(s) for the block ""Valve"" are: " & _
    vbCrLf & vbCrLf & strAttributes

' Get the normal attributes for the block reference.
varAttributes = objBlockRef.GetAttributes

' Initialize string.
strAttributes = ""

' Iterate all normal attributes and create a string.
For intCounter = LBound(varAttributes) To UBound(varAttributes)

    strAttributes = strAttributes & " Tag: " & _
        varAttributes(intCounter).TagString & vbCrLf & _
        " Value: " & varAttributes(intCounter).textString & vbCrLf & vbCrLf

Next

' Show the user the normal, nonconstant attributes.
MsgBox "The normal attributes for the block ""Valve"" are: " & _
    vbCrLf & vbCrLf & strAttributes

End Sub
```

Block Attributes

- The **AddAttribute** method creates an attribute definition.
- A **BlockRef** object's **GetAttributes** method retrieves the attributes associated with the block.
- A **BlockRef** object's **HasAttributes** property allows you to determine if a block has any attributes.
- The **GetConstantAttributes** method must be used to retrieve **Constant** attributes because the **GetAttributes** method does not retrieve them.

Exercise 11-3

Create the macros described below. All macros should be created in the **ThisDrawing** module of your MyMacros.dvb project. Provide all necessary error checking and control. Run and test each macro.

1. Create a macro named ex11_AttribBlock that creates a block of a grid bubble named GRIDBUBA. Use the specifications outlined in #1 in Exercise 11-1 with the exception of substituting the text with an attribute definition that has the properties:
   Text style: STANDARD
   Height: 1/4"
   Justification: Middle center
   Attribute prompt: Grid bubble number
   Attribute tag: GRIDNO
   Default value: A
2. Create a macro named ex11_InsertAttribs that uses the GRIDBUBA block created in #1 above to create a grid plan with 10 columns (labeled A thru J) and 10 rows (labeled 1 thru 10) with 10'-0" × 10'-0" spacing between each column and row. Save the drawing as C:\VBA for AutoCAD\Drawings\Grid_PlanA.dwg.

External References

An *external reference,* better known as an xref, is a special type of block that is not inserted into a drawing, but rather attached, or linked, as an external drawing file. A link is simply the path to another drawing. Each time a drawing with an attached xref is opened, the links are read and the specified drawing is loaded into the drawing. This allows you to include the latest information from a saved drawing file as a block in your drawing, as well as share drawing information between multiple drawings. Xrefs provide all of the benefits of "regular" blocks plus the following benefits:

- The ability to share up-to-date drawing information with multiple team members simultaneously.
- The ability to "reload" xrefs at any time and view latest saved version.
- The ability to reduce drawing size even further than regular blocks because all that is stored in the drawing is the link to the xref.

A good example of using xrefs to separate drawing information is the drawing 8th Floor.dwg located in the AutoCAD \Sample folder. This drawing consists of six separate xrefs. Each xref has its own unique drawing content related to the following building disciplines:

- Architectural
- Mechanical
- Lighting
- Electrical
- Plumbing

You can list all of the xrefs and their status using the **Xref Manager** in the AutoCAD drawing editor, as shown in **Figure 11-10.**

The two different types of xrefs are attach and overlay. Each type exhibits different behavior. An *attached xref* will also attach any xrefs that are attached to itself. This is referred to as *nesting* and can be seen in a hierarchal tree view in the **Xref Manager**, as shown in **Figure 11-11.** In this case, the 8th Floor Plan.dwg is attached to all of the xrefs in the drawing 8th Floor.dwg, so it appears as nested. This is done because the 8th Floor Plan.dwg consists of the architectural and structural features (walls, doors, windows, columns, etc.) that must be referenced when laying out the various discipline information in the individual drawings. It is pretty hard to locate an HVAC system without knowing where the walls are!

An *overlay xref* breaks the nesting chain and only loads the top-level xref. Sometimes, this approach is preferred so that unneeded xrefs are not loaded every time you open a drawing. If the 8th Floor Plan.dwg is changed to an overlay in all of the discipline drawings, the tree view of the **Xref Manager** looks like **Figure 11-12.**

It is also important to note that when an xref is attached, all of its named objects, such as layers, lintypes, text styles, etc., are temporarily renamed so that their origin can be identified. Each symbol name is prefixed with the name of the xref and a vertical bar (|). For instance, **Figure 11-13** shows the layer names in the 8th Floor.dwg as they appear in AutoCAD's **Layer Properties Manager**.

Figure 11-10.
In the AutoCAD drawing editor, the **Xref Manager** dialog box lists xrefs and their status.

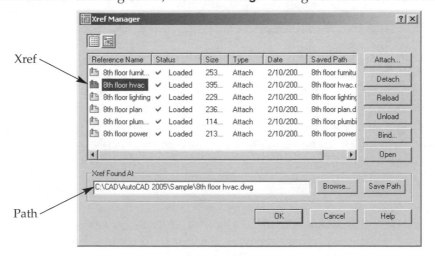

Figure 11-11.
Nested xrefs can be seen in the **Xref Manager** dialog box when the tree view is displayed.

Xref — Nested xref

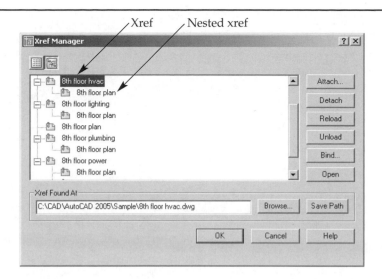

Figure 11-12.
When nested xrefs are changed to the overlay type they are not displayed in the **Xref Manager** dialog box.

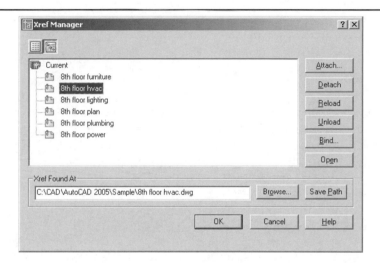

Figure 11-13.
Named objects in an xrefed drawing have their names prefixed, as shown here.

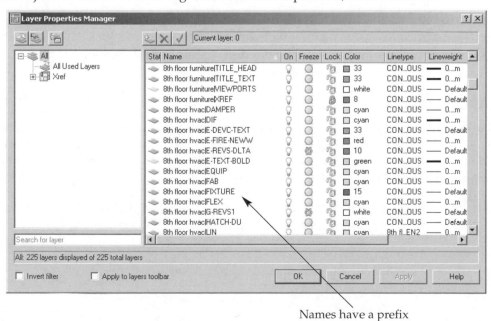

Names have a prefix

Figure 11-14.
When an xref is attached as a "bind" type, its named objects are permanently renamed.

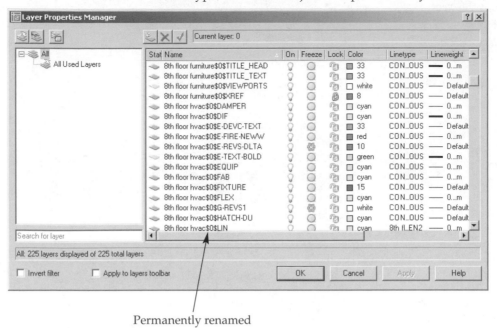

Permanently renamed

An xref can be made part of the current drawing using the xref "bind" option. Binding an xref converts it into a block in the drawing and breaks the link to the original xref. Sometimes this is necessary in order to transport a drawing. Otherwise, you must include the drawing and all of its xref files. Binding xrefs has two distinct *disadvantages:*

- The drawing may no longer contain current, up-to-date information because the xref link is broken.
- The drawing size is increased substantially.

Binding an xref is considered a last resort because of these issues. But, if you must, there are two ways to bind an xref: "bind" type and "insert" type. When "bind" type is selected, all of the named objects are renamed permanently to include the xref name with the string 0 replacing the vertical bar, as shown in **Figure 11-14.**

If you opt to bind as an "insert" type, no renaming occurs and all of the named objects retain their original names. The xref simply becomes a block in the drawing. Attaching and managing xrefs is discussed in detail in the following sections.

Attaching Xrefs

Attaching xrefs using VBA is very similar to inserting blocks, just as it is in the AutoCAD drawing editor. The major difference is that you must supply a path and whether you want the xref to be of the "overlay" or "attach" type. All of the other arguments are the same.

The **AttachExternalReference** method attaches an xref as an **ExternalReference** object. If successful, it returns a reference to the newly created **BlockReference** object. The signature is:

   *objXRef = Space.*AttachExternalReference (*Path, Name, InsertPt, XScale,* _
      YScale, ZScale, Rotation, Overlay)

where *objXRef* is the **ExternalReference** object. *Space* is the **ModelSpace** or **PaperSpace** collection. *Path* is a **String** that is the path to the xref. *Name* is a **String** that is the xref name. *InsertPt* is a **Variant** three-element array of **Double** data types that is the insertion point. *XScale*, *YScale*, and *ZScale* are **Double** data types that are the scale factors on the respective axes. *Rotation* is a **Double** data type that is the rotation angle, in radians. *Overlay* is a **Boolean** where **True** indicates the overlay type and **False** indicates the attach type.

The following code attaches the 8th Floor Plan.dwg file from the AutoCAD \Sample folder:

```
Sub Ch11_AttachXref()

    Dim dblInsertPt(0 To 2) As Double
    Dim strXrefPath As String

    ' Define the external reference to be inserted.
    strXrefPath = _
        "C:\Program Files\AutoCAD 2005\Sample\8th Floor Plan.dwg"

    ' Define the insertion point at 0,0,0.
    dblInsertPt(0) = 0
    dblInsertPt(1) = 0
    dblInsertPt(2) = 0

    ' Attach the external reference to the drawing.
    ThisDrawing.ModelSpace.AttachExternalReference strXrefPath, _
        "8th Floor Plan", dblInsertPt, 1, 1, 1, 0, False

    ' Zoom extents.
    ZoomExtents

    ' Tell the user.
    MsgBox "8th Floor Plan.dwg attached to the current drawing at 0,0,0."

End Sub
```

Professional Tip

There are two schools of thought regarding how to specify the path when attaching an xref. You can supply the complete path to locate the xref (hard-pathed), or you can rely on the AutoCAD search path or project path to locate the xref (soft-pathed). Relying on the search path is typically preferred because it allows you more flexibility. If xrefs move or folders change, you can simply update the search path in one spot. Hard-pathed xrefs must have their path updated manually in each drawing in which they are xrefed. Soft-coding xrefs also makes it much easier to transfer drawings to clients or subconsultants.

Detaching Xrefs

If you no longer need to reference an xref drawing, you can detach it. The **Detach** method will detach an **ExternalReference** object from a drawing. The signature is:

objXRef.Detach

where *objXRef* is the **ExternalReference** object to detach.

The following code detaches the 8th Floor Plan xref from the current drawing:

```
Sub Ch11_DetachXref()

    ' Error means the xref is not attached.
    On Error GoTo NOTFOUND

    ' Detach the xref via the Blocks collection.
    ThisDrawing.Blocks.Item("8th Floor Plan").Detach

    ' Tell the user.
    MsgBox "8th Floor Plan.dwg was detached from the current drawing."

    Exit Sub

    ' Xref not found.
    NOTFOUND:

    MsgBox "8th Floor Plan.dwg was not attached to this drawing."

End Sub
```

Caution You cannot detach an xref that is attached, or nested, in another currently attached xref.

Unloading Xrefs

Sometimes, it is necessary to temporarily unload an xref. An xref that is unloaded is still attached to a drawing, but is not visible or affected by any drawing calculations or drawing regenerations until it is reloaded. Unloading an xref reduces overhead and clutter caused by too much information. It will also help a drawing open faster.

The **Unload** method temporarily unloads an **ExternalReference** object from a drawing. The signature is:

objXRef.Unload

where *objXRef* is the **ExternalReference** object to unload.

The following code unloads the 8th Floor Plan xref from the current drawing:

```
Sub Ch11_UnloadXref()

    ' Error means the xref is not attached.
    On Error GoTo NOTFOUND

    ' Unload xref via the Blocks collection.
    ThisDrawing.Blocks.Item("8th Floor Plan").Unload

    ' Tell the user.
    MsgBox "8th Floor Plan.dwg was unloaded from the current drawing."

    Exit Sub

    ' Xref not found.
    NOTFOUND:

    MsgBox "8th Floor Plan.dwg was not attached to this drawing."

End Sub
```

Reloading Xrefs

After an xref has been unloaded it can be reloaded. The **Reload** method reloads an **ExternalReference** object that has been unloaded from a drawing. The signature is:

objXRef.Reload

where *objXRef* is the **ExternalReference** object to reload.

The following code reloads the 8th Floor Plan xref in the current drawing:

```
Sub Ch11_ReloadXref()

    ' Error means the xref was not attached.
    On Error GoTo NOTFOUND

    ' Reload the xref via the Blocks collection.
    ThisDrawing.Blocks.Item("8th Floor Plan").Reload

    ' Tell the user.
    MsgBox "8th Floor Plan.dwg was reloaded into the current drawing."

    Exit Sub

    ' Xref not found.
NOTFOUND:

    MsgBox "8th Floor Plan.dwg was not attached to this drawing."

End Sub
```

Binding Xrefs

As mentioned earlier, sometimes it is necessary to "bind" an xref so that it becomes part of the current drawing. This makes it possible to transport drawings without having to worry about including all of a drawing's attached xrefs.

There are two possible ways to bind an xref: "insert" (block) type or "bind" type. How an xref is bound determines how named objects, like layers, linetype, text styles, etc., are treated during the bind process. Named objects in a "bind" type operation are prefixed with the xref name and 0, as seen in **Figure 11-14.** The "insert" type operation keeps all of the original object names intact.

The **Bind** method binds an **ExternalReference** object to a drawing. The signature is:

objXRef.Bind *BindType*

where *objXRef* is the **ExternalReference** object to bind. *BindType* is a **Boolean** where **True** is the "insert" type and **False** is the "bind" type.

The following code binds the 8th Floor Plan xref to the current drawing as a "bind" type. The xref name and 0 will be prefixed to all named objects.

```
Sub Ch11_BindXref()

    ' Error means the xref was not attached.
    On Error GoTo NOTFOUND

    ' Bind the xref via the Blocks collection—include prefixes.
    ThisDrawing.Blocks.Item("8th Floor Plan").Bind False

    ' Tell the user.
    MsgBox "8th Floor Plan.dwg was bound to the current drawing."

    Exit Sub

    ' Xref not found.
    NOTFOUND:

    MsgBox "8th Floor Plan.dwg was not attached to the drawing."

End Sub
```

Caution

If the "insert" type is specified and duplicate named objects exist, AutoCAD uses the symbols already defined in the current drawing.

Let's Review...   External References

- The **AttachExternalReference** method attaches an xref to the current drawing at a specified insertion point, scale, and rotation.
- An **ExternalReference** object's **Detach** method detaches the xref from the current drawing.
- An **ExternalReference** object's **Unload** method unloads the xref from the current drawing.
- An **ExternalReference** object's **Reload** method reloads the xref into the current drawing.
- An **ExternalReference** object's **Bind** method binds the xref in the current drawing.

Exercise 11-4

Create the macros described below. All macros should be created in the **ThisDrawing** module of your MyMacros.dvb project. Provide all necessary error checking and control. Run and test each macro.
1. Create a macro named ex11_AttachXref that attaches the drawing C:\VBA for AutoCAD\Drawings\Grid_Plan.dwg created in #2 in Exercise 11-1 as an "overlay" xref type at 0,0,0 with a scale of 1.0 and rotation angle of 0.0 degrees.
2. Create a macro named ex11_BindXref that binds the Grid_Plan xref attached in #1 above as a "bind" type.

Chapter Test

Write your answers on a separate sheet of paper.

1. Explain a *block* and how it is used in AutoCAD.
2. List three advantages of using named blocks in AutoCAD.
3. Explain the difference between a *block definition* and a *block reference.*
4. List the four pieces of information stored with a block reference.
5. Explain the process of creating a new block that includes drawing objects.
6. Why can you not create a block named ModelSpace or PaperSpace?
7. How do you redefine a block?
8. When can a block definition *not* be deleted?
9. Which object type is created when a block is inserted into a drawing?
10. List the five arguments you must supply when inserting a block using the **InsertBlock** method.
11. What is the best way to retrieve a block reference from a drawing so that the block can be modified?
12. Which VBA method can be used to write a block to disk?
13. List three benefits of using block attributes in AutoCAD.
14. List the four attribute modes.
15. Which AutoCAD system variable controls the display of attributes?
16. Which property of the **BlockRef** object can be checked to determine whether or not a block has attributes?
17. Which VBA method must be used to retrieve attributes that were created using the **Constant** mode?
18. List three benefits of using external references in AutoCAD.
19. Explain the difference between an *"overlay" type* xref and an *"attach" type* xref.
20. What are the two different ways in which you can bind an xref?

Programming Problems

Create the macros described below. All macros should be created in the **ThisDrawing** module of your MyMacros.dvb project. Provide all necessary error checking and control. Run and test each macro.

1. Write a macro named p11_CreateTitleBlock that creates a block named TitleBlock. The block should be made up of a title block and border of your own design for a D-size sheet (22″ × 34″). Provide the following title text information:
   A. Designed by
   B. Drawn by
   C. Checked by
   D. Date
   E. Drawing name/number

2. Create a macro named p11_WriteTitleBlock that writes the TitleBlock block created in Problem 11-1 to a drawing file named C:\VBA for AutoCAD\Drawings\TitleBlock.dwg.

3. Create a macro named p11_TitleTextBlock that writes the TitleBlock block created in Problem 11-1 to a file named C:\VBA for AutoCAD\Drawings\TitleText.dwg with the following attribute definitions for the title text information:

Attribute Tag	Mode	Description
DESIGNBY	Normal	Designed by field.
DRAWNBY	Normal	Drawn by field.
CHKDBY	Normal	Checked by field.
DATE	Normal	Date field.
DRAWNO	Normal	Drawing number.

Provide prompts for those attributes you feel require prompts. After completing this problem, you will have a block named C:\VBA for AutoCAD\Drawings\TitleBlock.dwg that consists primarily of linework and a block named C:\VBA for AutoCAD\Drawings\TitleText.dwg made up of all of the dynamic title text information defined as attributes.

4. Create a macro named p11_AttachTitleBlock that does the following.
    A. Attaches the drawing C:\VBA for AutoCAD\Drawings\TitleBlock.dwg created in Problem 11-2 as an xref at the insertion point 0,0,0, with a scale of 1.0 and a rotation angle of 0.
    B. Inserts the attributed block C:\VBA for AutoCAD\Drawings\TitleText.dwg created in Problem 11-3 at the insertion point 0,0,0 and updates all of the attributes with new values of your choice.

CHAPTER 12

Layouts, Plot Configurations, and Plotting

Learning Objectives

After completing this chapter, you will be able to create VBA macros that:

- Reference a layout.
- Iterate all layouts in a drawing.
- Create a new layout.
- Make a layout current.
- Rename a layout.
- Delete a layout.
- Reference a plot configuration.
- Iterate all plot configurations in a drawing.
- Create, rename, and delete a plot configuration.
- Set the plot device.
- Set the plot style table and pen assignments.
- Set the paper size and units.
- Set the plot scale and plot area.
- Adjust the plot origin and rotate a plot.
- Preview a plot.
- Plot to a device or file.
- Plot multiple copies and multiple layouts.

Layouts

A *layout* is a 2D representation of a sheet of paper that exists, not surprisingly, in paper space. Remember that paper space is the 2D environment in AutoCAD used primarily for plotting. Model space is where you draw the 3D representation of your "model." See the section Model Space vs. Paper Space in Chapter 5 for a detailed description of the two drawing environments.

A layout typically includes a title block, general annotation features, and, most importantly, plot settings. Some of the plot settings managed via layouts include:

- Output device (printer/plotter)
- Paper size

- Pen table/Pen weights
- Plot scale

The beauty of layouts is that you can have more than one. This gives you the ability to set up multiple ways to look at and plot your drawing. For instance, you can create multiple layouts, each with its own unique paper size and scale. It is even possible to turn different data on and off per layout and viewport using the layer "freeze by viewport" feature.

A good example of utilizing multiple layouts is the 8th Floor.dwg located in AutoCAD's \Sample folder, **Figure 12-1.** The different layouts are listed on the tabs across the bottom of the screen above the command line. To see all of the tabs, you may need to use the navigation buttons to the left of the tabs. The 8th Floor.dwg contains six different layouts, each representing information for a different discipline. There are separate layouts for the following disciplines:

- Architectural (8th Floor Plan).
- Furniture (8th Floor Furniture Plan).
- HVAC (8th Floor HVAC Plan).
- Lighting (8th Floor Lighting Plan).
- Power (8th Floor Power Plan).
- Plumbing (8th Floor Plumbing Plan).

Each layout contains its own unique title block information, views, and plot settings. As you can see, the possibilities are endless. You are only limited by your imagination.

Figure 12-1.
The 8th Floor.dwg sample drawing contains multiple layouts.

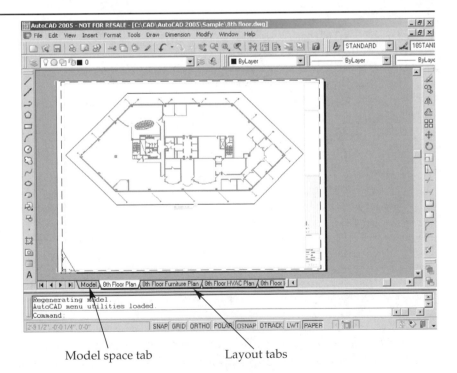

Model space tab   Layout tabs

Understanding the Layout and Block Relationship

Layouts are represented a little bit differently in the AutoCAD object model than they are in the AutoCAD drawing editor. In the object model, the content of a layout is broken down into two separate objects—the **Layout** object and the **Block** object. The **Layout** object contains all of the plot settings and layout definition information. The **Block** object contains all of the information about the drawing objects and their geometry. Every **Layout** object is associated with one **Block** object. You access the **Block** object via the **Layout** object's **Block** property as follows:

```
Dim objBlock As AcadBlock
Set objBlock = ThisDrawing.ActiveLayout.Block
```

The block name of the active paper space layout is always *PAPER_SPACE. Any other paper space layouts have blocks named *PAPER_SPACEn, where n is an integer that increases by one each time a new layout is added. When a layout is made active, it swaps block names with the formerly active layout so that the active layout block is always named *PAPER_SPACE. By default, the layout blocks in a new drawing have the names listed in **Figure 12-2.**

Professional Tip

You can determine a block's type via its **IsLayout** and **IsXRef** properties. If the **IsXRef** property is **True**, then the block is an external reference. If the **IsLayout** property is **True**, then the block contains the drawing objects and geometry associated with a layout. If both of these properties are **False**, it is a regular AutoCAD block.

Figure 12-2.
Default layout block names.

Block Name	Description
*MODEL_SPACE	The model space layout. There is only *one* model space layout per drawing. Accessible via the **ModelSpace** collection.
*PAPER_SPACE	The first paper space layout created. If model space is active, this block contains the last active paper space layout.
*PAPER_SPACE0	The second paper space layout created. When this layout is made active, it is renamed to *PAPER_SPACE and becomes accessible via the **PaperSpace** collection. The previous layout's block is renamed to *PAPER_SPACE0.

Layouts Collection

Each layout in a drawing is represented by a **Layout** object that is part of the drawing's **Layouts** collection. Object collections and their usage are discussed in Chapter 2. The following sections show you how to manage a drawing's **Layouts** collection and its **Layout** objects so you can:

- Reference an existing layout in a drawing.
- Iterate all of the layouts in a drawing.
- Create a new layout.
- Make a layout current.
- Rename a layout.
- Delete a layout.

Referencing a Layout

You can get a reference to an existing **Layout** object by either specifying the index number in the **Layouts** collection or by specifying the layout name. Specifying the name is the preferred method when working with named objects, like layouts.

The following code creates a reference to the Layout1 **Layout** object in the **Layouts** collection and displays its associated plotting device and paper size:

```
Sub Ch12_GetLayout()

    Dim objLayout As AcadLayout

    ' Go to NOTFOUND if the layout does not exist.
    On Error GoTo NOTFOUND:

    ' Get Layout1 from the Layouts collection.
    Set objLayout = ThisDrawing.Layouts.Item("Layout1")

    ' Display the plot device and paper size for Layout1.
    MsgBox "The plotter and paper size for Layout1 are:" & vbLf & vbLf & _
        "Plotter: " & objLayout.ConfigName & vbLf & _
        "Paper size: " & objLayout.CanonicalMediaName

    Exit Sub

NOTFOUND:

    ' Layout1 does not exist.
    MsgBox "Layout1 not found."

End Sub
```

Iterating the Layouts Collection

You can step through all of the layouts in a drawing by using a **For Each...** loop to iterate the **Layouts** collection. This approach was first introduced in Chapter 2 and can be used to iterate any of the named symbol table collections.

The following code iterates the **Layouts** collection and displays a list of all the layouts defined in the current drawing:

```
Sub Ch12_IterateLayouts()

    Dim strLayouts As String
    Dim objLayout As AcadLayout

    ' Initialize string.
    strLayouts = ""

    ' Step through all layouts defined in the drawing.
    For Each objLayout In ThisDrawing.Layouts
        strLayouts = strLayouts & vbTab & objLayout.name & vbCrLf
    Next

    ' Display the layouts to the user.
    MsgBox "Layouts defined in the current drawing: " & vbCrLf & vbCrLf _
        & strLayouts

End Sub
```

Creating a New Layout

To create a new layout using VBA and the AutoCAD object model, simply add a new **Layout** object with the desired name to the **Layouts** collection. After it is added, you can get a reference to it using the methods described earlier. Once you have a reference to the new **Layout** object, you can set any of its properties or use any of its methods.

The **Add** method adds a **Layout** object with the specified name to the **Layouts** collection. The signature is:

objLayout = Layouts.Add(*Name*)

where *objLayout* is the **Layout** object and *Name* is a **String** that is the name of the layout to add.

The following code adds a layout named My Layout to the current drawing:

```
Sub Ch12_AddLayout()

    ' Add the layout "My Layout" to the drawing.
    ThisDrawing.Layouts.Add "My Layout"

    ' Display to the user.
    MsgBox "The layout ""My Layout"" was added to this drawing"

End Sub
```

Making a Layout Current

The current layout is controlled via the **ActiveLayout** property of the **ThisDrawing** object. To make a layout current, set the **ActiveLayout** property to an existing **Layout** object. This requires getting a reference to the desired **Layout** object from the **Layouts** collection and then assigning it to the **ActiveLayout** property.

The following code gets a reference to the My Layout **Layout** object and then makes it current via the **ActiveLayout** property:

```
Sub Ch12_ActiveLayout()

    Dim objLayout As AcadLayout

    ' Go to NOTFOUND if the layout does not exist.
    On Error GoTo NOTFOUND:

    ' Get "My Layout" from the Layouts collection.
    Set objLayout = ThisDrawing.Layouts.Item("My Layout")

    ' Make the layout current.
    ThisDrawing.ActiveLayout = objLayout

    Exit Sub

NOTFOUND:

    ' "My Layout" does not exist.
    MsgBox "Layout ""My Layout"" not found."

End Sub
```

Renaming a Layout

You can rename a layout. To do so, first get a reference to the desired **Layout** object. Then, simply change its **Name** property to the new name.

The following code changes a layout name from My Layout to Your Layout:

```
Sub Ch12_LayoutRename()

    Dim objLayout As AcadLayout

    ' Go to NOTFOUND if the layout does not exist.
    On Error GoTo NOTFOUND:

    ' Get "My Layout" from the Layouts collection.
    Set objLayout = ThisDrawing.Layouts.Item("My Layout")

    objLayout.name = "Your Layout"

    Exit Sub

NOTFOUND:

    ' "My Layout" does not exist.
    MsgBox "Layout ""My Layout"" not found."

End Sub
```

Deleting a Layout

It is possible to delete a layout from a drawing's **Layouts** collection, as seen in the section Adding Objects to and Removing Objects from Object Collections in Chapter 2. It is even possible to delete a layout that is currently active! The **Delete** method deletes a **Layout** object from the **Layouts** collection. The signature for the **Delete** method is:

objLayout.Delete

where *objLayout* is the **Layout** object to delete.

The following code deletes the layout named Your Layout from the current drawing:

```
Sub Ch12_LayoutDelete()

    Dim objLayout As AcadLayout

    ' Go to NOTFOUND if the layout does not exist.
    On Error GoTo NOTFOUND:

    ' Get "Your Layout" from the Layouts collection.
    Set objLayout = ThisDrawing.Layouts.Item("Your Layout")

    ' Delete the layout.
    objLayout.Delete

    ' Tell the user.
    MsgBox "The layout ""Your Layout"" was deleted."

    Exit Sub

NOTFOUND:

    ' "Your Layout" does not exist.
    MsgBox "The layout ""Your Layout"" was not found."

End Sub
```

Layouts and the Layouts Collection

Let's Review...

- The content of a layout is broken down into two separate objects—the **Layout** object and the **Block** object.
- The **Layout** object contains all of the plot settings and layout definition information.
- The **Block** object contains all of the information about the drawing objects in the layout and their geometry.
- Each layout in a drawing is represented by a **Layout** object that is part of the drawing's **Layouts** collection.
- You get a reference to an existing **Layout** by specifying the layout name in the **Layouts** collection.
- You can step through all of the layouts in a drawing by using a **For Each...** loop to iterate the **Layouts** collection.
- A new layout can be created by adding a new **Layout** object with the desired name to the **Layouts** collection.
- To make a layout current, the **ThisDrawing.ActiveLayout** property must be set to reference an existing **Layout** object.
- A layout can be renamed by changing the **Layout** object's **Name** property.
- The **Delete** method deletes a **Layout** object from the **Layouts** collection.

Plot Configurations

The **PlotConfiguration** object is very similar to the **Layout** object, except it does not contain any drawing information. The **PlotConfiguration** object is used solely to manage plot settings. Since there are no drawing objects, there is no need for a separate **Block** object.

In AutoCAD, a **PlotConfiguration** object is represented via a user-defined "page setup." In the AutoCAD drawing editor, a page setup is saved using the **Page Setup Manager**, **Figure 12-3**. To add a new setup, pick the **New...** button to display the **New Page Setup** dialog box, **Figure 12-4**. You can then supply a unique name for the page setup.

Figure 12-3.
Pick the **New...** button in AutoCAD's **Page Setup Manager** dialog box to begin creating a new page setup.

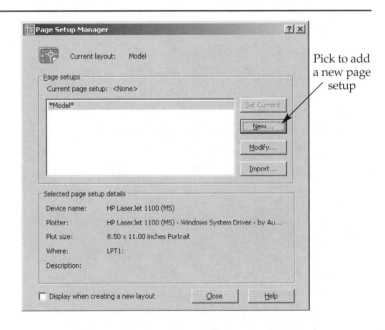

Pick to add a new page setup

Figure 12-4.
Creating a new user-defined page setup.

Name the page setup

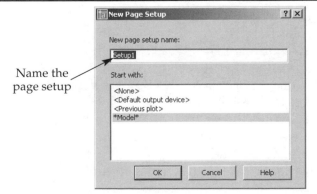

PlotConfigurations Collection

Each plot configuration in a drawing is represented by a **PlotConfiguration** object that is part of the drawing's **PlotConfigurations** collection. Object collections and their usage are discussed in Chapter 2. The following sections show you how to manage a drawing's **PlotConfigurations** collection and its **PlotConfiguration** objects so you can:

- Reference an existing plot configuration in a drawing.
- Iterate all of the plot configurations in a drawing.
- Create a new plot configuration.
- Rename a plot configuration.
- Delete a plot configuration.

Referencing a Plot Configuration

You can get a reference to an existing **PlotConfiguration** object by either specifying the index number in the **PlotConfigurations** collection or by specifying the plot configuration name. Specifying the name is the preferred method when working with named objects, like plot configurations.

The following code creates a reference to the **PlotConfiguration** object My Page Setup and displays its associated plotting device and paper size:

```
Sub Ch12_GetPlotCfg()

    Dim objPlotCfg As AcadPlotConfiguration

    ' Go to NOTFOUND if the plot configuration does not exist.
    On Error GoTo NOTFOUND:

    ' Get "My Page Setup" from the PlotConfigurations collection.
    Set objPlotCfg = ThisDrawing.PlotConfigurations.Item("My Page Setup")

    ' Display the plot device and paper size for "My Page Setup".
    MsgBox "The plotter and paper size for ""My Page Setup"" are:" & vbLf _
        & vbLf & "Plotter: " & objPlotCfg.ConfigName & vbLf & _
        "Paper size: " & objPlotCfg.CanonicalMediaName

    Exit Sub

NOTFOUND:

    ' "My Page Setup" does not exist.
    MsgBox """My Page Setup"" was not found."

End Sub
```

Iterating the Plot Configurations Collection

You can step through all of the plot configurations in a drawing by using a **For Each...** loop to iterate the **PlotConfigurations** collection. This approach was first introduced in Chapter 2 and can be used to iterate any of the named symbol table collections.

The following code iterates the **PlotConfigurations** collection and displays a list of all of the plot configurations defined in the current drawing:

```
Sub Ch12_IteratePlotCfgs()

    Dim strPlotCfgs As String
    Dim objPlotCfg As AcadPlotConfiguration

    ' Initialize string.
    strPlotCfgs = ""

    ' Iterate all page setups defined in the drawing.
    For Each objPlotCfg In ThisDrawing.PlotConfigurations
        strPlotCfgs = strPlotCfgs & vbTab & objPlotCfg.name & vbCrLf
    Next

    ' Display the page setups to the user.
    MsgBox "Page setups defined in the current drawing: " & vbCrLf & _
        vbCrLf & strPlotCfgs

End Sub
```

Creating a New Plot Configuration

To create a new page setup using VBA and the AutoCAD object model, simply add a new **PlotConfiguration** object with the desired name to the **PlotConfigurations** collection. Once it is added, you can get a reference to it using the methods described earlier. After you have a reference to the new **PlotConfiguration** object, you can set any of its properties or use any of its methods.

The **Add** method adds a **PlotConfiguration** object with the specified name to the **PlotConfigurations** collection. The signature is:

objPlotCfg = PlotConfigurations.Add(*Name*[, *Space*])

where *objPlotCfg* is the **PlotConfiguration** object and *Name* is a **String** that is the name of the page setup to add. *Space* is a **Boolean** where **True** means the layout applies to model space and **False** means the layout applies to all layouts.

The following code adds a plot configuration named My Page Setup to the current drawing:

```
Sub Ch12_AddPlotCfg()

    ' Add the page setup "My Page Setup" to the drawing.
    ThisDrawing.PlotConfigurations.Add "My Page Setup", True

    ' Display to the user.
    MsgBox "The page setup ""My Page Setup"" was added to the drawing."

End Sub
```

Renaming a Plot Configuration

The **PlotConfiguration** object's **Name** property controls the plot configuration name. You can rename a plot configuration by getting a reference to the desired **PlotConfiguration** object and then simply changing its **Name** property to the new name.

The following code changes a plot configuration name from My Page Setup to Your Page Setup:

```
Sub Ch12_PlotCfgRename()

    Dim objPlotCfg As AcadPlotConfiguration

    ' Go to NOTFOUND if the setup does not exist.
    On Error GoTo NOTFOUND:

    ' Get "My Layout" from the PlotConfigurations collection.
    Set objPlotCfg = ThisDrawing.PlotConfigurations.Item("My Page Setup")

    objPlotCfg.name = "Your Page Setup"

    Exit Sub

NOTFOUND:

    ' "My Page Setup" does not exist.
    MsgBox "The page setup ""My Page Setup"" was not found."

End Sub
```

Deleting a Plot Configuration

It is possible to delete a plot configuration from a drawing's **PlotConfigurations** collection, as seen in the section Adding Objects to and Removing Objects from Object Collections in Chapter 2. The **Delete** method deletes a **PlotConfiguration** object from the **PlotConfigurations** collection. The signature is:

objPlotCfg.Delete

where *objPlotCfg* is the **PlotConfiguration** object to delete.

The following code deletes the plot configuration named Your Page Setup from the current drawing:

```
Sub Ch12_PlotCfgDelete()

    Dim objPlotCfg As AcadPlotConfiguration

    ' Go to NOTFOUND if the setup does not exist.
    On Error GoTo NOTFOUND:

    ' Get "Your Page Setup" from the PlotConfiguration collection.
    Set objPlotCfg = ThisDrawing.PlotConfigurations.Item("Your Page Setup")

    ' Delete the setup.
    objPlotCfg.Delete

    ' Tell the user.
    MsgBox "The page setup ""Your Page Setup"" was deleted."

    Exit Sub

NOTFOUND:

    ' "Your Page Setup" does not exist.
    MsgBox "The page setup ""Your Page Setup"" was not found."

End Sub
```

Plot Configurations

- Each named page setup in a drawing is represented by a **PlotConfiguration** object that is part of the drawing's **PlotConfigurations** collection.
- You get a reference to an existing **PlotConfiguration** by specifying the plot configuration name in the **PlotConfigurations** collection.
- You can step through all of the plot configurations in a drawing by using a **For Each...** loop to iterate the **PlotConfigurations** collection.
- A new plot configuration can be created by adding a new **PlotConfiguration** object with the desired name to the **PlotConfigurations** collection.
- A plot configuration can be renamed by changing a **PlotConfiguration** object's **Name** property.
- The **Delete** method deletes a **PlotConfiguration** object from the **PlotConfigurations** collection.

Exercise 12-2

Create a macro named ex12_MakePageSetup that makes a plot configuration named Plot to DWF File. The macro should be created in the **ThisDrawing** module of your MyMacros.dvb project. Provide all necessary error checking and control. Run and test the macro.

Controlling Plot Settings

Now that you know where all of the plot settings are stored and managed, you probably wonder how to control them. The **Layout** and **PlotConfiguration** objects control most of the same plot settings. Some of the plotting settings at your control include:

- Plot device and/or plot configuration file (PC3).
- Pen table/pen weights.
- Paper size.
- Plot scale.
- Plot origin.
- Plot area.

In the AutoCAD drawing editor, plot settings are managed via either the **Plot** or **Page Setup** dialog box, which look almost exactly the same. The **Plot** dialog box is shown in **Figure 12-5.** You can configure the plotter/printer, select the paper size, set the plot area and scale, and make other settings.

How plot settings are controlled using VBA and the object model is explained in the following sections. Since the **Layout** and **PlotConfiguration** objects share the same properties and methods in regard to plotting, the **Layout** object is used in most of the code examples. You can simply substitute the **PlotConfiguration** object in place of the **Layout** object if programming for that object.

Figure 12-5.
AutoCAD's **Plot** dialog box allows you to control and fine-tune the plot.

Pick to configure the
printer/plotter

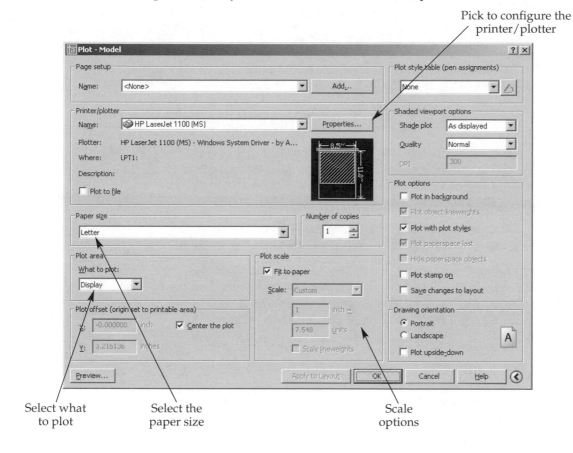

Select what
to plot

Select the
paper size

Scale
options

Setting the Plot Device

In AutoCAD, the available printers and plotters are controlled via plotter configuration (PC3) files. A PC3 file controls information specific to a plot device, such as:

- Printer/plotter name.
- Print driver.
- Port.
- UNC path if on network.
- Valid paper sizes.

A number of default PC3 files are supplied with AutoCAD. These are typically stored in the user's \Plotters folder under \Documents and Settings. To create a new plotter configuration (PC3) file, use the **Add-A-Plotter** wizard in the **Plotter Manager** in AutoCAD.

In order to use a PC3 file, it must be associated with a layout or page setup. The **ConfigName** property controls which PC3 file is associated with a layout or page setup.

The following code sets the plot device to plot a Design Web Format Version 6 (DWF6) file:

```
Sub Ch12_SetPlotDevice()

    Dim objLayout As AcadLayout

    ' Go to NOTFOUND if the layout does not exist.
    On Error GoTo NOTFOUND:

    ' Get Layout1 from the Layouts collection.
    Set objLayout = ThisDrawing.Layouts.Item("Layout1")

    ' Display the current plot device and paper size for Layout1.
    MsgBox "The current plotter and paper size for Layout1 are:" & vbLf & _
        vbLf & "Plotter: " & objLayout.ConfigName & vbLf & _
        "Paper size: " & objLayout.CanonicalMediaName

    ' Change the plot device to print to a DWF file.
    objLayout.ConfigName = "DWF6 ePlot.pc3"

    ' Display the new plot device and paper size for Layout1.
    MsgBox "The new plotter and paper size for Layout1 are:" & vbLf & _
        vbLf & "Plotter: " & objLayout.ConfigName & vbLf & _
        "Paper size: " & objLayout.CanonicalMediaName

    Exit Sub

NOTFOUND:

    ' Layout1 does not exist.
    MsgBox "Layout1 was not found."

End Sub
```

Professional Tip

There is no need to include the complete path when specifying any of the plotter-related support files as their locations are determined via AutoCAD's Printer Support File Path. This path is set in the **Files** tab of AutoCAD's **Options** dialog box.

Setting the Plot Style Table and Pen Assignments

A plot style table is a collection of plot styles assigned to a layout or page setup. There are two types of plot style tables: color-dependent plot style tables (CTB) and named plot style tables (STB).

Color-dependent plot style tables use a drawing entity's color to determine the printed characteristics of the entity, such as lineweight, grayscale, and screening. There are 256 plot styles in a color-dependent plot style table, one for each color in the AutoCAD Color Index (ACI).

Named plot style tables contain user-defined plot styles and also control an entity's printed characteristics. The difference between color-dependent and named plot styles is that named plot styles can be assigned to an object directly, including layers, similar to other object properties. A named plot style table can contain as many named plot styles as needed for the desired output.

A plot style table is assigned to a layout or page setup. The **StyleSheet** property controls which plot style table is associated with a layout or page setup.

The following code sets the plot style to the color-dependent plot style table DWF Virtual Pens.ctb to Layout1:

```
Sub Ch12_SetPlotStyle()

    Dim objLayout As AcadLayout

    ' Go to NOTFOUND if the layout does not exist.
    On Error GoTo NOTFOUND:

    ' Get Layout1 from the Layouts collection.
    Set objLayout = ThisDrawing.Layouts.Item("Layout1")

    ' Display the current plot style table for Layout1.
    MsgBox "The current plot style table for Layout1 is:" & vbLf & vbLf & _
        "Plot style table: " & objLayout.StyleSheet

    ' Change the plot device to print to a DWF file.
    objLayout.StyleSheet = "DWF Virtual Pens.ctb"

    ' Display the new plot device and paper size for Layout1.
    MsgBox "The new plot style table for Layout1 is:" & vbLf & vbLf & _
        "Plot style table: " & objLayout.StyleSheet

    Exit Sub

NOTFOUND:

    ' Layout1 does not exist.
    MsgBox "Layout1 was not found."

End Sub
```

Setting the Paper Size and Units

The paper size of a plot is directly related to the plotting device selected. Obviously, you cannot print to a D-size (22″ × 34″) sheet on a laser printer that only accepts up to A-size (8 1/2″ × 11″) paper. For this reason, it is good practice to select a plotter device prior to choosing a paper size.

CanonicalMediaName Property

The **CanonicalMediaName** property controls the paper size associated with a layout or page setup. The available paper sizes are determined by the associated PC3 file.

The following code sets the paper size to an ANSI B (17″ × 11″) sheet size:

```
Sub Ch12_SetPaperSize()

    Dim objLayout As AcadLayout

    ' Go to NOTFOUND if the layout does not exist.
    On Error GoTo NOTFOUND:

    ' Get Layout1 from the Layouts collection.
    Set objLayout = ThisDrawing.Layouts.Item("Layout1")

    ' Display the current plot device and paper size for Layout1.
    MsgBox "The current plotter and paper size for Layout1 are:" & _
        vbLf & vbLf & "Plotter: " & objLayout.ConfigName & vbLf & _
        "Paper size: " & objLayout.CanonicalMediaName

    ' Change the plot device to print to a DWF file.
    objLayout.ConfigName = "DWF6 ePlot.pc3"
```

```
' Change the paper size to ANSI B.
objLayout.CanonicalMediaName = "ANSI_B_(17.00_x_11.00_Inches)"

' Display the new plot device and paper size for Layout1.
MsgBox "The new plotter and paper size for Layout1 are:" & vbLf & _
    vbLf & "Plotter: " & objLayout.ConfigName & vbLf & _
    "Paper size: " & objLayout.CanonicalMediaName

' Zoom all.
ZoomAll

Exit Sub

NOTFOUND:

    ' Layout1 does not exist.
    MsgBox "Layout1 was not found."

End Sub
```

PaperUnits Property

The **PaperUnits** property controls in which units the plot settings are specified. The **PaperUnits** property can be set to the AutoCAD constants shown in **Figure 12-6.**

The following code sets the paper units to millimeters:

```
Sub Ch12_SetPaperUnits()

    Dim objLayout As AcadLayout

    ' Go to NOTFOUND if the layout does not exist.
    On Error GoTo NOTFOUND:

    ' Get Layout1 from the Layouts collection.
    Set objLayout = ThisDrawing.Layouts.Item("Layout1")

    ' Set the units to metric.
    objLayout.PaperUnits = acMillimeters

    ' Tell the user.
    MsgBox "The paper units for Layout1 are now millimeters."

    ' Zoom all.
    ZoomAll

    Exit Sub

NOTFOUND:

    ' Layout1 does not exist.
    MsgBox "Layout1 was not found."

End Sub
```

Figure 12-6.
The AutoCAD constants for the **PaperUnits** property.

Constant	Units
acInches	Inches
acMillimeters	Millimeters
acPixels	Pixels

Setting the Plot Scale

One of the most important aspects of a plot is its scale. A drawing is pretty useless if it is not at a specific scale. The scale is the relationship between a printed drawing and the real world. For this reason, there are a number of standard scales used in the AEC industry. Most of these are provided within AutoCAD. Sometimes, though, it is necessary to specify a custom scale. Both approaches are explained in the following sections.

UseStandardScale Property

The **UseStandardScale** property is used to set a plot scale to one of the industry standard scales provided in AutoCAD. In VBA, the standard plot scales are represented by the AutoCAD constants shown in **Figure 12-7**.

Figure 12-7.
The AutoCAD constants for standard plot scales.

Constant	Scale
acScaleToFit	Scale to Fit
ac1_128in_1ft	1/128"= 1'
ac1_64in_1ft	1/64"= 1'
ac1_32in_1ft	1/32"= 1'
ac1_16in_1ft	1/16"= 1'
ac3_32in_1ft	3/32"= 1'
ac1_8in_1ft	1/8" = 1'
ac3_16in_1ft	3/16"= 1'
ac1_4in_1ft	1/4" = 1'
ac3_8in_1ft	3/8" = 1'
ac1_2in_1ft	1/2" = 1'
ac3_4in_1ft	3/4" = 1'
ac1in_1ft	1"= 1'
ac3in_1ft	3"= 1'
ac6in_1ft	6"= 1'
ac1ft_1ft	1'= 1'
ac1_1	1:1
ac1_2	1:2
ac1_4	1:4
ac1_8	1:8
ac1_10	1:10
ac1_16	1:16
ac1_20	1:20
ac1_30	1:30
ac1_40	1:40
ac1_50	1:50
ac1_100	1:100
ac2_1	2:1
ac4_1	4:1
ac8_1	8:1
ac10_1	10:1
ac100_1	100:1

The following code sets the plot scale to 2:1:

```
Sub Ch12_SetStdPlotScale()

    Dim objLayout As AcadLayout

    ' Go to NOTFOUND if the layout does not exist.
    On Error GoTo NOTFOUND:

    ' Get Layout1 from the Layouts collection.
    Set objLayout = ThisDrawing.Layouts.Item("Layout1")

    ' Change the plot device to print to a DWF file.
    objLayout.StandardScale = ac2_1

    ' Tell the user.
    MsgBox "The plot scale is now set at 2:1."

    Exit Sub

NOTFOUND:

    ' Layout1 does not exist.
    MsgBox "Layout1 was not found."

End Sub
```

Note: If you ran the previous macro (SetPaperUnits) the plot scale is changed to 1:12.7 because there are 25 millimeters per inch (25 ÷ 2 = 12.7).

SetCustomScale Method

The **SetCustomScale** method allows you to specify a scale other than the standard scales listed in **Figure 12-7.** The signature is:

Object.SetCustomScale *Numerator, Denominator*

where *Object* is the **Layout** or **PlotConfiguration** object. *Numerator* is a **Double** data type that is the numerator in the scale ratio. *Denominator* is a **Double** data type that is the denominator in the scale ratio.

The following code sets a custom plot scale of 3:4 for Layout1:

```
Sub Ch12_SetCustomPlotScale()

    Dim objLayout As AcadLayout

    ' Go to NOTFOUND if the layout does not exist.
    On Error GoTo NOTFOUND:

    ' Get Layout1 from the Layouts collection.
    Set objLayout = ThisDrawing.Layouts.Item("Layout1")

    ' Set the standard scale flag to false.
    objLayout.UseStandardScale = False

    ' Set a custom scale of 3:4.
    objLayout.SetCustomScale 3#, 4#

    ' Display the plot device and paper size for Layout1.
    MsgBox "The plot scale is now set at 3:4."

    ' Regen the drawing.
    ThisDrawing.Regen acAllViewports

    Exit Sub

NOTFOUND:

    ' Layout1 does not exist.
    MsgBox "Layout1 was not found."

End Sub
```

Figure 12-8.
The AutoCAD constants for determining the portion of the drawing to plot.

Constant	Description
acDisplay	Prints everything that is in the current display.
acExtents	Prints everything that falls within the extents of the drawing.
acLimits	Prints everything that is within the limits of model space.
acView	Prints the view named by the **ViewToPlot** property.
acWindow	Prints everything in the window specified by the **SetWindowToPlot** method.
acLayout	Prints everything within the current paper space layout.

Setting the Plot Area

There are five ways in which you can specify the area of a drawing that you want to plot:

- Plot using the drawing limits.
- Plot to the extents of the drawing.
- Plot the current display.
- Plot a specific named view.
- Plot a defined window.

All of these options are available when plotting in VBA. The **PlotType** property determines what area of the drawing you want to plot. The AutoCAD constants shown in **Figure 12-8** are used to represent the different options.

The following code sets the plot area to the extents of the drawing:

```
Sub Ch12_SetPlotArea()

    Dim objLayout As AcadLayout

    ' Go to NOTFOUND if the layout does not exist.
    On Error GoTo NOTFOUND:

    ' Get Layout1 from the Layouts collection.
    Set objLayout = ThisDrawing.Layouts.Item("Layout1")

    ' Set the plot area to the extents of the layout.
    objLayout.PlotType = acExtents

    ' Tell the user.
    MsgBox "The plot area is now set to extents."

    Exit Sub
NOTFOUND:

    ' Layout1 does not exist.
    MsgBox "Layout1 was not found."

End Sub
```

Caution
The **ViewToPlot** property or **SetWindowToPlot** method must be called before you can set the **PlotType** property to **acView** or **acWindow**.

Adjusting the Plot Origin

The plot origin determines where the lower-left corner of a plot is located on the sheet of paper. It is possible to move the plot origin from the default location of 0,0. The **PlotOrigin** property controls the plot origin.

The following code moves the plot origin to the coordinate location (0.5,0.5):

```
Sub Ch12_SetPlotOrigin()

    Dim objLayout As AcadLayout
    Dim dblPlotOrigin(0 To 1) As Double

    ' Go to NOTFOUND if the layout does not exist.
    On Error GoTo NOTFOUND:

    ' Get Layout1 from the Layouts collection.
    Set objLayout = ThisDrawing.Layouts.Item("Layout1")

    ' Set the plot origin to 0.5,0.5.
    ' Must convert to metric!!!
    dblPlotOrigin(0) = (0.5 * 25.4)
    dblPlotOrigin(1) = (0.5 * 25.4)

    ' Set the plot origin.
    objLayout.PlotOrigin = dblPlotOrigin

    ' Tell the user.
    MsgBox "The plot origin is now set to (0.5,0.5)."

    Exit Sub

NOTFOUND:

    ' Layout1 does not exist.
    MsgBox "Layout1 not found."

End Sub
```

Professional Tip

It is possible to center a plot by setting the **CenterPlot** property to **True**:

> *objLayout*.CenterPlot = True

The **CenterPlot** property cannot be set to **True** on a layout object whose **PlotType** property is set to **acLayout**.

Rotating a Plot

It is possible to rotate a plot in 90° increments. The **PlotRotation** property can be used to rotate a plot to one of four different rotation angles. The AutoCAD constants shown in **Figure 12-9** are used to represent the different angles. All angles are measured counterclockwise with 0° oriented to the right (east).

Figure 12-9.
The AutoCAD
constants for the
plot rotation.

Constant	Rotation
ac0degrees	0°
ac90degrees	90°
ac180degrees	180°
ac270degrees	270°

The following code rotates the plot of the active layout by 90°.

```
Sub Ch12_SetPlotRotation()

    Dim objLayout As AcadLayout

    ' Go to ERROR if a problem occurs.
    On Error GoTo ERROR:

    ' Get the active layout.
    Set objLayout = ThisDrawing.ActiveLayout

    ' Rotate the existing plot rotation by 90 degrees.
    If objLayout.PlotRotation < ac270degrees Then
        objLayout.PlotRotation = objLayout.PlotRotation + ac90degrees
    Else
        objLayout.PlotRotation = ac0degrees
    End If

    ' Tell the user.
    MsgBox "The plot has been rotated 90 degrees."

    Exit Sub
ERROR:

    ' Error rotating the plot.
    MsgBox "Error rotating plot."

End Sub
```

Controlling Plot Settings — Let's Review...

- The **ConfigName** property controls which PC3 file is associated with a layout or page setup.
- The **StyleSheet** property controls the plot style table associated with a layout or page setup.
- The **CanonicalMediaName** property controls the paper size associated with a layout or page setup.
- The **PaperUnits** property controls whether plot settings are specified in inches or millimeters.
- The **UseStandardScale** property sets a plot scale to one of the standard scales provided in AutoCAD.
- The **SetCustomScale** method allows you set a custom plot scale.
- The **PlotType** property determines which area of the drawing to plot.
- The **PlotOrigin** property controls where the lower-left corner of a plot is located on the paper.
- The **PlotRotation** property can be used to rotate a plot in increments of 90°.

Exercise 12-3

Create the macros described below. All macros should be created in the **ThisDrawing** module of your MyMacros.dvb project. Provide all necessary error checking and control. Run and test each macro.

1. Create a macro named ex12_SetupLayouts that sets the following plot settings for the layouts created in #1 in Exercise 12-1:

    ANSI A-8.5 × 11
    PC3 file: Default Windows System Printer.pc3
    Plot style table: Monochrome.ctb
    Paper size: 8.5" × 11.0"
    Scale: 1:1
    What to plot: Layout

    ANSI B-11 × 17
    PC3 file: Default Windows System Printer.pc3
    Plot style table: Monochrome.ctb
    Paper size: 11.0" × 17.0"
    Scale: 1:1
    What to plot: Layout

    ANSI C-17 × 22
    PC3 file: Default Windows System Printer.pc3
    Plot style table: Monochrome.ctb
    Paper size: 17.0" × 22.0"
    Scale: 1:1
    What to plot: Layout

    ANSI D-22 × 34
    PC3 file: Default Windows System Printer.pc3
    Plot style table: Monochrome.ctb
    Paper size: 22.0" × 34.0"
    Scale: 1:1
    What to plot: Layout

2. Create a macro named ex12_SetupPlotCfg that sets the following plot settings for the page setup created for #2 in Exercise 12-1:
    Plot to DWF File

    PC3 file: DWF6 ePlot.pc3
    Plot style table: Acad.ctb
    Paper size: 8.5" × 11.0"
    Scale: 1:1
    What to plot: Layout

Plotting Using the Plot Object

Once all of the necessary plot settings have been made and everything is set up to produce the desired output, you should be ready to plot. This is achieved in the AutoCAD object model by using the **Plot** object. The **Plot** object is accessed via the **ThisDrawing** object as follows:

    ThisDrawing.Plot

The **Plot** object provides methods that allow you to preview a plot, plot to a particular device, and even plot to file. These and other **Plot** object methods and properties are discussed in the following sections.

Previewing a Plot

It is always a good idea to preview a plot before actually sending it to the printer. Many times fine tuning is needed in order to get the desired output. The **DisplayPlotPreview** method displays a plot preview of the current layout using the current settings. The signature is:

    Plot.DisplayPlotPreview *Preview*

Preview is the **acPreviewMode** enum, where **acPartialPreview** is a partial preview mode and **acFullPreview** is a full preview mode.

A partial preview shows an accurate representation of the plot area relative to the paper size. A full preview displays the drawing on the screen as it will appear when plotted on paper.

The following code displays a full plot preview:

```
Sub Ch12_PlotPreview()

    ' Display a full plot preview.
    ThisDrawing.Plot.DisplayPlotPreview acFullPreview

End Sub
```

Plotting to a Device

Once you have specified all of the desired plot settings and you have done a plot preview, it is time to plot. You can send the plot to the current plotter specified in the **ConfigName** property or override the current plotter and send the plot to a specific device.

The **PlotToDevice** method sends a plot to the specified device (PC3) using the current settings. If no device is specified, the plotter specified in the **ConfigName** property is used. The signature for the **PlotToDevice** method is:

    ReturnVal = Plot.PlotToDevice(*[PC3_File]*)

ReturnVal is a **Boolean** where **True** means the plot was successful and **False** means the plot failed. *PC3_File* is an optional **String** that is the plotter configuration file (PC3).

The following code sends a plot to the device specified in the **ConfigName** property:

```
Sub Ch12_PlotToDevice1()

    ' Plot to the current plot device with the current settings.
    ThisDrawing.Plot.PlotToDevice

End Sub
```

The code in the next example sends a plot to the default Windows system printer by specifying its PC3 file:

```
Sub Ch12_PlotToDevice2()

    Dim blnPlotOK As Boolean

    ' Plot to the default Windows system printer.
    blnPlotOK = ThisDrawing.Plot.PlotToDevice _
        ("Default Windows System Printer.pc3")

    ' Check to see if the plot was successful and inform the user.
    If blnPlotOK Then
        MsgBox "Plot successfully sent."
    Else
        MsgBox "Plot request failed."
    End If

End Sub
```

Professional Tip

If the configuration file is not found at the specified path, AutoCAD will search the Printer Support File Path described earlier. If the PC3 file is still not found, the method defaults to the current configuration

Plotting to a File

Sometimes, it might be necessary to create a plot file rather than sending a plot directly to a plot device. Plot files can be copied to a plot device later as long as the device type is the same as was specified when the plot file was created.

The **PlotToFile** method creates a plot file using either the current plot device set in the **ConfigName** property or the PC3 file specified. The signature for the **PlotToFile** method is:

ReturnVal = Plot.PlotToFile(*PlotFile*, [*PC3_File*])

ReturnVal is a **Boolean**, where **True** means the plot was successful and **False** means the plot failed. *PlotFile* is a **String** that is the name for the plot file. *PC3_File* is an optional **String** that is the plotter configuration file (PC3).

The following code creates a plot file named My Plot.plt:

```
Sub Ch12_PlotToFile()

    Dim blnPlotOK As Boolean

    blnPlotOK = ThisDrawing.Plot.PlotToFile("My Plot")

    ' Check to see if the plot was successful and inform the user.
    If blnPlotOK Then
        MsgBox "The plot file ""My Plot"" was successfully created."
    Else
        MsgBox "Plot file request failed."
    End If

End Sub
```

If a file extension is not provided in the *PlotFile* argument, then an extension is automatically generated based on the default extension for the specified driver or device. If a specific drive and folder are not included in the file name, the file is saved to the current working folder (as indicated by the **DWGPREFIX** system variable).

Plotting Multiple Copies

It is possible to create more than one copy of a plot at a time. The **NumberOfCopies** property allows you to specify the desired number of copies to plot.

The following code creates three copies of a plot:

```
Sub Ch12_PlotCopies()

    ' Plot three copies.
    ThisDrawing.Plot.NumberOfCopies = 3

    ' Plot to the current plot device with the current settings.
    ThisDrawing.Plot.PlotToDevice

End Sub
```

Plotting Multiple Layouts

It is possible to plot multiple layouts at one time. Using this approach you can plot all of the layouts in a drawing in a single operation. The **SetLayoutsToPlot** method plots one or more layouts consecutively. The signature is:

Plot.SetLayoutsToPlot *Layouts*

where *Layouts* is a **Variant** data type that is an array of the layout names.

The following code creates DWF files for all of the layouts in a drawing:

```
Sub Ch12_PlotAllLayouts()

    Dim strLayouts() As String
    Dim varLayoutList As Variant
    Dim objLayout As AcadLayout
    Dim intLayoutNo As Integer
    Dim intCounter As Integer

    ' Zoom all before creating the DWF.
    ZoomAll

    ' Get the names of all of the layouts in the drawing.
    For Each objLayout In ThisDrawing.Layouts
        intLayoutNo = intLayoutNo + 1
        ReDim Preserve strLayouts(1 To intLayoutNo)
        strLayouts(intLayoutNo) = objLayout.name
    Next

    ' Convert to a Variant, which is expected by the SetLayoutsToPlot method.
    varLayoutList = strLayouts

    ' Run in quiet mode so the batch is not interrupted.
    ThisDrawing.Plot.QuietErrorMode = False

    ' Set to one copy.
    ThisDrawing.Plot.NumberOfCopies = 1

    ' Start the batch plot with the number of layouts to plot.
    ThisDrawing.Plot.StartBatchMode intLayoutNo

    ' Plot all layouts to DWF files.
    ' Must be called every time.
    ThisDrawing.Plot.SetLayoutsToPlot varLayoutList

    ' Plot to DWF file format.
    ThisDrawing.Plot.PlotToDevice "DWF6 ePlot.pc3"

    ' Tell the user.
    MsgBox "DWF files created for all layouts in the drawing."

End Sub
```

Professional Tip

If you plot multiple layouts to a file (instead of a plot device) using the **SetLayoutsToPlot** method, the output plot files are automatically named by concatenating the drawing name with the layout name. By default, the plot files are saved to the current working folder indicated by the **DWGPREFIX** system variable.

Plotting Using the Plot Object   Let's Review...

- The **Plot** object provides methods that allow you to preview a plot, plot to a particular device, and plot to file.
- The **DisplayPlotPreview** method displays a plot preview of the current layout using the current settings.
- The **PlotToDevice** method sends a plot to the specified device using the current settings.
- The **PlotToFile** method creates a plot file.
- The **NumberOfCopies** property allows you to specify the desired number of copies to plot.
- The **SetLayoutsToPlot** method plots one or more layouts consecutively.

Exercise 12-4

Create the macros described below. All macros should be created in the **ThisDrawing** module of your MyMacros.dvb project. Provide all necessary error checking and control. Run and test each macro.

1. Create a macro named ex12_MakeDWF that plots the current drawing display to a DWF file named ex12-04.dwf.
2. Create a macro named ex12_PlotLayouts that plots all of the layouts created in #1 in Exercise 12-1 to the default Windows system printer.

Chapter Test

Write your answers on a separate sheet of paper.

1. Explain a *layout* and how it is used in AutoCAD.
2. List three plot settings managed via layouts.
3. List the two VBA objects that make up a layout and describe for what each object is used.
4. What is *always* the block name of the active paper space layout?
5. Which two properties can be used to determine a block's type?
6. Explain the difference between a **Layout** object and a **PlotConfiguration** object.
7. To what is a **PlotConfiguration** object referred as in the AutoCAD drawing editor?
8. What is a *PC3 file* and for what is it used?
9. Which property is used to control the PC3 file associated with a layout or page setup?
10. List the two different kinds of plot style tables and provide a brief explanation of each.
11. Which property is used to control the plot style table associated with a layout or page setup?
12. Which property is used to control the paper size associated with a layout or page setup?
13. Which method allows you to set a custom plot scale and how is it used?
14. List five ways you can specify the area of the drawing that you want to plot.
15. Which property can be used to center a plot on a piece of paper?
16. Which VBA object provides all of the necessary methods and properties needed to plot a drawing?
17. When a plot is sent using VBA, how can you tell if it was successfully sent?
18. Which **Plot** object method can be used to plot more than one layout at a time?

Programming Problems

Create the macros described below. All macros should be created in the **ThisDrawing** module of your MyMacros.dvb project. Provide all necessary error checking and control. Run and test each macro.

1. Write a macro name p12_NewLayout that creates a new layout named ANSI D-22 × 34 and makes it current. Run the macro once and then run the p11_AttachTitleBlock macro from Problem 11-4. Save the drawing as p12-01.

2. Create a macro name p12_LayoutSettings that establishes the following settings for the ANSI D-22 × 34 layout created in Problem 12-1:

   PC3 file: Default Windows System Printer.pc3
   Plot style table: Monochrome.ctb
   Paper size: 22.0″ × 34.0″
   Scale: 1:1
   What to plot: Layout
   Save the drawing as p12-02.

3. Create a macro named p12_PlotDefault that plots the ANSI D-22 × 34 layout in drawing p12-02 to the default Windows system printer.

4. Create a macro name p12_PlotDWF that plots the ANSI D-22 × 34 layout in drawing p12-02 to a DWF file.

Controlling Pull-Down Menus and Toolbars

Learning Objectives

After completing this chapter, you will be able to create VBA macros that:

- Reference a menu group.
- Iterate through all menu groups currently loaded.
- Load a menu group.
- Save a menu group to a file.
- Unload a menu group.
- Add a pull-down menu to the menu bar.
- Remove a pull-down menu from the menu bar.
- Add menu items to a pull-down menu.
- Add a separator to a pull-down menu.
- Remove a menu item from a pull-down menu.
- Create a cascading submenu.
- Add a new toolbar menu.
- Add a toolbar button.
- Specify a toolbar button icon.
- Add a toolbar button separator.
- Remove a toolbar button.
- Create a toolbar flyout menu.
- Control the size and location of a toolbar.

Pull-Down Menus and Toolbars

Like most Windows applications, AutoCAD contains pull-down menus and toolbars for issuing commands, setting options, controlling object properties, and generally interacting with the program. These graphic components are often referred to collectively as an application's *graphical user interface (GUI)*.

Unlike most other Windows applications, the AutoCAD GUI is highly customizable. In AutoCAD, it is possible to create a completely customized menu system consisting of different pull-down menus and toolbars. The ability to customize AutoCAD in this fashion has been available to the average user for years. The **MENU** and **MENULOAD** commands can be used to load and unload different menu files. The **CUSTOMIZE** command allows you to create and customize your own toolbars and toolbar buttons. You can even create your own toolbar icons within AutoCAD.

It is possible to customize menus and toolbars using VBA and the AutoCAD object model. All of AutoCAD's pull-down menus and toolbars are stored as **MenuGroup** objects that are, in turn, part of a **MenuGroups** collection. Menu groups can be added to and removed from the **MenuGroups** collection using loading and unloading methods similar to those provided in the AutoCAD drawing editor. Loading a menu group makes it part of the **MenuGroups** collection. Once a menu group is loaded, you can get a reference to its corresponding **MenuGroup** object. The **MenuGroup** object provides control of all of a menu group's pull-down menus and toolbars. The following sections explain how to manage and control menu groups so that you can create custom pull-down menus and toolbars via the AutoCAD object model.

MenuGroups Collection

The **MenuGroups** collection is a collection of **MenuGroup** objects that represents the menu group currently loaded in the AutoCAD session. The **MenuGroups** collection resides directly below the AutoCAD **Application** object in the AutoCAD object model as seen in **Figure 13-1**.

The following sections show you how to manage the **MenuGroups** collection and its **MenuGroup** objects so you can:

- Reference a currently loaded menu group.
- Iterate all the menu groups loaded in the current AutoCAD session.
- Load a menu group (full and partial).
- Save a menu group to a menu file.
- Unload a menu group.

Caution   Before running any of the code in this chapter, make a backup copy of the acad.mns menu file in the AutoCAD \Support folder so that the original menu file is not affected by any changes.

Figure 13-1.
The **MenuGroups**
collection.

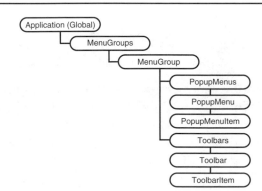

Referencing a Menu Group

You can get a reference to a currently loaded **MenuGroup** object by specifying the menu group name in the **MenuGroups** collection. The following code gets a reference to the ACAD **MenuGroup** object in the **MenuGroups** collection and displays the path and file name of the menu file from which it was loaded:

```
Sub Ch13_GetMenuGroup()

    Dim objMenuGroup As AcadMenuGroup

    On Error GoTo ERROR:

    ' Get the menu group ACAD from the MenuGroups collection.
    Set objMenuGroup = ThisDrawing.Application.MenuGroups("ACAD")

    ' Display the menu file path for the menu group ACAD.
    MsgBox "The file name for the menu group ""ACAD"" is:" _
        & vbLf & vbLf & objMenuGroup.MenuFileName

    Exit Sub
ERROR:

    ' Error retrieving the menu group ACAD.
    MsgBox "Error retrieving ""ACAD"" menu group."

End Sub
```

Iterating the MenuGroups Collection

You can step through all of the menu groups currently loaded in an AutoCAD session by using a **For Each...** loop to iterate the **MenuGroups** collection. The following code iterates the **MenuGroups** collection, displays a list of all of the menu groups currently loaded, and indicates whether they are a base menu group or a partial menu group:

```
Sub Ch13_IterateMenuGroups()

    Dim strBaseMenus As String
    Dim strPartialMenus As String
    Dim objMenuGroup As AcadMenuGroup

    ' Initialize strings.
    strBaseMenus = ""
    strPartialMenus = ""

    ' Iterate all menu groups in the drawing.
    ' Delineating between base and partial menus.
    For Each objMenuGroup In ThisDrawing.Application.MenuGroups
        If objMenuGroup.Type = acBaseMenuGroup Then
            strBaseMenus = strBaseMenus & vbTab & objMenuGroup.name _
                & vbCrLf
        Else
            strPartialMenus = strPartialMenus & vbTab & _
                objMenuGroup.name & vbCrLf
        End If
    Next

    ' Display the loaded menus to the user.
    MsgBox "Base menu groups loaded: " & vbCrLf & vbCrLf & _
        strBaseMenus & vbCrLf & _
        "Partial menu groups loaded: " & vbCrLf & vbCrLf & _
        strPartialMenus

End Sub
```

Figure 13-2.
AutoCAD menu file types.

File Type	Description
MNU	An ASCII text file, with formatting and comments, that defines the menu. Menu customization and edits are typically made in this file.
MNS	An ASCII-based menu definition source file minus formatting and comments. This file is updated automatically by AutoCAD.
MNL	The AutoLISP program file associated with the menu that typically contains menu support code. It is loaded automatically when the associated menu file is loaded.
MNR	The menu resource file. This file contains bitmap images, in binary format, used by the toolbar buttons. It is created automatically when the menu file is compiled and the MNC menu file is created.
MNC	The compiled menu file. It is created automatically when the menu is loaded and has been updated. This is a binary menu file used internally by AutoCAD.

MenuGroup Object

As mentioned earlier, the **MenuGroup** object is the key to accessing all of a menu group's pull-down menus and toolbars. But what is a menu group exactly? A *menu group* contains all of the pull-down menus and toolbars for AutoCAD. It is defined in an external, ASCII-based text file that is typically referred to as an *AutoCAD menu file*. There are actually a number of different related files that make up a complete menu system. They all share the same root name, but rely on different file extensions to indicate their types and usage. The different menu file types and their descriptions are listed in **Figure 13-2.**

The MNU file contains the definitions for all of the pull-down menus and toolbars in ASCII format and can be edited using a simple text editor. Customizing menu files via a text editor approach is described in detail in the Customization Guide found in AutoCAD's online developer documentation. Later in this chapter, you will learn how to update a menu directly using VBA code. First, however, you need to know how to load a menu using VBA.

Loading a Menu Group

There are two ways to load a menu group in AutoCAD—full and partial. The full load method is used to load what is known as a base menu. The *base menu* contains most of the menus, toolbars, and mouse button definitions. A partial menu load allows you to load subsequent specific menus that provide additional functionality on top of the base menu. For example, a partial menu might define additional pull-down menus that perform specific, related tasks.

In AutoCAD, a full menu load is accomplished using the **MENU** command, which displays the **Select Menu File** dialog box shown in **Figure 13-3.** The **MENULOAD** command performs a partial menu load in the AutoCAD drawing editor via the **Menu Customization** dialog box shown in **Figure 13-4.**

Figure 13-3.
Performing a full menu load using the **Select Menu File** dialog box.

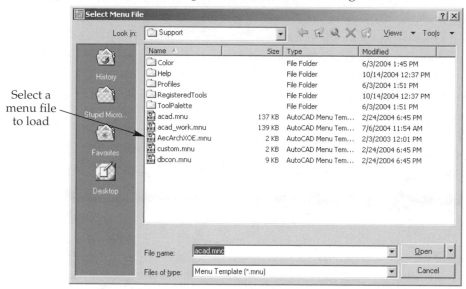

Select a
menu file
to load

Figure 13-4.
Performing a partial menu load using the **Menu Customization** dialog box.

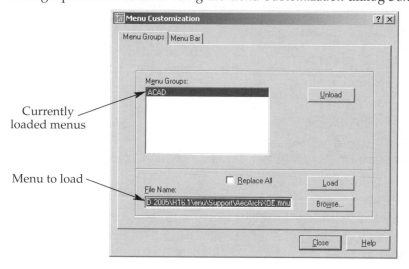

Currently
loaded menus

Menu to load

Both the full and partial methods of loading menu files are provided in the AutoCAD object model via the **MenuGroups** collection **Load** method. The signature for the **Load** method is:

objMenuGroup = MenuGroups.Load (*MenuFile, FullLoad*)

where *objMenuGroup* is the **MenuGroup** object. *MenuFile* is a **String** that is the menu file name (MNC, MNS, or MNU file type). *FullLoad* is a **Boolean** where **True** means a full menu load and **False** means a partial menu load.

The following code performs a full load of the default acad.mns base menu. Note: If the acad menu is loaded when you run this macro, an error is generated.

```
Sub Ch13_LoadMenuGroupFull()

    Dim strMenuFileName As String
    Dim objMenuGroup As AcadMenuGroup

    On Error GoTo NOTLOADED:

    ' Set the menu file name.
    strMenuFileName = "ACAD.MNS"

    ' Load the menu as a base menu.
    Set objMenuGroup = _
        ThisDrawing.Application.MenuGroups.Load(strMenuFileName, True)

    ' Tell the user of success.
    MsgBox """ACAD.MNS"" was successfully loaded."

    Exit Sub

NOTLOADED:

    ' Could not load the menu.
    MsgBox """ACAD.MNS"" could not be loaded for the following reason:" _
        & vbLf & vbLf & Err.Description

End Sub
```

All that is necessary to perform a partial load is to set the **Load** method's *FullLoad* **Boolean** argument to **False**. The following code performs a partial load of the menu file C:\VBA for AutoCAD\Menus\MyMenu.mns:

```
Sub Ch13_LoadMenuGroupPartial()

    Dim strMenuFileName As String
    Dim objMenuGroup As AcadMenuGroup

    On Error GoTo NOTLOADED:

    ' Set the menu file name and path.
    strMenuFileName = "C:\VBA for AutoCAD\Menus\MyMenu.mns"

    ' Load the menu as a partial menu.
    Set objMenuGroup = _
        ThisDrawing.Application.MenuGroups.Load(strMenuFileName, False)

    ' Tell the user of success.
    MsgBox """MyMenu.mns"" was successfully loaded."

    Exit Sub

NOTLOADED:

    ' Could not load the menu.
    MsgBox """MyMenu.mns"" could not be loaded for the following reason:" _
        & vbLf & vbLf & Err.Description

End Sub
```

Saving a Menu Group

It is possible to save a currently loaded menu group to a menu file using the **MenuGroup** object's **Save** method. This allows you to save any changes you make to a menu through code using VBA. Customizing pull-down menus and toolbars using VBA and the AutoCAD object model is discussed later in this chapter. The signature for the **Save** method is:

```
MenuGroup.Save MenuFileType
```

MenuFileType is an **acMenuFileType** enum, where **acMenuFileCompiled** is a compiled menu file (MNC) and **acMenuFileSource** is a source menu file (MNS).

The following code saves the MyMenu.mns partial menu. Note: If the menu is not loaded, a run-time error is generated.

```
Sub Ch13_SaveMenuGroup()

    Dim objMenuGroup As AcadMenuGroup

    On Error GoTo ERROR:

    ' Get the menu group MyMenu from the MenuGroups collection.
    Set objMenuGroup = ThisDrawing.Application.MenuGroups("MyMenu")

    ' Save the menu as a source menu file (MNS).
    objMenuGroup.Save acMenuFileSource

    ' Tell the user.
    MsgBox "MyMenu.mns was saved successfully."

    Exit Sub
ERROR:

    ' Error saving MyMenu.mns.
    MsgBox "The menu group ""MyMenu"" could not be saved."

End Sub
```

Unloading a Menu Group

Unloading a menu group removes it from the **MenuGroups** collection. Once unloaded, the menu's pull-down menus and toolbars are no longer available. The signature for the **Unload** method is:

```
MenuGroup.Unload
```

The following code unloads the MyMenu menu group:

```
Sub Ch13_UnloadMenuGroup()

    Dim objMenuGroup As AcadMenuGroup

    On Error GoTo ERROR:

    ' Get the menu group MyMenu from the MenuGroups collection.
    Set objMenuGroup = ThisDrawing.Application.MenuGroups("MyMenu")

    ' Unload the menu.
    objMenuGroup.Unload

    ' Display the menu file path for the menu group MyMenu.
    MsgBox "The menu group ""MyMenu"" was successfully unloaded."

    Exit Sub
ERROR:

    'Error unloading the menu group MyMenu.
    MsgBox "The menu group ""MyMenu"" could not be unloaded."

End Sub
```

Caution Delete any references to toolbars and menus that are in a menu group to be unloaded before you unload the menu group because these references will become invalid.

Let's Review...

MenuGroups Collection and MenuGroup Object

- Each menu group loaded in a drawing is represented by a **MenuGroup** object that is part of the drawing's **MenuGroups** collection.
- You get a reference to a **MenuGroup** by specifying the menu group name in the **MenuGroups** collection.
- You can step through all of the menu groups loaded in a drawing by using a **For Each...** loop to iterate the **MenuGroups** collection.
- The **Load** method loads a menu file and adds it to the **MenuGroups** collection.
- The **Load** method can be set to do either a partial menu load or full menu load.
- The **Save** method saves a menu group to a specified menu file name and type.
- The **Unload** method unloads a menu group.

Exercise 13-1

Create the macros described below. All macros should be created in the **ThisDrawing** module of your MyMacros.dvb project. Provide all necessary error checking and control. Run and test each macro.

Important: Before starting this exercise, copy the acad.mns menu file from the AutoCAD \Support folder to the C:\VBA for AutoCAD\Menus folder so that the original menu file is not affected by any changes.

1. Create a macro named ex13_UnloadMenu that unloads the default ACAD menu group.
2. Create a macro named ex13_LoadMenu that loads the copy of the acad.mns file (C:\VBA for AutoCAD\Menus\acad.mns).

Pull-Down Menus

Pull-down menus are located at the top of the AutoCAD application window and provide access to AutoCAD commands and features. Selecting the top menu item, such as **Draw**, displays the menu's first level, **Figure 13-5**.

Most Windows applications share a similar pull-down menu interface. In fact, the first six pull-down menus—**File**, **Edit**, **View**, **Insert**, **Format**, and **Tools**—can be found in the same location in most Microsoft Office applications. The content of each menu might vary from one application to another, but the locations are the same. This makes it easier for Office users to switch between Windows programs without having to learn a different UI.

All of the pull-down menus are implemented as the **PopupMenus** object collection in the AutoCAD object model. Managing the **PopupMenus** collection and customizing pull-down menus are explained in the following sections.

Figure 13-5.
The first level of AutoCAD's **Draw** pull-down menu is displayed here.

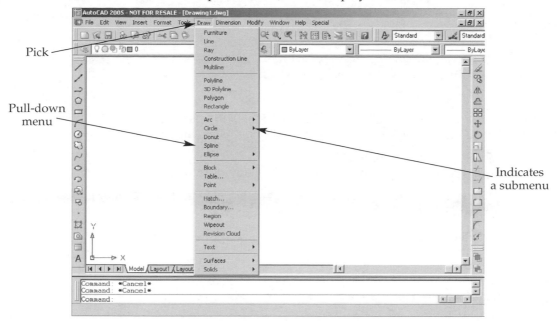

PopupMenus Collection

As seen in object model diagram shown in **Figure 13-1,** each pull-down menu in a menu group is represented by a **PopupMenu** object that is part of the **MenuGroup** object's **PopupMenus** collection. The following sections show you how to manage the **PopupMenus** collection so you can:

- Add a pull-down menu to the menu bar.
- Remove a pull-down menu from the menu bar.
- Add pull-down menu items.
- Add a pull-down menu separator.
- Remove pull-down menu items.
- Create a cascading submenu.

Adding a Pull-Down Menu to the Menu Bar

The **InsertMenuInMenuBar** method adds a pull-down menu to the menu bar. The signature is:

    Menus.InsertMenuInMenuBar *MenuName, Index*

where *MenuName* is a **String** that is the name of the pull-down menu name to add. *Index* is a **Variant** that is the index number or pull-down menu name *left* of which the menu is to be inserted. Index numbers must be between 0 and *n–1*, where 0 is the leftmost menu and *n* is the number of pull-down menus. Menu names must include accelerator keys (indicated by &) in menu name.

The following code adds an empty pull-down menu named **My Menu** to the menu bar directly before (to the left of) the **Help** menu. Note: The menu MyMenu must be loaded or an error is generated.

```
Sub Ch13_AddPullDownMenu()

    Dim objMenuGroup As AcadMenuGroup
    Dim objPopupMenu As AcadPopupMenu

    On Error GoTo ERROR:

    ' Get the menu group MyMenu from the MenuGroups collection.
    Set objMenuGroup = ThisDrawing.Application.MenuGroups("MyMenu")

    ' Create the new menu.
    Set objPopupMenu = objMenuGroup.Menus.Add("M&y Menu")

    ' Display the menu on the menu bar before the standard Help menu.
    objMenuGroup.Menus.InsertMenuInMenuBar "M&y Menu", "&Help"

    Exit Sub

ERROR:

    ' My Menu pull-down could not be added.
    MsgBox "The pull-down menu ""My Menu"" could not be added."

End Sub
```

Removing a Pull-Down Menu from the Menu Bar

The **RemoveMenuFromMenuBar** method removes a pull-down menu from the menu bar. The signature is:

Menus.RemoveMenuFromMenuBar *MenuName*

where *MenuName* is a **String** that is the name of the pull-down menu to remove.

The following code removes the **My Menu** pull-down menu from the menu bar. Note: The menu MyMenu must be loaded and the **My Menu** pull-down menu must be on the menu bar or a run-time error is generated.

```
Sub Ch13_RemovePullDownMenu()

    Dim objMenuGroup As AcadMenuGroup

    On Error GoTo ERROR:

    ' Get the menu group MyMenu from the MenuGroups collection.
    Set objMenuGroup = ThisDrawing.Application.MenuGroups("MyMenu")

    ' Remove the My Menu pull-down menu from the menu bar.
    objMenuGroup.Menus.RemoveMenuFromMenuBar "M&y Menu"

    Exit Sub

ERROR:

    ' Error removing the pull-down menu.
    MsgBox "An error occurred trying to remove the pull-down menu ""My Menu""."

End Sub
```

Adding Menu Items

The **AddMenuItem** method adds an item to a pull-down menu at a specified location in the menu. The item contains the desired label and corresponding menu macro. The signature for the **AddMenuItem** method is:

objMenuItem = PopupMenu.AddMenuItem (*Index, Label, Macro*)

VBA for AutoCAD

where *objMenuItem* is the **PopupMenuItem** object. *Index* is a **Variant** that is the location in the pull-down menu where the item is to be added. The new menu item is added before the specified index location. Index numbers must be between 0 and *n*–1, where 0 is the first menu item and *n* is the total number of menu items. To add the new menu item to the end of a menu, set the index to be greater than *n*. *Label* is a **String** that is the label for the menu item. This string may contain DIESEL string expressions and accelerator keys. Accelerator keys are defined with an ampersand (&) in front of the mnemonic character. *Macro* is a **String** that is the macro associated with the menu item.

Menu macros are simply text strings that are processed as commands at the AutoCAD command line when a menu item is picked. The standard format is to start a menu macro with two cancels so that any active commands will be canceled before the macro is run. In VBA, a cancel is issued using the ESC character sequence. Also, an AutoCAD command macro must end with either a space or the semi-colon (;) character. Both of these characters represent pressing the space bar or [Enter] so that the macro is processed. For detailed information about creating menu macros, refer to the Customization Guide in AutoCAD's online developer documentation.

The following code creates the **My Menu** pull-down menu and adds two menu items to it. The first menu item invokes the **LINE** command and the second menu item invokes the **CIRCLE** command. Note: This code adds the pull-down menu before adding the menu items. Therefore, the pull-down menu must not be displayed on the menu bar before running the macro or a run-time error is generated. You may also need to restart AutoCAD after removing the pull-down menu before running the macro.

```
Sub Ch13_AddMenuItems()

    Dim objMenuGroup As AcadMenuGroup
    Dim objPopupMenu As AcadPopupMenu
    Dim strMenuMacro As String

    On Error GoTo ERROR:

    ' Get the menu group MyMenu from the MenuGroups collection.
    Set objMenuGroup = ThisDrawing.Application.MenuGroups("MyMenu")

    ' Create the new menu.
    Set objPopupMenu = objMenuGroup.Menus.Add("M&y Menu")

    ' Add a macro to start the line command: "ESC ESC _line ".
    strMenuMacro = Chr(3) & Chr(3) & "_line" & Chr(32)

    ' Add the macro to the My Menu pull-down menu.
    objPopupMenu.AddMenuItem objPopupMenu.Count + 1, "&Line", _
            strMenuMacro

    ' Add a macro to start the circle command: "ESC ESC _circle ".
    strMenuMacro = Chr(3) & Chr(3) & "_circle" & Chr(32)

    ' Add the macro to the My Menu pull-down menu.
    objPopupMenu.AddMenuItem objPopupMenu.Count + 1, "&Circle", _
            strMenuMacro

    ' Display the menu on the menu bar before the standard Help menu.
    objMenuGroup.Menus.InsertMenuInMenuBar "M&y Menu", "&Help"

    Exit Sub

ERROR:

    ' Error adding menu items.
    MsgBox "The menu items could not be added."

End Sub
```

Figure 13-6.
The pull-down menu
My Menu is added to
the menu bar.

Running this Ch13_AddMenuItems macro creates the **My Menu** pull-down menu shown in **Figure 13-6.**

Professional Tip

The **Count** property keeps track of how many menu items a pull-down menu contains. You can use this property to add menu items to the end of a pull-down menu by increasing it by one and using the result to specify the new menu item's index, as seen in the Ch13_AddMenuItems macro above.

Adding a Menu Item Separator

The **AddSeparator** method adds a separator, or line, between menu items. This allows similar menu items to be visually grouped. The signature for the **AddSeparator** method is:

> *objMenuItem* = PopupMenu.AddSeparator (*Index*)

where *objMenuItem* is the **PopupMenuItem** object. *Index* is a **Variant** that is the location in the pull-down menu where the separator is to be added. The separator is added before the specified index location. Index numbers must be between 0 and *n*–1, where 0 is the first menu item and *n* is the total number of menu items.

The following code adds a menu separator to the last position in the **My Menu** pull-down menu:

```
Sub Ch13_AddMenuSeparator()

    Dim objMenuGroup As AcadMenuGroup
    Dim objPopupMenu As AcadPopupMenu
    Dim strMenuMacro As String

    On Error GoTo ERROR:

    ' Get the menu group MyMenu from the MenuGroups collection.
    Set objMenuGroup = ThisDrawing.Application.MenuGroups("MyMenu")

    ' Get My Menu.
    Set objPopupMenu = objMenuGroup.Menus.Item("M&y Menu")

    ' Add a separator to the end of the menu.
    objPopupMenu.AddSeparator objPopupMenu.Count + 1

    Exit Sub

ERROR:

    ' Error adding separator.
    MsgBox "The menu separator could not be added."

End Sub
```

Running the Ch13_AddMenuSeparator macro adds a separator to the bottom of the **My Menu** pull-down menu, as shown in **Figure 13-7.**

Figure 13-7.
A separator is added
to the pull-down
menu **My Menu**.

Separator
added

Caution

⚠️

The first item in a menu cannot be a separator. Therefore, you cannot add a separator at index position 0. You also cannot add a separator immediately next to another separator.

Removing Menu Items

You can remove a menu item by getting a reference to the menu item and calling its **Delete** method. The signature for the **Delete** method is:

objMenuItem.Delete

where *objMenuItem* is the **PopupMenuItem** object to delete.

The following code removes the first menu item (**Line**) from the **My Menu** pull-down menu:

```
Sub Ch13_DeleteMenuItem()

    Dim objMenuGroup As AcadMenuGroup
    Dim objPopupMenu As AcadPopupMenu
    Dim strMenuMacro As String

    On Error GoTo ERROR:

    ' Get the menu group MyMenu from the MenuGroups collection.
    Set objMenuGroup = ThisDrawing.Application.MenuGroups("MyMenu")

    ' Get My Menu.
    Set objPopupMenu = objMenuGroup.Menus.Item("M&y Menu")

    ' Remove the first menu item.
    objPopupMenu.Item(0).Delete

    Exit Sub

ERROR:

    ' Error deleting the menu item.
    MsgBox "Error deleting the menu item."

End Sub
```

Creating Cascading Submenus

A cascading submenu is a menu contained within a pull-down menu. The **AddSubMenu** method adds a cascading submenu with the desired label to a pull-down menu at a specified location. The signature for the **AddSubMenu** method is:

objPopupMenu = PopupMenu.AddSubMenu (*Index, Label*)

---

where *objPopupMenu* is the **PopupMenu** object. *Index* is a **Variant** that is the index number or menu item name *above* which the submenu is to be inserted. Index numbers must be between 0 and *n–1*, where 0 is the first menu item and *n* is the total number of menu items. To add the submenu to the end of a menu, set the index to be greater than *n*. *Label* is a **String** that is the label for the submenu. This string may contain DIESEL string expressions and accelerator keys. Accelerator keys are defined with an ampersand (&) in front of the mnemonic character.

The following code adds a submenu, itself containing two menu items, to the **My Menu** pull-down menu with the label **File Commands**. The first item in the submenu issues the **OPEN** command and the second item in the submenu issues the **SAVE** command:

```
Sub Ch13_AddSubMenu()

    Dim objMenuGroup As AcadMenuGroup
    Dim objPopupMenu As AcadPopupMenu
    Dim objSubMenu As AcadPopupMenu
    Dim strMenuMacro As String

    On Error GoTo ERROR:

    ' Get the menu group MyMenu from the MenuGroups collection.
    Set objMenuGroup = ThisDrawing.Application.MenuGroups("MyMenu")

    ' Get My Menu.
    Set objPopupMenu = objMenuGroup.Menus.Item("M&y Menu")

    ' Add the submenu.
    Set objSubMenu = objPopupMenu.AddSubMenu(objPopupMenu.Count + 1, _
        "&File Commands")

    ' Add a macro to start the open command: "ESC ESC _open ".
    strMenuMacro = Chr(3) & Chr(3) & "_open" & Chr(32)

    ' Add a menu item to the submenu.
    objSubMenu.AddMenuItem objPopupMenu.Count + 1, "&Open", _
        strMenuMacro

    ' Add a macro to start the close command: "ESC ESC _save ".
    strMenuMacro = Chr(3) & Chr(3) & "_save" & Chr(32)

    ' Add a menu item to the submenu.
    objSubMenu.AddMenuItem objPopupMenu.Count + 1, "&Save", _
        strMenuMacro

    Exit Sub

ERROR:

    ' Error adding submenu.
    MsgBox "Error adding the cascading menu."

End Sub
```

Running the Ch13_AddSubMenu macro adds the **File Commands** submenu to the bottom of the **My Menu** pull-down menu, as shown in **Figure 13-8.**

Figure 13-8.
The submenu **File Commands** is added to the pull-down menu **My Menu**.

Submenu added

Exercise 13-2

Create the macros described below. All macros should be created in the **ThisDrawing** module of your MyMacros.dvb project. Provide all necessary error checking and control. Run and test each macro.

1. Create a macro named ex13_InsertPullDown that creates a pull-down menu named **VBA for AutoCAD** and adds it to the menu bar directly to the left of the **Help** pull-down menu.
2. Create a macro named ex13_CreateMenuItems that adds the following two menu commands to the **VBA for AutoCAD** pull-down menu created in #1 above:
Load MyMacros—Loads the file MyMacros.dvb at the command line.
Unload Macros—Unloads the file MyMacros.dvb at the command line.

Toolbars

Toolbars provide access to AutoCAD commands and features via groups of related buttons that show graphic representations (icons) of the commands the buttons invoke. In addition to the icon on a button, text feedback in the form of a "tooltip" is displayed when the cursor is held over the button. **Figure 13-9** shows the **Standard** toolbar with a tooltip displayed for the **Copy to Clipboard** button.

Like pull-down menus, most Windows applications share a similar toolbar menu interface. In fact, a number of toolbar buttons are shared by many different programs. Most people are familiar with the button with an image of a floppy disk that saves a file or the button with an image of a printer that prints a file. This is just another tactic that makes it easier for a user to seamlessly switch between programs.

Some of the main features of toolbars are that they can be turned on and off, moved, and resized. Toolbars can be made to "float," so that they can be dragged around the screen and placed in convenient locations, or they can be "docked" on one of the four

Figure 13-9.
A tooltip is displayed when the cursor is paused over a button.

sides of the AutoCAD drawing window. All of these features allow a user to easily customize their setup so the most-often tools and commands are easily accessible.

In AutoCAD, toolbars can be turned on and off using the **Customize** dialog box, **Figure 13-10.** The **Customize** dialog box can also be used to create custom toolbars and toolbar buttons via the **Commands** tab, **Figure 13-11.** To add a button for one of AutoCAD's built-in commands to any visible toolbar, simply drag the "command" from the tab and drop it onto the desired toolbar.

Figure 13-10.
Toolbars can be turned on and off in the **Customize** dialog box.

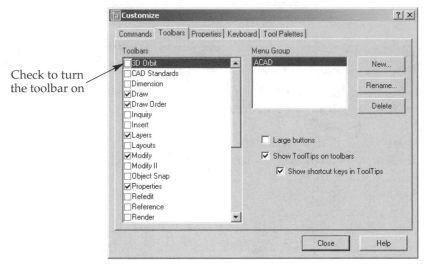

Figure 13-11.
The **Commands** tab of the **Customize** dialog box can be used to add buttons to toolbars.

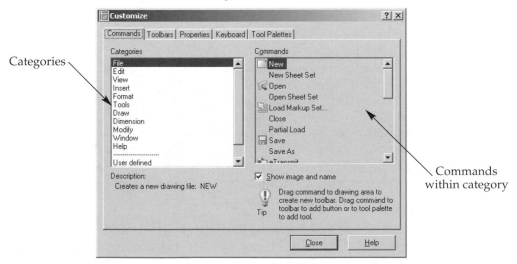

It is even possible to create new buttons that activate user-defined menu macros. The images on these buttons may be selected from a library or they can be custom images. First, add a user-defined button to a toolbar from the **Commands** tab. Then, pick on the new blank button to display the **Button Properties** tab in the **Customize** dialog box, **Figure 13-12.**

In the **Button Properties** tab, you can define all facets of a toolbar button. It is even possible to create custom toolbar icons via the built-in **Button Editor** dialog box shown in **Figure 13-13.** As you can see, just about every aspect of toolbars and their buttons is customizable within AutoCAD. Fortunately, this same level of customization is also possible using VBA and the AutoCAD object model.

All of the toolbar menus are implemented as the **Toolbars** object collection in the AutoCAD object model. Managing the **Toolbars** collection and customizing toolbar menus and buttons is explained in the following sections.

Figure 13-12.
The **Button Properties** tab of the **Customize** dialog box is used to define a button.

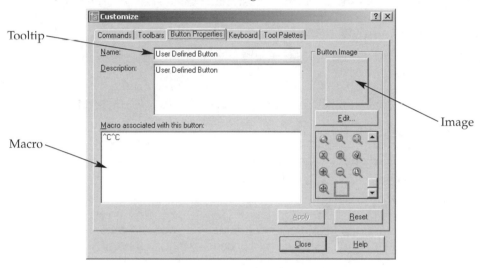

Figure 13-13.
The **Button Editor** dialog box is used to edit or create a button image.

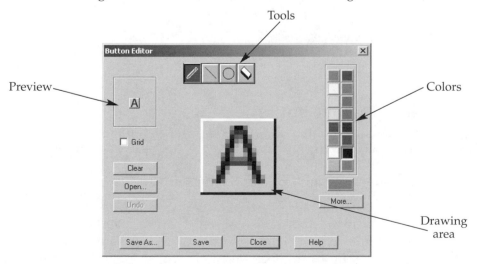

Toolbars Collection

As seen in the object model diagram shown in **Figure 13-1,** each toolbar in a menu group is represented by a **Toolbar** object that is part of the **MenuGroup** object's **Toolbars** collection. The following sections show you how to manage the **Toolbars** collection so you can:

- Add a new toolbar.
- Add toolbar buttons.
- Specify a toolbar button icon (image).
- Add a toolbar separator.
- Remove toolbar buttons.
- Create a toolbar flyout.
- Control the size and location of a toolbar.

Adding a New Toolbar

The **Add** method creates an empty toolbar by adding a **Toolbar** object with the specified name to the **Toolbars** collection. The signature for the **Add** method is:

objToolbar = Toolbars.Add(*Name*)

where *objToolbar* is the **Toolbar** object and *Name* is a **String** that is the name of toolbar to add.

The following code adds a toolbar menu named **MyToolbar** to the MyMenu menu group:

```
Sub Ch13_CreateToolbar()

    Dim objMenuGroup As AcadMenuGroup
    Dim objToolbar As AcadToolbar

    On Error GoTo ERROR:

    ' Get the menu group MyMenu from the MenuGroups collection.
    Set objMenuGroup = ThisDrawing.Application.MenuGroups("MyMenu")

    ' Create the new toolbar.
    objMenuGroup.Toolbars.Add ("MyToolbar")

    Exit Sub

ERROR:

    MsgBox "Error creating the toolbar."

End Sub
```

Adding a New Toolbar Button

A new toolbar is pretty useless unless you add at least one button to invoke a command. The **AddToolbarButton** method adds a button to a specified toolbar. The signature is:

objToolbarButton = Toolbar.AddToolbarButton (*Index, Name, Helpstring,* _
    Macro, [Flyout])

where *objToolbarButton* is the **ToolbarItem** object. *Index* is a **Variant** that is the index location in the toolbar where the item is added. The new item is added before the specified index location. Index numbers must be between 0 and *n*–1, where 0 is the first toolbar button and *n* is the total number of toolbar buttons. To add the new toolbar button to the end of a toolbar, set the index to be greater than *n* or an empty string (""). *Name* is a **String** that is the name for the toolbar button. This string is displayed as the tooltip. *Helpstring* is a **String** that is displayed in the AutoCAD status line when the cursor is placed over the toolbar button. *Macro* is a **String** that is the menu macro associated with the toolbar button. *Flyout* is an optional **Boolean** where **True** means the button is a flyout and **False** means the button is not a flyout. If not a flyout, this can be omitted.

The following code adds two toolbar buttons to the **MyToolbar** toolbar menu created in the previous section. The first toolbar button invokes the **LINE** command and the second toolbar button invokes the **CIRCLE** command:

```
Sub Ch13_CreateToolbarButtons()

    Dim objMenuGroup As AcadMenuGroup
    Dim objToolbar As AcadToolbar
    Dim strMenuMacro As String

    On Error GoTo ERROR:

    ' Get the menu group MyMenu from the MenuGroups collection.
    Set objMenuGroup = ThisDrawing.Application.MenuGroups("MyMenu")

    ' Get the toolbar MyToolbar.
    Set objToolbar = objMenuGroup.Toolbars.Item("MyToolbar")

    ' Add a macro to start the line command: "ESC ESC _line ".
    strMenuMacro = Chr(3) & Chr(3) & "_line" & Chr(32)

    ' Add a Line button to the toolbar.
    objToolbar.AddToolbarButton "", "Line", "Draws a line", strMenuMacro

    ' Add a macro to start the circle command: "ESC ESC _circle ".
    strMenuMacro = Chr(3) & Chr(3) & "_Circle" & Chr(32)

    ' Add a Circle button to the toolbar.
    objToolbar.AddToolbarButton "", "Circle", "Draws a circle", strMenuMacro

    Exit Sub

ERROR:

    MsgBox "Error creating the toolbar buttons."

End Sub
```

Running the Ch13_CreateToolbarButtons macro creates the **Line** and **Circle** toolbar buttons on the **MyToolbar** toolbar menu, as shown in **Figure 13-14.** Notice anything wrong with the toolbar? It does not have proper toolbar icons. The AutoCAD default question mark clouds are displayed instead. The visual cue provided by the button image is probably the most important part of the toolbar button. This is how the user navigates. How you create a toolbar image and assign it to a toolbar button is explained in the next section.

Figure 13-14.
Two buttons have been added to the toolbar **MyToolbar**. Note the default images.

Creating a Toolbar Button Image

AutoCAD relies on bitmap images stored in the BMP file format for the images displayed on toolbar buttons. Since toolbar buttons can be set by the AutoCAD user to be displayed in small or large format, you must assign two files for each button. Small buttons are 16 pixels × 16 pixels, while large buttons are 32 pixels × 32 pixels. You can create your own buttons using the AutoCAD **Button Editor** shown in **Figure 13-13.** This dialog box allows you to perform a "save as" operation to save a BMP file for both small and large toolbar buttons. The size of the saved image is based on whether or not the **Large Buttons** check box is checked in the **Toolbars** tab of the **Customize** dialog box.

Once both small and large bitmap files have been created, the **SetBitmaps** method can be used to assign them to the desired toolbar button. The signature for the **SetBitmaps** method is:

ToolbarItem.SetBitmaps *SmallBMPFile, LargeBMPFile*

where *SmallBMPFile* is a **String** that is the file name and path of a 16 × 16 bitmap file and *LargeBMPFile* is a **String** that is the file name and path of a 32 × 32 bitmap file.

The following code assigns bitmap files representing a line and a circle to the **Line** and **Circle** toolbar buttons on the **MyToolbar** toolbar menu.

```
Sub Ch13_SetButtonIcons()

    Dim objMenuGroup As AcadMenuGroup
    Dim objToolbar As AcadToolbar
    Dim objToolBarButton As AcadToolbarItem
    Dim strMenuMacro As String
    Dim strBitmap16 As String
    Dim strBitmap32 As String

    On Error GoTo ERROR:

    ' Get the menu group MyMenu from the MenuGroups collection.
    Set objMenuGroup = ThisDrawing.Application.MenuGroups("MyMenu")

    ' Get the toolbar MyToolbar.
    Set objToolbar = objMenuGroup.Toolbars.Item("MyToolbar")

    ' Get the Line toolbar button.
    Set objToolBarButton = objToolbar.Item("Line")

    ' Change the icon for the new toolbar button.
    strBitmap16 = "C:\VBA for AutoCAD\Menus\Line16.bmp"
    strBitmap32 = "C:\VBA for AutoCAD\Menus\Line32.bmp"

    ' Set the line bitmap image.
    objToolBarButton.SetBitmaps strBitmap16, strBitmap32

    ' Get Circle toolbar button.
    Set objToolBarButton = objToolbar.Item("Circle")

    ' Change the icon for the new toolbar button.
    strBitmap16 = "C:\VBA for AutoCAD\Menus\Circle16.bmp"
    strBitmap32 = "C:\VBA for AutoCAD\Menus\Circle32.bmp"
```

Figure 13-15.
The buttons on the
toolbar **MyToolbar** now
have images associated
with them.

```
        ' Set the circle bitmap image.
        objToolBarButton.SetBitmaps strBitmap16, strBitmap32

        Exit Sub

    ERROR:

        MsgBox "Error creating toolbar button icons."

    End Sub
```

Running the Ch13_SetButtonIcons macro assigns the line and circle bitmap icons to the **MyToolbar** toolbar menu, as shown in **Figure 13-15.**

Adding a Toolbar Button Separator

The **AddSeparator** method adds a separator, or line, between toolbar buttons so buttons that perform similar commands can be grouped together. The signature for the **AddSeparator** method is:

objToolbarButton = Toolbar.AddSeparator (*Index*)

where *objToolbarButton* is the **ToolbarItem** object. *Index* is a **Variant** that is the index location in the toolbar where the item is added. The separator is added before the specified index location. Index numbers must be between 0 and $n-1$, where 0 is the first toolbar button and n is the total number of toolbar buttons. To add the separator to the end of a toolbar, set the index to be greater than n.

The following code adds a toolbar button separator to the second position in the **My Toolbar** toolbar menu:

```
Sub Ch13_AddToolbarSeparator()

    Dim objMenuGroup As AcadMenuGroup
    Dim objToolbar As AcadToolbar

    On Error GoTo ERROR:

    ' Get the menu group MyMenu from the MenuGroups collection.
    Set objMenuGroup = ThisDrawing.Application.MenuGroups("MyMenu")

    ' Get the toolbar MyToolbar.
    Set objToolbar = objMenuGroup.Toolbars.Item("MyToolbar")

    ' Add a separator to the new toolbar.
    objToolbar.AddSeparator ""

    Exit Sub

ERROR:

    MsgBox "Error creating the toolbar separator."

End Sub
```

<table>
<tr><td>

Caution

</td><td>

The first item in a toolbar cannot be a separator. Therefore, you cannot add a separator at index position 0. You also cannot add a separator immediately next to another separator.

</td></tr>
</table>

Removing a Toolbar Button

You can remove a toolbar button by getting a reference to the button and using its **Delete** method. The signature for the **Delete** method is:

objToolbarButton.Delete

where *objToolbarButton* is the **ToolbarItem** object to delete.

The following code removes the first toolbar button from the **My Toolbar** toolbar:

```
Sub Ch13_DeleteToolbarButton()

    Dim objMenuGroup As AcadMenuGroup
    Dim objToolbar As AcadToolbar
    Dim objToolBarButton As AcadToolbarItem

    On Error GoTo ERROR:

    ' Get the menu group MyMenu from the MenuGroups collection.
    Set objMenuGroup = ThisDrawing.Application.MenuGroups("MyMenu")

    ' Get the toolbar MyToolbar.
    Set objToolbar = objMenuGroup.Toolbars.Item("MyToolbar")

    ' Remove the first toolbar button.
    objToolbar.Item(0).Delete

    Exit Sub

ERROR:

    MsgBox "Error removing the toolbar button."

End Sub
```

Creating a Toolbar Flyout

A flyout is a button that, when picked, displays another toolbar from which to select a command. A flyout button is indicated by a small triangle in the lower-right corner of the button. A toolbar flyout menu is created by attaching the desired toolbar menu to an existing toolbar button using the **AttachToolbarToFlyout** method. The signature for the **AttachToolbarToFlyout** method is:

ToolbarItem.AttachToolbarToFlyout *MenuGroupName, ToolbarName*

where *MenuGroupName* is a **String** that is the name of the menu group where toolbar menu is defined and *ToolbarName* is a **String** that is the name of toolbar menu to attach.

The following code adds a flyout toolbar button to the end of the **MyToolbar** toolbar menu. This is done by first setting the button's **Flyout** property to **True** when the button is created using the **AddToolbarButton** method. Then, a newly created toolbar named **MyFlyout** is attached using the **AttachToolbarToFlyout** method. The new toolbar contains toolbar buttons that invoke the **OPEN** and **SAVE** commands.

```
Sub Ch13_CreateFlyout()

    Dim objMenuGroup As AcadMenuGroup
    Dim objToolbar1 As AcadToolbar
    Dim objToolbar2 As AcadToolbar
    Dim objToolBarButton1_3 As AcadToolbarItem
    Dim objToolBarButton2_1 As AcadToolbarItem
    Dim objToolBarButton2_2 As AcadToolbarItem
    Dim strMenuMacro As String
    Dim strBitmap16 As String
    Dim strBitmap32 As String

    On Error GoTo ERROR:

    ' Get the menu group MyMenu from the MenuGroups collection.
    Set objMenuGroup = ThisDrawing.Application.MenuGroups("MyMenu")

    ' Get the toolbar MyToolbar.
    Set objToolbar1 = objMenuGroup.Toolbars.Item("MyToolbar")

    ' Add a flyout button to the toolbar.
    Set objToolBarButton1_3 = objToolbar1.AddToolbarButton("", "Flyout", _
        "Flyout", "MyFlyout", True)

    ' Create the flyout toolbar.
    Set objToolbar2 = objMenuGroup.Toolbars.Add("MyFlyout")

    ' Add a macro to start the open command: "ESC ESC _open".
    strMenuMacro = Chr(3) & Chr(3) & "_open" & Chr(32)

    ' Add an Open button to the toolbar.
    Set objToolBarButton2_1 = objToolbar2.AddToolbarButton("", "Open", _
        "Opens a drawing", strMenuMacro)

    ' Change the icon for the new toolbar button.
    strBitmap16 = "C:\VBA for AutoCAD\Menus\Open16.bmp"
    strBitmap32 = "C:\VBA for AutoCAD\Menus\Open32.bmp"

    ' Set the bitmap icon.
    objToolBarButton2_1.SetBitmaps strBitmap16, strBitmap32

    ' Add a macro to start the save command: "ESC ESC _save".
    strMenuMacro = Chr(3) & Chr(3) & "_save" & Chr(32)

    ' Add a Close button to the toolbar.
    Set objToolBarButton2_2 = objToolbar2.AddToolbarButton("", "Save", _
        "Saves a drawing", strMenuMacro)

    ' Change the icon for the new toolbar button.
    strBitmap16 = "C:\VBA for AutoCAD\Menus\Save16.bmp"
    strBitmap32 = "C:\VBA for AutoCAD\Menus\Save32.bmp"

    ' Set the bitmap icon.
    objToolBarButton2_2.SetBitmaps strBitmap16, strBitmap32

    ' Attach the flyout.
    objToolBarButton1_3.AttachToolbarToFlyout objMenuGroup.Name, _
        objToolbar2.Name

    ' Set the toolbar visibility.
    objToolbar1.Visible = True
    objToolbar2.Visible = False
```

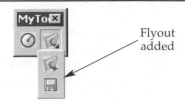

Figure 13-16.
A flyout has been
added to the toolbar
MyToolbar.

Flyout
added

```
    ' Save the menu.
    objMenuGroup.Save acMenuFileCompiled

    Exit Sub

ERROR:

    MsgBox "Error creating toolbar flyout."

End Sub
```

Running the Ch13_CreateFlyout macro attaches the **MyFlyout** toolbar menu to the existing **MyToolbar** toolbar menu as a flyout menu, as shown in **Figure 13-16.**

Controlling the Size and Location of a Toolbar

You can float a toolbar on the screen by using its **Float** method to specify its top and left location in pixels and the number of rows or columns of buttons to display. The signature for the **Float** method is:

> Toolbar.Float *Top, Left, NumberOfRows*

where *Top* is an **Integer** that is the pixel location of the top edge of the toolbar and *Left* is an **Integer** that is the pixel location of the left edge of the toolbar. *NumberOfRows* is an **Integer** that is the number of rows of buttons to create on a horizontal toolbar or number of columns for a vertical toolbar.

The following code floats AutoCAD's **Draw** toolbar, places it at the top left of the screen (0 pixels from the top and 0 pixels from the left), and sets it to have two rows:

```
Sub Ch13_FloatToolbar()

    Dim objMenuGroup As AcadMenuGroup
    Dim objToolbar As AcadToolbar

    On Error GoTo ERROR:

    ' Get the menu group ACAD from the MenuGroups collection.
    Set objMenuGroup = ThisDrawing.Application.MenuGroups("Acad")

    ' Get the Draw toolbar.
    Set objToolbar = objMenuGroup.Toolbars.Item("Draw")

    ' Position the toolbar and set it to two rows.
    objToolbar.Float 0, 0, 2

    Exit Sub

ERROR:

    MsgBox "Error positioning the toolbar."

End Sub
```

Running the Ch13_FloatToolbar macro floats the AutoCAD **Draw** toolbar in the upper-left of the screen as seen in **Figure 13-17**.

You can dock a toolbar to one of the four sides of the AutoCAD application window using the **Dock** method. The signature for the **Dock** method is:

Toolbar.Dock *Side*

where *Side* is the **acToolbarDockStatus** enum. See **Figure 13-18**.

Figure 13-17.
The AutoCAD **Draw** toolbar is floating at the top-left corner of the screen and is displayed with two rows of buttons.

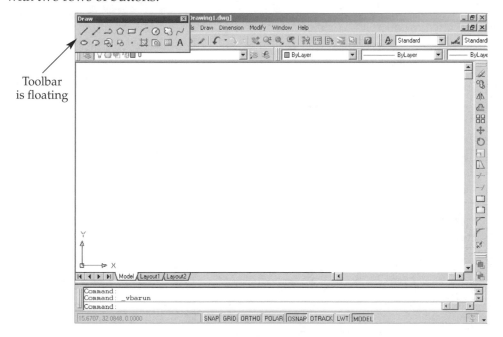

Toolbar
is floating

Figure 13-18.
The docking enums.

Enumerator	Location
acToolbarDockTop	Top of the screen.
acToolbarDockBottom	Bottom of the screen.
acToolbarDockLeft	Left side of the screen.
acToolbarDockRight	Right side of the screen.

The following code docks AutoCAD's **Draw** toolbar on the left side of the AutoCAD application window:

```
Sub Ch13_DockToolbar()
    Dim objMenuGroup As AcadMenuGroup
    Dim objToolbar As AcadToolbar

    On Error GoTo ERROR:

    ' Get the menu group ACAD from the MenuGroups collection.
    Set objMenuGroup = ThisDrawing.Application.MenuGroups("Acad")

    ' Get the Draw toolbar.
    Set objToolbar = objMenuGroup.Toolbars.Item("Draw")

    ' Dock the toolbar on the left side of the screen.
    objToolbar.Dock acToolbarDockLeft

    Exit Sub

ERROR:

    MsgBox "Error docking the toolbar."

End Sub
```

Running the Ch13_DockToolbar macro docks the AutoCAD **Draw** toolbar on the left side of the AutoCAD window as seen in **Figure 13-19.**

Professional Tip   You can check to see if a toolbar is docked by querying its **DockStatus** property. The **DockStatus** property returns **True** if the toolbar is docked and **False** if the toolbar is floating.

Figure 13-19.
The AutoCAD **Draw** toolbar has been docked on the left side of the AutoCAD screen.

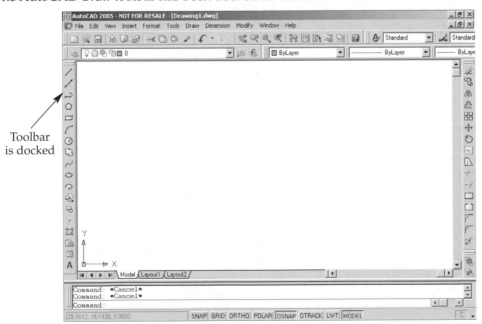

Toolbar is docked

Toolbars and the Toolbars Collection

- Each toolbar in a menu group is represented by a **Toolbar** object that is part of the menu group's **Toolbars** collection.
- The **Add** method creates an empty toolbar.
- The **AddToolbarButton** method adds a toolbar button to a toolbar.
- The **SetBitmaps** method assigns bitmap images to a toolbar button.
- The **AddSeparator** method adds a toolbar button separator.
- The **Delete** method removes a toolbar button.
- The **AttachToolbarToFlyout** method attaches a toolbar flyout to a toolbar button.
- A **Toolbar** object's **Float** and **Dock** methods allow you to control the size and location of a toolbar.
- You can check a **Toolbar** object's **DockStatus** property to determine whether or not the toolbar is docked.

Exercise 13-3

Create the macros described below. All macros should be created in the **ThisDrawing** module of your MyMacros.dvb project. Provide all necessary error checking and control. Run and test each macro.

1. Write a macro named ex13_CreateToolbar that creates a toolbar named **VBA for AutoCAD**.
2. Create a macro named ex13_CreateToolbarButtons that adds the following two toolbar buttons to the **VBA for AutoCAD** toolbar menu created in #1:
   Load MyMacros—Loads the MyMacros.dvb file at the command line.
   Unload Macros—Unloads the MyMacros.dvb file at the command line.
3. Create a macro named ex13_CreateToolbarIcons that sets small and large icon BMP images of your choice to the toolbar buttons created in #2. Dock the toolbar on the right side of the AutoCAD screen.

Chapter Test

Write your answers on a separate sheet of paper.

1. Describe a *pull-down menu* and how it is used.
2. Which two AutoCAD commands can be used to load and unload AutoCAD menus?
3. Menus and menu groups are implemented as part of which object collection in the AutoCAD object model?
4. List the five types of menu files that make up a menu group and provide a brief description of each.
5. Explain the difference between a *full menu load* and a *partial menu load*.
6. Which **MenuGroups** collection method can be used to perform either a full or a partial menu load?
7. Pull-down menus are represented by which object in the AutoCAD object model?
8. Which **Menus** collection method allows you to add a new pull-down menu to the menu bar?
9. How do you specify where a pull-down menu is inserted on the menu bar?

10. Which **PopMenu** property can be used to determine how many menu items a pull-down menu contains?
11. How is a cancel specified at the beginning of a menu macro in VBA?
12. What are the two possible characters that menu macros should always end with?
13. Which **PopupMenu** object method allows you to create a cascading submenu?
14. Toolbars are represented by which object in the AutoCAD object model?
15. What is a toolbar button *helpstring?*
16. Which **Toolbar** object method is used to add a toolbar button to a toolbar menu?
17. How do you determine where a toolbar button is inserted on a toolbar?
18. What are the two different sizes, in pixels, for toolbar button images?
19. Explain how you might create and assign toolbar button images for both small and large toolbar buttons.
20. Which **ToolbarItem** object method allows you to create a toolbar flyout menu?
21. List the two **Toolbar** object methods that control the size and location of a toolbar.

Programming Problems

Create the macros described below. All macros should be created in the **ThisDrawing** module of your MyMacros.dvb project. Provide all necessary error checking and control. Run and test each macro.

Important: Before completing the following problems, copy the acad.mns menu file from your default AutoCAD \Support folder to the C:\VBA for AutoCAD\Menus folder and rename it to Prob13.mns.

1. Create a macro named p13_Loadp13Menu that unloads the default ACAD menu group and then loads the C:\VBA for AutoCAD\Menus\Prob13.mns menu .

2. Write a macro named p13_PullDownMenu that creates a pull-down menu named **Drawing Utilities**, adds it in the menu bar before the **Help** pull-down menu, and adds the following five menu items and associated macros:

   New D-Size Layout—Runs the p12_NewLayout macro.
   Setup D-Size Layout—Runs the p12_LayoutSettings macro.
   Attach Title Block—Runs the p11_AttachTitleBlock macro.
   Plot D-Size Layout—Runs the p12_PlotDefault macro.
   Create D-Size DWF File—Runs the p12_PlotDWF macro.

3. Write a macro named p13_ToolbarMenu that creates a toolbar menu named **Drawing Utilities** with the following five toolbar buttons and associated macros:

   New D-Size Layout—Runs the p12_NewLayout macro.
   Setup D-Size Layout—Runs the p12_LayoutSettings macro.
   Attach Title Block—Runs the p11_AttachTitleBlock macro.
   Plot D-Size Layout—Runs the p12_PlotDefault macro.
   Create D-Size DWF File—Runs the p12_PlotDWF macro.

   Create and set both small and large bitmap icons for all toolbar buttons. Dock the toolbar on the left side of the AutoCAD window.

CHAPTER 14

Programming Using VBA Forms

Learning Objectives

After completing this chapter, you will be able to:

- Insert a new form into a VBA project.
- Change the properties of a form.
- Add controls to a form using the VBA **Toolbox**.
- Control the size and placement of a control.
- Change the properties of a control.
- Add code to a form and its controls.
- Display a form in AutoCAD.
- Unload a form.

Programming dialog boxes with VBA is similar to programming them using AutoCAD's Dialog Control Language (DCL) interface…but much easier. Both languages allow you to create macros that have a dialog box-driven graphical user interface (GUI).

This chapter explains how to create an event-driven dialog box using VBA. The following sections outline the steps to create the dialog box shown in **Figure 14-1.** This **Add Text** dialog box allows the user to enter text in the text edit box, which is then inserted into the current drawing at the point 0,0,0 when the **Add Text** button is picked.

Figure 14-1.
The **Add Text** dialog box that is created in this chapter.

Creating a Dialog Box Using VBA

In VBA, dialog boxes are called *forms.* A form is basically an empty dialog box. Forms are created graphically in VBA. Yes, VBA provides a graphical user interface for creating a graphical user interface!

A dialog box is created by simply inserting a form into a VBA project. Once you insert a form, all of the command buttons, list boxes, check boxes and other control features you need can be added by dragging and dropping them from the VBA **Toolbox**. Then, all that needs to be done is add some code. Fortunately, the coding process is greatly simplified in VBA.

AutoLISP vs. VBA

A major difference between VBA and DCL is that with DCL you must define dialog boxes using an ASCII text file with a .dcl file extension. This DCL file contains information and properties about all of the graphic features of a dialog box, including each feature's size and location. One of the most cumbersome aspects of DCL is that the location of features is determined using a system of rows, columns, and spacers. This can get very confusing. Designing dialog boxes using DCL is a seemingly endless process of trial and error involving editing the DCL file and loading it in AutoCAD to see if the dialog box is correct.

Programming a Dialog Box Using VBA

In VBA, all of the associations between dialog box features (controls) and code are automatic. When you drag and drop a control onto a form, all of its associated code comes along with it. Well, not all of the code. You have to do something. The code that is transferred is a series of functions that respond to different events related to that control. Events were introduced in Chapter 2. To review, events, as they relate to controls, are different actions that occur when a program is running that you can respond to with a function. For instance, every button has a "click" event to which you can respond via code. All you have to do is add the code you want executed to the **Sub** named **CommandButton_Click** that is automatically added to your project when you insert the control. Now, when a user picks the button during program runtime the code is executed.

When programming a dialog box using DCL, you have to associate each control with what is referred to as a callback function. A callback function is the AutoLISP function that is run when a control is selected and/or modified. For instance, when a user selects the **OK** button in a dialog box, a function is executed that might do some cleanup and exit the dialog box gracefully. With DCL and AutoLISP, this association must be explicitly created and maintained using "action requests" and "callback functions."

Inserting a Form into a Project

The first thing you need to do when creating a dialog box-driven VBA macro is insert a VBA form into your project. This is the "blank slate" to which you add all of the desired controls. To insert a new form, select **Userform** from the **Insert** pull-down menu in the **Visual Basic Editor**. This creates a new form named UserForm1 and displays the VBA **Toolbox** as shown in **Figure 14-2.**

You can resize the form by dragging the edge or corner of the form using typical Windows "click and drag" methods. A grid is provided to help you locate controls when you drag them from the VBA **Toolbox** and drop them onto the form. The grid properties can be changed in the **Options** dialog box, which is opened by selecting **Options...** in the **Tools** pull-down menu in the **Visual Basic Editor**.

Figure 14-2.
A blank form is added to the project.

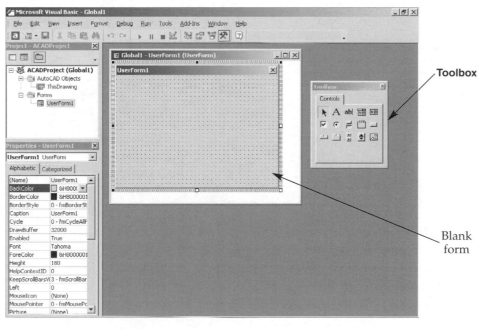

Toolbox

Blank form

Figure 14-3.
The name of the
form is changed to
frmAddText using the
Properties window
in the **Visual Basic
Editor**.

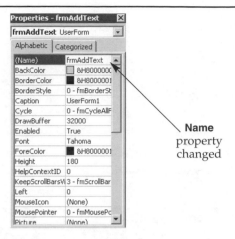

Name
property
changed

Changing the Properties of a Form

Once a form is added to a project, it is a good idea to rename the form to something other than the default name UserForm1. This can be accomplished by changing the form's **Name** property via the **Properties** window, as shown in **Figure 14-3.** In this example, the form is renamed to frmAddText.

The frm prefix is typically used when naming forms. In fact, there are a number of standard prefixes that are used when naming **Form** objects and other VBA controls. These suggested standard prefixes are similar to the Hungarian notation variable naming convention discussed in Chapter 1. The typical standard prefixes used for most controls are listed in **Figure 14-4.**

Another important aspect of any dialog box is the text that appears in the title bar. This text should describe the purpose of the dialog box. The title bar text is controlled via the form's **Caption** property. In **Figure 14-5,** the **Caption** property has been changed to Add Text.

Figure 14-4.
Typical prefixes for
VBA controls.

Prefix	VBA Control Type
cbo	**ComboBox**
chk	**CheckBox**
cmd	**CommandButton**
dir	**DirListBox**
drv	**DriveListBox**
file	**FileListBox**
fra	**Frame**
frm	**Form**
hsb	**HScrollBar**
img	**Image**
lbl	**Label**
lin	**Line**
lst	**ListBox**
mnu	**Menu**
ole	**OLE**
opt	**OptionButton**
pic	**PictureBox**
tmr	**Timer**
txt	**TextBox**
vsb	**VScrollBar**

Figure 14-5.
The title bar for the
dialog box (form) is
changed to **Add Text**
via the form's **Caption**
property.

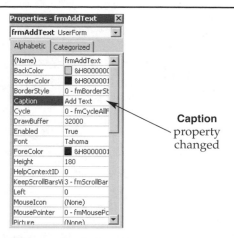

Caption
property
changed

If you look at the **Properties** window in the **Visual Basic Editor**, you will see that there are a number of other properties you can control on the form. You can change the color of the form, its border style, fonts, and so on. The **Properties** window is your one-stop shop for managing a form's appearance and behavior.

Professional Tip

A control is really just another object in VBA. Most of the properties managed in the **Properties** window in the **Visual Basic Editor** can also be controlled via code at program run-time using the approaches explained in earlier chapters. A control also has its own methods, just like other objects. In fact, the **Form** object's **Show** method is how you display a form in a VBA macro. The **Show** method is discussed later in this chapter when it is used to display the **Add Text** dialog box.

Adding Controls to a Form

Controls are added to a form by dragging them from the VBA **Toolbox** and dropping them onto the form. The arrow on the top row on the far left is the selector tool and is used to move and resize controls that have already been placed on a form. **Figure 14-6** identifies the other tools.

The tools shown in **Figure 14-6** are the standard tools. It is possible to add even more controls to the VBA **Toolbox** using the **Additional Controls** dialog box. This dialog box is displayed by selecting **Additional Controls...** from the **Tools** pull-down menu. Only standard controls are used on the **Add Text** dialog box.

First, add a **TextBox** control to the form by dragging it from the **Toolbox** and dropping it onto the form near the top-right corner. This is the control that is going to be used to obtain text from the user that will be placed on the drawing.

Next, add two **CommandButton** controls to the form. These will provide two ways to close and exit the **Add Text** dialog box. One **CommandButton** control will be used to exit the dialog box and add the text in the **TextBox** control to the drawing. The other **CommandButton** control will be used to cancel out of the dialog box without doing anything. See **Figure 14-7**.

Figure 14-6.
The standard tools in the VBA **Toolbox**. Additional tools can be added.

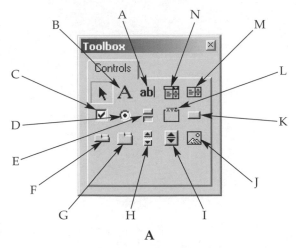

A

Letter	Tool	Description
A	**TextBox**	For text that the user can either enter or change.
B	**Label**	Static text that cannot be changed by a user, such as a caption.
C	**CheckBox**	A box that the user can mark to indicate if something is true or false or to display multiple choices for multiple selections.
D	**OptionButton**	Used to display multiple choices from which a user can select only one.
E	**ToggleButton**	A button that toggles on and off.
F	**TabStrip**	Defines multiple pages for dialog box.
G	**MultiPage**	Presents multiple screens of information as a single set.
H	**ScrollBar**	A graphic tool for navigating through a long list of items or a large amount of information.
I	**SpinButton**	A control to increase and decrease the value of numbers. It can also be used to scroll back and forth through a range of values or a list of items.
J	**Image**	Displays an image on the form from a bitmap, icon, or other metafile.
K	**CommandButton**	A button the user can select to carry out a command.
L	**Frame**	Used to create a graphic or functional grouping of controls
M	**ListBox**	Displays a list of items from which the user can choose.
N	**ComboBox**	A combination of a list box and text box. The user can either choose an item from the list or enter a value in the text box.

B

Figure 14-7.
A **TextBox** and two **CommandButton** controls are added to the form.

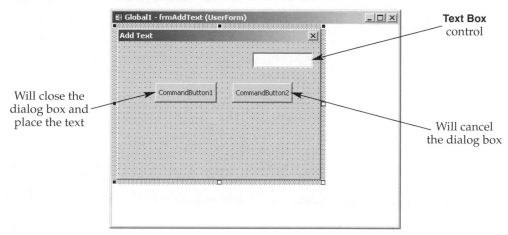

It is always good programming practice to provide a way to cancel a dialog box. In fact, **CommandButton** controls have a **Cancel** property that can be set to **True** in order to make them the default cancel button. The **Cancel** property is discussed in the section Changing the Properties of a Control later in this chapter.

The last control that needs to be added to the form is a **Label** control. This control will provide a label for the **TextBox** control to indicate the purpose of the **TextBox** control. Remember, the **TextBox** control is where the text to add to the drawing should be entered by the user. Add the **Label** control to the left of the **TextBox** control.

Changing the Size and Placement of a Control

After you place a control on a form, you can move and resize it using standard Windows mouse "click and drag" methods. Once all of the desired controls have been added to the form, you can resize and relocate them as shown in **Figure 14-8.** The form is beginning to look like the finished product shown in **Figure 14-1.** All that remains to be done is change a few control properties and add some code.

Figure 14-8.
A **Label** control is added to the form. All components are also resized and moved as needed.

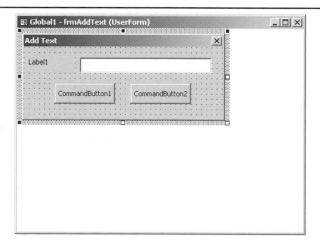

Now, update the **Caption** property of the controls added in the last section. The **Caption** property controls the text displayed on a control. Typically, the caption should be changed to indicate what the control does. However, in the case of the **Label** control, the caption indicates what the user should enter in the **TextBox** control.

Select the **Label** control on the form. Then, in the **Properties** window, change the **Caption** property to Text to add:. The **Label** control on the form is updated when you press [Enter].

Now, change the **CommandButton** controls. The left-hand button, CommandButton1, will be used to add the text to the drawing. Therefore, change its **Caption** property to Add Text using the **Properties** window.

Next, define an accelerator key for CommandButton1. *Accelerator keys* allow a user to navigate to a control via the keyboard by pressing the [Alt] key in combination with the mnemonic character (underlined letter). The control's **Accelerator** property is used to designate its accelerator key. In the **Properties** window, enter A for the **Accelerator** property. An underscore now appears on the A in Add Text on the button.

The last control that needs to be changed is the CommandButton2 button. This button is going to provide the user a way to exit, or cancel, the dialog box without executing the macro. First, select the button on the form. Then, change the **Caption** property to Cancel in the **Properties** window. Also, set the button's **Cancel** property to **True**. Setting the **Cancel** property to **True** links the command button with the [Esc] key on the keyboard. In this way, a user can exit the dialog box by simply pressing [Esc].

The properties of the controls have now been set. See **Figure 14-9.** Next, the associated code needs to be added to the form and the controls.

Figure 14-9.
The properties of the controls have been changed.

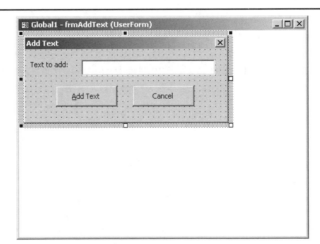

Adding Code to Forms and Controls

Now that the form and all of its controls are set up and appear the way you want, it is time to add some code. The easiest way to display the **Code** window is to simply double-click on the control to which you wish to add code. You can also display the **Code** window for a specific control by selecting the desired control from the **Object** list box at the top left of the **Code** window, as shown in **Figure 14-10**. Remember, every time you add a control from the VBA **Toolbox**, the code structure that supports the control is added to the project as well. This code structure includes all of the possible events that can occur for that particular control.

The concept of events was first introduced in Chapter 2 in the section Understanding Program Events. In a nutshell, an event is an action occurring at run time that you can react to with code of your own (hence the name "reactors" in Visual LISP). The example given in Chapter 2 is an **OK** command button in a dialog box being associated with code to perform some action and exit the dialog box gracefully.

When you add a control to a form, you are really just adding an object of that control type. The object automatically contains predefined **Subs** that represent every possible event type, or action, of which the control is capable. All of the control's possible events are listed in the **Procedure** list box at the top right of the **Code** window when you make the control the current object in the **Object** list box. The event procedures for the **CommandButton** control are shown in **Figure 14-11**.

Selecting one of the event procedures adds a **Sub** to the project with a name created automatically by concatenating the name of the control with the name of the event procedure. In **Figure 14-12**, the **Click** event procedure has been selected for the CommandButton1 control, so a **Sub** named CommandButton1_Click has been added to the project. All you have to do now is add the code you want to run when the button is picked somewhere between the **Sub** name and the **End Sub** statement. The following code creates single line text at 0,0,0 using the text string entered by the user in the **Text to add:** edit box. The text string is obtained via the TextBox1 control's **Value** property.

Figure 14-10.
Select a control from the **Object** list box.

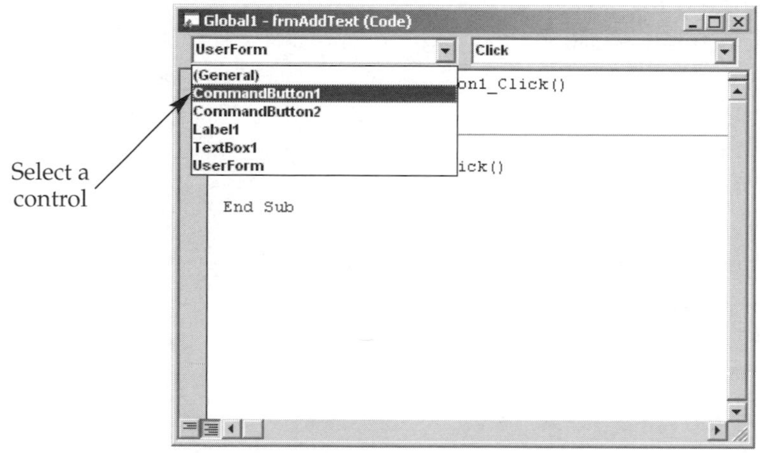

Figure 14-11.
Select an event
procedure from the
Procedure list box.

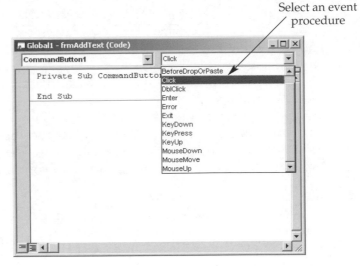

Select an event
procedure

Figure 14-12.
A **Click** event
procedure is added
to the form for
CommandButton1.

Add code here

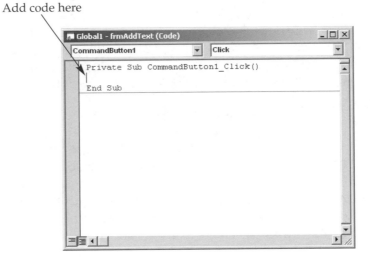

```
' Create the Add Text button.
Private Sub CommandButton1_Click()

    Dim objText As AcadText
    Dim dblInsertPt(0 To 2) As Double
    Dim strText As String

    ' Insert point (0,0,0).
    dblInsertPt(0) = 0
    dblInsertPt(1) = 0
    dblInsertPt(2) = 0

    ' Get the text from the TextBox control.
    strText = TextBox1.Value

    ' Set the text height to 1/8".
    dblHeight = 0.125

    ' Add the text to the current drawing.
    ThisDrawing.ModelSpace.AddText strText, dblInsertPt, dblHeight

    ' Zoom extents.
    ZoomExtents

End Sub
```

The dialog box is now almost done. However, there still needs to be some way to display the dialog box so the macro can be executed. This is accomplished by creating a VBA macro in the **ThisDrawing** object that, when run, "shows" the dialog box. This is described in the following section.

Using DCL, the association between an action, or event, and the code to be executed has to be explicitly created and maintained using cryptic "action requests" and "callback functions." In VBA, this process is automated.

AutoLISP vs. VBA

Displaying and Unloading Forms

A macro containing a VBA form begins when the main form, or dialog box, is displayed. This allows the user to begin interacting with the dialog box, which, in turn, triggers events that call your code. Displaying a form is accomplished via a **Form** object's **Show** method. You can even add code to a **Form** object's **Initialize** method that is run automatically when a form is first displayed. This is where you would add code that helps set up and initialize a dialog box with any default values or settings.

Show Method

To display the **Add Text** dialog box, use the form's **Show** method to display and activate the form. Add the Ch14_AddText macro shown below to the **ThisDrawing** object.

```
' Macro to initialize the Add Text dialog box.
Sub Ch14_AddText()

    ' Set the default text in the TextBox control.
    frmAddText.TextBox1.Value = "Hello World!"

    ' Show the Add Text form.
    frmAddText.Show

End Sub
```

This macro first sets the default value of the **Text to add:** text box to Hello World!. This is done by setting the **TextBox** object's **Value** property. The code then displays the form by calling the form's **Show** method.

Unload Method

All that is needed now is some way to exit the dialog box once it is displayed. This is accomplished using the **Unload** method. The **Unload** method exits a form and releases it from memory. First, add the **Click** event procedure for the CommandButton2 control. Then, enter the following code to implement the **Unload** method.

```
' Cancel button.
Private Sub CommandButton2_Click()

    ' Unload the Add Text form.
    Unload Me

End Sub
```

Now, when the user picks the **Cancel** button in the **Add Text** dialog box, the dialog box is closed and the macro is exited.

Professional Tip

The **Me** keyword in the example on the previous page refers to the currently loaded form. It is used throughout VBA to refer to the specific instance of the class, or object, where the code is executing.

Running the AddText Macro

Now, the dialog box is completely done. It is time to run the Ch14_AddText macro and see what happens. When you run the macro, the dialog box shown in **Figure 14-13** should be displayed. Picking the **Add Text** button in the dialog box will add the text displayed in the **Text to add:** text box to the current drawing at 0,0,0 and perform a zoom extents. See **Figure 14-14.**

Try experimenting with all of the controls on the **Add Text** dialog box. Think about how the macro and dialog box might be improved, what other options might be included, or how it might be used for similar tasks. This basic form is just the tip of the iceberg. As you may imagine, it is possible to create very complex, dialog box-driven macros using VBA.

Figure 14-13.
The **Add Text** dialog box is displayed when the Ch14_AddText macro is run.

Figure 14-14.
When the **Add Text** button is selected in the **Add Text** dialog box, the text in the **Text to add:** text box is placed in the drawing.

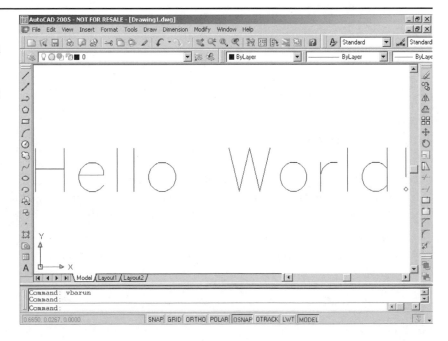

Remember, you can add more controls to the VBA **Toolbox** via the **Additional Controls** dialog box. There are controls that do just about everything. There is even a control that allows you to place a preview of an AutoCAD drawing on a form.

Programming Using VBA Forms   Let's Review...

- All of the graphic control features that make up a dialog box, such as command buttons, list boxes, check boxes, and the other features found in the VBA **Toolbox**, are referred to as controls.
- To insert a new form in a project, select **Userform** from the **Insert** pull-down menu in the **Visual Basic Editor**.
- The properties of a form and all of its controls are managed via the **Properties** window in the **Visual Basic Editor**.
- A control is considered a VBA object and has properties and methods.
- Controls can be resized using standard Windows "click and drag" methods.
- The **Caption** property controls what text is displayed on a control.
- An acceleratory key is the underlined character (mnemonic character) on a control that can be used in conjunction with the [Alt] key to navigate a form using the keyboard.
- A control's **Accelerator** property is used to designate its accelerator key.
- Predefined event procedures are added to a project automatically when a control is placed on a form.
- Double-clicking on a control displays the **Code** window for the control.
- Adding code to a control's predefined event procedure allows the code to be executed when that event occurs at run-time.
- A **Form** object's **Show** method displays the form and begins execution of a macro.
- The **Unload** method exits a form and releases it from memory.

Exercise 14-1

Create the macros described below. All macros should be created in the **ThisDrawing** module of your MyMacros.dvb project. Provide all necessary error checking and control. Run and test each macro.

1. Create a macro named ex14_EditText that allows the user to select text in a drawing, displays the text on a VBA form so that it can be edited, and then updates the drawing when the user picks the **OK** button.
2. Create a macro named ex14_EditTextProps that updates the ex14_EditText macro and its associated VBA form so that the user can also update the text height, layer, and text style properties.

Chapter Test

Write your answers on a separate sheet of paper.

1. Explain the major differences between creating a dialog box using VBA and creating a dialog box using DCL.
2. What are VBA *controls* and where are they located?
3. How do you insert a blank form into a VBA project?
4. List 15 of the standard prefixes typically used to identify a control when setting a control's **Name** property.
5. Which control property controls the text string that is displayed on a control?
6. List all of the standard controls found in the VBA **Toolbox** and provide a brief description of each.
7. How can you add additional controls to the VBA **Toolbox**?
8. For what is the **Cancel** property of a command button used?
9. Which property controls the underlined text in a command button that allows you to navigate controls by using the [Alt] key on the keyboard?
10. Explain an *event procedure* and how it is used to program using forms.
11. Which **Form** object method is used to display a form?
12. Which **Form** object method is run automatically when a form is loaded (if it exists)?
13. Which **Form** object method is used to exit and close a form?
14. Explain the VBA **Me** keyword and how it is used.
15. Custom controls are stored as which type of file in the Windows \System folder?

Programming Problems

Create the macro described below. The macro should be created in the **ThisDrawing** module of your MyMacros.dvb project. Provide all necessary error checking and control. Run and test the macro.

1. Create a macro named p14_DrawingSetup to display a form named frmDwgSetup that allows the user to perform the following functions.
   A. Create a D-size layout via the p12_NewLayout macro.
   B. Setup a D-size layout via the p12_LayoutSettings macro.
   C. Attach a title block via the p11_AttachTitleBlock macro.
   D. Update the following attribute information using five **TextBox** controls:
      Designed by:
      Drawn by:
      Checked by:
      Date:
      Drawing name/number:
   E. Plot the drawing via the p12_PlotDWF macro.

CHAPTER 15

Utilizing ActiveX and Programming with AutoCAD Events

Learning Objectives

After completing this chapter, you will be able to do the following:

- Access another application's object model by referencing the type library.
- Create an instance of another application using its class name.
- Utilize another application's object model.
- Export block attributes to an Excel spreadsheet.
- Import block attributes from an Excel spreadsheet.
- Create an events class module.
- Enable application level events.
- Create a macro that runs when an AutoCAD system variable changes.
- Enable document level events.
- Create a macro that runs when any AutoCAD drawing entity is added or modified.
- Enable object level events.
- Attach a macro to a specific object, which then runs when the object is modified.

Utilizing ActiveX Automation

The concept of ActiveX Automation is explained in detail in Chapter 2. In a nutshell, ActiveX Automation is simply the process of accessing and using another application's object model from within your own macro. Most Microsoft Office programs have their own object model just like AutoCAD. Every program's object model has an **Application** object as its top level, or root object, that is exposed to other programs. All you have to do in your macro is get a reference to another program's **Application** object and you have access to all of that program's objects, properties, and methods.

All of an application's objects, properties, and methods exposed by ActiveX Automation are contained in a type library. A *type library* is a file or part of a file that describes the object model for an ActiveX application. Before you can access another application's object model, you must first reference its type library. You can create references to one or more type libraries via the **References** dialog box described in the next section.

Figure 15-1.
Referencing a type library via the **References** dialog box.

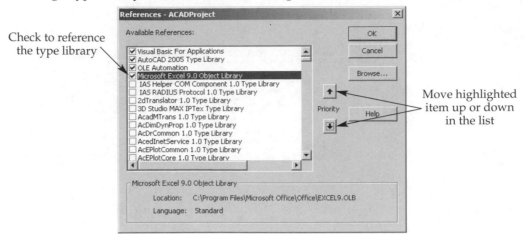

Accessing Another Application's Object Model

In order to access another application's object model, you must first reference its type library via the **References** dialog box, as shown in **Figure 15-1.** To open this dialog box, select **References...** from the **Tools** pull-down menu in the **Visual Basic Editor**.

In the example in this chapter, you will create a reference to the object model for Microsoft Excel. The following sections explain how you can create an instance of Excel in an AutoCAD VBA macro and then use the Excel object model to share AutoCAD block attribute information between the two programs.

Creating an Instance of Another Application

After referencing an application's type library, you get access to it by creating an "instance" of the library. All this means is that you must get a reference to the program's **Application** object, and in order to do that, the application must be running. VBA provides you with two options: you can get a reference to an application that is currently running or you can start the application yourself.

The **GetObject** method will get a reference to an application that is currently running. The signature is:

   objApplication = GetObject (*[PathName]*, *[Class]*)

where *objApplication* is the **Application** object. *PathName* is an optional **Variant** that is the full path and name of the application. *Class* is an optional **Variant** that is the class name of the object.

The **CreateObject** method will start an application and return a reference to it. The signature is:

   objApplication = CreateObject (*Class*, *[ServerName]*)

where *objApplication* is the **Application** object. *Class* is a **Variant** that is the class name of the object. *ServerName* is an optional **Variant** that is the name of the server on which to create the object.

The following code gets an instance of Microsoft Excel by either getting a reference to the application that is currently running or by starting Excel and then getting a reference to it.

```
Sub Ch15_GetApplication()

    Dim appExcel As Excel.Application

    On Error Resume Next

    ' Check to see if Excel is already running and get the current application.
    Set appExcel = GetObject(, "Excel.Application")

    ' Excel is not running; need to start it.
    If appExcel Is Nothing Then

        ' Clear the above error.
        Err.Clear

        ' Start Excel.
        Set appExcel = CreateObject("Excel.Application")

        ' Could not start Excel.
        If Err.Number <> 0 Then
            MsgBox "Could not start Excel. Ensure the program is installed.", _
                vbCritical, "Excel Error"
            Exit Sub
        End If

    End If

    ' Make the Excel window visible.
    appExcel.Visible = True

    ' Tell the user.
    MsgBox "Excel application object created."

    ' Quit Excel.
    appExcel.Application.Quit

End Sub
```

Now that you have a reference to Excel's **Application** object, you can use any of its objects, properties, or methods…if you know what they are and how to use them, that is. The following section shows you an easy way to find out.

Investigating Another Application's Objects

Most of the object models for Microsoft's Office products can be viewed via the online documentation in each application. Graphic representations of each object model hierarchy are provided, in a similar fashion to the AutoCAD object model, to allow you to quickly navigate to a specific object and determine its properties and methods. Picking on a property or method will display information related to that item. The ActiveX object model for Excel is shown in **Figure 15-2.**

ActiveX Automation Example

The following sections provide an example of using ActiveX to get a reference to Microsoft Excel and its object model so that data can be shared between an AutoCAD drawing and an Excel worksheet. You must have Microsoft Excel installed on your computer in order to run the following code examples. You will also need to open the Office.dwg drawing file located in the \Drawings folder on the Student CD before proceeding.

Figure 15-2.
Microsoft Excel's ActiveX object model.

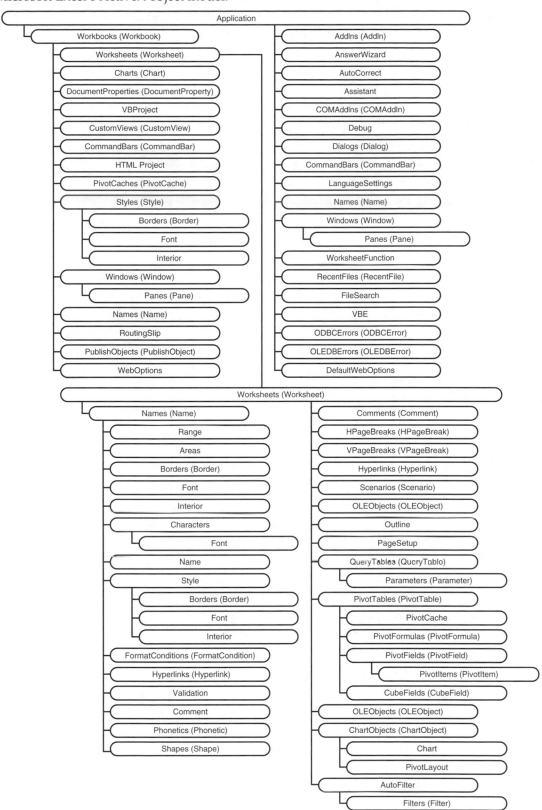

Exporting Block Attributes to an Excel Spreadsheet

The following code gets all instances of the block named Computer in the drawing file Office.dwg and exports all of the block attributes and their values to an Excel spreadsheet named C:\VBA for AutoCAD\Drawings\Computers.xls:

```
Sub Ch15_ExportAttributes()

    Dim objSSet As AcadSelectionSet
    Dim objBlockRef As AcadBlockReference
    Dim intDxfCode(0 To 1) As Integer
    Dim varDxfValue(0 To 1) As Variant
    Dim intCounter1 As Integer
    Dim intCounter2 As Integer
    Dim varAttributes As Variant
    Dim strAttTag As String
    Dim strAttValue As String
    Dim intRow As Integer
    Dim appExcel As Excel.Application
    Dim objWorksheet As Worksheet
    Dim objWorkbook As Workbook

    On Error Resume Next

    ' Create a new selection set.
    Set objSSet = ThisDrawing.SelectionSets.Add("SS1")

    ' Set the entity DXF code to match the Insert entity type.
    intDxfCode(0) = 0
    varDxfValue(0) = "INSERT"

    ' Set the entity name DXF code to match the Computer block name.
    intDxfCode(1) = 2
    varDxfValue(1) = "Computer"

    ' Get all instances of the Computer block in the drawing.
    objSSet.Select acSelectionSetAll, , , intDxfCode, varDxfValue

    ' Get the attributes if any blocks were found.
    If objSSet.Count > 0 Then

        ' Start Excel.
        Set appExcel = CreateObject("Excel.Application")

        ' Could not start Excel.
        If Err.Number <> 0 Then
            MsgBox "Could not start Excel. Ensure the program is installed.", vbCritical, _
                "Excel Error"
            objSSet.Delete
            Exit Sub
        End If

        On Error GoTo ERRORHANDLER

        ' Create a new workbook and get the active sheet.
        Set objWorkbook = appExcel.Workbooks.Add
        Set objWorksheet = appExcel.ActiveSheet

        ' Save the workbook.
        objWorkbook.SaveAs "C:\VBA for AutoCAD\Drawings\Computers.xls"

        ' Set to first row.
        intRow = 1
```

```
' Format the header (first row).
objWorksheet.Rows("1:1").Font.Bold = True
objWorksheet.Cells(intRow, 1).value = "Computer ID"
objWorksheet.Cells(intRow, 2).value = "Manufacturer"
objWorksheet.Cells(intRow, 3).value = "Computer Type"
objWorksheet.Cells(intRow, 4).value = "Employee Number"
objWorksheet.Cells(intRow, 5).value = "Location"

' Parse all blocks in the selection set.
For intCounter1 = 0 To objSSet.Count - 1

    ' Check to see if the block has attributes.
    If objSSet.Item(intCounter1).HasAttributes Then

        ' Increment row.
        intRow = intRow + 1

        ' Get the attributes.
        varAttributes = objSSet.Item(intCounter1).GetAttributes

        ' Extract attributes and place them in the Excel worksheet.
        For intCounter2 = LBound(varAttributes) To UBound(varAttributes)

            ' Attribute tag.
            strAttTag = varAttributes(intCounter2).TagString

            ' Attribute value.
            strAttValue = varAttributes(intCounter2).TextString

            ' Place each attribute in the correct column based on the tag.
            If strAttTag = "COMP_ID" Then
                    objWorksheet.Cells(intRow, 1).value = strAttValue
            Elself strAttTag = "MANUFACTURER" Then
                    objWorksheet.Cells(intRow, 2).value = strAttValue
            Elself strAttTag = "TYPE" Then
                    objWorksheet.Cells(intRow, 3).value = strAttValue
            Elself strAttTag = "EMPLOYEE" Then
                    objWorksheet.Cells(intRow, 4).value = strAttValue
            Elself strAttTag = "LOCATION" Then
                    objWorksheet.Cells(intRow, 5).value = strAttValue
            End If

        ' End parse attributes.
        Next

    End If

Next

' Format columns.
objWorksheet.Columns("A:E").EntireColumn.AutoFit

' Save the workbook and close and exit Excel.
objWorkbook.Save
objWorkbook.Close
appExcel.Application.Quit

' No computer blocks in the drawing.
Else

    MsgBox "The ""Computer"" block is not inserted in this drawing."

End If
```

```
            ' Delete the selection set.
            objSSet.Delete

            ' Tell the user everything was a success.
            MsgBox "C:\VBA for AutoCAD\Drawings\Computers.xls created successfully.", _
                vbInformation

            ' Exit Sub.
            Exit Sub

    ' Error handler.
    ERRORHANDLER:

            MsgBox "Export attributes error " & Err.Number & " (" & Err.Description _
                & ") from " & Err.Source, vbCritical, "Export Attributes"

            ' Delete the selection set.
            objSSet.Delete

            ' Quit Excel.
            appExcel.Application.Quit

    End Sub
```

Importing Block Attributes from an Excel Spreadsheet

The following code imports the values stored in the Computers.xls Excel spreadsheet created by the Ch15_ExportAttributes macro and updates the Computer block attributes based on its Comp_ID attribute tag in the drawing Office.dwg:

```
    Sub Ch15_ImportAttributes()

            Dim objSSet As AcadSelectionSet
            Dim objBlockRef As AcadBlockReference
            Dim intDxfCode(0 To 1) As Integer
            Dim varDxfValue(0 To 1) As Variant
            Dim intCounter1 As Integer
            Dim intCounter2 As Integer
            Dim intCounter3 As Integer
            Dim varAttributes As Variant
            Dim intRow As Integer
            Dim appExcel As Excel.Application
            Dim objWorksheet As Worksheet
            Dim objWorkbook As Workbook
            Dim strCompID As String
            Dim strManufacturer As String
            Dim strType As String
            Dim strEmployee As String
            Dim strLocation As String
            Dim blnRcrdFound As Boolean

            On Error Resume Next

            ' Create a new selection set.
            Set objSSet = ThisDrawing.SelectionSets.Add("SS1")

            ' Set the entity DXF code to match the Insert entity type.
            intDxfCode(0) = 0
            varDxfValue(0) = "INSERT"

            ' Set the entity name DXF code to match the Computer block name.
            intDxfCode(1) = 2
            varDxfValue(1) = "Computer"
```

```vba
' Get all instances of the Computer block in the drawing.
objSSet.Select acSelectionSetAll, , , intDxfCode, varDxfValue

' Get the attributes, if any blocks were found.
If objSSet.Count > 0 Then

    ' Start Excel.
    Set appExcel = CreateObject("Excel.Application")

    ' Could not start Excel.
    If Err.Number <> 0 Then
        MsgBox "Could not start Excel. Check if program installed.", vbCritical, _
            "Excel Error"
        objSSet.Delete
        Exit Sub
    End If

    On Error GoTo ERRORHANDLER

    ' Open the Computers.xls workbook created
    ' for the Ch15_ExportAttributes macro.
    Set objWorkbook = appExcel.Workbooks.Open _
        ("C:\VBA for AutoCAD\Drawings\Computers.xls")
    Set objWorksheet = appExcel.ActiveSheet

    ' Parse all blocks in the selection set.
    For intCounter1 = 0 To objSSet.Count - 1

        ' Check to see if the block has attributes.
        If objSSet.Item(intCounter1).HasAttributes Then

            ' Get the attributes.
            varAttributes = objSSet.Item(intCounter1).GetAttributes

            ' Extract attributes and place them in the Excel worksheet.
            For intCounter2 = LBound(varAttributes) To UBound(varAttributes)

                If varAttributes(intCounter2).TagString = "COMP_ID" Then

                    strCompID = varAttributes(intCounter2).TextString
                    blnRcrdFound = False
                    intRow = 2

                Do While objWorksheet.Cells(intRow, 1).value <> "" And _
                            Not blnRcrdFound
                    If objWorksheet.Cells(intRow, 1).value = strCompID Then
                            strManufacturer = objWorksheet.Cells(intRow, 2).value
                            strType = objWorksheet.Cells(intRow, 3).value
                            strEmployee = objWorksheet.Cells(intRow, 4).value
                            strLocation = objWorksheet.Cells(intRow, 5).value
                            blnRcrdFound = True
                    End If
                    intRow = intRow + 1
                Loop

            End If

        ' End parse attributes.
        Next

        ' Record with the same computer ID found; fill in the rest of the attributes.
        If blnRcrdFound Then

            For intCounter3 = LBound(varAttributes) To UBound(varAttributes)
```

```
                         ' Place the attribute in the correct column based on its tag.
                         If varAttributes(intCounter3).TagString = "MANUFACTURER" Then
                                 varAttributes(intCounter3).TextString = strManufacturer
                         ElseIf varAttributes(intCounter3).TagString = "TYPE" Then
                                 varAttributes(intCounter3).TextString = strType
                         ElseIf varAttributes(intCounter3).TagString = "EMPLOYEE" Then
                                 varAttributes(intCounter3).TextString = strEmployee
                         ElseIf varAttributes(intCounter3).TagString = "LOCATION" Then
                                 varAttributes(intCounter3).TextString = strLocation
                         End If

                     ' End parse attributes.
                     Next

                 ' Record found in a spreadsheet.
                 End If

             End If

         Next

         ' Close the workbook and exit Excel.
         objWorkbook.Close
         appExcel.Application.Quit

         ' No Computer blocks in the drawing.
         Else

             MsgBox "No instances of ""Computer"" block found in drawing."

         End If

         ' Delete the selection set.
         objSSet.Delete

         ' Tell the user everything was a success.
         MsgBox "Information from Computers.xls imported successfully", _
             vbInformation

         ' Exit Sub.
         Exit Sub

' Error handler.
ERRORHANDLER:

         MsgBox "Import attributes error " & Err.Number & " (" & Err.Description _
             & ") from " & Err.Source, vbCritical, "Import Attributes"

         ' Delete the selection set.
         objSSet.Delete

         ' Quit Excel.
         appExcel.Application.Quit

End Sub
```

To really see the full affects of this code, first open the Computer.xls spreadsheet created by the previous macro, change some of the values, and save the file. Then, run the Ch15_ImportAttributes macro again and watch the attribute values update. Theoretically, you can now manage all of the Computer block's attributes externally via the Computer.xls spreadsheet. All you have to do is make sure to run the Ch15_ImportAttributes macro each time the drawing is opened.

You can ensure the Ch15_ImportAttributes macro gets run each time a drawing is opened by utilizing the AcadDoc.lsp file. If you locate a file named AcadDoc.lsp in the AutoCAD search path, the file is loaded each time a drawing is opened. All you need to do is add the following code:

```
(defun S::STARTUP()
    (command "_-vbaload" "examplecode.dvb")
    (command "_-vbarun" "Ch15_ImportAttributes")
)
```

Using ActiveX Automation

- ActiveX Automation is the process of analyzing and utilizing another application's object model from within your own macro.
- All of an application's objects, properties, and methods exposed by ActiveX Automation are contained in the application's type library.
- A type library is a file or part of a file that describes the object model for an ActiveX application.
- You must reference another application's type library to access its object model.
- The **GetObject** method will get a reference to an application that is currently running.
- The **CreateObject** method will start an application and return a reference to it.
- An **Application** object's **Visible** property can be used to control whether or not an application is visible.
- Use the Microsoft Office online documentation to view the ActiveX object model hierarchy for other applications.
- VBA macros can be run from the AcadDoc.lsp file so that they execute each time a drawing is opened.

Exercise 15-1

Create a macro named ex15_ExportGridBubs that exports the GRIDNO attribute value of all the GRIDNOA grid bubble blocks in the drawing C:\VBA for AutoCAD\Drawings\Grid_PlanA.dwg, which was created in #2 in Exercise 11-3, to an Excel spreadsheet named C:\VBA for AutoCAD\ex15-01.xls. The macro should be created in the **ThisDrawing** module of your MyMacros.dvb project. Provide all necessary error checking and control. Run and test the macro.

Programming with AutoCAD Events

Remember from Chapter 2 that there are three different levels of events in AutoCAD—application, document, and object levels. Application level events react to changes in the AutoCAD application and its environment. This includes things like:

- Changes to the application window.
- Opening, saving, closing, and plotting drawings.
- Issuing of AutoCAD commands.
- Loading or unloading of ARX and LISP applications.
- Changes to system variables.

Document level events react to changes to a specific drawing or its contents. This includes things like:

- Changes to the drawing window.
- Drawing regeneration.
- Activation of a shortcut menu.
- Switching between layouts.
- Changes in the "pick first" selection set.
- Addition, deletion, or modification of objects.

Object level events react to changes made to a specific object. There is only one object level event. This occurs when an object has been modified.

When programming for form-based events (discussed in Chapter 14), the relationship between a form (control event) and the **Sub** (event handler) called when an event occurs is pretty much automated when the form is created. Programming for AutoCAD events, however, takes a little more work. You are simply linking a **Sub** to run when a particular event occurs, it is just that the events are a little different and you must manually create the link.

The link between an AutoCAD event and the **Sub** function to run is managed using your own events class module. The events class module is where you create the **Subs** you want to be associated with the different AutoCAD events. It is also where you indicate the event levels you want to be able to react to using the **WithEvents** VBA keyword. The **WithEvents** keyword is used in an object variable declaration to enable the object to respond to events triggered by other ActiveX objects. The **WithEvents** keyword is valid only in class modules.

For example, the following three lines of code enable events for all three AutoCAD levels by declaring an object for each level using the **WithEvents** keyword:

```
Public WithEvents AcadApp As AcadApplication
Public WithEvents AcadDoc As AcadDocument
Public WithEvents Object As AcadText
```

The first line declares an object named *AcadApp* as an AutoCAD **Application** object. The second line declares an object named *AcadDoc* as an AutoCAD **Document** object. The third line declares an object named *Object* as an AutoCAD **Text** object. Then, dimension a variable in the **ThisDrawing** object to be the new event class. Assuming the event class is named **clsEvents**, the **Dim** statement is:

```
' Dimension the event class.
Dim X As New clsEvents
```

The final step is to initialize the events by assigning the objects you declared **WithEvents** above to their corresponding AutoCAD object:

```
' Link the clsEvents Application object with the
' currently running AutoCAD application.
Set X.AcadApp = ThisDrawing.Application

' Link the clsEvents Document object with the current drawing.
Set X.AcadDoc = ThisDrawing

' Link the clsEvents Object object with the newly created text object.
Set X.Object = objText
```

Now when an event occurs, its corresponding **Sub** will be called from the *clsEvents* object named *X*. Information contained in events, such as the system variable name and value in the **SysVarChanged** event, are passed to event handlers as arguments.

That is all there is to it. By the end of this chapter, not only will you be able to program with AutoCAD events, you will also have created your very own custom object. That is basically what you have done when you create a new events class module. How this is achieved is explained in the next section.

Creating an Events Class Module

To insert a new class module, select **Class Module** from the **Insert** pull-down menu in the **Visual Basic Editor**. This class module is where you will be creating the **Subs** that are called when an AutoCAD event occurs.

For this example, insert a new class module and then change its name to clsEvents via the **Properties** window, **Figure 15-3.** The next step is to dimension the new class in the **ThisDrawing** object. Enter the following in the **Code** window for **ThisDrawing**, as shown in **Figure 15-4:**

```
' Force variable declaration.
Option Explicit

' Dimension event class.
Dim X As New clsEvents
```

Figure 15-3.
A class module is inserted and renamed.

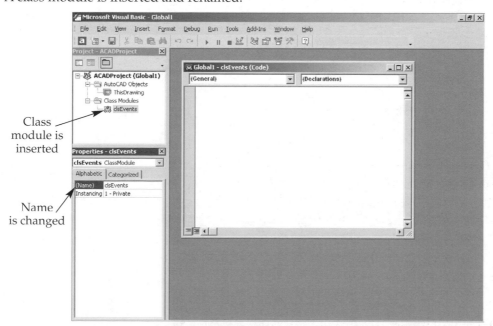

Class module is inserted

Name is changed

Figure 15-4.
Dimensioning a new class.

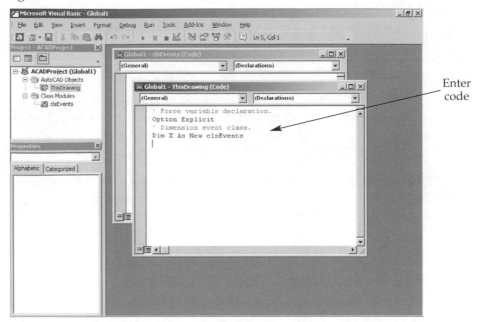

Now that the AutoCAD event structure is created, you can start adding some code. A good place to start is at the top with some code that reacts to an application level event, as described in the next section.

Application Level Events

Application level events react to changes in the AutoCAD application and its environment. **Figure 15-5** lists all of the application level events to which a macro can react.

Enabling Application Level Events

Application level events must be enabled. This is done by declaring an AutoCAD **Application** object with the **WithEvents** keyword at the top of the clsEvents class module, as shown in **Figure 15-6:**

```
Public WithEvents AcadApps As AcadApplication
```

Figure 15-5.
Application level events to which a macro can react.

Event Name	Description
AppActivate	Triggered just before the main application window is activated.
AppDeactivate	Triggered just before the main application window is deactivated.
ARXLoaded	Triggered when an ObjectARX application has been loaded.
ARXUnloaded	Triggered when an ObjectARX application has been unloaded.
BeginCommand	Triggered immediately after a command is issued, but before it completes.
BeginFileDrop	Triggered when a file is dropped into the main application window.
BeginLISP	Triggered immediately after AutoCAD receives a request to evaluate an AutoLISP expression.
BeginModal	Triggered just before a modal dialog box is displayed.
BeginOpen	Triggered immediately after AutoCAD receives a request to open an existing drawing.
BeginPlot	Triggered immediately after AutoCAD receives a request to print a drawing.
BeginQuit	Triggered just before an AutoCAD session ends.
BeginSave	Triggered immediately after AutoCAD receives a request to save the drawing.
EndCommand	Triggered immediately after a command completes.
EndLISP	Triggered on completion of evaluating an AutoLISP expression.
EndModal	Triggered just after a modal dialog box is dismissed.
EndOpen	Triggered immediately after AutoCAD finishes opening an existing drawing.
EndPlot	Triggered after a document has been sent to the printer.
EndSave	Triggered when AutoCAD has finished saving the drawing.
LISPCancelled	Triggered when the evaluation of an AutoLISP expression is canceled.
NewDrawing	Triggered just before a new drawing is created.
SysVarChanged	Triggered when the value of a system variable is changed.
WindowChanged	Triggered when there is a change to the application window.
WindowMovedOrResized	Triggered just after the application window has been moved or resized.

Figure 15-6.
Enabling an application level event.

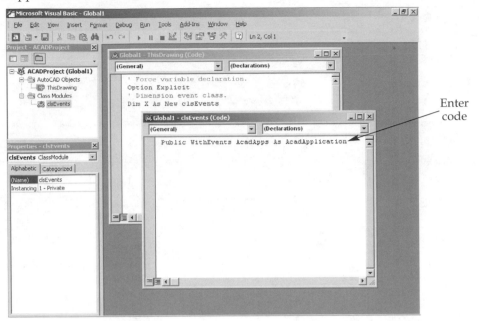

System Variable Changed Event

Once an **Application** object has been declared, it can be selected in the **Object** list box on the top left of the **Code** window. Also, a list of all of its available event procedures is provided in the **Procedure** list box in the **Code** window, as shown in **Figure 15-7**.

Selecting the **SysVarChanged** procedure from the list adds a **Sub** named AcadApp_SysVarChanged to the clsEvents class module that will run anytime the value of a system variable is changed. Now you need to add your own code.

The following code displays a system variable name and its new value in a VBA message box when the system variable is changed:

```
Private Sub AcadApps_SysVarChanged(ByVal SysvarName As String, _
    ByVal newVal As Variant)

    ' Show which variable changed and its new value.
    MsgBox "System variable changed: " & SysvarName & vbLf & vbLf & _
        "New value: " & newVal, vbInformation, "Application Level Event"

End Sub
```

The last thing that needs to be done for the code to run is initialize the application level events.

Initializing Application Level Events

Initializing the application level events is accomplished by assigning the clsEvents AutoCAD **Application** object to the currently running AutoCAD application via object *X* in the **ThisDrawing** module. The following code sets *X.AcadApp* to reference the **ThisDrawing.Application** object:

```
Sub Ch15_InitializeAppEvents()
    Set X.AcadApps = ThisDrawing.Application
End Sub
```

Figure 15-7.
The **Procedure** list box shows the available events.

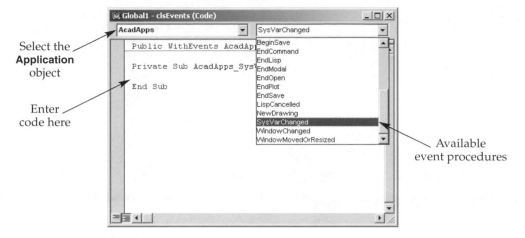

Select the
Application
object

Enter
code here

Available
event procedures

Figure 15-8.
This message box
indicates that the
application level
event—a change in
system variable
settings—has occurred.

After running the Ch15_InitializeAppEvents macro, anytime an AutoCAD system variable is changed a message box like the one shown in **Figure 15-8** is displayed. In this example, the **BLIPMODE** system variable has been turned on.

Document Level Events

Document level events react to changes to a specific drawing or its contents. **Figure 15-9** lists all of the document level events to which a macro can react.

Enabling Document Level Events

Document level events are enabled by declaring an AutoCAD **Document** object with the **WithEvents** keyword at the top of the clsEvents class module:

```
Public WithEvents AcadDoc As AcadDocument
```

Figure 15-9.
Document level events to which a macro can react.

Event Name	Description
Activate	Triggered when a document window is activated.
BeginClose	Triggered just before a document is closed.
BeginCommand	Triggered immediately after a command is issued, but before it completes.
BeginDoubleClick	Triggered after the user double-clicks on an object in the drawing.
BeginLISP	Triggered immediately after AutoCAD receives a request to evaluate an AutoLISP expression.
BeginPlot	Triggered immediately after AutoCAD receives a request to print a drawing.
BeginRightClick	Triggered after the user right-clicks in the drawing window.
BeginSave	Triggered immediately after AutoCAD receives a request to save the drawing.
BeginShortcutMenuCommand	Triggered after the user right-clicks in the drawing window and before the shortcut menu appears in command mode.
BeginShortcutMenuDefault	Triggered after the user right-clicks in the drawing window and before the shortcut menu appears in default mode.
BeginShortcutMenuEdit	Triggered after the user right-clicks in the drawing window and before the shortcut menu appears in edit mode.
BeginShortcutMenuGrip	Triggered after the user right-clicks in the drawing window and before the shortcut menu appears in grip mode.
BeginShortcutMenuOsnap	Triggered after the user right-clicks in the drawing window and before the shortcut menu appears in osnap mode.
Deactivate	Triggered when the drawing window is deactivated.
EndCommand	Triggered immediately after a command completes.
EndLISP	Triggered on completion of evaluating an AutoLISP expression.
EndPlot	Triggered after a document has been sent to the printer.
EndSave	Triggered when AutoCAD has finished saving the drawing.
EndShortcutMenu	Triggered after the shortcut menu appears.
LayoutSwitched	Triggered after the user switches to a different layout.
LISPCancelled	Triggered when the evaluation of an AutoLISP expression is cancelled.
ObjectAdded	Triggered when an object has been added to the drawing.
ObjectErased	Triggered when an object has been erased from the drawing.
ObjectModified	Triggered when an object in the drawing has been modified.
SelectionChanged	Triggered when the current "pick first" selection set changes.
WindowChanged	Triggered when there is a change to the document window.

Figure 15-10.
The **Procedure** list box shows the available events.

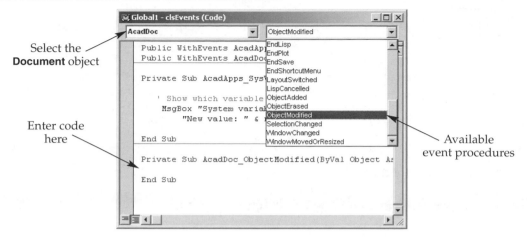

Select the **Document** object

Enter code here

Available event procedures

Object Modified Event

Once a **Document** object has been declared, you can select it in the **Object** list box on the top left of the **Code** window. A list of all of its available event procedures is provided in the **Procedure** list box, as shown in **Figure 15-10**. Selecting the **ObjectModified** procedure from the list adds a **Sub** named AcadDoc_ObjectModified to the clsEvents class module that will run anytime an object is modified. Then, you need to add your own code. (Initially, a **Sub** named AcadDoc_BeginSave appears in the **Code** window; delete this **Sub**.)

The following code displays a VBA message box indicating the type of object that was modified:

```
Private Sub AcadDoc_ObjectModified(ByVal Object As Object)

    ' Show the user the type of object that was modified.
    MsgBox "Object type modified: " & Object.ObjectName, vbInformation, _
            "Document Level Event"

End Sub
```

Professional Tip

Not only do modified drawing objects trigger the **ObjectModified** event, the event is also triggered when any named symbol table object is modified. This includes adding new named objects to a symbol table, such as creating a new layer or a new linetype.

Initializing Document Level Events

The last thing you need to do for your code to run is initialize the document level events. This is accomplished by assigning the clsEvents AutoCAD **Document** object to the current drawing via object *X* in the **ThisDrawing** module.

The following code sets *X.AcadDoc* to reference the **ThisDrawing** object:

```
Sub Ch15_InitializeDocEvents()
    Set X.AcadDoc = ThisDrawing
End Sub
```

Figure 15-11.
This message box indicates that the document level event has occurred.

After running the Ch15_InitializeDocEvents macro, anytime an AutoCAD object is modified a message box like the one shown in **Figure 15-11** is displayed. In this case, a line has been modified.

Object Level Events

Object level events react to changes to a specific object. There is only one object level event: the **Modified** event. It is triggered when an object is modified in any fashion.

Enabling Object Level Events

Object level events are enabled by declaring an AutoCAD object of the type you want with the **WithEvents** keyword at the top of the clsEvents class module:

```
Public WithEvents Object As AcadText
```

Modified Event

Once an object has been declared, you can select it in the **Object** list box on the top left of the **Code** window. The **Modified** procedure can also be selected in the **Procedure** list box, **Figure 15-12.** Notice that there is only one procedure in the list box.

Selecting the **Modified** procedure from the list adds a **Sub** named Object_Modified to the clsEvents class module that will run anytime the object is modified. Now you need to add your own code.

Figure 15-12.
The **Procedure** list box shows the available events. In the case of an **Object** object, there is only one possible event.

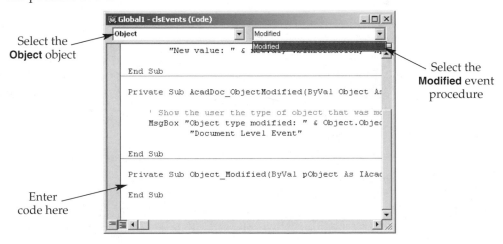

The following code displays a VBA message box that informs the user that text has been modified:

```
Private Sub Object_Modified(ByVal pObject As IAcadObject)

    ' Tell the user that text was modified.
    MsgBox "Text modified.", vbInformation, "Object Level Event"

End Sub
```

Initializing Object Level Events

The last thing you need to do for your code to run is initialize the object level events. This is accomplished by assigning the clsEvents AutoCAD **Object** object to the desired object via object *X* in the **ThisDrawing** module.

The following code sets *X.Object* to reference a newly created **Text** object:

```
Sub Ch15_InitializeObjEvents()

    Dim objText As AcadText
    Dim strText As String
    Dim dblInsPt(0 To 2) As Double
    Dim dblHeight As Double

    ' Set the text string to "Hello World!"
    strText = "Hello World!"

    ' Insert at 0,0,0.
    dblInsPt(0) = 0#
    dblInsPt(1) = 0#
    dblInsPt(2) = 0#

    ' Text height 0.25".
    dblHeight = 0.25

    ' Add text.
    Set objText = ThisDrawing.ModelSpace.AddText(strText, dblInsPt, _
        dblHeight)

    ' Attach the reactor to the text object.
    Set X.Object = objText

End Sub
```

After running the Ch15_InitializeObjEvents macro, anytime the new **Text** object (Hello World!) is modified a message box like the one shown in **Figure 15-13** is displayed.

Figure 15-13.
This message box indicates that the object level event has occurred.

Programming with AutoCAD
Events

- There are three levels of AutoCAD events—application, document, and object.
- Application level events react to changes in the AutoCAD application and its environment.
- Document level events react to changes to a specific drawing or its contents.
- Object level events react to changes to a specific object.
- The **WithEvents** VBA keyword is used to enable events for each level.
- Event handling **Subs** must be located in their own class module.
- Insert a new class module by selecting **Class Module** from the **Insert** pull-down menu in the **Visual Basic Editor**.
- You can select an object's available event procedures from the **Procedure** list box after the object has been enabled using the **WithEvents** keyword.
- Application level events are initialized by assigning the **Application** object that was declared with the **WithEvents** keyword to the **ThisDrawing.Application** object.
- Document level events are initialized by assigning the **Document** object that was declared with the **WithEvents** keyword to the **ThisDrawing** object.
- Object level events are initialized by assigning the object that was declared with the **WithEvents** keyword to a specific AutoCAD drawing object.

Exercise 15-2

Create the event procedures described below. All event **Subs** should be created in a class module named clsEvents in your MyMacros.dvb project. Provide all necessary error checking and control. Enable each event as follows so that you can test each **Sub** after it has been initialized:

```
AcadApp As AcadApplication
AcadDoc As AcadDocument
Object As AcadText
```

1. Create a **Sub** named AcadApp_BeginFileDrop that displays in a VBA message box the name of a file dragged by the user and dropped into the AutoCAD window, and then cancels the file loading process. Initialize the event via a macro named ex15_InitializeAppEvents in the **ThisDrawing** module.
2. Create a **Sub** named AcadDoc_ObjectAdded that displays in a VBA message box the name of a layer added by the user. Initialize the event via a macro named ex15_InitializeDocEvents in the **ThisDrawing** module.
3. Create a **Sub** named Object_Modified that is executed when the diameter of a specific circle changes from a default value of 2.0 inches. Initialize the event via a macro named ex15_InitializeObjEvents in the **ThisDrawing** module that creates a circle with a default diameter of 2.0 inches and then attaches the **Modified** event to the object.

Chapter Test

Write your answers on a separate sheet of paper.

1. What is the top-level object that is used to access the object model for all ActiveX programs?
2. What is a *type library* and how is it used?
3. How do you access another application's object model?
4. Which two methods allow you to create an instance of another ActiveX application?
5. Explain a Visual Basic *class* and what it is used for.
6. Which **Application** object property controls whether or not a program is shown on the computer screen?
7. What is the best way to determine how to program using another Windows application's object model?
8. How can you ensure that a particular VBA macro is run each time a drawing is opened?
9. List the three different levels of AutoCAD events with a description of each.
10. For what is the VBA **WithEvents** keyword used?
11. How do you initialize an object that was declared using the **WithEvents** keyword?
12. How do you create a new class module in VBA?
13. List ten application level events and provide a brief description of each.
14. List ten document level events and provide a brief description of each.
15. What is the only object level event?

Programming Problems

For Problem 1, create the macro described below. It should be created in the **ThisDrawing** module of your MyMacros.dvb project. Provide all necessary error checking and control. Run and test the macro.

1. Create a macro name p15_ExportTitleInfo that exports the attributes defined in the block C:\VBA for AutoCAD\Drawings\TitleText.dwg created in Problem 11-3 to a Microsoft Excel spreadsheet named C:\VBA for AutoCAD\p15_TitleInfo.xls. Use the following format:

Drawing	**DWGNAME** system variable
Name/Number	DRAWNO attribute value
Date	DATE attribute value
Design By	DESIGNBY attribute
Drawn By	DRAWNBY attribute value
Checked By	CHDKBY attribute value

   Include formatted header information and set the column width to "autofit" after data are exported.

For Problems 2 through 4, create the event procedures described. All event **Subs** should be created in a class module named clsEvents in your MyMacros.dvb project. Provide all necessary error checking and control. Enable each event as follows so that you can test each **Sub** after it has been initialized:

AcadApp As AcadApplication
AcadDoc As AcadDocument
Object As AcadText

2. Create a **Sub** named AcadApp_EndPlot that writes out information about a completed plot to a Microsoft Excel spreadsheet named C:\VBA for AutoCAD\p15_PlotInfo.xls. Use the following format:

Drawing	**DWGNAME** system variable
Plot Device	**ConfigName** property
Paper Size	**CanononicalMediaName** property
Plot Origin	**PlotOrigin** attribute
Rotation	**PlotRotation** property

Include formatted header information and set the column width to "autofit" after data are exported. Initialize the event via a macro named p15_InitializeAppEvents located in the **ThisDrawing** module.

3. Create a **Sub** named AcadDoc_BeginDocClose that purges all unreferenced objects whenever a user closes a drawing and then saves the drawing quietly (without any user interaction). Initialize the event via a macro named p15_InitializeDocEvents located in the **ThisDrawing** module.

4. Create a **Sub** named Object_Modified that is executed whenever a drawing object's layer is changed to check if the new object layer is one of the following standard layers:

CENTER
DIMENSION
HIDDEN
OBJECT
PHANTOM
TEXT

If the layer is not one of the standard layers, display a message box informing the user that the object has been moved to a nonstandard layer. Initialize the event via a macro named p15_InitializeObjEvents that attaches the **Modified** event to any drawing object using standard object selection methods.

Glossary

A

Accelerator keys: Allow a user to navigate to a control via the keyboard by pressing the [Alt] key in combination with the mnemonic character (underlined letter).

ActiveX Automation: A means of programming using a predefined ActiveX object model that allows you to share data between various Windows-based applications. Sometimes referred to as the Component Object Model (COM).

Application level events: Events related to the AutoCAD application and its environment.

Arguments: Values that are passed to a procedure that can then be used within the procedure itself.

Arithmetic operators: Used to perform mathematical calculations.

Array: A collection, or list, of values of the same data type that is treated as a single unit.

Attached xref: Any xrefs that are attached to itself are also attached. This is referred to as *nesting*.

B

Base menu: Contains most of the menus, toolbars, and mouse button definitions.

Binding: Declaring a variable to be a particular data type.

Block: Multiple lines of code. Also used to refer to a named collection of one or more AutoCAD drawing entities.

Block attributes: Special dynamic text that can be updated with different alphanumeric information when the block is inserted or anytime after that.

Block table: Contains all of the block definitions, including anonymous blocks generated by the **HATCH** command and associative dimensioning. Each block definition contains the entities that make up that block as it is used in the drawing.

Break mode: A temporary suspension of program execution in the development environment. In break mode, you can examine, debug, reset, step through, or continue program execution. Sometimes referred to as "debug mode."

Breakpoints: Markers that allow you to suspend execution at a specific statement in a procedure. In this way, you can isolate where you might think there is a potential for errors in the program or examine the value of a specific variable or expression.

By reference: Passing a variable by reference allows you to change the original value of the variable in memory.

By value: Passing a variable by value makes a copy of the argument variable so that any changes made in the procedure only affect the copy and not the original variable.

C

Calling: Referencing, or invoking, a procedure.

Comparison operators: Used to perform comparisons and return a Boolean value of true or false.

Concatenation operators: Used to combine strings.

Constants: Values assigned to a descriptive name that, once assigned, can never be changed within the program.

Controls: All of the graphic control features that make up a dialog box.

D

Data type: A classification identifying one of various types of data stating the possible values for that type, the operations that can be done on that type, and the way the values of that type are stored.

Database preferences: Represent all of the options in AutoCAD's **Options** dialog box that reside in the drawing, not in the system registry.

Decision structures: provide a means of testing a condition, or multiple conditions, in your program and then performing different operations based on the result.

Design mode: When no code is running; when you are adding code. This is the mode in which you create and edit your code.

Design time: Before the program is run.

Dimension override: A temporary change made to a specific setting in the current dimension style that overrides the default setting of the style.

Dimension styles: Stored dimension settings that control the appearance of dimensions in a drawing; used to help maintain dimension standards.

Document level events: Events related to the current drawing in AutoCAD.

Double *data type:* Double-precision floating-point value stored as a 64-bit (8-byte) floating-point number ranging in value from $-1.79769313486231E308$ to $-4.94065645841247E-324$ for negative values and from $4.94065645841247E-324$ to $1.79769313486232E308$ for positive values.

Drawing scale factor: Multiplier that determines the size of annotation features, such as text height, dimension features, and linetype appearance, when a drawing is printed; typically the reciprocal of the plot scale or view scale.

DXF group codes: A numerical system used to represent different AutoCAD drawing objects and their properties.

Dynamic array: Nonfixed array type used when you do not know how many elements are needed or if the number of elements will change.

E

Early binding: An explicitly declared variable. The variable's data type is resolved before the program is run.

Element: Each value in an array; referenced by its location in the list.

Embedded: Residing within a drawing.

Embedding: Making a project part of the current drawing. An embedded project is loaded automatically each time the drawing is opened.

Enum: (enumerated constant) A Visual Basic data type that is a collection of related constants.

Error code: A unique number to which the **Err.Number** property is set when a run-time error occurs.

Event handler: Programming code that is executed when an event occurs. Example of events include a mouse click or the creation of a drawing entity.

Events: Actions that occur when a program is running.

Explicitly declare: The process of declaring a variable to only store a specific data type. Declaring variables explicitly reduces run-time errors and increases program performance. If a variable is not declared explicitly, the variable defaults to the generic **Variant** data type so that data types must be determined at program run time.

External reference: A special type of block that is not inserted into a drawing, but rather attached, or linked, as an external drawing file; better known as an xref.

F

Fixed length array: Used when you know how many elements are needed in an array, and that this number will not change.

Floating viewports: Viewports created in paper space that can be modified using standard AutoCAD commands such as **MOVE**, **COPY**, and **ROTATE**. Unlike model space viewports that must abut each other (tiled) with no space in between them, paper space viewports can have space between them and can even overlap (floating).

Forms: The VBA term for dialog boxes.

Form variable: A global variable that is declared outside of all procedures. Also known as a module variable.

Function procedure: A named collection of programming code that, when called, is executed and returns a value. The same as a Sub procedure except that it returns a value.

G

Global: Available in multiple drawings and on multiple computer systems. A global project must be loaded into AutoCAD before any of the project's macros are available.

Global variable: A variable whose scope allows it to be referenced anywhere in your application.

Graphical user interface (GUI): The pull-down menus and toolbars for issuing commands, setting options, controlling object properties, and generally interacting with the program.

H

Hungarian notation: A voluntary variable naming convention that makes VB/VBA code easier to understand and maintain. All of the variable names have a three-character, descriptive prefix indicating their data type.

I

Index: An element's location in an array or collection.

In-process: A program written using VBA that runs in the same memory space as the application that was used to create it.

Integrated Development Environment (IDE): Where all of your program development is done.

Iteration: A means of stepping through each object in a collection so that you can access the object's properties and methods.

L

Late binding: Occurs when variables are not declared explicitly. Late binding of variables causes programs to run slower because validity checking is done while the program is running. Late binding also increases the possibility of run time errors.

Layout: A 2D representation of a sheet of paper that exists in paper space that is used for laying out a drawing for plotting.

Linetypes: Unique line patterns used to graphically represent different features on a drawing.

Local variable: A variable that is declared within a procedure. Its value can only be set or retrieved from within the procedure in which the variable is declared.

Logical conjunction: Logical operator that results in **True** if both of the operands are **True**.

Logical disjunction: Logical operator that results in **True** if either of the operands is **True**.

Logical equivalence: Logical operator that results in **True** if both of the operands are **True** or if both of the operands are **False**.

Logical exclusion: Logical operator that results in **True** if one, and only one, of the operands is **True**.

Logical implication: Logical operator that results in **True** if both of the operands are **True**, both of the operands are **False**, or the first operand is **False** and the second operand is **True**.

Logical negation: Logical operator that inverts the logical value of an operand so that **True** becomes **False** and **False** becomes **True**.

Logical operations: Operations that combine two or more comparison tests into a single, compound comparison expression that returns a Boolean value of **True** or **False.**

Logical operators: Used to combine two or more comparison tests into a single, compound comparison expression that returns a Boolean value of **True** or **False.**

Loop structures: Provide a means of repeating a series, or block, of statements.

M

Macro: A **Sub** that is declared **Public** in a VBA project that can be run from within AutoCAD using the **VBARUN** command.

Menu group: Contains all of the pull-down menus and toolbars for AutoCAD. It is defined in an external, ASCII-based text file that is typically referred to as an *AutoCAD menu file.*

Methods: The functions, or procedures, that can be used to manipulate an object.

Model space: The 3D drawing environment typically used for drawing the "model," or 3D representation of your design. Model space contains most of the text and line work that makes up a drawing.

Modular programming: Breaking up the program into small chunks that perform certain tasks.

Module variable: A variable that is declared outside of all procedures.

Mutliline text: Lines of text in paragraph form that are treated as a single unit, which is defined by a user-defined boundary.

N

Named view: A rectangular area of the drawing, defined by the user, that can be redisplayed later.

Nesting: Including control structures within other control structures. See also *attached xref.*

O

Object: A predefined programming component consisting of *properties* and *methods* that exists with other predefined *objects* in a hierarchy known as an object model.

Object class name: How an object is represented internally in the AutoCAD object model.

Object collection: A predefined group of the same type of objects.

Object *data type:* Can be used to represent any object type in the ActiveX Object Model.

Object level events: Events related to individual drawing entities in AutoCAD.

Object model: The hierarchy of objects that represents an application.

Object-oriented programming: Computer programming paradigm in which a software system is modeled as a set of objects that interact with each other.

Obliquing angle: Determines the forward or backward slant of the text; a way of creating italic type.

Operators: Allow you to perform different data operations in your program.

Out-of-process: A program written using VBA that does not rely on a host application.

Overlay xref: Breaks the nesting chain and only loads the top-level xref.

P

Paper space: The 2D environment used for creating multiscaled layouts of the model space information for plotting purposes. A paper space layout usually consists of a title block and one or more views of the model space information.

Private variable: A variable whose scope is limited to the module or form in which the variable is declared.

Procedure: Programming code that is grouped together and assigned a unique name that can then be referenced anywhere in the program.

Program debugging: The act of examining your code while a program is running so that you can isolate and fix "bugs," or errors, as they occur.

Programming comments: Describe what is intended by the programmer.

Project: A collection of one or more different modules (collections of procedures), and often forms (dialog boxes), that performs a given function or functions.

Prompt: A static form of communication that simply tells the user something; no input is required.

Properties: The data that describe and define the object.

Run mode: Code is running.

Run time: When the program is running.

S

Scope: The variable scope determines where and when you can retrieve or set the value of the variable.

Selection set: One or more selected objects that are treated as a unit by a command.

Selection set filters: The ability to select drawing entities based on one or more of their properties by filtering out entities that do not share the same properties.

Signature: The method's name and its arguments.

Single *data type:* Single-precision floating-point value stored as a 4-byte floating-point number ranging in value from $-3.402823E38$ to $-1.401298E-45$ for negative values and from $1.401298E-45$ to $3.402823E38$ for positive values.

Single line text: Each line of text treated as a single AutoCAD object; the "original" type of text in AutoCAD.

Standard modules: Used to locate generic code that can be shared with the rest of your program.

Static variable: A local variable whose value is not erased when you exit a procedure.

Subentity: An entity that is part of a larger complex object, such as a block or an xref.

Sub *procedure:* A named collection of programming code that, when called, is executed. The most basic procedure type.

T

Tag: A unique identifier that defines and references attribute information in a block.

Text generation flag: Used to make the text display backward, upside down, or both.

Text style: Defines how the text looks in a drawing by controlling the font, height, and effects (oblique angle, width, etc.).

Tiled viewports: Viewports created in model space that must abut each other with no space in between them. Unlike paper space floating viewports, tiled viewports cannot be modified using the standard modify commands.

Top-down conditional testing: Sometimes referred to as waterfall or cascade programming because, like water falling over a waterfall, code is executed as control falls through the program.

Type library: A file or part of a file that describes the object model for an ActiveX application.

Type mismatch: Error generated whenever an attempt is made to assign a variable with a data value that does not match the variable's declared data type.

V

Variable: Named storage location that can contain data. The data can be modified during program execution.

Variant *data type:* Special data type that can store any kind of data except fixed-length **String** data.

Variant variable: Can be set to many different data types at program run time.

Viewports: Allow you to display multiple views of a drawing at the same time.

Visual Basic: A graphic implementation of the BASIC programming language.

Visual Basic for Applications (VBA): Implementation of the Visual Basic programming language that is built into AutoCAD, all of the Microsoft Office applications, and a few other applications.

W

Watch expressions: User-defined expressions that enable you to observe the behavior of a variable or expression.

Index

Public keyword, 51
Pull-down menus, 367–368, 374–381
    adding menu items, 376–378
    adding menu item separator,
        378–379
    adding to menu bar, 375–376
    creating cascading submenus,
        379–381
    PopupMenus collection, 375
    removing from menu bar, 376
    removing menu items, 379
Purging drawings, 138
PViewport object, 295

Q

Quick Select dialog box, 224–225

R

Ray object, 173
RealToString method, 158–159
Rectangular arrays, 205–206
ReDim statement, 27
References dialog box, 409–410
Referencing,
    block definition, 306
    layers, 238–239
    layouts, 342
    linetypes, 251
    model space viewports,
        289–290
    named views, 282–283
    text styles, 263
Regenerating drawings, 138
Regen method, 138
Reloading xrefs, 335
Reload method, 335
RemoveItems method, 230–231
RemoveMenuFromMenuBar method,
    376
Renaming,
    blocks, 309
    dimension styles, 274
    layers, 241
    layouts, 344
    linetypes, 255
    plot configurations, 348–349
    views, 285
Resume Next statement, 59–60
Retrieving system variables, 136
Rotate method, 70, 212–213
Rotating plots, 358–359
Run mode, 103
Running VBA macros, 99–100
Run time, 22
Run to Cursor command, 104

S

Save As dialog box, 85
SaveAs method, 134–135
SaveAsType property, 120
Save method, 134, 372–373
Saving projects, 84–85
Scale, 256–258, 298–299, 355–356
    drawing scale factor, 257

global linetype, 257
    setting linetype, 257–258
    UseStandardScale property,
        355–356
ScaleEntity method, 213–214
Scope, 50–53
SelectAtPoint method, 222
SelectByPolygon method, 223
Select Case... decision structure,
    34–36
Selection mode, 232–233
    PickFirst property, 232
    PickfirstSelectionSet property,
        232–233
Selection set filters, 217
SelectionSet object, 219
Selection sets, 217–234
    accessing and iterating,
        227–228
    adding entities, 220–224
    AddItems method, 220
    Clear method, 229
    controlling mode, 231–233
    creating, 219–220
    determining amount of
        entities, 228
    Erase method, 230
    filters, 224–226
    referencing objects, 227
    RemoveItems method, 230–231
    removing entities, 229–231
    SelectAtPoint method, 222
    SelectByPolygon method, 223
    SelectionSets collection, 218
    Select method, 221–222
    SelectOnScreen method,
        223–224
SelectionSets collection, 218
Select Menu File dialog box,
    370–371
Select method, 221–222
SelectOnScreen method, 223–224
SendCommand method, 159–160
SetBitmaps method, 386
SetCustomScale method, 356
SetLayoutsToPlot method, 363–364
SetProjectFilePath method, 115
Set statement, 65, 73
Setting system variables, 135–136
SetVariable method, 135, 275
SetView method, 284–285
Show method, 405
Signature, 70
Single data type, 26
SingleDocumentMode property, 123
Single-line text, 177–178
Solid object, 187–188
Spline object, 169–171
Split method, 292
Splitting model space viewports,
    292
Standard modules, 97
StandardScale property, 298–299
Statements,
    Case, 77
    Case Else, 35
    Dim, 64
    End If, 32
    Exit Function, 48
    On Error Goto..., 56–59

Open Explicit, 21
Option Explicit, 53
ReDim, 27
Resume Next, 59–60
Set, 65, 73
Static keyword, 52
Static variables, 52
Step Into button, 99–100
Step Into command, 104
Step keyword, 37
Step Out command, 104
Step Over command, 104
String data type, 22–23
StyleSheet property, 352
Subentity, 147
Sub procedures, 43–44
System variable changed event, 424
System variables,
    ANGBASE, 143, 145
    ATTDISP, 319
    DWGPREFIX, 363
    LTSCALE, 257
    MAXACTVP, 294
    PDMODE, 186
    PROJECTNAME, 116
    setting and retrieving,
        135–136
    TILEMODE, 288
SysVarChanged procedure, 424

T

Tag, 318
TextBox control, 399–401
Text generation flag, 267–268
TextGenerationFlag property,
    267–268
Text object, 177–179, 202–204, 420
    changing height, 202–203
    changing text string, 203–204
    multiline text, 178–179
    single-line text, 177–178
TextString property, 203–204
Text Style dialog box, 262
TextStyle object, 262
Text styles, 261–270
    creating new, 264
    deleting, 268–269
    generation flag, 267–268
    height, 266
    making current, 264–265
    managing fonts, 265–266
    obliquing angle, 266–267
    referencing, 263
TextStyles collection, 262–270
    iterating, 263–264
ThisDrawing.ActiveSpace property,
    287
ThisDrawing.MSpace property, 298
ThisDrawing object, 95, 420
Tiled viewports, 288
ToolbarItem object, 384
Toolbar object, 384
Toolbars, 367–368, 381–393
    adding button separator, 387
    adding buttons, 384–385
    adding new, 384
    controlling size and location,
        390–392

creating button images,
386–387
creating flyouts, 388–390
removing buttons, 388
Toolbars collection, 384–393
Toolbox window, 96
Top-down conditional testing, 34
Type library, 79, 409
Type mismatch, 21

U

Unloading projects, 86
Unloading xrefs, 334
Unload method, 334, 373, 405–406
User interaction, 139–159
    initializing input, 148–153
    input, 140–148
    prompting, 139–140
UseStandardScale property, 355–356
Utility methods, 155–159
Utility object, 140

V

Variables, 20–22, 24
    naming conventions, 24
Variable scope, 50–53
    global variables, 51
    local variables, 50
    module and form variables,
    51
    private variables, 51
    procedure scope, 52–53
    static variables, 52
Variant data type, 22

Variant variable, 21
VBA,
    arrays, 26–29
    AutoCAD commands, 107
    binding, 22
    coding conventions, 53–55
    constants, 25–26
    conversion functions, 22–24
    decision structures, 31–36
    definition, 19
    error handling, 55–60
    loop structures, 37–41
    nested control structures, 42
    operators, 29–31
    procedure arguments, 46–50
    procedures, 43–46
    project structure, 94–99
    projects and macros, 83–109
    Toolbox, 396
    variable naming conventions,
    24
    variables and data types, 20–22
    variable scope, 50–53
VBA Manager, 84–88
    creating projects, 84–85
    embedding projects, 86–87
    extracting projects, 87
    loading projects, 86
    saving projects, 85
    unloading projects, 86
vbCrLf constant, 54
View object, 282
Viewport object, 289
Viewports, 287–300
    model space, 288–294
    paper space, 294–300
Viewports collection, 289
Viewports dialog box, 288–289

Views collection, 282–286
    creating new named view, 284
    deleting, 286
    iterating, 283
    making current, 284–285
    referencing, 282–283
    renaming, 285
Visual Basic Editor, 88–94
    Code window, 90–94
    debug windows, 90
    Project Explorer window, 89
    Properties window, 90
Visual Basic for Applications
    (VBA), definition, 19

W

Watch expressions, 102
Watch window, 90
Watches window, 102–103
WBlock method, 315–316
Windows, debug, 101–103
WindowState property, 112
WithEvents keyword, 420, 422, 425,
    428

X

XLine object, 172–173
Xref Manager dialog box, 330–331
Xrefs, 329–336
    attaching, 332–333
    binding, 335–336
    detaching, 333–334
    reloading, 335
    unloading, 334